Benevolent Empire

PENNSYLVANIA STUDIES IN HUMAN RIGHTS

Bert B. Lockwood, Jr., Series Editor

A complete list of books in the series is available from the publisher.

BENEVOLENT EMPIRE

U.S. Power, Humanitarianism,
and the World's Dispossessed

Stephen R. Porter

PENN

UNIVERSITY OF PENNSYLVANIA PRESS

PHILADELPHIA

Published by
University of Pennsylvania Press
Philadelphia, Pennsylvania 19104-4112
www.upenn.edu/pennpress

Printed in the United States of America on acid-free paper
10 9 8 7 6 5 4 3 2 1

Library of Congress Cataloging-in-Publication Data
ISBN 978-0-8122-4856-2

CONTENTS

Introduction

The United States has long reached out to aid some of the world's most vulnerable persons, but only in the twentieth century did the practice become an important way in which both the American state and civil society staked a claim for their country as a truly global power. The term "benevolent empire" emerged in the nineteenth century as a moniker for the explosion of Protestant missionary societies that spanned the continent and lands beyond to spread the Gospel and, often, the purported benefits of American civilization.[1] By the early twentieth century, the enterprise had begun to morph into something less overtly sacred, more diversified in its participants, committed to the modern tenets of "scientific charity" and social work, and above all tied to the project of promoting American authority not just abroad, but at home too. The phrase "benevolent empire" may have fallen out of favor by the time armies of Americans committed themselves to unprecedentedly vast humanitarian projects during the era of the First World War, but the label still proved apt, albeit in altered ways, as the United States marched boldly through the new century. When Americans now thought of themselves as part of an imperial venture, it was likely to be at least as much about country as God.[2] And though twentieth-century America would never quite mirror European-style territorial empires, Americans often implicitly conceptualized their country's dramatic new extensions of global power through an imperial prism that partially but significantly justified America's influence over foreign populations by its benevolent intentions for the most vulnerable and needy among them.[3] John Winthrop's City upon a Hill had grown big, and it refused to stay put.

Benevolent Empire interrogates this phenomenon by examining political-refugee aid initiatives and related responses to humanitarian crises led by American people and institutions from World War I through the 1960s. These developments open an important window onto what has been called the Short American Century, when the United States rose to a position of a major world power, and the American state and civil society profoundly retooled the way they organized social life at home. Chronicling both international relief efforts and domestic resettlement programs aimed at dispossessed populations of foreign nationals, this study asks how, why, and with what effects American actors took responsibility for millions of victims of war, persecution, and political upheaval during these decades. It argues that the U.S. ascendance to and maintenance of a position of elite global power was significantly justified and fueled by the proposition that the country's objects of philanthropic concern might potentially include any vulnerable people across the globe. *Benevolent Empire* is thus simultaneously a history of the United States and the world beyond, embedding its narrative in several signal markers of the twentieth century, including massive human-made crises, organized efforts to assuage their effects, and the emergence of the United States as a world power.

The book advances and challenges several issues that have animated conversations in a variety of fields of U.S. and international history. As an exploration of American governing strategies, it engages with studies in the history of politics, law, welfare, and institutions that have, for the past several decades, comprised a field often referred to as American Political Development (APD). Initially an effort by political historians and historically inclined social scientists to "bring the state back" into U.S. history after the Social and Cultural Turns had, for a time, pushed it to the margins, the first wave of APD scholarship offered important insights into the intricacies of public power, but sometimes did so by emphasizing the state at the expense of other factors that helped to organize American society. Recent work in the field has begun correcting for earlier overreaches, in part by studying the many ways in which non-state organizations have, in pursuit of objectives, served as critical conduits between American society and formal government. This phenomenon has especially prevailed when overt, robust state action alone would have run counter to prevailing trends in American political culture. Whereas understanding the machinations of public power does indeed behoove nuanced attention to official government, some of the more recent APD scholarship demonstrates that it is, in fact, often the linkages—the associations—between the state and organized civil society that best illuminate the processes of governance. Historian Brian Balogh argued in 2015 that enough work had emerged on this front to suggest the outlines of a new "associational synthesis" to explain how American people and institutions have governed the country over the past century. The "associational turn" that Balogh posits offers a potent interpretive paradigm, but it remains hindered by the fact that most APD scholarship has focused overwhelmingly on America's domestic arena, leaving the profound and manifold governing innovations responsible for the tremendous rise of the United States as a global power in the twentieth century both insufficiently described and, consequently, inadequately understood.[4]

Benevolent Empire offers a corrective contribution to this emerging synthesis. It shows how associational governing techniques (also referred to here as "hybrid" or "public-private") were central to how a diverse array of persons and institutions, ones collectively representing *the United States*, presented themselves to the world, both explicitly and implicitly, genuinely and duplicitously: as a benevolent empire, a new kind of global hegemon. Whether implemented abroad or in the United States, aid initiatives on behalf of refugees and other vulnerable persons represented a vast project of hybrid governance. The interests of official government actors in refugee and related humanitarian crises rarely mirrored but often overlapped with those of American civil society and private sectors, behooving each to forge extensive, if sometimes dysfunctional, working relationships with the other. This collaboration between the American state and myriad philanthropies, religious organizations, ethnic aid associations, political advocacy groups, and, at times, business interests produced a capacious and kinetic field of American governance to which no one set of actors could lay sole claim as representative of the United States. In the process, the relationship of the American state and the country's humanitarian based voluntary agencies underwent a profound transformation with ramifications for decades to come.

As a transnational history that systematically explores developments within and beyond formal U.S. borders, *Benevolent Empire* also engages with the historiographical field frequently in recent years called "U.S. in the World." Like APD, U.S. in the World owes some of the impetus for its emergence (or resurgence, as some might prefer) to the intellectual energy produced by the social and cultural turns of the 1970s through 1990s, when the tight focus on elite state actors by diplomatic historians came to be seen by many observers as both antiquated and exclusive. By the new millennium, a generation of historians had begun to explore the international dimensions of U.S. history by attending to a source base and set of historical actors that was considerably more diverse than scholars had typically engaged with before. The New International Historians, as they have also been called, additionally employed a range of innovative interpretive devices, often previously honed by those social and cultural historians who had concentrated more squarely on the domestic dimensions of U.S. history. This flurry of scholarly activity has come to be recognized for the international turn it navigated, constituting in what historian Erez Manela has called, with justification, an "overarching trend that charts the most exciting recent changes in the American historical profession across its various fields."[5]

Echoing some studies in the more domestically focused field of APD, a subset of U.S. in the World scholarship has produced meaningful insights into the ways that the American state and civil society organizations collaborated with one another to extend the country's reach in the twentieth century. Some of this work also shares with *Benevolent Empire* an interest in specific humanitarian-based initiatives of American actors. Much of the best work in this vein has understandably trained its sights especially on the first few decades of the twentieth century, a period that historian Ellis Hawley years ago marked as perhaps the key era of American associationalism. The scholarship has additionally tended to concentrate on a single agency, such as the Red Cross, or an outsized public figure, such as Herbert Hoover.[6]

This study certainly finds ample reason to engage with both that particular organization and man. But it also traces projects of associational governance over a longer chronology and wider array of people and institutions. In doing so, it tells a longer and broader tale of the ways in which the United States extended its authority during the Short American Century through initiatives explicitly framed as humanitarian. Narrating these developments includes following the paths of lesser-known persons and organizations alongside the more prominent. It entails systematically examining associational governing arrangements on behalf of refugees and other dispossessed persons into and past the World War II era, when American statism is now commonly understood to have been at its zenith. The book demonstrates something about the United States' role in the world during the Short American Century that is still insufficiently understood: the United States presented itself to the world during this critical period of American influence not only as a benevolent power, but also a decidedly hybrid and, at times, even schizophrenic one.

The half century of aid initiatives described in this book composed far more than the deployment of what international relations historians and political scientists call "soft power."[7] Humanitarian projects could exercise profound authority, not only because they were often part and parcel of diplomatic strategies of the American state in the country's official relations with other states. American institutions, both governmental and nongovernmental, actively assumed extensive degrees of responsibility for significant numbers of the world's dispossessed people, whether by caring for millions of them abroad or by legally admitting to the United States, and then resettling systematically over one million of them in thousands of communities across the United States as "new Americans." As these persons were commonly claimed by America's enemies as their own citizens, such self-described humanitarian endeavors often amounted to forceful and highly controversial extensions of American power—sometimes even sovereignty—over new global populations and foreign territories.

Such developments speak to a vibrant literature examining the intersection of ethics and the modern international order. *Benevolent Empire* joins conversations advanced by such theorists, historians, and social scientists as Judith Shklar, Thomas Haskell, Lynn Hunt, Samuel Moyn, and Michael Barnett in asking why feelings of responsibility by certain groups of persons have attached themselves to the perceived plight of different, often physically distant persons in certain historical contexts. Whether these phenomena manifested themselves as humanitarianism, human rights, or related discourses of justice, this book inquires into their emergence and consequences, paying special attention to what it refers to as the various "philanthropic identities" claimed by a diverse array of Americans. It explores the more general tension that Seyla Benhabib describes as being between the "sovereign self-determination claims" by nation-states to assist foreigners as the nation-states and their members see fit on the one hand and "adherence to universal human rights principles on the other."[8]

If the massive overseas programs of humanitarian aid explored in this study signaled a dramatically new level of commitment to such endeavors by America's state and voluntary sectors, so too did the related projects of refugee admissions and resettlement represent a novel development in American immigration history.[9] Scholarship on the history of refugee admissions informs us that, beginning in the aftermath of the Second World War, for the first time the United States began purposely admitting large numbers of immigrants specifically because they were deemed to be vulnerable to certain kinds of persecution in their homelands or places of temporary asylum. (Typically, this was persecution as committed by American adversaries but not allies.) That is, American immigration policy began regularly recognizing the political refugee as a distinct category of immigrant, worthy of legally entering the country outside of the restrictive mainstream of U.S. immigration law. The two most important studies on U.S. refugee admissions policies during the Cold War are Gil Loescher and John Scanlan's *Calculated Kindness* and Carl Bon Tempo's *Americans at the Gate*. The latter has become the definitive text on U.S. refugee admissions during the Cold War, due in no small measure to its keen analysis of the actual implementation of refugee admissions policies.[10]

Benevolent Empire builds upon the perceptive insights of *Americans at the Gate* while breaking new scholarly ground and, in the process, suggesting some alternative readings of American refugee affairs in the twentieth century. This study proposes a different periodization than that offered by Bon Tempo and other scholars, a periodization that, for several intertwined reasons, has not yet been systematically explored. First, it demonstrates how the history of refugee admissions into the United States was tied to a broader history of humanitarian-based endeavors outside American borders on behalf of not only refugees, but also other dispossessed civilians. Second, while the state was central to many of the international and domestic dimensions of these endeavors, a fuller understanding of them requires sustained attention to the associative governing relationships forged by both state and non-state representatives and their institutions. The nature of these institutions and the relationships between them underwent fundamental transformations during the First World War, Great Depression, and Second World War.

Finally, if, as this study argues, international humanitarian aid serves as one important counterpart to U.S. refugee admissions, then the institutional resettlement of refugees after entry into the United States serves as another. *Benevolent Empire* parts with other studies of U.S. refugee affairs—including the extensive literature on the exclusion of Jewish refugees in the 1930s—by suggesting an earlier beginning to the history of those U.S. policies aimed specifically at admitting large groups of persecuted refugees.[11] It does this by revealing how a grand bargain of sorts was struck, rather surreptitiously, in the midst of the Great Depression between private citizens advocating for the right of Jewish refugees to secure haven in the United States and a handful of federal immigration officials. The agreement, as Chapter 2 elaborates, tied the state's admission of some refugees to a guarantee by voluntary aid organizations that the latter would help admitted refugees in their adjustment to life in the United States without the need for state support. *Benevolent Empire* argues that this link between admissions decisions and organized resettlement came to define who was treated distinctly as a *refugee* in U.S. immigration policy, at least as much as did the persecution to which a victim had been subjected.

The book traces the often contentious evolution of this agreement involving the admissions-resettlement nexus—sometimes explicit, sometimes muted—

as part of the study's larger examination of the persistent debates over who should ultimately assume responsibility for the refugees: the American state and its attendant national community or private organizations and the more particular American populations they represented. The core narrative of *Benevolent Empire* concludes in the 1960s with the Cuban Refugee Program because, whereas the promise of institutional welfare support remained tied to admissions decisions, a sea change had nevertheless occurred in U.S. refugee policies as the federal government began assuming, for the first time, significant degrees of responsibility for the welfare of admitted refugees. It was an arrangement that would endure into the twenty-first century, albeit with notable evolutions, as explored in the Epilogue.

Each chapter of *Benevolent Empire* presents a case study of a major humanitarian initiative abroad or refugee resettlement program in the United States, a case in which the international and domestic phenomena affected and illuminated one another. Proceeding chronologically, the flow and focus of the chapters are designed to uncover both persistence and change in both American refugee affairs and attendant humanitarian projects. Though boasting roots from earlier American missionary movements, immigrant aid efforts, and occasional state-supported humanitarianism abroad, the studies of this book chart an unprecedented explosion of American-led activities directed toward those non-Americans publicly deemed in special need of assistance, be it a result of violent dislocation, vulnerability to persecution, or both. Many thousands of Americans enlisted in these efforts, whether contributing to projects directed by nongovernmental organizations, state bureaus, intergovernmental agencies, or a hybrid conglomeration of two or more of them. Motivated variously by cultural ties, geopolitical imperatives, humanitarian sensibilities, and even economic profit, the Americans engaging in these endeavors initially dedicated most of their labors to a wide swath of those Europeans victimized by the two World Wars, Nazism, and Soviet rule, until Castro's 1959 Cuban Revolution began turning the attention of the American refugee aid community elsewhere. Well over one million of these dispossessed and displaced people found refuge in the United States during the book's time period, with many millions more such persons receiving American support outside U.S. territory. While the state played an important role in these operations throughout the book's narrative arc, its commitment expanded over time, recharging long-standing debates over whether certain of the world's vulnerable populations should be the primary responsibility of the U.S. government, its voluntary sector, or neither.

Chapter 1 engages with what has been called "America's Humanitarian Awakening," the bold foray of American people, money, goods, and state power into the vast expanse of human suffering that blanketed Europe and the Middle East during World War I and, especially, its aftermath. Initially offering a wide view of the crisis itself, it surveys the multiple institutional outlets through which millions of Americans could express their philanthropic identities. Sometimes such expression meant alleviating the suffering of the war's victims, while at others, it meant, by offering welfare assistance to combatants, greasing the machinery of war. The chapter then focuses on the ground-level experience of one young American who, like so many others, was pulled into the field of war relief through an overlapping and evolving set of loyalties and attendant empathetic sensibilities. His experiences reveal that, amid the mass of human suffering that marked large swaths of the world after the Great War, there was a hierarchy to the plight, one that could deepen and bend the commitments of those agencies and persons attempting to address the worst instances of inhumanity. Whereas in the past, however, such advocates for the most vulnerable Europeans often worked to alleviate humanitarian crises by facilitating many victims' immigration to the United States and other receiving countries, the gates of entry were, in the 1920s, now fast closing. This development seemed especially foreboding for overseas Jews and their American advocates.

Covering the twelve years of Nazi rule, Chapter 2 reveals what we might think of as an incubation period for a nascent refugee resettlement regime. It explores the collaborations of a handful of government officials and a small army of private welfare and immigrant aid personnel who toiled below the radar to fuse federal admissions decisions on behalf of refugees with the promise of organized resettlement assistance, all with the goal of providing refuge for as many European Jews as possible amid a hostile environment in the United States of tight immigration restrictions and anti-Semitism. This study complicates the traditional scholarly approach to examining U.S. refugee policies during the Nazi era, one which has, until now, emphasized the myriad missed opportunities to create a separate wing of U.S. immigration law, one sympathetic to the special needs of the dispossessed. It demonstrates that, on the contrary, and with full acknowledgment of the tragic consequences of restrictive U.S. immigration policies, when one digs below the conspicuous events of high politics, mass rallies, and public figures, the foundations of a distinct refugee policy can be unearthed, situated at least a decade earlier than when others have typically placed it. This development emerged through new working agreements between private refugee advocates and federal immigration officials, whereby the advocates could help to secure legal haven for refugees as long as those immigrants were guaranteed access to private rather than public institutional welfare support.

Chapter 3 explores how an explosion of philanthropic activity by millions of Americans on behalf of World War II's civilian victims overseas in turn prompted the federal government to capture that energy in a nearly unprecedented wave of civil society regulation. The state then "recruited" those transformed war philanthropies for America's vast international relief and rehabilitation operations during and after the war. The chapter argues that these public-private endeavors produced a massive hybrid welfare state that was exported to a war-torn world abroad as a critical part of America's rise to a position of global superpower. The chapter concludes by exploring the fleeting attempts of voluntary humanitarian aid personnel to use the cultural currency they had amassed during the war, a currency accrued to promote a nongovernmental style of diplomacy. This was to be a diplomacy that might maintain friendly ties across a rising Iron Curtain at a moment when state-to-state relations between East and West were in a state of geopolitical free fall. While that project failed, the ties forged between the private American agencies and the state during the war would help to fuel a decades-long maturation of a powerful network of civil society organizations engaged in humanitarian work on behalf of displaced and other dispossessed people. In other words, important seeds for what would later be called an "NGO Revolution" were sown with the deep involvement of a powerful government.

Chapter 4 refocuses the lens on domestic resettlement, examining the U.S. Displaced Persons Program of 1948 to 1952. It asks whether America's international hybrid welfare state, and the often-professed humanitarian and human rights rationales justifying it, could be transported back to American territory to aid the nearly half a million European "displaced persons" admitted to the United States in the country's first Congressionally legislated large-scale refugee admissions and resettlement program. The lofty goals of American refugee advocates came under fire, within an ideologically charged early Cold War environment, as stories emerged that many thousands of Central and Eastern European refugees were being resettled in highly exploitative living and working arrangements, including as debt-bound cotton sharecroppers and sugarcane stoop laborers throughout the Deep South. Some of the same federal officials who had pushed America's postwar vision for human and civil rights onto an international stage made a difficult choice. To make the "DP" Program operate at full capacity in the sometimes harsh reality of the American labor market and an ascendant rights rhetoric that prioritized formal equality over substantive social justice, they opted to scale back the range of rights they had demanded for those refugees resettling inside the United States.

The narrative next invites a deeper look into American refugee affairs at mid-century with two companion chapters on the Hungarian Refugee Program. Together the two chapters offer comparative gazes, both backward to previous endeavors and across the geography that separated international aid from domestic resettlement. The Hungarian Refugee Program provides a useful opportunity to take stock of the country's initiatives on behalf of refugees, but not because it represented the largest, longest, or most challenging of such projects. It did not. Rather, the relatively modest size and duration of the crisis gave refugee advocates a nearly ideal opportunity to demonstrate that America's system for sharing its benevolence with the world's dispossessed was as sound in design as it was genuine in intention. With both a population of refugees ripe for portrayal as heroic, anti-communist "freedom fighters" and an American economy in the middle of its postwar economic boom, the stage seemed set for success. The significant challenges that soon arose, however, on both the international and domestic sides of the Hungarian program, in turn revealed growing tensions over how American refugee aid should be governed, particularly with regard to the proper balance between the roles of state and voluntary actors.

The first of these chapters addresses the American overseas aid operations that took place on behalf of nearly two hundred thousand Hungarian refugees who fled Soviet troops and a Soviet-backed Hungarian government after a failed uprising. It demonstrates how flawed management of the situation in the refugee camps in Austria prompted vociferous but ultimately and largely unheeded calls from Herbert Hoover and others to increase significantly the U.S. government's role in such endeavors. In what had become a pattern in America's international and domestic management of such crises, the ambivalent commitment of the state once again frustrated the coveted Cold War message that the victims of communist oppression would indeed fare much better by throwing their lot in with the Free World's superpower rather than with the regimes they had fled.

Chapter 6 explores the domestic side of the Hungarian Refugee Program, allowing for a comparison of how these initiatives operated both abroad and on U.S. soil. This includes the ways challenges faced by the resettlement of thirty-eight thousand Hungarians were, in certain ways, even more troubling than the problems encountered with the resettlement of displaced persons after World War II. A recession quickly turned a narrative of successful resettlement into one of unemployment, frustration, and even voluntary repatriations to communist Hungary. These events penned an unwelcome script for refugees and their advocates: even during the country's boom years, newly arrived refugees were subject to the vagaries of economic cycles and to an institutional resettlement system that seemed to neglect them almost as quickly as it had initially embraced them. The chapter then revisits the issue of race and refugee resettlement, one explored previously with the Displaced Persons Program. It follows the controversy that erupted when a Hungarian refugee crossed the color line at a historically black university in the U.S. South. Unlike the situation with the refugee sharecroppers after World War II, however, the events at the university occurred just as the Civil Rights Movement was starting to saturate American public life. And they involved someone whose label as a "freedom fighter" failed to match the welcome he received from his new homeland. In this, his experience echoed that of the young African Americans simultaneously fighting for their own set of freedoms in the United States.

Chapter 7 highlights a sea change in American refugee resettlement policies—sparked by Fidel Castro's rise to power in Cuba—when the federal government began, for the first time, directly channeling vast amounts of public resources to newly arrived refugees to aid in their resettlement. These developments fueled the ire of American citizens who resented the specter of non-citizens receiving welfare support from the federal government. Ultimately, though, an unusually long and large refugee influx joined with Cold War political imperatives to ensure that the federal government maintained its newfound role in resettlement. The changes initiated with the Cuban program set a mold that would largely persist into the twenty-first century. Refugee admissions would continue to be tied to special guarantees for the welfare of refugee immigrants, but with the federal government assuming a significant degree of those promises.

The Epilogue demonstrates that, though the admission of hundreds of thousands of Indochinese beginning in the mid-1970s represented a significant change in the geographical and cultural composition of the refugees entering the United States, American refugee affairs betrayed significant continuities in the way that the institutions of America's state and civil society sectors would help them adjust to life in their new homeland. The federal government funneled funds through the voluntary agencies who maintained their new roles as subcontractors for the state, engaging directly with the refugees, but on a more limited basis than in the past. The changes in resettlement assistance initiated with the Cuban and Indochinese programs were formalized in 1980 with the country's first comprehensive refugee law. Almost as soon as the law was passed, however, refugee resettlement became entangled in a wider web of the anti-welfare politics of Reagan-Era America. Over the ensuing years, the federal government remained deeply involved in refugee resettlement—but also, and in general, committing itself to ever-decreasing levels of support. As the Cold War imperatives that once justified American refugee aid faded over the 1990s, so too did the political pressure to assist admitted refugees at levels sufficient to help them adjust successfully to life in America. As the voluntary agencies now proved no longer equipped, as they had once been, to handle the lion's share of refugees' needs, American refugee affairs limped into the twenty-first century.

CHAPTER 1

A New Benevolent Empire?

What's in a uniform? What meanings does a uniform convey to the person it envelops or to those seeing it worn? Created to symbolize a stable connection between someone donning it and an institution, a uniform sometimes fails its job, especially in environments defined by instability. In the summer of 1920, a Fiat carrying two uniformed men rattled along a Ukrainian country road into such a frenetic scene. As it approached the village of Yarmolintsy, several Russian cavalrymen of the Red army emerged from a ditch shouting for the car to halt, "*stoy!*" On approaching the car, the Russians identified the passengers as Polish army officers, apparently unaware that Yarmolintsy had been taken recently by the Red army unit as part of the Russian Civil War and related regional violence in the aftermath of the Great War. Only moments later, however, the Russians may have wondered why war-seasoned Polish officers would be sprinting away from their automobile in panic. The cavalrymen would learn later that day that the fleeing men were not militants at all, but American philanthropists wearing uniforms bearing a striking but unintentional resemblance to those of Polish army officers. Israel Friedlaender and Bernard Cantor were in the area not to wage war but to alleviate the human costs of war by helping dispossessed civilians who had been brutalized in recent years by both opposing armed forces and civilian neighbors. The men's uniforms belonged to the recently formed Joint Distribution Committee (JDC), and like the uniforms of other American relief agencies, they were intended to resemble U.S. army uniforms in an effort to lend vulnerable aid workers an aura of authority associated with the rapidly ascending military and diplomatic heft of the American state. That the uniforms of the U.S. military—and thus, the JDC—happened to resemble those worn by Polish army officers proved an ironic stroke of misfortune that sent Cantor and

Friedlaender scrambling for their lives on the wrong side of a front line they had unwittingly crossed.[1]

In several ways, the encounter that morning offers an entrée into a formative period in the history of American efforts to aid refugees and other civilian victims of war and related upheavals. First, Friedlaender and Cantor were part of something big. The American philanthropists were far from the safety of their homes in New York City, yet far from alone in the type of work they were doing. Thousands of Americans joined the two in dramatically extending the international presence of American people and institutions during the Great War and its aftermath through humanitarian projects they commonly referred to as "relief." Whether organized through the American government, civil society associations, or a combination of both, a cluster of aid agencies deployed thousands of Americans throughout Europe and the Near East during the Great War and, especially, its aftermath to operate feeding centers, medical facilities, orphanages, schools, and immigration programs for millions of displaced and dispossessed victims of violence, persecution, and political chaos whose very lives often depended on such American support. These "missions" comprised not only, in the words of one historian, a "nation's humanitarian awakening," but also a significant extension of American authority abroad, an important if underappreciated part of America's ascent as a world power in the era of the First World War. American overseas aid operations nurtured and protected enormous foreign populations, rebuilt infrastructures, and stabilized states, sometimes at the purposeful expense of adversarial political factions.[2]

Second, as Israel Friedlaender and Bernard Cantor learned harrowingly, the chaos and scale of the period's humanitarian crises fostered a field of organized responses where murkiness and fluidity often trumped clarity and stability. Whether through uniforms or otherwise, the lines of affiliation between a diverse array of aid organizations and their personnel could be hard to ascertain and subject to regular misunderstandings amid the kinetic nature of war, political turmoil, and mass suffering. The same can be said of the working relationships between the institutions themselves, with new organizations replacing older ones overnight, and lesser-known agencies operating under the nominal umbrella of better-known entities at one point while working independently at another. The ever-shifting involvement of the American state furthermore waxed and waned in aid operations in manifold ways that made calling American war relief a "public" or "private" endeavor as deceptive as it could be revealing. Sometimes least clear of all were the lines of responsibility between American aid organizations and the broad range of suffering persons they might potentially assist. Unlike the charge a nation-state officially had for its citizens, or even an empire for its subjects, the duty of an American relief association to a vulnerable non-American generally rested on a softer normative foundation, one where the connection between institution and victim was something to be developed and negotiated more than presumed.

The flip side of the liminal and opaque nature of the field of American war relief reveals that its myriad organizations offered a diverse array of Americans the opportunity to express what we might think of as their *philanthropic identities* and attendant senses of obligation, whether to their nation, government, particular cultural group, or wider conception of humanity. In this, overseas aid served as a counterpart to both military service and home front voluntarism during the wartime era.[3] Americans seeking an outlet for their patriotic fervor and belief in international camaraderie could turn to large entities like the American Red Cross and the various agencies directed by Herbert Hoover, all with their own close operational ties to the American state and symbolic association to the broad contours of the American nation.[4] But Americans were also pulled into war relief along other, more particular registers of identification, often animated by their ethnoreligious affinities. They joined organizations like the YMCA, YWCA, Knights of Columbus, American Friends Service Committee (AFSC), and JDC, not only as good Americans but also as good Protestants, Catholics, Quakers, Jews, French Americans, Italian Americans, Polish Americans, and so on. Some negotiated what were often overlapping philanthropic identities by migrating between agencies or even serving more than one at a time. Two and a half years before Israel Friedlaender found himself fleeing Bolshevik soldiers in Ukraine, for instance, he joined an American Red Cross mission slated for Palestine to investigate the humanitarian needs of Jews there as, simultaneously, an official JDC representative.[5]

A final way in which the events near Yarmolintsy begin opening a window onto American overseas humanitarian aid in the era of the Great War pertains to the intertwined issues of profound vulnerability and the use of immigration to escape it. That is, it pertains to refugees, or at least to those persons who would have become refugees if afforded the mobility, people whose circumstances were dire enough that fleeing their homelands in fear seemed a reasonable goal among unreasonably bad options. While many Americans were deeply moved by the considerable suffering of those with whom they felt an

affinity abroad, for some American communities, the plight that they sought
to address was worse and more stubborn than others. The people that Cantor
and Friedlaender had hoped to visit that July morning fit such a description.
Residents of the Jewish shtetl of Sokolavka on the outskirts of Yarmolintsy,
their numbers had been dwindling steadily over the previous two decades as
a result of recurring, murderous pogroms and of emigration to avoid the next
one. Many of those persons who had fled had then resettled in cities of the
northeastern United States, part of a great wave of twenty million immigrants,
most of them European, who had entered the country since the 1880s.[6]
Founded in the early months of the Great War to assist victims of anti-Semitic
persecution, the American-led JDC was initially reluctant to give immigration assistance to the overseas Jews it aimed to help, instead prioritizing aiding
needy Jews "where they are."[7] As JDC personnel like Friedlaender and Cantor
witnessed the ferocious anti-Semitism that had left hundreds of thousands
dead, wounded, and homeless throughout the region, it became increasingly
apparent that many Jews would not live a secure existence in the postwar
Europe that the JDC and other American organizations were trying to help
rebuild.

But as the material impediments that had dramatically hindered intercon-
tinental migration to the United States during the World War began to ease,
legal ones were emerging to take their place. The U.S. Congress stood poised
to curtail legal immigration radically, using a formula based on national origins that would purposely shut off most immigration from Eastern and
Southern Europe, the very areas producing many of the worst humanitarian
crises for Jews and others. And so, as thousands of American philanthropists
ventured overseas in their array of uniforms, the prospect loomed that when
they left, immigration to the United States might no longer offer the salve it
long had for the people that poet Emma Lazarus had in 1883 sympathetically
called "homeless, tempest-tossed" "huddled masses" yearning to find refuge
on the other side of America's "golden door."[8]

A World Safe for and from War

The humanitarian enterprise to which Bernard Cantor, Israel Friedlaender,
and thousands of others committed themselves proved grossly outmatched by
the crises it addressed. The suffering and chaos caused by the First World War
and the various conflicts that arose in its shadows and wake were vast, almost

incomprehensibly so. Nearly twenty million soldiers and civilians were killed with another twenty million wounded, most of them in Europe and the Near East. Almost countless numbers of widows and orphans were created during the war, all left to destroyed infrastructures, economies, and other mechanisms of social support. Four major empires collapsed—Ottoman, Austrian, German, and Czarist Russian—to be replaced by fragile nation-states and fervent nationalisms hostile to minority populations. The Great War begat other conflicts doing even more devastation into the early 1920s that included fighting between revolutionary Bolshevik Russians, anti-revolutionary White Russians, Poles, Ukrainians, Turkish nationalists, and Christian states in the Balkans.[9]

The Great War and its aftermath not only dislocated people on a scale never before witnessed, but it also helped to make the phenomenon of massive refugee crises a perpetual feature of the international order in the century that followed. Nearly ten million refugees were produced by military fighting, deportations, population swaps, and people's attempts to flee persecution and destitution. The demographic dislocations included two million Poles; two million Russians and Ukrainians; two million more Muslims and Christians exchanged between Turkey, Greece, and Bulgaria; one million ethnic Germans; and a quarter of a million Hungarians. When considering the number of people displaced internally within a state or empire, the numbers grow further. At the beginning of the Bolshevik Revolution in 1917, for instance, six million people were uprooted in the Russian Empire. To put this in perspective, all Russian industrial workers—the proletariat at the purported heart of the revolution—numbered only three and a half million. Russian cities often counted refugees as one in ten of their inhabitants.[10]

During most of the period of U.S. neutrality from 1914 to 1917, the American public generally resisted involvement in such a destructive affair far from the country's shores, but the specter of suffering war victims generated a notable exception to such isolationist impulses. Spurred by the German occupation of Belgium and northern France in the late summer of 1914, millions of Americans rushed to offer their contributions in cash, kind, and labor to war sufferers abroad. Their commitment was encouraged by anti-German lectures, posters, and theater performances across the country decrying "the Hun's Rape of Belgium" and the like. Beginning in 1915, reports of Ottoman atrocities against Armenian and Syrian Christians further fueled American sympathy born of outrage. Significant if smaller offerings were sent to Russia, Serbia, Romania and other Entente countries farther east. Many of the eight million Americans of German and Austrian heritage sent at least $2 million in aid to the Central Powers, a sometimes risky act in a public culture growing increasingly hostile to all things German.[11]

The verve and diversity of Americans' desire to support overseas civilians initially outpaced the institutional capacity to receive and distribute it. While scores of relatively small organizations developed their own means of collecting and distributing aid throughout wartorn Europe and the Near East, many contributions were given without a clear path for finding their intended targets. Vast amounts of money arrived at national organizations like the American Chamber of Commerce as well as such government offices as the U.S. embassy in Paris, often without suitable plans for dispensation. Though the American state stood largely to the side of such philanthropic endeavors during the period of neutrality, the U.S. ambassador to France, Myron Herrick, offered a glimpse of a more active government role in the near future when, to gain control of the situation, he helped to form the private War Relief Clearing House for France and Her Allies. Led by such prominent business leaders as Cornelius Vanderbilt and the president of General Electric, the Clearing House received contributions in cash, food, construction and agricultural tools, medical supplies, clothing, and children's toys from over six thousand private American organizations, bodies that included various social welfare groups, immigrant and nationality aid societies, religious associations, patriotic clubs, and industrial manufacturers. The Clearing House liaised with French and American officials to secure coveted transoceanic shipping space for these contributions across the sea, customs-free, before French rail cars took them to points of distribution inland. The Congressionally chartered American Red Cross funneled significant resources through the Clearing House along with other humanitarian agencies in the United States and abroad. Supplementing these various activities was the Rockefeller Foundation, which funded major health campaigns during and after the period of neutrality, the anti-typhus campaign it ran with the American Red Cross in Serbia being particularly notable.[12]

The largest institutional outlet for American relief contributions during the neutrality period was the Commission for Relief in Belgium. Led by Herbert Hoover, the successful mining engineer with a fast-growing reputation for managing vast and Byzantine international projects, the CRB convinced both British and German governments to let enough food pass through military barriers to feed nearly ten million people in German-occupied Belgium and Northern France during the war. Many of them otherwise would have been in danger of starving. It was a Herculean feat both diplomatically and logistically, and would set critical precedents for even larger relief projects directed by Hoover later in the war and in its aftermath.[13] Taking a cue from the CRB, the Committee for Armenian and Syrian Relief (later, Near East Relief) was formed in 1914, raising $100 million over the next decade for operations directed overwhelmingly at Christians in the region.[14]

The American Red Cross (ARC) additionally contributed to civilian relief through its own institutional channels. Considered by some persons in the late nineteenth century a fledgling and amateurish organization, it had since secured two Congressional charters and various proclamations naming it the country's premier disaster and war relief organization. Though supported by private contributions and, generally, run by private individuals, its connections with the state were legion, including the U.S. President serving at the head of the organization and the government promoting Red Cross fundraisers. This quasi-private, quasi-public institution (a descriptor used then and since) boasted twenty thousand members and one hundred fifty chapters during the neutrality period, sending 341 of its own "mercy ships" to Europe. The vessels carried enough medical personnel and equipment to build and operate sixteen hospitals in seven belligerent countries. Though the lion's share of these resources went to the Allied countries of England, France, Belgium, Russia, and Serbia, about one fifth benefited the Central Powers of Germany and Austria-Hungary.[15]

The ARC's operational focus during American neutrality, however, was not only on aiding refugees and other civilian victims of war, but also on providing medical care and shelter for wounded and sick combatants who had been charged with perpetrating the conflict's violence. It was a role that had centrally defined the organization since its founding in 1881, and was echoed in the work of other national Red Cross societies along with that of the International Red Cross in Geneva. Over twenty thousand such military personnel from countries on opposing sides of the conflict were treated by the ARC during the period before the United States officially entered the war in 1917. At once a humanitarian and military-support endeavor, Red Cross assistance not only helped soldiers return to battle, but also arguably allowed belligerent states to commit more resources to weapons and other technologies of martial violence that would have otherwise been required to maintain the health of their fighting forces. Despite what some observers perceived as a hypocritical tension between the simultaneous support of war-relieving and war-making, enthusiasm for the organization remained robust throughout the conflict, especially after the United States entered the war. In 1918, thirty-one million American women, men, and children claimed ARC membership, composing one third of the U.S. population. While many members volunteered little more than their name and a modest financial donation, such mass support proved profoundly important in the aggregate. During the decade after 1914, the ARC raised over $400 million for its domestic and overseas programs, to which tens of thousands of American social workers, medical professionals, sanitation experts, and others contributed their labor.[16]

Once the United States entered the war on April 6, 1917, opportunities for Americans to support endeavors that simultaneously promoted war-making and war-relieving expanded both within and well beyond the ARC, with the country's voluntary sector emerging as a critical surrogate arm of the American state in the latter's project of fighting the war. The responsibility for many of the welfare services provided to U.S. military personnel by the voluntary agencies during the First World War would be taken over by the military itself by during the Second World War. This transition had the effect, for years thereafter, of hardening the line between troop support and humanitarian civilian aid, a line that often had operated more flexibly for war workers during the First World War. Mirroring the blurred distinction between troop and civilian aid were the associational governing methods deployed by the voluntary and state spheres. To address human hardship during the period troop support and civilian war relief combined with each other, forming an international counterpart to numerous domestic projects. It operated through the combined efforts of state entities and civil society organizations. These were groups that confronted such social challenges as child and mother welfare, urban blight, labor conditions, natural resource management, and immigrant incorporation.[17] Ellis Hawley and Christopher Capozzola have shown how the public-private nature of Progressive-Era governance was similarly deployed on the American home front to mobilize the country for the Great War, with countless Americans volunteering their resources to help the state raise money to fund the conflict, conserve and produce war-related materials, recruit and enlist men for military service, and, demonstrating the coercive side of such activities, police those persons whose support for the war was considered suspect.[18] The war also invited Americans to export such patterns of hybrid governing activity abroad. As Julia Irwin has noted, "this associational form of social organization, so typical of the Progressive Era United States, shaped American approaches to world affairs."[19]

The leaders of the Red Cross and YMCA stepped forward first, immediately offering their full assistance to the government's war efforts. As had happened on a much smaller scale during the recent war with Mexico and the Spanish American War before it, the government invited the organizations to help the troops. While the Red Cross continued its historic responsibility for military medical care, the YMCA and six smaller national voluntary agencies formed the National War Work Council to coordinate with the War and Navy Departments to offer a wide array of "temporal" and "spiritual" troop welfare services. Most were religiously affiliated, and included the Salvation Army, Knights of Columbus, Jewish Welfare Board (JWB), and the YWCA. They represented older social welfare organizations or, in the case of the JWB, a new conglomeration of them. Though not representing an absolute consensus among American voluntary aid organizations—the pacifist Quakers, for instance, were leery of helping the military so directly—the agencies of the National War Work Council expressed their support for the government's war efforts, coupled with a confidence in their ability to do so with benevolent aims. National Commander for the Salvation Army, Evangeline Booth, matched the pitch of others in the Council when exclaiming that her organization stood "ready, trained in all necessary qualifications in every phase of humanitarian work, and the last man will stand by the President for execution of his Orders."[20]

The connections forged during the war between the American state and the troop welfare agencies boasted both material and symbolic dimensions. As for the former, the services the agencies provided the troops went well beyond merely supplemental support to include the provision of food, surgical supplies, uniforms, mail and telegraph services, recreation, and spiritual and emotional counsel. Many of the responsibilities that the U.S. military would bring in house by the Second World War were provided by the country's voluntary sector during the Great War, especially in its early stages when state capacity lagged considerably behind the needs of fighting the war. The U.S. Medical Department, for instance, initially counted only 403 nurses in the regular army compared to eight thousand in the Red Cross. And although the Army Nurse Corps ballooned to twenty-one thousand by war's end, Red Cross medical resources proved critically important in the early stages.[21] By the end of the Armistice period in 1919, the organizations in the War Work Council collectively worked with over five million U.S. soldiers, sailors, and marines, and nearly twenty million Allied personnel overall. The YMCA alone boasted twenty-six thousand paid staff and thirty-five thousand volunteers. Hundreds of service organization workers were killed, wounded, and taken prisoner, with scores receiving war decorations from the Allies.[22]

Among the more emblematic ties between state and civil society were uniforms and rank. The expansive guidelines created by the Wilson administration for the voluntary agencies wanting to work with the government went so far as to painstakingly describe the design of the uniforms that the personnel of the non-state organizations would wear. Each agency was assigned a slightly different uniform resembling those of the U.S. army to greater and lesser degrees. Even voluntary agency personnel like the Joint Distribution Committee's Bernard Cantor and Israel Friedlaender, who were involved not with troop support but civilian humanitarian aid, adopted the practice of wearing uniforms. It served as a marker of the often close connection not only between state and voluntary institutions, but also between troop welfare and civilian relief programs among American civil society organizations. Voluntary personnel working with U.S. troops were additionally given "assimilated" military rank. Officially just honorary titles, the ranks were nevertheless designed to strengthen the connection between the military and voluntary organizations, granting a further modicum of authority to the latter in the process.[23]

Privately resourced troop welfare programs were not alone in institutionally integrating the state and civil society in overseas wartime endeavors while simultaneously blurring the lines between supporting the state's war aims and mitigating the effects of the conflict's violence through humanitarian aid for civilians. The vast aid initiatives directed by Herbert Hoover formed another critical pillar for these phenomena. The several organizations led before, during, and after the war by the man commonly known by his admiring subordinates as "Chief" were sometimes funded by the United States and other governments, at other times supported predominantly by private contributions, or, on occasion, fueled by a balance of state and non-state resources. After two and a half years of leading the Commission for Relief in Belgium, Hoover was asked by President Wilson to direct American operations for feeding both the military and often starving civilian populations of the countries recently allied with the United States since the latter's declaration of war. Moving from a nongovernmental position with the CRB to that of a state official with the newly created U.S. Food Administration (USFA), Hoover spent the twenty-six months of America's formal involvement in the war and Armistice period using $3.5 billion in federal Treasury loans to purchase (mostly American) grain and other foodstuffs. Under Hoover's direction, the USFA then arranged for the remarkably complex distribution of these 23 million metric tons of supplies throughout a geographically vast expanse that stretched from

Bordeaux, France, to Vladistovok, Siberia, and countless points in between. Helping to ship and distribute the goods were noncombatants from the Allied militaries (when available), relief agencies of the various recipient countries, and personnel from American voluntary agencies, groups that included the Joint Distribution Committee, Red Cross, YMCA, AFSC, American National War Work Council, and other American voluntary organizations.[24]

Hoover continued his direction of massive war relief programs after the war ended, both during the Armistice period in the first half of 1919 and the Reconstruction period that lasted for several years thereafter. As director of general relief for the Allies during the Armistice, Hoover commanded the governmental contributions of the winning countries, $805 million of which (72 percent of the total) was provided by the U.S. Treasury under the auspices of two federal entities: the USFA, as it phased out in the first part of 1919, and, beginning in late February of that year, the first of several relief organizations under Hoover's direction that went by the name, American Relief Administration (ARA). These operations focused especially on the victims of the worst famine that Central and Eastern Europe had witnessed in three hundred years, helping perhaps one hundred fifty million persons, many of whom would otherwise likely have died. The first ARA was followed by three other Hoover-directed relief operations with similar names but funded with a significantly smaller proportion of government contributions in comparison to privately derived resources. Two of these concentrated on feeding children (1919–1923) while the other addressed a terrible famine in large swaths of Soviet Russia and the Ukraine. Though officially distinct, the array of aid entities under Hoover's command was commonly referred to collectively at the time as the "American Mission," the "Relief Commission" or simply "Hoover's operations."[25]

Historian Bruno Cabanes has demonstrated that Hoover's missions joined the contemporary initiatives of such other prominent humanitarian advocates as René Cassin and Fridtjof Nansen in building a normative architecture for humanitarian-based rights, an architecture that would be remodeled continuously throughout the twentieth century. In many ways, however, Hoover's approach to his own work emphasized the nuts and bolts of effective administration at least as much as it did the ideals of justice.[26] The Chief ruled over his various relief missions with an authoritative and innovative hand. Hoover perpetually found ways to secure resources from both states and private contributors for his array of relief organizations. As the USFA wound down in early 1919, for instance, he successfully lobbied for a $100 million grant from

Congress to fund the first incarnation of the ARA. He additionally commanded surplus American food stocks previously earmarked for war use, along with vast supplies requisitioned from the defeated Central Powers. To help meet labor needs, Hoover arranged for two thousand five hundred U.S. military personnel to be transferred to his command after the war, many, hand selected young officers of Ivy League pedigree. By most accounts, the commitment of these servicemen transferred easily to America's civilian relief Chief, who, in the words of his biographer, garnered "almost boundless devotion" from the relief personnel under his charge. Or as stated by one such aid worker, Gilchrist Stockton, Hoover "has no idea of our absolute loyalty." A civilian government official with his own loyal army of relief workers, in the Armistice period alone, Hoover directed the distribution of over $1 billion of aid to two dozen countries in Europe and the Near East.[27]

As wartime turned to a postwar period focused on negotiating a peace and rebuilding the shattered territories of Europe and the Near East, the avenues through which a range of Americans could express their philanthropic identities multiplied. Many of the U.S. military personnel working for the initial incarnation of the ARA decided to remain active in war relief after the Armistice ended in mid-1919, and Hoover's relief operations transitioned from state to predominantly privately run and funded entities. Some remained under the Chief's direction while others joined a range of overseas civilian aid operations including those run through the Red Cross and Anti-Typhus Commission or one of the private American agencies like the YMCA, Knights of Columbus, JDC, or American Friends Service Committee that typically attracted volunteers based on their religious or ethnic identity. Additionally, the voluntary agencies themselves were often incorporated under the larger umbrella of either the Red Cross or Hoover's organizations, all part of the diversity of options Americans had to engage overseas during the war.[28]

Serving America by Saving the World

James Becker was among the many Americans who saw in the intersecting lines of overseas war work an opportunity to express the multiple solidarities that moved him to action. If war encourages extraordinary hatred for a defined set of others, so too can it foster exceptional empathy for people both close by and far away, empathy that can grow into profound feelings of re-

Figure 1. U.S. Food Administration. "Exhibit by the U.S. Food Administration for Indiana in the Liberty Loan Parade, April 6, 1918." Records of the U.S. Food Administration, RG 4-G. NARA, B 3, F 24.

sponsibility for others, whether of a patriot and citizen for a nation and its government, a cosmopolitan idealist for an expansively imagined humanity, or a member of an ethno-religious group for cultural comrades overseas. In the span of several years, James Becker embraced each of these types of empathetic sensibilities in simultaneously overlapping and evolving ways. A snapshot of his young adult life offers a close look at the phenomenon of wartime empathy, revealing how people's expressions of philanthropic commitment were commonly channeled through the wartime institutions available to them, institutions which in turn afforded them potentially life altering opportunities. Becker's experience furthermore lends to almost incomprehensibly vast phenomena a more approachable scale, humanizing the complex choices and horrors confronted by thousands of Americans hoping to do some good in an unusually frenetic and dark time. Finally, it serves as a reminder that, although the era of the Great War produced tremendous suffering across diverse populations and vast expanses, the communities that some Americans tried to help were in considerably worse shape and with bleaker prospects than others. It was a realization that ultimately steered Becker's path across those of Bernard Cantor and Israel Friedlaender, as all three men were ushered into an emerging era where the world's most dispossessed people found progressively fewer outlets for refuge.

"Jimmie" Becker had just completed his freshman year at Cornell University when Austria's Archduke Franz Ferdinand was assassinated on June 28, 1914, sparking the conflict that would stir the young man to patriotically inspired service before his graduation three years later.[29] The beneficiary of a privileged upbringing that emphasized giving back to the community, the Becker family epitomized the type of American success story that was becoming increasingly attainable by the turn of the century for Reform Jews of Germanic background. Born in 1894, Jimmie Becker was raised in an affluent part of the Hyde Park neighborhood on Chicago's South Side, surrounded by other Jews who could also typically claim at least a generation or two of family presence in the United States. His parents, Kittie and Abraham, afforded their son and his three sisters a "harmonious life filled with love and mutual respect," their handsome home hosting "many joyous family festivities, friends and parties."[30] As a teenager, Jimmie spent an entire summer touring northwestern Europe.[31] His father used the considerable profits from his fast-growing investment banking business to become one of the city's more prominent philanthropists for both civic and Jewish institutions, endeavors in which his young son took a considerable interest.[32] A self-described "greasy grind" in high school whose intellectual fixations crowded out other pursuits, Becker spread his wings at Cornell. He continued to be a serious and gifted student who took time to assist the less fortunate around him, but also engaged in sports and a range of social activities.[33]

The United States entry into the war in early April 1917 would dramatically change Jim, his preferred name by that time, as it did so many of his generation—although the change came too slowly for Becker's taste. Set to graduate Phi Beta Kappa, he watched the large majority of his classmates leave school early to support their country in the war, whether through the military, voluntary agencies providing troop welfare overseas, or for those governmental or commercial enterprises feverishly mobilizing the country's agricultural and industrial resources for the task ahead.[34] After receiving a tepid response from his parents to his plea to volunteer for combat service, he agreed to their suggestion that he find work at the bottom rung of a company in order to give the privileged young man some real-world business experience in preparation for his presumed career with the family bank. Even though he acquiesced, Becker found a way to play a role in the conflict nonetheless, working for a gun factory in Massachusetts that made rifles and bayonets for one of America's new partners in the war, the Imperial Russian army.[35]

Gun manufacturing would prove only the first of several ways in which

Becker supported his country's war effort as he strove toward his goal of serving overseas. While not initially called into service after registering for the draft on June 5, 1917, with nearly ten million other men between the ages of twenty-one and thirty, by middle summer, he obtained the opportunity to move a little closer to the action. Accepting a job in Washington, D.C., with a government office eventually known as the War Trade Board, Becker helped with the regulation of shipping food, munitions, and other materials important to the war effort. Predicting to his parents that "my work promises to be wonderful," he nevertheless kept his sights on serving for the U.S. military abroad. The next summer, he received half of that wish when he was finally called for military duty. But instead of being shipped overseas to fight, he wore his U.S. army uniform at a desk located just up the street from his old job, doing similar work for the War Department's Purchase, Storage, and Traffic Division. And so for the final half year of fighting, Becker remained intimately involved with the conflict, yet far from the action of which he wanted to be a part.[36]

As the war ended on November 11, 1918, Becker remained committed to serving his country overseas, even though it could no longer be in a combat role. The day after the Armistice, Becker, bedraggled from celebrating with other service members the day before, asked his parents to give "serious consideration" to allowing him to help with the postwar rebuilding work in Europe should the opportunity arise. Possibly raising an eyebrow from his banker father, the young man explained that he wanted to put his talents "to some use other than merely money making." Opining "how narrow is the life of the ordinary person during ordinary times," he predicted that "the post war period will be one of the most interesting in the history of the world," especially in Europe.[37] Just after the New Year, he was "tickled to death" to learn that an old friend had come through for him. Lewis Strauss, Hoover's personal assistant (who would later gain fame by charging nuclear scientist Robert Oppenheimer with national disloyalty while Strauss served as head of the Atomic Energy Commission in 1954), was instrumental in reassigning Lieutenant James Becker from his position with the War Department in Washington to Hoover's U.S. Food Administration in Paris. Becker reflected in his diary that it was an opportunity to "see our job through."[38] If the "job" for Jim was no longer about military victory, it was nonetheless a chance to perform his patriotic duty in the center of the action, on behalf of a world that needed what America had to offer. Becker acknowledged to his parents that he knew "nothing about the work" he would be doing other than that he would keep his present army rank, but he nevertheless believed it to be "one of the grandest chances a young fellow could possibly get—and just to work under Mr. Hoover is a great treat." "Today," he told them, "I am in high spirits and looking forward to the most interesting events of my life."[39]

After a farewell weekend of wining and dining in Manhattan with family and friends, Becker set off to Paris for his new adventure. His passage on the *U.S.S. Agamemnon*, a military transport ship until the Armistice, foreshadowed the mix of opulent prestige and martial grit that would mark his early tenure with Hoover's American mission in Europe. On the one hand, he both met fellow "Cornell men" and encountered the entire Chinese delegation for the peace conference that had just begun in Paris, each reminders that not only that he was heading toward a major endeavor unfolding in Europe, but also that he had been chosen as a select member of that undertaking. Less appealing to the privileged young man were the dirty linens, bad food, and cacophonous band that endlessly played in the officers' dining room, all quite different from his "crossing on a commercial liner" as a youth.[40] Adding to the contrasting and liminal nature of the wider endeavors upon which Becker embarked, he was also one of twenty-five hundred U.S. service members recruited to work for the U.S. government's civilian-directed postwar relief operations—first, through the USFA, and by late February, its successor, the federal ARA—which were in turn supported robustly by both public tax dollars and non-state contributions.[41]

Arriving for work at Paris's stately Hotel Crillon on January 23, 1919, Becker's appetite to serve his country while engaging with the world must have seemed well on its way to being satiated.[42] He had entered the nerve center of postwar planning, a fact which delighted him. Not only did many of the delegates tasked with negotiating the postwar peace agreement, including President Woodrow Wilson himself, stay and work at the hotel, but the postwar relief operations under Hoover's direction were just ramping up in dozens of bustling offices at the Crillon too. Hoover's command center pulsed, in the Chief's later words, with:

> the clatter of typewriters, adding machines, [and] telegraph instruments . . . the walls covered with ocean maps upon which every morning little flags showed where our hundreds of ships were and where they were going; charts of twentyfive [sic] countries showing what their stocks of food were at the last date and what they would need in the next month.[43]

The energy extended to the hotel's restaurant, which Becker found to be "splendid," boasting not only close proximity to "generals, admirals, statesmen galore," but also more "Cornell men," who helped make "Paris feels like home." Becker spent his first afternoon of work with Lewis Strauss and Lieutenant Robert Byfield, a mutual friend of theirs also recently recruited to the relief mission, sitting in on Hoover's conferences with the types of important men Jim had dined near at lunch. That night, the three friends convened in Hoover's "beautiful" suite at the hotel where they had "a truly European party" consisting of a "fine meal with a good bottle of red wine." It was, he reflected before drifting off to sleep that night, "the most eventful day of my young life!"[44]

As Becker and fellow members of the American mission fanned out by train from Paris in early February to establish various regional relief operations in Central and Eastern Europe, he relished feeling connected to a country, organization, and boss often publicly revered by the community leaders, public officials, and other locals whom he encountered. He deemed it "a wonderful experience to be selected for a mission like this and I appreciate it more every day. What a rare opportunity to meet people and see things." Echoing the enthusiasm of others working under Chief Hoover's command, Lieutenant Becker marveled at the stature of the former mining engineer and his operations among top U.S. military brass and foreign leaders alike, filling his journal and private correspondence with such exaltations as "oh Hoover, what wonders are worked in thy name!" and "the power of the Relief Commission is startling—makers and breakers of governments, because none of the governments of Central or Southeastern Europe can stand without being fed by the Commission."[45] Becker and the other uniformed men of the American mission enjoyed being "gaped at" on the streets, fed extravagant meals, and treated "like kings," including regularly enjoying opera from the choicest boxes in the house. When the orchestra at the Warsaw opera played the Star Spangled Banner in their honor, "the people all arose, looked up at our boxes, cheered, clapped, etc." This event, among many gestures Becker received, indicated to him "how grateful they all are to America." The attention also included having "a great time with the girls," with Jim predicting that "if I only had time to play with them I surely could make hay."[46] Ascribing the welcome attention to more than whatever romantic charisma he possessed, Becker observed that "the girls all make a great fuss over my uniform—they like the pockets, the bars, the eagles, the collar etc. It is funny to hear them—'tres chick' [sic]. It is a good looking uniform if I say so myself."[47]

If Lieutenant Becker's uniform told one story of his identity as he traveled eastward with the American mission, the specific duties he had been assigned offered another, purposely less visible one that he would embrace increasingly over time. Before Becker left Paris, Strauss had explained that while Jim would indeed work in the "Administration of Relief"—that is, in the official, public domain of Hoover's operations—he was being given a "secret and specific purpose too." Strauss and Hoover had been discussing troubling rumors from Central and Eastern Europe about the unusually difficult situation of Jewish communities there. Not only had Jews suffered tremendous persecution at the hands of governments, armies, and civilian neighbors—including pogroms that had likely killed thousands—but also the desperately needed supplies sent by Hoover's operations were reportedly being purposefully withheld from Jews by the local governments and charities.[48] Though Hoover rather conspicuously used his various postwar relief organizations to support the White Russians against the Bolsheviks in the Russian Civil War, he was more committed to the principle of humanitarian neutrality when it came to religion and ethnicity.[49] So, along with his and Strauss's old friend, Byfield, who was also Jewish, Becker would travel to Eastern Europe to "send back confidential reports by secret courier telling about conditions and treatment of Jews in these places and whether there was any truth in the reported persecutions and unfair treatment which they were receiving." Becker was initially to operate in Poland, with Byfield going to Austria and Romania. They were charged, in other words, with setting up Jewish relief operations in Eastern Europe for the nascent relief mission there, but were to do so surreptitiously so as not to spark anti-Semitic backlash among the local Gentile communities.[50]

The problem of anti-Semitism was not, however, only with Europeans but also with the U.S. diplomatic corps and Military Intelligence Division, both of which would be critically important liaisons for the work of Hoover's mission. Operating with a military and civilian staff of fourteen hundred by the end of the war, MID officials in Paris regularly accepted specious reports from their military attachés stationed in cities throughout Europe and the Near East that the Jewish personnel of the Joint Distribution Committee who increasingly populated the beleaguered regions in the war's aftermath were in fact Bolshevik agents masquerading as welfare workers. Sometimes relying on dubious intelligence from foreign governments, MID officials claimed that JDC personnel and other Jewish aid workers systematically sought to thwart anti-Bolshevik forces that included White Russians and Polish, Ukrainian, and Romanian nationalists. They also charged both the JDC and Hebrew Immigrant Aid Society with purposefully helping pro-Bolshevik Jewish refugees to immigrate to the United States in an effort to subvert the American government in favor of Communism. In time the MID even succeeded in placing some JDC workers on passport refusal lists. Both diplomatic officials stationed in places like Poland and Romania as well as the military attachés of the MID who briefed them were known to discount reports of mass attacks against Jewish civilians as targeted military responses to allegedly armed and hostile Jews rather than pogroms. The anti-Jewish attitude reached the upper echelon of Hoover's relief operations as well, with one remarking in his diary, "on with the pogroms," after having described the "greasy beards" of the Orthodox people he had recently seen in "90% Jew country" while traveling to Prague.[51]

Adding another layer of complexity to the situation, prominent American officials of the Joint Distribution Committee had worked out an arrangement with Hoover whereby money raised in American Jewish communities for overseas Jewish relief would be transferred by the JDC into the bank accounts of the federal government's ARA, where it could then be earmarked for distribution as material aid to Jews and, sometimes, to non-Jews as well. At the beginning of the Armistice, and to varying degrees for a year or more thereafter, the JDC had little to no operational presence in those areas where Jews were hit worst by the war and the brutal discrimination and pogroms that followed it. Local Jewish charities struggled to regain their footing, and while JDC personnel labored to establish relief conduits through local organizations, they were often stymied in doing so by the continuing violence, lawlessness and, above all, feverish anti-Semitism. This proved most true in the very areas where Jews suffered most, especially in the Pale of Settlement, now a chaotic place of emerging states and warring forces that included Poland, Romania, Ukraine, and the western edge of a mutating Russian Empire. While JDC leaders would have preferred to have had a more direct hand in managing Jewish relief, especially in the early stages of the postwar period, they often needed to channel aid through Hoover's operations for the institutional reach and geopolitical heft they provided.[52] People like Becker and Byfield thus became the JDC's "secret" intermediaries on the inside of Hoover's mission. So too, as it happens, was Strauss, who had been recruited the previous July by JDC chairman Felix Warburg to serve as a middleman between the JDC and Hoover's operations, an engineer for a part of America's relief mission that required robust action and yet needed to fly below the radar.[53]

Jewish officials in Hoover's operation like Becker, Strauss, and Byfield also periodically liaised with a JDC advisory council of several prominent

American Jews who were in Paris during the first half of 1919 to observe and advise in the creation of the Minority Treaties and other developments tied to the peace talks.[54] Beginning with the first of the Minority Treaties, for the newly configured state of Poland in June of that year, such legal agreements to protect religious and ethnic minorities proved tragically ineffective in significantly stemming the level of persecution in the Eastern European states required to accept the treaties. Strident disagreements among some of the Jewish leaders themselves over the issue of Zionism failed to help matters.[55]

JDC personnel worked especially diligently, and often warily, with officials from the State Department, U.S. military, Hoover's relief missions, and the Red Cross to help navigate the particularly rocky waters around the field of Jewish humanitarian assistance. At times, this situation meant that the JDC made its supplies available to suffering Gentile communities as well as to area Jews in order to curb potentially violent resentment that Jews, though often worse off, might nevertheless be receiving more aid from what were in fact sometimes the JDC's better supplied operations.[56] JDC officials fastidiously cleared their proposals for international operations with the State Department, even when not officially required, intensely mindful of maintaining the good graces of government officials in a department with a reputation for strains of anti-Semitism. Such interactions occurred regularly between both mid- and high-level officials in the JDC and State that included frequent correspondences between Woodrow Wilson's secretary of state Robert Lansing and JDC chairman Felix Warburg.[57] Among other things, the JDC commonly needed the Department to smooth the way with foreign governments and military commanders in order to ensure that JDC money, food, medical supplies, clothes, and other relief items would go where they were needed. Proposals consisting of the transfer of funds and materials were typically given the Department's blessing, but until the later stages of the war, the government discouraged operations requiring JDC personnel on the ground in the war zones for fear of complicating American diplomacy and, after America's entry into the war in April 1917, strategic operations. As a result, during much of the fighting the JDC had to channel its funds and relief materials—considerable though they were—from its New York headquarters through intermediary banks and distribution centers in Europe and the Near East to local Jewish agencies operating in and near the war zones.[58]

Becker faithfully heeded the charge to mute the Jewish nature of his responsibilities, particularly in the early stages of his work. For instance, before his departure from Paris, when he met with Zionist leaders Chaim Weizmann and Nahum Sokolow to be briefed on the condition of the devastated Jewish shtetls of Eastern Europe, the young lieutenant hid from the men that he had been placed specifically in charge of Jewish affairs for the U.S. government's relief organization. Initiating a disciplined habit he would continue as he moved into the devastated East, Becker presented himself to the two men primarily as a dispassionate federal official "merely representing the Food Administration and not the Jewish Interests." Becker noted in his journal that he "did not want them to know my real mission."[59] When meeting with local Jews in Poland, including much older community leaders, Becker adopted an officious, sometimes even paternalistic tone of a U.S. government official just looking "to see that everyone got a fair deal," rather than a fellow Jew who understood that Jewish communities frequently required disproportionate help.[60]

Even after being shaken in mid-February 1919 by his first direct evidence of a recent pogrom, Becker nonetheless maintained his official pose, although his personal reflections suggested that an internal struggle was brewing. While touring the Jewish quarter of Lemberg, Poland that had been destroyed in November, the Lieutenant was unclear whether the atrocities were perpetrated by the Polish military or Ukrainian nationals—both had been complicit in similar attacks on Jews—but the effects of the massacre were obvious. He learned that during three days of horror, the Jewish quarter was sealed off, with fifty-four houses being burned and shelled to smoking rubble. The synagogue and stores met a similar fate. Over thirteen thousand people were robbed of their belongings and cash. Jewish women were systematically raped, four hundred people were wounded, and seventy-three killed. As he visited the sick, wounded, and orphaned victims over the coming days, he found their condition "beyond belief," surmising that the milk he procured through the American mission for an orphanage was the only thing keeping the children from starving to death. The stories about such pogroms making their way westward were, in Becker's description, "far too weak" when compared to the reality he was witnessing.[61] The Lemberg pogrom in fact was credited with helping to reignite a wave of dozens of others in the region. The massacres of the late 1910s and early 1920s accounted for nearly two hundred thousand Jewish deaths alone in the eastern part of Poland, where Becker was assigned, along with neighboring Ukraine where matters were rumored to be even worse partly because war conditions prevented Western relief agencies from setting up operations.[62]

While clearly distraught by what he had witnessed, the young American still initially found it difficult—or perhaps more accurately, unwarranted—to trade his U.S. army boots for the shoes of the vulnerable Jews he spent hours working to help. In a "heated" living-room debate Becker took issue with a group of Lemberg's prominent Jews who defended their decision to remain neutral in the war between the Poles and Ukrainians since both sides mistreated them regardless. Becker "strenuously objected" to their position, making his case with an analogy colored by his particular understanding of national civic duty, a conception that seemed to his hosts a poor application to their predicament wherein nationalism was perpetually used to exclude and oppress rather than unite and reward. The U.S. army lieutenant lectured that if such a separatist position ruled in the United States, "there would be no American nation," adding that, "America did not want anyone who in her hour of need would forsake his America for the land of his birth." Lieutenant Becker believed Polish officials to be "right when they say that such a stand cannot exist and therefore you are either for us or against us—either friend or enemy." Becker's embrace of Polish nationalism and frustrations with reticent Polish Jews was not so different than that of many of his U.S. army comrades stationed in the area. The U.S. ambassador to Poland, Hugh Gibson, reported that American soldiers were "first amused by the costume of the Jews, their beards, their habits and are then incensed by their lack of patriotism." While Becker was undoubtedly more sympathetic to the plight of the region's Jews, he nevertheless assigned some blame to the victims. "Of course the pogroms were horrible and inexcusable," he reflected that night in his journal, "but one can understand how they happened." Continuing to analogize the local situation with that in his home country, he predicted that the United States would have "adopted the same course" had Americans of German descent similarly refused to fight for their country in the Great War. "If Poland was good enough to live in," the patriotic young lieutenant reasoned, "it was good enough to die for."[63]

As exceptionally callous as such sentiments might seem in hindsight, they were echoed and nurtured by a political culture on the American home front where the difference between dissidence and treason against one's state was blurred considerably during the era of the Great War. As enforced by a wide array of voluntary associations and the government alike, one's loyalty to the nation-state regularly trumped that to any cultural group or political position, particularly when the former diverged from the latter two. The use of German, for instance, was forcibly curtailed in schools, churches, and other public spaces. Extra-legal violence, including lynching, was sometimes tolerated as a form of vigilante coercion against those suspected of being disloyal to or even reticent about the American war effort. In another articulation of the powerful norm of national obligation during the period, just weeks after Becker's confrontation with the Jewish leaders of Lemberg, America's iconic progressive Supreme Court Justice Oliver Wendell Holmes, Jr., explained his majority decision in the unanimously decided *Schenck* case to limit legally acceptable free speech during war time by opining that, "when a nation is at war many things that might be said in time of peace are such a hindrance to its effort that their utterance will not be endured so long as men fight." And so, if the confluence of circumstances confronted by Becker in the Lemberg living room were exceptional, the conclusions he applied to them about conformity and patriotic duty should be seen as less so given the broader context of contemporary American political culture.[64]

This is not to say, however, that Becker's sense of patriotism and the proper role he saw for his country in the world was shared by all or even most other Americans. At least partly as a result of his familial upbringing and education, he was motivated by a cosmopolitanism that differed from many of his contemporary citizens who believed that their country should exit the troubled international stage now that the war had concluded. As with many others working for American relief organizations after the war, Becker believed that his country had an obligation and unique ability to help heal a broken world, and as a patriotic American citizen, he had a duty to aid in those efforts. In his journal and letters from the period, he betrayed a perspective that historians have variously termed "liberal internationalist," "progressive internationalist," or "Wilsonian internationalist." That is, Becker joined many others working in overseas American war relief in his belief that such humanitarian action would benefit both the United States and the world, and that there was no inherent conflict between an embrace of benevolently inspired multilateral cooperation and the confidence that his country knew better than others the best way forward.[65] Even though Becker differed from most other members of the American relief mission in his "secret" assignment as a cultural minority tasked with looking after an especially traumatized group, his response to the Jewish leaders of Lemberg suggests that, at this early stage of his relief work, the part of him identifying as a patriotic citizen of a nation-state overrode that of a Jew empathizing with the suffering of other Jews.

The young U.S. army lieutenant proved to be on the cusp of changing, however, as he witnessed not only the results of more massacres and discrimination against Jews, but also direct threats to his life that included encounters with the type of combat in which he had once pined to engage. Upon seeing the "disfigured faces" of soldiers wounded in the first battle he witnessed, he declared that "the glory of war does not enter military hospitals." After weeks of hearing the screams of artillery shells flying over his head as Ukrainian nationalists launched recurrent attacks on Polish-held Lemberg, Becker refused to leave the town even though he predicted that "there is bound to be a terrible slaughter with no mercy shown to any of us."[66] Recalling the admonition from his mother that "now that the war is over I am unwilling for you to run any risks," he admitted that he was nonetheless becoming "every day more and more of a fatalist," even contemplating writing his parents a farewell letter that could be sent to them upon his death. To keep critical relief supplies flowing, he sloshed through muddy combat trenches, placed luggage against train windows as "a sort of protection against bullets," and avoided being on a plane hit by "70 bullets" only because of a miscommunication over its scheduled departure.[67] Fearing that he "would never see dear old Chicago again," he refused "to regret having come here—how could one when there is such suffering going on and such need for help . . . which perhaps I alone can get for them?" Justifying his decision to push forward in the face of danger, Becker hoped that even his mother would "want me to see the job through" if only she "knew the conditions here."[68]

Figure 2. Underwood and Underwood, photographer. "Hungry Russian Women Kneel Before American Relief Administration Officials." New York: Underwood and Underwood, 1922. Library of Congress, Prints and Photographs Division: Miscellaneous Items in High Demand. FSS-Famines-Russia-1922.

Evolving Loyalties

As the winter of 1919 turned to spring, Becker's writing betrayed someone transitioning between two *mentalités*. On the one hand was the U.S. army lieutenant conscientiously, if surreptitiously, discharging duties for his government's humanitarian aid agency. But assuming more and more influence within the young man was a sober, and even somber, American Jew expressing a passionate commitment for his Eastern European "co-religionists," as he increasingly came to call them.[69] The army officer who had previously opined that Jewish pogrom victims were partly complicit in their own plight increasingly turned his critical sights on the ruling authorities and majority populations he had previously defended. The month after his February argument with the Jews of Lemberg, Becker decided that Poland was in fact "the land of hate and prejudice, and the very air is tainted."[70] Less than two months later, in May, Becker had seen enough hate and prejudice to determine that "half of these countries are not worth fighting for." The college student who in mid-1917 had begged for his parents' permission to fight for his country was by mid-1919 scoffing at the prospect of his country ever again raising "another army 'to save the world for Democracy.'"[71]

After approximately half a year of service for Hoover's operations, Becker made his transition official in the middle of 1919, letting his military commission expire so he could begin to work for the Joint Distribution Committee as it continued to build its operational presence across Europe and the Near East. The nature of his work was in many ways similar to that which he had been doing for Hoover's mission during the previous months. Upon arriving in a new area, he would establish contact with the local Jewish leaders in nearby cities and towns, gathering information on the needs of the Jewish communities in each. This included learning whether the municipal welfare bureaus and charities had been withholding food, clothing, soap, medicine, and other relief supplies from the Jewish population, a common practice throughout the regions where Becker worked. During his work with both the ARA and the JDC, he accordingly made contact with the leaders of such mainstream relief organizations in an effort—sometimes successful, sometimes not—to give Jews more equitable treatment. In his efforts to persuade local officials, Becker commonly worked to leverage his connections with sympathetic officials in the higher ranks of the ARA, U.S. military, and American State Department. As with other American aid officials, Becker placed suffering populations in various categories according to their perceived needs, be they orphans requiring institutional guardians; the infirmed, wounded, or elderly demanding medical treatment and sanitary conditions; the malnourished pining for food; or displaced refugees needing shelter and protection, and when the circumstances allowed, passage to temporary havens of asylum or new homelands of resettlement. Whatever their need or needs, the people who fell under Becker's purview shared in a state of dispossession. Becker also demanded that Jewish charity officials within a given city or town unite under a single federation to make the distribution of relief supplies from the American entities he represented more streamlined and efficient. Becker was acutely aware that he was sometimes the only outsider working to deliver relief to marginalized and exceptionally needy populations, often making such observations in his correspondence and journal as "the Jews of Lemberg know that I am here and they are starting to flock to me." As all of this occurred, Becker communicated with his colleagues to the West—typically in Paris and Washington for the ARA, and in Paris and New York for the JDC—to make arrangements for shipment of the necessary material relief supplies and, sometimes, cash that Becker had calculated the various Jewish communities in his region required. Upon arrival, Becker was often responsible for seeing that local aid organizations distributed the relief fairly.[72]

Through the spring of 1920, Becker was responsible mainly for establishing JDC relief operations for the Jews of Romania, another area riddled by political instability and profound anti-Semitic persecution. By mid-1920, Becker had seen his responsibilities for the JDC expand. This included serving as acting director general of the JDC's expansive array of European operations for the final few months of 1920 before he finally returned home to Chicago to take up his place with the family's investment business. Assuming an astonishing degree of responsibility for someone still in his mid-twenties, Becker's innovative administrative skills and fervent perseverance earned him the reputation among his superiors at the JDC as a highly valued asset of the organization. In a confidential letter from March 1920, high ranking JDC official Julius Goldman reported to JDC chairman Felix Warburg that Goldman had not "come across in any of the work that has been done by anybody on behalf of the J.D.C." someone betraying "more intelligent, conscientious, and humane action." Even more noteworthy was that "a young man of barely twenty-five years should have been able to develop such an insight into the conditions that must have been entirely strange to him."[73] Another JDC official, who already thought Becker was "a wonder" based on distant observation alone, came to "think ten times of him" after observing the young man operate first hand.[74]

As Becker's committed solidarity with the suffering Jews of Eastern Europe intensified, he grew to cast a more critical eye on his privileged and relatively insulated upbringing in Chicago. During his youth, Becker had only limited exposure to the types of Yiddish-speaking, Orthodox, Eastern European Jews he later encountered constantly abroad. His family's stately lakeside home and their Reformed Temple Sinai must have seemed an ocean away from the overcrowded immigrant dwellings of Chicago's Maxwell Street ghetto except when young Jimmie visited the charities his father bankrolled for the poor residents of the neighborhood.[75] As was often the case in other American cities, the charities serving Chicago's Orthodox and Reformed Jewish communities largely operated separately from one another, echoing broader divisions between the cultures.[76] At about the time of Becker's move from the American Relief Administration to the JDC, he lamented to his parents the religious instruction he received at Sinai had been "too reformed" and not offering "enough of the old Jewish traditions and customs." It was something he planned to rectify upon his eventual return stateside by making "a late start."[77]

Becker's criticism was sometimes cast more widely toward the set of affluent Jews, friends and business associates of his parents, who had watched him grow up. One such occasion occurred at a Chicago banquet held "In Honor of Lieutenant James Becker" in April 1920 during his first and only visit home during his two year relief tour overseas. After the attendees applauded and laughed during the light-hearted introduction of their hometown "hero," "Jimmie," by Chicago judge and future Illinois governor Henry Horner, Becker stepped up to the podium and brought the mood down at the tony Standard Club. Expressing embarrassment that such an event would be held in his honor, Becker explained that though the previous year had at times given him considerable fulfillment and even happiness, it had also been the "saddest year of my life." He proceeded to speak for at least an hour, providing a somber, painstakingly detailed, and sometimes ghastly account of the devastation he had witnessed accompanied by the measures he had implemented to help the battered communities of Eastern Europe rebuild. Turning the spotlight on the people in front of him, he lamented reports that American Jews were "skeptical as to the need" of the Jews in Europe, and had consequently refrained from contributing financially to their plight as much as Becker believed they could have. He assured his audience that if they had witnessed the "horror and misery" he had seen, "those stricken Jews would have all the money they need."[78]

At another speech in Chicago, Becker's frustration proved less inhibited, tying such a lack of commitment to the disaster overseas to a "damnable internal anti-Semitism" held by well assimilated American Jews of Germanic background for recent Ashkenazi Jewish immigrants from Eastern Europe.[79] In cities throughout the country, America's better established Jewish communities were known to express fear that the immigration of over two and a half million Eastern European Jews to the United States since the early 1880s would, in the words of one contemporary observer, bring the wrong kind of "attention" from the "general population."[80] Many from this relatively well established, economically viable American Jewish population had arrived from provinces in the German Confederation and other parts of Central Europe decades earlier in the mid-nineteenth century, and might just as likely consider the newer, poorer immigrants, with their Orthodox practices, strange language, and unfamiliar appearances more as foreigners than as fellow Jews.[81] One American Jewish philanthropist of German descent was noted to have stood apart from certain colleagues in his elite circle for believing that "even Jews in Romania were human beings."[82] Though New York City was best known for these phenomena, with the resentful condescension of some "uptown Jews" toward the newer arrivals crowded into the Lower East Side, Becker spread the blame, accusing Chicago's better assimilated "North Side Jews and South Side Jews" attending his talk of alienating themselves from the "West Side" Jews of the Maxwell Street ghetto. Becker continued that his experiences had taught him that "the non-Jew" who was responsible for "pogroms and prejudice and hatred and bigotry" saw no such distinctions, only "plain Jews." Becker wondered aloud if the suffering of Jews thousands of miles away was in fact "God punishing us for our own anti-Semitism."[83]

Even as Becker fiercely embraced his role from the second half of 1919 through 1920 as a Jew working for a Jewish organization serving Jewish communities, he nonetheless continued to wear the uniform of a U.S. military officer affiliated with Hoover's great American relief mission. He did this both figuratively and literally. As for the former, he often found it prudent to let those persons with whom he worked assume that he was still with the American Relief Administration rather than the JDC. He did this to minimize anti-Semitic discrimination while benefiting from the reputational heft of both Hoover's operations and the U.S. military. When a sympathetic U.S. army officer working for the ARA wrote Becker letters of introduction to other American relief officials across Romania—letters that intimated an authority for him over ARA operations that Becker in fact did not possess—Becker decided happily that "no one will be wiser and we will just go along on this assumption." Such an assumption also undoubtedly helped Becker deal with Romanian officials who could otherwise resist working with personnel from the JDC. Becker capitalized on his presumed stature by taking over key parts of the ARA's distribution pipeline so that local Romanian officials could no longer purposefully withhold American aid—whether from the ARA or American Red Cross—from Jewish communities. With this and related initiatives, even after Becker had fully committed himself to helping Jews through a Jewish organization, he sometimes still embraced a role similar to the one assigned to him by Lewis Strauss when Becker began his work for Hoover's operations at the beginning of January 1919. That is, he kept the Jewish nature of his working profile low when he deemed it strategically sensible, maximizing the leverage he could attain from an affiliation with the postwar prestige of the United States of America.[84]

Becker also continued wearing the uniform of a U.S. military officer in the literal sense. Evidence indicates that he did so, along with other JDC staff who possessed U.S. army uniforms, while working in less stable areas where there was a greater chance of being accosted or receiving friction from local civilian authorities, military personnel, or civilians themselves. While Becker's early references to his uniform tended to emphasize the favorable attention it garnered from young women, he nonetheless developed a greater appreciation for its less romantic benefits as time wore on, making such observations as, "the presence in uniform of American Jews in Eastern Europe has had an effect, the importance of which cannot be exaggerated, in preventing all kinds of excesses against the Jew," including mass murders.[85]

It was a safety measure, however, that the U.S. government formally banned in May 1920, publicizing a new policy stating that the relief personnel of American voluntary agencies could no longer wear U.S. military uniforms or replicas of them. The order explained that foreign governments had complained of various problems arising from the difficulty in differentiating between American military members and uniformed American aid workers.[86] In what turned into a months-long struggle between the government and the JDC, the uneven enforcement of the rule soon suggested that the policy may have also been motivated by anti-Semitic officials in the military and diplomatic corps who resented the specter of Jews being confused with U.S. servicemen. JDC officials complained to U.S. officials that members of such non-Jewish organizations as the American Red Cross, YMCA, and Anti-Typhus Commission were regularly spotted wearing U.S. army uniforms or

close replicas while JDC workers received stern reminders to avoid the practice by wearing uniforms that looked quite different from those worn by military servicemen. As JDC official Isidore Hirshfield intimated to the U.S.
Ambassador to Poland, Hugh Gibson, the ability of JDC personnel to "wear a
distinguishing uniform, particularly our field men" was critically important
for Jewish aid workers in violent areas saturated with anti-Semitism. Presumably knowing that Gibson had publicly interpreted some previous pogroms as
merely military encounters between Poles and armed Jewish Bolsheviks,
Hirshfield insisted to Gibson that "the reasons for this are quite obvious and
fully understood by you." Written and photographic evidence indicates that
JDC personnel often violated the policy in practice by continuing to wear
uniforms resembling those of the U.S. army.[87]

In the late spring of 1920, at nearly the same time that the War Department announced its policy, university professor and JDC official Israel Friedlaender entered war torn Ukraine with the uniform of a U.S. army major, or
at least one of its likeness. By early summer, he was working with a small
group of JDC personnel that included Bernard Cantor to develop Jewish relief
operations in Ukraine's Podolia region which had, until recently, been deemed
too dangerous for nearly any American relief personnel to work, much less
Jews.[88] Earlier, in February, after meeting with two other members of the
group in Bucharest, James Becker had expressed concern that the men the
organization was planning to send into Ukraine lacked the experience necessary to navigate Ukraine's exceptionally tenuous environment.[89]

He may have been right. After Friedlaender and Cantor were ordered by
the Bolshevik cavalrymen from their Fiat on that July morning outside the
village of Yarmolintsy, eye witness accounts suggest that the Americans pan-
icked in their decision to flee. A subsequent JDC investigation into the events
that morning failed to reveal whether the tension might have been allayed had
the two Americans chosen to stand their ground more calmly. Nor could it
predict whether the men's prospects might have improved had they had not
been wearing uniforms resembling those of the U.S. army and, thus, also of
the Polish army. What is known is that the men were targeted because they
were mistaken for enemy Polish officers, and were killed while attempting to
escape. The twenty-eight-year-old cantor, a rabbi from New York, was shot
dead before he could sprint off the road. Forty-three-year-old Friedlaender
was soon thereafter shot and bayoneted to death in a neighbor's yard after
butting one of the soldiers in the chest with a rifle he had managed to wrest
free from his pursuer. A professor of biblical literature in New York, Fried-

laender left behind a wife and six children as he died in the very region from which he had fled as a child before returning to offer a modicum of protection for the area's vulnerable Jews. Boasting to nearby residents and their commander that they had killed Polish officers, the Russians may not have realized initially that they had slain Jews, much less Americans. After all, the relatively clean-shaven Americans bore a remarkably different appearance from that of the Orthodox men in the area with whom the Russians would have associated with being Jewish. It was only after their uniforms had been removed, revealing that each was circumcised, when observers recognized them as Jews.[90]

Even after the subsequent JDC investigation suggested that the men's uniforms led to the misidentification that spelled their doom, JDC officials continued to question the American government's prohibitionist policy. In October, for instance, Becker impressed upon JDC chairman Felix Warburg that it was "absolutely essential" that JDC workers be permitted to wear uniforms that evoked a connection to the authority of the United States. Apparently deeming the Yarmolintsy incident an exception that proved the rule, Becker and other JDC officials remained convinced that the intense and ubiquitous vulnerability of Jews in the region nevertheless behooved Jewish aid workers to capitalize on whatever associations with the authority of the American nation-state they could.[91]

If news of the killings reminded many overseas JDC personnel of their vulnerability, Becker must have been struck especially hard that the fates of the dead aid workers might well have been his. Earlier that year, in January, he became the first JDC aid worker to enter wartorn Ukraine to survey the condition of Jews in the area, rumored to be even worse than what Becker had witnessed during his months working in Poland and Romania. It was an audacious decision, one apparently initiated by Becker against the strong recommendations of those within his own organization, U.S. authorities, and the local government officials and Jews with whom he had been working in Romania. His harrowing journey in the bitter cold included a "hard battle with heavy ice and a swift current" across the Dniester River that separated Romania from the Polish-occupied part of Ukraine. Becker spent the next two weeks witnessing evidence of atrocities that, after all the previous suffering he had already seen in Poland and Romania, convinced him that he had only now reached "the heart of the worst pogrom territory," a "living hell," as he later described it, where "the thousands who were murdered . . . were the luckiest." Wearing his uniform for protection during his stay in the Ukraine, Becker would have recognized that the area's environment of anti-Semitism, lawlessness, and violence that had ravaged scores of thousands of Jews in the area might well make him a vulnerable target too, traveling as he was alone and without armed protection. He gathered that he was the first American that most, if not all the Jews he encountered had seen.[92]

Whether as measured calculation or uncontrollable reaction, he seems to have channeled whatever danger he sensed into sympathetic anguish and the rage of retribution. Whereas Jim had once tended to withhold in letters to his parents the worst things he encountered overseas, the "wicked cowardly cruelty" he witnessed in Ukraine overwhelmed any policy of censorship. After visiting many Jewish victims of recent pogroms at hospitals and orphanages, he told his parents of retreating troops making ritual cuts "across the scalp" of their victims, of the commonality of entire "platoons of soldiers raping a single young girl or woman," of "men women and children [who] were thrown out of windows . . . [and] cut to pieces," and of the "special pastime" of these "devilish dogs" in taking "children by the feet and bashing out their brains against a wall." The young man who early the previous year delighted in sharing with his parents descriptions of the stunning European food, architecture, and young women he encountered on his exciting overseas journey admitted that "the spirit of revenge is wide awake in me and I should love to herd together the makers of these pogroms and boil them alive in hot oil." Though acknowledging that his parents "probably shudder to read what I write," he explained that "being in the midst of such things it is only natural that I am aroused to such an extent that you, from a distance, cannot comprehend."[93] As Kittie and Abraham Becker read their son's report from "the heart of the worst pogrom territory," it could not have escaped them how much he had changed since having predicted barely a year earlier that the opportunity to be a part of the postwar rebuilding projects in Europe "would be a wonderful education and would have a broadening influence."[94] The latter had proven undoubtedly true, though the world had clearly lost some of its alluring wonder for their son.

As James returned home in December of 1920 after completing his two years of aid work overseas, he solemnly estimated to a gathering of JDC leaders in New York that "90 percent of the Jews" of Central and Eastern Europe "would like to emigrate, if there was any possibility of their getting out."[95] Their dim prospects, shared by Jews in the Near East and elsewhere in Europe, stemmed especially from two sources. One was potentially temporary, while the other loomed as a longer-term threat.

As for the first, many of the region's countless Jews could not leave, possessing neither the financial resources nor access to transcontinental transportation required to emigrate to the United States or other places of refuge that might be willing to take them could they make the journey. Such impediments were made more challenging by a continuing dearth of available shipping space and foreign consulates overwhelmed by applicants for immigration. Both the Hebrew Immigrant Aid Society and the JDC were doing what they could to help, the latter having only entered the field of immigration aid after confronting the unviable conditions for Jews in a wide swath of territories. But the resources of both were utterly outmatched by scope of the problem. In an example of the gravity of the situation, at the December meeting of JDC leadership, Becker explained with dark irony to the wealthy financiers and others gathered that the organization's Czechoslovakia operations offered a rare bright spot, at least in terms of the budget, because the one time "problem had disappeared." "The problem" had been the many thousands of Jewish refugees gathered in Prague during the war and Armistice. Some had managed to emigrate to the United States, Germany, or other destinations where they hoped to remain safe, but most were forced by the Czech government into Poland, where Becker's intelligence suggested that over three quarters of them "died either of hunger or were killed." The Jewish refugee problem elsewhere, however, persisted even as the mass killings and deaths from starvation and disease continued.[96] Nearly one million Jews in Poland alone were later estimated to be refugees or, for those who lacked the mobility to flee the multiple wars that continued to rage there, starving.[97]

Making the outlook for the Jews of Europe and the Near East bleaker was a longer term threat to U.S. immigration, a legal one, as the U.S. Congress steadily pushed toward legislation that would dramatically reduce immigration into the United States, the place where two and a half million Eastern European Jews had sought refuge since the early 1880s.[98] A full third of Eastern Europe's Jews fled their homelands in this period, with 80 percent headed for the United States.[99] The Russian Empire saw eight in ten of its Jews leave, largely as a result of pogroms and related oppression.[100] Whereas many of those arriving in the United States—Jews and others, during these decades of unprecedented immigration—had fled considerable hardship that included persecution, no group had arrived as battered, vulnerable, and unlikely to return as were Jews from Eastern Europe. As one telling metric of this, 25 percent of all immigrants to the United States in 1914 eventually went back to their former homelands, whereas only 5 percent of Jewish immigrants returned. The mass arrival of these and the many millions of other immigrants—Jews composed about 10 percent of the total[101]—fueled a vigorous anti-immigration movement. One federal law after another was passed during these years to reduce immigration. At first, primarily targeting Asians, the Nativist proponents of the restrictions increasingly took aim at those persons arriving from Southern and Eastern Europe, from where most of the era's immigrants hailed. The anxiety felt by some of the more established Jews would be reinforced as the anti-alien fervor eventually culminated in the 1924 Johnson-Reed Act. Applying a system of "national origins" quotas that went into effect later in the decade, the law was designed to curtail dramatically immigration to the United States, especially from Eastern, Southern, and Central Europe, from whence the vast majority of Jewish immigrants hailed, not to mention the millions of Roman Catholic, Orthodox Christian, Slav, and other groups purposely targeted by the law.[102]

The rest of the world offered only limited alternatives for refugees and would-be refugees. After a brief surge in refugee immigration in the early 1920s, legal and economic impediments increasingly closed off opportunities as the decade progressed. In the words of historian Michael Marrus, after Canada imposed significant restrictions on immigration in 1923, "other countries followed suit. . . . The Jews were to remain, therefore, on the European continent." France proved an exception to a wider trend of immigration restrictionism, inviting one and a half million immigrant laborers—most from the battered regions of Europe and the Near East—to help replace the millions of absent French men of working age who had been killed or wounded in the war. But when Britain was granted its mandate for Palestine in 1922, the hope that the area would become a panacea for fleeing Jews proved short lived. Arab resistance to Jewish immigrants, coupled with economic challenges, helped prompt British officials to keep immigration to Palestine far below demand. A similar trend emerged in the British metropole. Long an important way station for Jews and other immigrants from the East on their way to the United States and elsewhere in the Americas, a wave of anti-immigrant sentiment, of which Jews were a particular focus, worked to reduce the opportunities for immigrants there, regardless of whether the immigrants were in search of temporary or longer-term shelter. As one indicator of the prospects for postwar refugees, the Atlantic Park Hostel in Southampton had been established after the war to offer temporary refuge to five thousand travelers from the East at a time looking for permanent resettlement across the Atlantic. Even with considerable financial commitment to the endeavor by American and British Jews, however, the immigration restrictions sweeping Britain, the United States, Canada, and elsewhere meant that the facility only housed three hundred persons by the end of 1924, mostly Jewish refugees stuck in limbo.[103]

Growing Up and Coming Home

Among the various parallels between James Becker's early adult life and the field of American war relief that he helped build, both were forced to grow up quickly. When Becker finished his freshman year in college, Americans interested in helping the vulnerable overseas could have trouble finding institutional outlets through which they could contribute. By the time he sailed into New York Harbor on his twenty-sixth birthday at the end of 1920, he had not only grown "considerably older"—his observation from earlier that year—but American aid organizations had matured dramatically as well, boasting operations across vast expanses in Eurasia and the Near East. The next period of Becker's life mirrored the wider sphere of American overseas relief too. Finally heeding his parent's pleas over the previous two years, he settled into his place in the family's successful investment firm headquartered in Chicago. He continued supporting the JDC, but in a reduced role, and mostly stateside.[104] While the American Relief Administration, American Red Cross, and YMCA maintained significant European operations in the early 1920s, responding to humanitarian crises that notably included a devastating famine in western Soviet Russia and eastern Ukraine, their overall commitment to the suffering foreigners overseas soon similarly receded. The ARA pulled out of the region by the end of 1922, the money from its Congressional grants and other contributions spent. An era of state-sponsored relief initiatives came to an effective close. The once robust war relief initiatives of the American Red Cross and YMCA also began to wane, their attention directed both back home and elsewhere in the world. The Red Cross greatly reduced its remaining presence in mid-1922, all but pulling out of the region a year later.[105]

American aid for vulnerable Jews, however, followed a different trajectory. Though officials with the Joint Distribution Committee had hoped to begin winding down the organization's operations alongside their American counterparts, the persistently brutal conditions of overseas Jews convinced them to carry forth. The JDC maintained a presence in the Soviet Union and its satellite states through the remainder of the decade and much of the next. At a time when both American and Soviet high politics made it increasingly difficult for the U.S. government to remain active in the Soviet East, the JDC earned the good graces of Soviet officials by importing enormous amounts of American corn seed, fleets of modern tractors, and efficient planting techniques to help feed the region's struggling populations, often both Jewish and Gentile. JDC officials parlayed these diplomatic dividends into a new project, Agro-Joint, that worked with the Soviet government to revitalize struggling Jewish communities in the Soviet Union through loans and the establishment of collective farms. Though Agro-Joint helped scores of Soviet Jews, most Jews would suffer a tragic fate, one enveloped by the emergence of the world's next great conflict. By 1940, the Agro-Joint's Russian leadership was killed as part of Stalin's purges. The next year, invading Nazi forces killed many of the Jews living in the farms and towns reorganized by Agro-Joint. Most of these Jews would have fled previously, but for Soviet policies that forbade emigration and the wave of anti-immigration laws enacted across the globe in the previous World War's aftermath.[106]

Nowhere did such laws have a greater impact on populations who would have otherwise sought refuge from violence and persecution than the immigration restrictions of the United States, affecting—as its supporters had intended—those persons hailing from Southern, Central, and Eastern Europe the most. The national origins system introduced with the 1924 immigration law was joined by administrative measures in America's immigration bureaucracy to keep out European Jews and others deemed undesirable. The Great Depression exacerbated the situation, helping to further close America's Golden Door on would-be immigrants during a decade and a half period that was marked by an even greater degree of mass violence and oppression in Europe than that witnessed during the Great War.[107] As other countries similarly restricted immigration during the era, the international community proved only marginally helpful. The Minority Treaties emerging from the First World War's peace agreements along with the refugee aid offices directed by Fridtjof Nansen proved inadequate in protecting the victims of persecution and violent atrocities.[108]

Beginning especially in the mid-nineteenth century and growing more common in the decades surrounding the turn of the century, American discourse used the terms "refugee" and "immigrant" interchangeably. The elision was partly an implicit recognition that a great many immigrants, even the relatively comfortable and secure, would not have made such a disruptive journey to a new homeland so far away without feeling pushes alongside pulls. The rhetorical practice also acknowledged, however, that most of the nearly countless Europeans who fled their homelands because their basic security, health, and even lives depended on it could in fact find haven in the United States provided they managed to arrive on her shores. But as James Becker and thousands of other American aid personnel returned home from the worst humanitarian disaster the world had yet seen, the figure of the *immigrant-refugee* was soon to become a much rarer phenomenon.

CHAPTER 2

Refugees in the Shadow of the New Deal

On a stormy late summer evening at a Midtown Manhattan auditorium in 1938, a group of America's leading Jewish refugee aid advocates wrestled with a horrible dilemma. The intensifying persecution of German Jews by the Third Reich had recently fueled a dramatic growth in the number of refugees entering the United States, arriving increasingly destitute and in need of institutionalized assistance. Feeling the financial pinch was a galaxy of immigrant welfare agencies caring for the newcomers, the vast majority of whom were entering through and settling in New York City. Exacerbating matters, the situation in Germany had prompted calls for a larger share of America's limited pool of Jewish philanthropic resources to be dedicated to the suffering of Jews overseas.[1]

Searching for ways to ease the financial stress, members of the meeting debated whether to move a group of chronically infirm refugees at a hospital on New York City's "Welfare Island" from private to public welfare rolls. Passing the bill onto the city's public welfare bureau would result in considerable savings for the Jewish agencies currently footing the bill and operating under the administrative umbrella of the National Coordinating Committee (NCC). The NCC officials at the meeting pondered what might happen if the refugee patients were deported for violating the "public charge" provision in U.S. immigration law since no patient had been in the country for five years, the time required before being allowed to accept government welfare support. Those members gathered contemplated the fact that, while not optimal, deportation might have its advantages since state hospitals in Germany were deemed of higher quality than those in New York. NCC executive director and longtime immigrant aid worker Cecilia Razovsky dampened the hopes for such a solution. She did so by passing on information she had recently received from a

U.S. State Department official who, on Razovsky's behalf, had previously asked a German government official about this possible scenario. Rather than receive care in a German hospital, it was relayed back, deported Jews would "be sent to concentration camps," where, presumably unable to work and follow orders, "they would be killed." Absorbing the sobering news, the participants of the New York meeting decided that the costly medical fees should be paid by private, not public sources, even if that decision ultimately diverted resources away from critical needs abroad.[2]

The previous chapter peered into the tight connections forged between American state and voluntary sectors in the management of humanitarian endeavors overseas during the era of the Great War. This chapter picks up that narrative a decade later on the American domestic front. It explores what transpired when another humanitarian crisis abroad challenged advocates for the dispossessed—advocates deeply animated by a particular philanthropic identity—to find innovative ways to offer critical assistance amid daunting obstacles.

The conundrum deliberated at that 1938 meeting raises an issue largely neglected in the well-developed literature on Jewish refugee affairs during the twelve years of Nazi rule from 1933 to 1945. Thousands of German Jews secured refuge in the United States from Nazi abuses during the period, many of whom required institutional support at a time when the New Deal welfare programs were reconfiguring the relationship between the American state and its people. Most historiography has either examined the degree to which European Jews were tragically excluded from the United States through restrictive immigration policies[3] or focused on the highly visible but relatively small number of extraordinary refugee scientists, intellectuals, and artists who fled to America from Europe during the period.[4] But the large majority of the one hundred and fifty thousand to three hundred thousand German Jews who managed to find haven from Nazism in the United States—the exact numbers are difficult to ascertain—were typically neither famous nor possessing exceptionally coveted skills.[5] Increasingly over the period, many refugees arrived emotionally traumatized, sometimes physically battered, and with little money or material resources to help them start life in America independently of outside support. The high unemployment rates of the Great Depression and a surge of anti-Semitism during the period made the situation even more daunting for the less fortunate among these newcomers. For many Americans, Jews among them, access to federally supported welfare provisions not only offered much needed relief from the era's economic vagaries, but also came to be considered a right, a way of confirming their membership in the national community. And so the tension that emerged for American refugee advocates like those in the 1938 meeting was not only born from the pressure to use precious philanthropic resources for needy refugees when public welfare coffers were ballooning for others. The prospect of denying them government support also forfeited an important opportunity, in the eyes of some refugee aid personnel, to forge a stronger connection between the refugees and their new homeland, to welcome them to America as *new Americans.*

The state played a variety of different and sometimes surprising roles in these domestic dimensions of American refugee affairs that unfolded during the overlapping eras of Nazi rule and the New Deal. On the one hand, it loomed as a threat to refugee advocates and those persons they sought to assist. Its immigration policies both erected enormous barriers to the admission of Jewish refugees, along with many others, and threatened deportation should refugee immigrants become public charges within five years of arriving. As a legal expert warned Cecilia Razovsky, "we all know that from time to time Congress gets stirred up about aliens . . . and there is likely some time or other . . . to be a general round-up and a good many deportations."[6] But as the above meeting begins to reveal, American refugee aid personnel also forged working relationships with pockets of the American state that proved extremely fruitful to their work. These included obtaining regular counsel from sympathetic government officials on how best to navigate the labyrinthine channels of American immigration policy that had been designed over the recent years and decades to keep poor Jews, Catholics, and other "undesirables" from Central, Eastern, and Southern Europe outside American borders. At least as importantly, it also included the exceptional move of U.S. immigration officials ceding to Jewish welfare organizations the state's traditional role in approving a critical part of immigration applications during the period, an American sponsor's affidavit of support promising that no prospective immigrants mentioned in the affidavit would become public charges.

A seemingly minor bureaucratic development, the effects of the state granting voluntary agencies the authority to "audit" affidavits were profound. This proved true not just for American refugee affairs during the period but for those that followed in their wake after the Second World War. It made it possible for thousands of refugees to enter the United States who likely otherwise would have been excluded for lack of an acceptable sponsor. Furthermore, the arrangement implied that should the sponsor of an approved affidavit renege, the private agency would assume responsibility for ensuring that refugees would remain off government support. In this, refugee admissions decisions that fell officially under the purview of the state, as with all immigration admissions decisions, became fused in practice, if not in explicit law, with the promise that "resettlement" assistance would be provided by a voluntary agency when needed.

Since the United States began explicitly admitting large groups of immigrants beyond mainstream immigration law as *refugees* in the aftermath of World War II, scholars and refugee advocates have long noted that American refugee policies have often prioritized racial, ethnic, religious, and geopolitical rationales above humanitarian ones for determining who is permitted to be categorized as an admissible refugee. "Calculated kindness," in the words of two such scholars, is said to have defined the country's refugee policies since they emerged after the Second World War even while the calculations themselves have changed considerably with the times and circumstances.[7] While this rendering is certainly accurate and important so far as it goes, the fusion in the 1930s of admissions decisions with resettlement aid promised by private organizations offers another—and in fact, more consistent—way of understanding how immigration policies that specifically targeted those persons deemed refugees came to differ from those for mainstream immigrants. This perspective invites us to reperiodize the beginning of large scale American refugee policies—or perhaps, at least, quasi or proto policies—a decade or more before the federal government formally admitted nearly half a million "displaced persons" outside of mainstream immigration law through both executive order and Congressional legislation.[8] It shows that, on shaky ground, the foundations for large-scale U.S. refugee policies were forged even while millions were denied haven in the United States. This phenomenon emerged not through the types of executive orders, legislative fiat, or other manner of official state actions typically understood to spawn public policy innovations. Rather, American refugee policies during the Nazi era were conceived and implemented through actions that systematically traversed the lines nominally dividing the spheres of state and civil society, of public and private.

Whether we think of the interstitial spaces where these activities occurred as *associational*, *public-private*, or *hybrid*, they betrayed several common features. Most notably, these included the perpetual collaboration of state officials and voluntary agency personnel engaged in critical governing decisions on behalf of persecuted Jews; the de facto appropriation of public authority by nongovernmental organizations engaged in refugee aid; and the institutional repetition of activities that, while often only partially articulated in or even explicitly permitted by law, nevertheless developed into a de facto refugee policy distinct in important ways from mainstream immigration policy. These developments not only saved thousands of lives under the most inhospitable circumstances, but they also laid the foundations for the most consistent defining feature of American refugee policies from the 1930s through the early twenty-first century: the tight linkage of immigration decisions with adequate institutional mechanisms for refugees' welfare in the United States. In a stroke of irony, however, many advocates who managed to crack open America's rusty Golden Door for Jews fleeing Nazism operated under the reasoned belief that the political conditions for refugee admissions required that the admitted refugees be kept out of the spotlight and off public support even when legally permissible. It proved an ambivalent welcome for the new Americans to their adopted homeland.

Quietly Building a Refugee Aid Network

The political and legal terrain of the United States during the 1930s and World War II hardly offered a fertile ground for the scattered seeds of American refugee policies to take root. The emergence of the Nazi-inspired refugee crisis coincided with a period marked by powerful anti-immigration and anti-Semitic forces in the United States. The formidable U.S. legal barriers created during the 1910s and 1920s to curtail European immigration were fortified by Great Depression-era fears that an influx of aliens would steal scarce American jobs, draw on the country's limited public resources, and infect its fragile political culture with leftist radicalism. This was especially true with poor and desperate Jews.[9] In the summer of 1938—the same period when the NCC wrestled over the hospitalized refugees—a public opinion poll showed that 67 percent of Americans were opposed to admitting refugees from Nazism to the United States. By April the following year the vicious anti-Semitic pogroms in Germany, Austria, and the Sudetenland had made headlines in American newspapers, yet that number had grown to 83 percent.[10]

Throughout the period of the Nazi refugee crisis, Congress threatened to curtail immigration laws much more often than liberalize them, but a bureaucratic directive proved even more responsible than the quota system for excluding victims of Nazi persecution. In 1930, President Herbert Hoover responded to depression-inspired fears of labor competition by directing American consuls abroad to apply an extremely strict interpretation of a decades-old public charge clause in federal immigration law in an effort to exclude all but those persons able to arrive in the United States with considerable means. The policy had its desired intent, dramatically reducing immigration well below the quota limits for most countries—including Germany—until late in the decade when American refugee advocates finally convinced immigration officials in the Roosevelt administration to liberalize the policy.[11]

During Hitler's reign, documented immigration to the United States was lower than any other twelve-year period since such records began being kept in the 1830s. Less than 20 percent of the of the nation's available immigration quotas—already considered appallingly low by immigration liberals—were filled over this period.[12] No special exception for the particular needs of political refugees found its way into legislation,[13] and American administrative and legislated law would not begin recognizing an alien's right to asylum for several decades.[14] New Deal liberalism thus seldom translated into liberalized immigration initiatives, and the ethnic and racial pluralism that helped to forge the New Deal political coalition only rarely fostered a widespread sympathy for Nazism's chief victims: Jews.

The options to immigrate elsewhere were generally at least as grim, with the Great Depression, xenophobia, and anti-Semitism typically playing similar roles as they did with U.S. immigration policy. A haven for hundreds of thousands of Jewish and other refugees during the 1920s, France curtailed immigration dramatically by the end of 1933. While Popular Front leadership in the mid-1930s eased barriers somewhat, persistently vocal anti-Jewish sentiments in French political culture worked to keep the numbers low. Likely no more than seventy thousand Jewish refugees from the Reich were present at any point, many there illegally. With no comparable recent claim as a place of asylum, Britain's exclusion of Jewish refugees from Nazism marked less of a shift. English ports served as important layovers to the Western Hemisphere for refugees sailing from Bremerhaven, Hamburg, and elsewhere, but the number of exiles that the Board of Deputies of British Jews and other advocates managed to keep in the country was small, with probably fewer than seven thousand Jewish refugees from Nazism in Britain at the time of the pogroms of Kristallnacht in late 1938. Among that group, many exiles were allowed to stay only by taking low-wage jobs in domestic service and other fields where they were prone to exploitation. The chances of Jewish refugees were rarely better in other European countries and were often worse. For instance, after Switzerland initially granted entry to the first wave of German refugees in 1933, it forbade further permanent settlement thereafter, at least partially a result of the growing proportion of Jews among the transient. In a similar vein, Hungary and Yugoslavia adopted a closed border policy throughout the period. It appeared for a time that British Palestine might offer a solution to the refugee crisis, particularly as its economy actually expanded during the first stages of the global depression. Two hundred fifteen thousand Jews settled in Palestine from 1933 to 1939, with most of the newcomers coming from Poland. However, by the time a notably larger proportion began arriving from the Reich later in the decade, British authorities had reduced immigration quotas. This shift took place because of the White Paper of 1939 and related developments and was partly prompted by a desire by British officials to secure Arab support for the looming war with Germany.[15]

In the early stages of this daunting environment for Jewish refugees, less than a year after Hitler's assumption of power, a handful of U.S. immigration officials began drafting what would become a blueprint for the governance of American refugee aid initiatives into the foreseeable future. Their primary attention, however, was much more modest and myopically focused. Since early 1933, U.S. officials had been bombarded by appeals from people and organizations looking for ways to help victims of oppressive Nazi policies either gain admission to the United States from abroad or be allowed to remain there on expired visitor or student visas. Public criticism of the Roosevelt administration's relative unresponsiveness to discriminatory Nazi policies had been mounting in recent months with little sign of dissipating. Most of the pleas had been arriving from both the wide range of active Jewish immigrant aid and social service agencies as well as from individual Americans with family and friends suffering in Germany. The Joint Distribution Committee created a Clearing Bureau later in the year to refer requests to private immigrant aid and welfare organizations, but U.S. immigration officials remained unsatisfied. The field of refugee affairs had intruded forcefully into the U.S. immigration bureaucracy, and federal officials moved to escort parts of it back out.[16]

The process began in earnest on December 23, 1933, when the recently appointed League of Nations' High Commissioner for German Refugees, American James McDonald, received a confidential memorandum from immigration officials within the U.S. State and Labor Departments.[17] Though the memorandum was unsigned, Charles E. Wyzanski, Jr., was almost surely one of those responsible for it. Wyzanski, a Jew, was solicitor of the Labor Department from 1933 to 1935, and highly involved with immigration matters concerning German Jews. The same month that the federal memorandum was sent to High Commissioner McDonald, in fact, Wyzanski spoke to HIAS officials regarding proposed changes to administrative law, slightly lowering the bar that Jewish applicants for immigration needed to hurdle to avoid being labeled excludable by State Department immigration authorities on public charge grounds.[18]

Indicating the matter's sensitivity, the note to McDonald advised that he "better not leave this memorandum around." Echoing some of the High Commissioner's own wishes, the federal memorandum urged that a single nongovernmental institution be established to both coordinate the myriad refugee aid efforts in the United States and serve as the official liaison between American civil society and both the United States and the League's High Commissioner in matters concerning the refugees. Beyond these two central tasks of multi-agency coordination and liaison between the non-state and governmental sectors, the memorandum spelled out in considerable detail what matters the proposed organization should take responsibility for coordinating. They included legal and administrative assistance on immigration matters, language and vocational training, job placement, settling the refugees in suitable communities, and the development of a system to help American sponsors draft affidavits of support on behalf of prospective immigrants.[19]

In the first months of 1934, McDonald and the federal officials began selling their idea to those in the nongovernmental sector who had been most active to that point with the mounting refugee problem. They initiated communications with the longtime immigrant aid and social welfare leader Cecilia Razovsky. As director of migration services of the country's largest Jewish immigrant adjustment organization, the National Council of Jewish Women (NCJW), Razovsky boasted decades of nearly unparalleled experience in the field and wide ranging professional contacts to boot in the United States and around the globe. Razovsky had worked extensively not only with Jewish community leaders and social workers affiliated with New York's umbrella welfare association, the Federation of Jewish Philanthropies, but also with myriad social service professionals beyond the Jewish community employed in both public and private welfare offices. Joining the conversation was Joseph P. Chamberlain, Columbia University professor of public law and President Roosevelt's U.S. representative to the High Commission for German Refugees. A Gentile, Chamberlain's range of pertinent connections, political acuity, and dogged commitment to the cause of refugee relief would prove to be impressive enough to rival Razovsky's over the twelve years of Nazi rule.[20]

Leaning especially upon Razovsky's relationships with the leaders of pertinent voluntary agencies, McDonald and Chamberlain convened a meeting in Washington, D.C., on March 9, 1934, of just over two dozen officials from nearly twenty agencies interested in managing the mounting refugee crisis. Though the meeting was dominated by such Jewish agencies as the NCJW, HIAS, and B'nai B'rith, Christian and nonsectarian organizations also participated, as had been the wish of federal immigration officials. These included the American Friends Service Committee, the American Christian Committee on Refugees, and the International Migration Service. Some of the Jewish agencies represented at the meeting had already taken initial steps toward combining their operations with one another, but this new prospect of forging a working relationship with federal officials offered an added incentive to take the process to a new level. With near unanimity, the meeting's participants agreed to forge a coordinating and liaison organization along the lines proposed by the federal immigration officials. Meeting several more times between March and June, the group fine-tuned their mission, establishing the National Coordinating Committee (NCC) by the beginning of summer.[21]

The choice behind the new agency's vague name foretold the constant balancing act its officials performed throughout the Nazi era. With popular sentiment overwhelmingly opposed to immigrants—particularly Jews—arriving in the United States, potentially competing in a weak job market, and vying for scarce public resources, refugee advocates strove to attract as little attention to their work as possible. This included avoiding publicizing the refugee aid organization as a Jewish agency. Though nearly half NCC's twenty affiliated agencies were Christian-based or nonsectarian, only the Friends were highly active among them throughout the Nazi era.[22] Much to the chagrin of a handful of people who tried, largely in vain, to alert American Christian communities to the suffering of various groups of Christians under Nazi rule, refugee aid during the period remained a phenomenon dominated by the Jewish community. When NCC officials reorganized their operations in the middle of 1939, the name they gave the new agency, the National Refugee Service (NRS), offered a similarly non-sectarian connotation even though the NRS would boast a more exclusively Jewish membership and operational focus than had its predecessor. In press releases and other publicity to broad audiences throughout most of the Nazi era, both organizations often refrained from using the word "Jew" when describing their activities.[23]

Responding to the growing numbers of increasingly destitute refugees arriving in the United States later in the decade, the new NRS was designed to assume more direct operational responsibility for the immigrants, expanding well beyond the largely coordinating role performed by the NCC. The demands placed on the new organization were considerable, a measure of the relative success with admissions that Jewish refugee advocates had considering the substantial legal, political and material obstacles in their way. Though proportionally and tragically small when compared to both the humanitarian needs born from the crisis and U.S. immigration law's available national immigration quotas for Nazi-controlled countries, the upward trajectory of refugee admissions during the period was nevertheless an impressive feat when measured against the daunting immigration constraints of the era. From 1933 through 1945 nearly a third of a million immigrants arrived in the United States from the twenty-two countries under Nazi rule at the time of immigration. Because U.S. immigration records categorized immigrants neither as refugees fleeing persecution nor by religion, it is difficult to establish with certitude exactly how many of these were Jewish refugees. But there exists both ample evidence from historical documents and a broad consensus across historical scholarship that the majority were in fact Jews fleeing Nazism.[24]

The figures calculated by the NCC and NRS can provide a conservative sense of the considerable growth in Jewish refugee admissions, conservative because voluntary agency officials systematically worked to diffuse opposition to refugee admissions, often inspired by anti-Semitism, by downplaying the number of Jewish immigrants arriving in the United States.[25] By 1935 the number of Jewish refugees annually migrating to the United States with permanent resident visas reached approximately six thousand, almost triple the figure from two years prior. It nearly doubled again the next year to over eleven thousand, continuing to double over each of the next two years. Over fifty-one thousand Jewish refugees from Nazism entered with permanent resident and temporary visas from mid-1938 to mid-1939, most settling in and around New York City. Over the next two years, seventy-one thousand more arrived.[26] The NRS, furthermore, estimated that many thousands of additional Jewish refugees remained in the United States during the Nazi era on temporary and expired visas. Though a strict State Department application of the public charge provision meant that the immigration quota failed to be filled for immigrants from Nazi-controlled countries for any year except for 1939, this growth of admissions was nevertheless a significant achievement considering the challenging context.[27]

While not all refugees required assistance from the NCC and NRS, a great many of them did. The NRS alone processed over one quarter of a million immigration cases and one hundred thousand "social adjustment" cases. The two organizations together provided direct financial assistance for thirty-eight thousand cases, representing both individuals and families in significant need of welfare support. The NRS found twenty-six thousand people work, provided business start-up loans to over five thousand people, and provided vocational training to many others. While the bulk of operations were concentrated around New York City, nearly fifteen thousand refugees resettled in hundreds of communities around the country with the agencies arranging for them to have jobs, housing, and social support upon arrival. In 1940, over five hundred were gainfully employed by the NRS, with many more volunteering their labors. To help pay for these services, the NCC originally relied mostly on the fundraising campaigns of member agencies and donations from the Joint Distribution Committee. When the NRS supplanted the NCC in 1939, the agency's budget derived primarily from the United Jewish Appeal, the collective funding arm for domestic aid operations performed by the NRS along with the international endeavors of the Joint Distribution Committee and United Palestine Appeal.[28]

As the aid agencies assisted these growing numbers of refugees, they were not merely responding to the admissions decisions made by U.S. immigration officials, but instead frequently playing a critical role in that process. Among the ways in which this occurred, the organizations' "Information and Liaison Office" grew deft at the often politically sensitive task of determining how to approach government officials with immigration requests, when to delay action pending more favorable circumstances, and when to remain silent. Joseph Chamberlain and Cecilia Razovsky traveled regularly to Washington, D.C., to meet with federal immigration officials. These meetings helped to prompt some important bureaucratic reforms that gradually eased refugee admissions procedures by the later 1930s and early 1940s. The expansion of Nazi persecution and simultaneous reduction of safe havens in Europe during the period worked to put additional pressure on the Roosevelt administration to implement reforms, however modest. On a less official level, sympathetic federal bureaucrats also kept the private agencies apprised about the best ways to assist individuals in filling out the daunting immigration applications. This included coaching American sponsors on completing affidavits of support so that they would stand the best chance of convincing an immigration official that the prospective immigrant would not require state support if admitted.[29]

Arguably no developments were more important to the relative liberalization of admissions decisions on behalf of immigrants from the Reich than were those developments that concerned affidavits of support. Virtually all

Jews applying to enter the United States to escape persecution abroad were required by the State Department Visa Division to have affidavits filed on their behalf by a sponsor in the United States promising to support the immigrant if granted admission. While other poor and potentially dependent immigrant applicants also had the affidavit requirement applied to them, contemporary refugee advocates and later observers have noted that it was applied much more strictly and systematically to the Jewish refugees, partially the result of strong pockets of anti-Semitism among American consuls abroad and their counterparts in Washington.[30] At least as important, however, were Nazi laws dictating that Jews leave their homelands impoverished. By the time the Nuremberg laws had stripped all German Jews of their citizenship in September 1935—and thus what little actually remained of their civil rights—most had already been robbed of the means to earn a sustainable livelihood. Making matters worse, the German government progressively limited the amount of capital and valuables with which emigrants were allowed to leave. By 1937 the level had dwindled to 10 Deutschmarks, equaling about $4 U.S.[31]

Since the inception of the NCC in 1934, the organization's top officials had worked to manage the affidavit process so as to maximize the number of successful visa applications. It did this both by having NCC's affiliate agencies solicit affidavits from prospective sponsors of immigrant applicants and by then advising those sponsors on how to produce an affidavit that stood the best chance of being approved by the notoriously fickle U.S. consuls. By traveling regularly to Washington, D.C. for meetings with federal immigration officials, Cecilia Razovsky and Joseph Chamberlain kept themselves as current as possible with the ever-shifting requirements and whims of consuls over what constituted acceptable affidavits. Presenting a significant problem to the overall situation was the fact that consuls were commonly skeptical of any affidavit not submitted by a close relative. Immigration officials claimed that affidavits from other persons held less weight than did those from close family members since it was presumed the promise to support immigrants from such sponsors was weaker. As the previous great wave of Jewish migration to the United States was composed overwhelmingly of Jews from Eastern Europe, not Germany, most immigrant applicants from the Reich in fact had few if any close relatives in the United States who could submit an affidavit of support on their behalf. The pressure to address the dilemma only intensified over the decade, especially since U.S. visa applications skyrocketed in 1938 as a direct result of the German acquisition of Austria in March and the pogroms of Kristallnacht in November.[32]

The solution that Razovsky, Chamberlain, and their liaisons in the federal immigration bureaucracy developed to address the matter constituted a critically important, but generally overlooked development in the history of American refugee policy. In many ways, the development proved to be a foundational one for the evolution of American refugee admissions and resettlement initiatives for decades to come. Playing a principal role was George Lewis Warren, who had served as a key conduit between the U.S. immigration bureaucracy and voluntary agency officials, especially Chamberlain and Razovsky. Since working with indigent immigrant groups in Boston while an undergraduate at Harvard in 1909 and 1910, Warren had made a career for himself in immigrant welfare and international humanitarian aid. He worked for the American Red Cross in Bridgeport, Connecticut, during the decade immediately after the First World War before serving as director of the International Migration Service from 1928 to 1938. Beginning in 1933, he also worked for the U.S. State Department as an adviser on the League of Nations Temporary Commission on Assistance to Indigent Aliens, which met periodically in Geneva. When President Roosevelt organized, in the summer of 1938 in the French resort town of Évian-les-Bains, a conference of thirty-two countries to discuss solutions for the refugee crisis, Warren was asked to serve as the chief advisor to the U.S. delegation. He assumed this position in his capacity as a member of Roosevelt's recently appointed Advisory Committee on Political Refugees, to which Chamberlain had also been named.[33]

While the Evian Conference has been remembered justifiably for its failure to find refuge for the victims of Nazi persecution, one action Warren performed just prior to his departure for the gathering did, in fact, actually work to improve the galling situation even though it has remained outside the standard history of the era's refugee affairs. Most likely after consulting with Chamberlain, and possibly Razovsky, in later June 1938, Warren sent a memorandum to his colleagues in the immigration offices of the U.S. State Department recommending the adoption of a new procedure, one whereby a private immigrant aid agency, accredited by the State Department, could legally both audit and approve immigration affidavits. Refugee advocates had previously hoped that affidavits the voluntary agencies themselves submitted directly would be acceptable to consuls, but consuls consistently accepted affidavits from individuals only, not institutions. As the NCC and its core affiliate agencies were included among those entities licensed by State, they thus would be eligible to conduct such audits under Warren's proposed policy, as had been his intention. Warren's intention, and what in fact ultimately transpired, was for consuls to look much more favorably on affidavits approved by the voluntary agency as strong evidence that an immigrant applicant otherwise admissible would not likely become a public charge.[34]

Once the policy was implemented shortly thereafter, a seemingly minor bureaucratic reform produced major changes in the governance of refugee admissions and resettlement. Beyond the fact that refugees began gaining admission at considerably higher rates than before, the new initiative effectively made the State Department and the voluntary agencies partners in the admissions process. The former officially entrusted the latter to guarantee that admitted refugees would be cared for without government assistance. The change represented both an explicit recognition that the voluntary agencies possessed the expertise to ferret out good affidavits from bad ones and, more important, an implicit understanding that private organizations would indeed take care of any dependent refugees whose sponsors reneged on their promise.[35]

The new policy demanded certain institutional innovations by voluntary agency personnel. In the coming months, NCC and NRS officials deliberated over how best to implement the new policy. This debate included the appointment of a standing committee that would work regularly with officials in the State Department to learn what criteria consuls wanted applied in the assessment of audits. A cyclical process then emerged wherein NCC officials conceived of ways in which they in turn could use that knowledge to help sponsors submit affidavits. These affidavits, it was argued, would meet the requirements of the voluntary agency auditors—requirements that the voluntary agencies had gleaned originally from their consultations with federal officials. An important example of this phenomenon concerned how consuls interpreted an affidavit. To the consuls, an affidavit was ironclad, regardless of whether it was submitted by a close family member, provided the affiant had, in Razovsky's words, given for each family sponsored a "guarantee of at least $500." Razovsky continued: "That is what the Consul wants: some concrete assurance that the person will not be dumped on New York City or any other community and need relief as soon as he arrives." NCC and NRS officials consequently developed a system whereby funds from affiliate voluntary agencies, both in New York and throughout the remainder of the country, would be made available to affiants, evidence of which was included as part of the submitted affidavits. The NRS eventually convinced federal officials to allow the voluntary agency to deposit a single blanket surety bond for all affidavits it approved, thereby freeing up critical resources that had been tied up by setting aside $500 for possible use by each affiant.[36]

In a great many other ways, however, the new policy effectively represented just the formal fruition of a practice begun several years earlier when private refugee advocates developed a system guaranteeing that needy refugees would be supported by private and not public means. For most of the case workers and other personnel working for the agencies affiliated with the NCC and NRS, their professional tasks remained much the same as before. They continued helping admitted refugees with such matters as learning English and new job skills, finding employment and housing, managing psychological trauma and family discord, paying bills, applying for citizenship, enrolling children in school, connecting with a suitable synagogue, sending money to family and friends overseas and, when possible, finding haven for those same loved ones, whether in the United States or elsewhere. After a meeting with State Department officials in 1941, where the policy was upheld, Chamberlain pointed to the committed tradition of NRS-affiliated agencies to the welfare of refugees in the country. He boasted that his government counterparts were convinced of the "responsibility" diligently assumed by the NRS in the conjoined admissions and resettlement process because "none of the immigrants who have entered this country from Europe and have come under [the agencies'] supervision has become a public charge."[37]

Voluntary agency personnel instituted another notable practice well after the implantation of the new policy. Refugee advocates maintained their established habit of keeping a low profile, lest the publicity of their activities bring unwanted attention to the presence of many thousands of needy Jewish refugees in the United States, potentially putting the viability of continued admissions in jeopardy. At a meeting in the fall of 1938, NCC official David M. Bressler urged his colleagues to produce "as little publicity as possible" about the recent changes to avoid arousing "a great deal of antagonism" from what he perceived were "the many people in the United States who are not at all friendly to the idea of what they call 'assisted immigration.'" On another occasion, Chamberlain explained to his colleagues that Immigration and Naturalization Service Commissioner Earl Harrison and "other high ranking members of the Justice Department" were "very anxious not to disturb" the country's delicate political atmosphere regarding refugees in the country. Cecilia Razovsky summarized her organization's guiding policy in its relations with government officials when she explained to her colleagues that, "we want to do our work as quietly as possible and always with the full knowledge and approval of the State and Labor departments," warning that "unorganized and unsupervised publicity could lead to very disastrous results."[38]

Whose New Deal? Whose America?

There was a diversity of opinion among refugee advocates, however, over whether the resettlement responsibility that their agencies were granted by the state was a positive or negative development. While leaders of the aid agencies and of America's Jewish communities more commonly believed that guaranteeing the welfare of admitted refugees solely through private means was

Figure 3. The Evian Conference of 1938 that the pictured participants helped plan was ultimately deemed a failure in its stated goal of finding places of haven for Jewish refugees from Nazism. While the events at Evian garnered considerable publicity, such refugee advocates as Joseph Chamberlain (partially concealed on the left) toiled largely behind the scenes to maximize refugee admissions to the U.S. by ensuring that refugees were cared for through private and not government resources. Pictured left to right: Professor Joseph P. Chamberlain, Assistant Secretary of State George S. Messersmith, Rabbi Stephen S. Wise, Treasury Secretary Henry Morgenthau, Reverend Samuel Cavert, Reverend Michael J. Ready, Labor Secretary Frances Perkins, and Lewis Kennedy. Harris and Ewing, photographer. "Aid to Refugees Planned at White House. Washington, D.C., April 13. Experts on the refugee problem shown leaving the White House today after conferring with President Roosevelt, the group met with the President to go over preliminaries to an international conference to help political refugees from Germany and Austria." Washington, D.C.: Harris and Ewing, April 13, 1938. Library of Congress, Prints and Photographs Division: Harris and Ewing Collection. LC-H22-D-3729.

critical to keeping government officials cooperative and the broader political environment engaged elsewhere, others disagreed. Notable among them were social workers and other rank and file personnel of the voluntary agencies who regularly interacted face-to-face with the refugees. Thus, they often understood the immigrant experience personally and frequently occupied the left end of the political spectrum. From their perspective, referring certain refugees to government welfare programs was a way for the newcomers to strengthen their bonds to the state and the national community it served. This was particularly true in the trying times of the Great Depression, and made even more legitimate by New Deal programs that claimed an unprecedented degree of responsibility for the country's poor.

America's Jewish community forged an interesting and somewhat ambivalent relationship with the New Deal welfare state. On the one hand, as a core part of Franklin Roosevelt's coalition of supporters, Jews tended to be strong supporters of New Deal welfare programs. New York City, where a great many of them lived, boasted the country's most robust local public welfare system, one that had expanded much further as copious federal funds flowed into what came to be known as the New Deal's "49th state." As one historian has noted, many New York Jews believed that "government welfare offered Jews the opportunity to integrate more fully within American culture, as both contributors to and beneficiaries of New Deal society," making federal assistance "one of the most cherished Jewish communal ideals."[39]

Another of those cherished communal ideals, however, was the field of Jewish philanthropy. At the outset of the Great Depression, American Jewish communities—especially those of New York City—claimed both a remarkably well developed network of private welfare agencies and a much touted, centuries-old tradition of "caring for our own." In the decades surrounding the turn of the century, Jewish settlement houses and welfare offices matured into a model for others to emulate. The development had been fueled by the pressing need to help two and a half million Jewish immigrants adjust to life in America, many arriving destitute and battered after having fled bitter persecution and violent pogroms in Eastern Europe during the decades surrounding the turn of the century. The various chapters of HIAS and the National Council of Jewish Women became regularly counted among the most sophisticated welfare agencies in the country during the Progressive Era, public or private.[40]

The Great Depression, however, sapped the resources of the charitable institutions, Jewish and other, requiring those that survived to accommodate themselves to their own reduced abilities, clientele in tremendous need, and an enormous new welfare state in the form of New Deal programs. Econo-mists Jonathan Gruber and Daniel M. Hungerman have quantified one aspect of this development, positing that New Deal government relief spending re-sulted in a 30 percent "crowd out" decrease in charitable giving to sectarian-based relief activities. Accelerating this process was the fact that the New Deal's foundational poor relief measure, the Federal Emergency Relief Ad-ministration, required that its funds be distributed only to public, not private agencies. During the Progressive Era many private welfare agencies had re-ceived regular cash subsidies from local and state governments to perform some of their operations, but the new federal initiatives considerably curbed that practice. New Deal welfare programs drew a starker line between public and private relief than had previously existed, with that line shifting to make more room for the growth of government agencies at the expense of the pri-vate. In response, most private welfare agencies largely forfeited their roles of providing financial "relief" and other material aid to federal New Deal pro-grams. These voluntary agencies accordingly tended to shift their organiza-tional priorities to emphasize a range of services that included familial and emotional counsel, vocational training and placement, and cultural support to help maintain community bonds.[41]

The earlier foundations on which Jewish charities had been built helped them weather the economic maelstrom somewhat better than some others, prompting an aide to federal welfare director Harry Hopkins to observe that "the dependency on the government felt in other parts of the city [New York] is not felt . . . among the Jews."[42] This said, even though New York City's Jewish welfare offices managed to support materially their poor clientele at higher rates than the city's overall population, 70 to 90 percent of New York City's Jewish welfare cases in 1934 received public relief.[43]

Whether New York's many aliens should be able to partake in the new welfare state proved a contentious and shifting matter. Despite the concerns at the 1938 NCC meeting about the hospitalized refugees, deportation often was not central to debates over the issue, both because the deportation of Europeans for public charge violations was rare and because most non-citizens had immigrated before the Great War and, thus, were not subject to immigration law's five-year window for public charge violations. In fact, New York City and state not only boasted arguably the country's most progressive public welfare programs in the 1930s, but also were particularly friendly to European aliens.[44] When a controversy arose in 1936 over such policies, the city's Emergency Relief Bureau (ERB) responded to its critics by defending "the soundness of the city, State and Federal policies that need should be the primary test in determining eligibility for relief and WPA [Works Progress Administration] employment," not citizenship status. Nearly one in five New York City residents at the time received ERB aid.[45] The ERB and federal WPA officials resisted for as long as possible demands that they make public the citizenship status of relief recipients. They justified their delay on the basis that the federal and state programs, on which a sizable portion of the city's relief budget relied, legally prohibited discrimination based on citizenship status for most types of relief. Indeed, federal and state authorities threatened to cut off relief funds to the city should aliens be denied public support.[46]

But the debates sometimes favored the other side too. Between 1937 and 1939, U.S. Congressional opponents of New Deal spending measures helped remove well over one hundred thousand legally documented aliens from WPA rolls across the nation. Approximately one quarter of those cut were New York City residents.[47] Advocates for the restrictions in New York sometimes used race to create a wedge between Fiorello La Guardia's administration and African Americans. Bronx alderman Joseph E. Kinsley, for example, charged that aliens took relief resources from black New Yorkers who, as citizens, were more deserving of public aid, but discriminated against.[48] Although many aliens remained legally eligible to receive WPA jobs if they had filed their "first papers" for naturalization by a particular date, thousands nevertheless stayed off the rolls.[49]

These and related developments prompted a sharp increase in naturalization rates among America's alien population during the New Deal era. Earlier in the decade, Immigration and Naturalization Service Commissioner Daniel W. MacCormack had suggested to a meeting of immigrant aid workers in New York that this increase was a result of immigrants wanting access to the "honey pot," referring to the fact that many states' old age and blind assistance limited benefits to American citizens. As these types of restrictions were applied on a national scale in the later 1930s, however, the rates of naturalization applications rose sharply. File clerks on Ellis Island could not keep up with the sudden influx of requests by immigrants for their ship registers as a part of the naturalization application process. They were sent digging through the countless brittle old pieces of faded yellow paper, some of which had not been touched for over twenty years. This was done at the urging of tens of thousands of aliens who were scrambling to negotiate a political environment that increasingly defined people's access to the country's public resources by their legal relationship to the nation-state.[50]

These episodes reveal how New Deal welfare programs nationalized the category of public welfare as never before, providing a new forum for debates over membership in the national community. Even before large numbers of aliens began being cut from public relief rolls in the later 1930s, a dominant discourse surrounding New Deal relief programs had emerged that linked entitlement to national citizenship. In her study of Chicago's industrial laborers historian Lizabeth Cohen demonstrated that the stigma of receiving public aid largely abated during the New Deal for the working class and poor because they "felt they deserved benefits as citizens."[51] But the debates over aliens' rights to public welfare exposed another, less inclusive dynamic of this phenomenon. In addition to class, ethnicity, and race, one's legal status vis-à-vis the national state could also be an important determinant for how groups vied for their rightful place within New Deal era America.

Throughout the operational tenures of the NCC and NRS, there had been calls from within the organizations to move refugee clientele to available public relief programs. Certain members argued for the shift for those refugees who had been in the country for five years, so that there was no danger of the refugees being deported. Other members downplayed the possibility of deportation, wanting the immigrants moved to state rolls sooner. These positions converged over the claim that New Deal welfare programs should be considered a right for those in need, a way for newcomers to connect with the state and nation of their adopted homeland. The case workers and political leftists who typically held this view were well outmatched throughout most of the 1930s by the more cautious personnel and leaders of the organizations. Although the self-described "community leaders" of the Executive Committee overseeing the refugee aid agencies—and the other Jewish leaders with whom they commonly worked—betrayed remarkable dedication to the refugee cause, they typically fought their battles on a higher plane of public and government relations. Their eyes were fixed on a wider field of public policy initiatives, especially postwar immigration reform and the overall reputation of American Jewry. They may have sympathized with the idea that it stigmatized the needy victims of Nazi anti-Semitism by keeping them away from public support and maybe even delayed the process of incorporation into the American fabric, but they had a different set of overall priorities than those who regularly and directly worked with the refugees themselves.[52]

By the late 1930s, however, evolving circumstances portended that the potential costs of keeping refugees off public rolls might have more material consequences. Refugee admissions increased considerably by the end of the decade, partly a result of the lobbying efforts of NRS leadership with their government liaisons, the ability of Jewish agencies to approve affidavits of support, and the track record of keeping admitted refugees off government support. While the State Department's Visa Division and its corps of Central European consuls continued to harbor strains of anti-Semitism and general callousness toward the refugees' plight throughout the period, the obstinate mood that prevailed earlier in the decade gradually softened, if only a little. To review, from mid-1936 to mid-1937, the number of Jewish refugees migrating to the United States with permanent resident visas had nearly doubled, from approximately six thousand to over eleven thousand. It continued to double over each of the next two years. Over fifty-one thousand Jewish refugees from Nazism entered the United States with permanent resident and temporary visas from mid-1938 to mid-1939, most continuing to settle in and around New York City. During the next two years, seventy-one thousand more arrived before the escalation of the war. The Nazi "Final Solution" for the Jews significantly cut off channels for escape and transcontinental travel.[53]

The newly arrived refugees placed tremendous pressure on the NRS, not only because of the spike in numbers, but also because of their deteriorating condition. Matters were exacerbated by the fact, as "enemy aliens" from Germany, Jewish refugees were initially legally forbidden from working many government-sponsored jobs related to war mobilization. Private employers additionally often refused jobs to German speakers during the war, an ironic twist of fate for refugees who fled Germany in fear. During 1939, the refugee agencies saw the number of financial relief cases (representing both families and individuals) on their books triple from one thousand to over three thousand. When war began in September that year, NRS offices in New York City alone fielded over one thousand requests for assistance per day, twice the load of three years prior despite the marked growth of a resettlement program that had begun systematically moving limited numbers of refugees away from New York. The case load only continued to swell into the early 1940s. From the war's outset to the end of 1940 just over a year later, the average length of time for a refugee family to remain on NRS relief doubled from less than six months to a year. Fifteen hundred "residual load of relief cases" crowded NRS client lists as the decade began, the clients they represented having little foreseeable likelihood of becoming independent of outside support. In the past, agency personnel had only been prepared to assume a small handful of such cases, perhaps several score. Not only were refugees arriving in the United States with fewer material resources, but growing numbers were too old to work productively as well and more likely to require expensive medical care. Only one of six refugees arriving in the United States in 1938 was over forty-four, whereas nearly one in three was in that age group by 1940.[54]

Making the situation more challenging, the war and heightened Nazi persecution meant that more human and financial resources were needed for overseas initiatives to help Jews escape the grip of Nazi authorities and secure temporary refuge and material relief until the war was over.[55] While the NCC and NRS were designed to provide aid to victims of Nazism domestically, even their leadership began focusing increasingly on the international situation. NRS director Joseph Chamberlain sat on the President's Advisory Committee on Political Refugees, the liaison body between Franklin Roosevelt and the Intergovernmental Committee on Refugees (IGCR), the latter created at the behest of FDR in 1938 to find resettlement opportunities around the world for refugees.[56] Receiving no funding from member governments, the IGCR relied on private contributions, particularly those from the American Jewish community. As was the case with the League of Nations High Commissioner for Refugees, the IGCR was administered primarily by voluntary refugee aid agencies, particularly Jewish-based organizations from the United States and Great Britain.[57] NRS executive director Cecilia Razovsky made regular trips to Latin American countries to persuade governments to accept refugee émigrés, either on a permanent or temporary basis. These agreements could be especially taxing on voluntary agency funds, often requiring the agency to put up expensive bonds for each admitted refugee. Sometimes government officials demanded bribe money as well.[58] These and such similar endeavors as the 1944 establishment of the War Refugee Board were considered critical to saving the lives of Jews, and thus became increasingly prioritized.[59]

As a result of these various developments, in 1940, Jewish refugees saw the private welfare they received cut for the first time during the era. Previously, the NCC and NRS commonly offered their clientele a more generous suite of support than other agencies, whether public or private. It was, after all, one of the chief ways that Jewish leadership over the years had managed to limit negative publicity, contain excessive anti-Semitism, and appease their contacts in the federal government. Now, however, National Refugee Service clients began to receive provisions below what most would have received had they gone on public support.[60] It must have been a humbling development considering that Jewish welfare personnel regularly criticized the quality of operations at government welfare departments.[61]

Throughout the war years, factions within the NRS engaged in increasingly heated debates over whether the agency should finally refer clients to government welfare offices, with the matter coming to a head during 1943 and 1944. In the summer of 1943, an NRS subcommittee released a report recommending that those NRS clients with five years residency in the United States, and thus no longer deportable on public charge grounds, be moved to public rolls. Making the case in largely financial terms, the study highlighted the strains placed on the agency by the growing number of "residual cases" of refugees who, typically because of age or health, required long-term support from the NRS. The five-year anniversary of the pogroms of Kristallnacht was only months away, an event that had helped trigger the dramatic rise in the number of refugees who began arriving in the United States requiring sustained institutional assistance. These people composed over one third of the agency's relief case load. Transferring them to public welfare rolls, in the subcommittee's view, would allow the NRS to divert a significant proportion of its operating budget to other pressing needs. In short, the agency could markedly improve its financial situation without putting the refugees at risk of deportation. Such an option had not been available to refugee advocates five years earlier as they briefly considered whether the chronically hospitalized Jews on New York's Welfare Island might be better served in German hospitals if removed from the United States for becoming wards of the state.[62]

What seemed to the subcommittee a straightforward solution to some of the agency's needs from a financial perspective was deemed more fraught in political terms by NRS leadership and the prominent people it consulted about the proposal. NRS Chairman Joseph Beck held meetings over the matter with Immigration and Naturalization Service Commissioner Earl Harrison and officers of several other leading Jewish organizations and alien advocacy groups that included the American Jewish Committee, the Anti-Defamation League, and the Common Council for American Unity. Even though the refugees under consideration were legally entitled to public support, it was decided that they would remain on private rolls because, "in the light of existing pressure in Washington for the curtailment of immigration, such referral would constitute a potential threat to continued immigration in the post-war period."[63] Factions in the U.S. Congress had been threatening to curtail immigration throughout the Nazi era, and wartime anxieties over the presence of "enemy aliens" in the United States could give them the type of political capital their campaign sought. The immigrant advocates who met over the subcommittee's report, on the other hand, had their sights set on lobbying for liberalized immigration reform after the war, and wanted no more impediments to that prospect than already existed. They reasoned that their campaign had a much better chance of succeeding if Jewish leaders could continue to boast that America's organized Jewish community had proven its ability to adjust poor and sick Jewish immigrants to American society successfully during the Nazi era without relying on public resources. The non-Zionist component of America's Jewish community, in particular, began seeing such legislative changes as one of the few panaceas for the lot of world Jewry after the war.[64]

Case workers in the Family the Family Services Division of the NRS expressed great frustration with the decision announced by their agency's Executive Committee. Though each group labored tirelessly in its respective ways on behalf of Jewish refugees, these groups could barely have been more different in experience and outlook. Predominantly women, many from the community of social workers had themselves come to the United States seeking haven from anti-Semitic pogroms, ones perpetrated during an earlier era in Eastern Europe. Frequently involved in socialist politics, they had long labored in the trenches of alien destitution, receiving their images of "how the other half lives" daily and first-hand. The Executive Committee, on the other hand, was composed mostly of men, and typically boasted comparatively longer roots in the United States: their respective families had largely arrived from the German speaking regions of Central Europe in more comfortable fashion than did the more recent groups of immigrants, who had instead fled the old Russian Pale of Jewish Settlement and Hitler's Germany. These bankers, lawyers, rabbis, scholars, and statesmen represented American Jewry's upper echelon and were well connected with prominent Gentiles in American civil society and government, especially fellow Democrats. Where the case workers' attention focused sharply on the neediest of the refugees for whom they cared, the leaders of the NRS tended to emphasize other considerations that included not only the prospects for future immigration legislation but also how a public backlash against the specter of destitute Jewish refugees receiving government welfare might affect the reputation of Jewish community more broadly.[65]

The social workers of the Family Services Division publicly charged the NRS Executive Committee and those with whom they had consulted of embracing an outdated and "professionally undeveloped method of work" with immigrants. The case workers marshaled arguments that drew from both New Deal inspired economic rights and the wartime message of the "Double

Victory" campaign that made the conflict not just about fighting totalitarianism abroad, but battling the illiberal aspects of American life on the home front. Rather than alienate the refugees from mainstream American society, offering the needy among them access to public welfare would hasten their "Americanization." Asking refugees to forego the legally available resources of the state to avoid political backlash suggested "to the refugee that in effect he forego certain of his democratic privileges because certain sections of the Jewish community have fears about the future of the alien in the United States." While still emphasizing the importance of the Jewish community maintaining some responsibility for the refugees, they insisted that public assistance "when needed has been established as a right in our democracy." Allowing refugees that right would represent just one more example of America's "increased public concern over unifying various parts of the nation" as it battled the Axis powers, not just militarily, but over competing ideologies about the value of cultural diversity and liberal inclusion. The caseworkers implored that, because the Jewish community had born the sole responsibility of caring for its own for long enough, it was now time for the broader American community to begin accepting its fair share of the responsibility.[66]

The pitch worked. The NRS decided in the summer of 1944 to begin referring their refugee clientele who had been in the country for five years to government welfare offices. The most vulnerable of a battered population of Jewish immigrants would, at least in this particular way, be encouraged by their host community to make their claim on the American nation-state. But as different sides on the immigration issue prepared for a postwar battle over the possible admission of a much larger and more diverse overseas population of the dispossessed, it seemed to some refugee advocates that they were rolling the dice.

CHAPTER 3

Recruiting Philanthropies for Battle

Two events in the midst of World War II open a window onto the unprecedented role assumed by the United States during that period in managing
humanitarian crises abroad. One occurred in dramatic fashion at the beginning of 1943; the other unfolded a year later in a staid office setting that belied
its global import. A commercial airplane leased by the U.S. War Department
took off from a military airstrip near Washington, D.C., in January 1943, des-
tined for North Africa, where the American and British armies had recently
achieved stunning victories over Axis occupying forces.[1] Hours later it crashed
into the dense jungles of Dutch Guiana on the northern coast of South America, killing all thirty-five persons on board. As details of the crash slowly
emerged, the once secret mission became widely known as the deadliest airplane disaster in American history and the second worst the world had yet
seen. Beyond the nine-member TWA crew, most of the twenty-six passengers
were military personnel.[2] One passenger, however, boasted a more civilian
and domestically focused professional résumé than most of his co-travelers.
His presence on the plane seemed out of place, at least at first glance.

    For the previous twenty years passenger William Hodson had been one of
America's preeminent social welfare leaders in both the private and public
sectors. Among his many accomplishments, he had unified New York City's
myriad private welfare societies into a single federation, successfully helped
lobby the U.S. Congress to pass the New Deal's major poor relief initiatives,[3]
and then harnessed unparalleled amounts of those federal funds into New
York City's Department of Public Welfare while serving as commissioner of
that bureau.[4] These achievements were all impressive ones, but what did the
expertise of a domestic welfare specialist have to do with secretive military
flights to North Africa in the chaos of mass war?

Although the larger overseas mission that Hodson had been slated to join would ultimately need to proceed without him, the reasons for his presence on that plane in the first place begin to illuminate the dramatic nature of the mission itself. Hodson had been preparing to serve on the front lines of two intertwined revolutions of American governance: one in welfare policy and the other in foreign policy. By the end of World War II the transformation occurring within these policy domains—traditionally considered distinct from each other—would merge into a massive new field of international humanitarian relief, a U.S.-sponsored welfare regime that dwarfed even that witnessed in the First World War. As Hodson boarded his plane in early 1943, this process was gaining momentum, but its shape was still emerging. The U.S. government was planning its first major overseas civilian relief operations of the war, and in Hodson, federal officials had found a "relief" administrator with nearly unparalleled experience in caring for large destitute populations. During the Great Depression his efforts had famously helped to provide millions of New Yorkers—both citizen and alien—with food, shelter, clothing, and medical care, relief provisions that many needed to survive. By 1943, the American wartime economy had greatly reduced the need for such massive poor relief programs at home, but many more millions of refugees and other civilians were now in dire need of similar relief services abroad. U.S. government officials increasingly embraced the position that international relief initiatives had become a critical component of American war strategies. As such Hodson's experience and skills were to have been transferred to the war cause.[5]

Perhaps the most appealing quality that Hodson would have brought to his new job was his depth of experience in working with both public and private (or "voluntary") welfare agencies. New York City owed its reputation for boasting the country's largest and arguably best organized social welfare system significantly to the collaborative working arrangements established during the Great Depression among the city's public welfare bureau and its many private aid agencies. The federal official responsible for conscripting Hodson to the field of overseas aid understood the role he had played in encouraging such relationships between the government and voluntary welfare sectors of New York. As director of the U.S. government's emerging relief efforts, former New York Governor Herbert Lehman had hoped that Hodson could foster such public-private collaboration on a far grander scale, in the field of international war relief.[6] Though Hodson would ultimately not be around to participate, the endeavor moved briskly forward regardless.

A year after Hodson's death, in a nondescript federal office building in

Washington D.C., Lehman presided over a critical meeting in the development of American policies of international humanitarianism. Gathered were two dozen representatives of the U.S. government, America's leading war relief charities, and the recently established intergovernmental organization, the United Nations Relief and Rehabilitation Administration, soon to be known worldwide as UNRRA. While the intergovernmental organization we associate today with the words "United Nations" would not come into being for nearly another year and a half, UNRRA represented the largest and most active of its institutional progenitors during World War II. Lehman, who had recently become UNRRA director, explained the purpose of the meeting to those present. The intergovernmental agency was poised to embark on its first major relief operation, to be conducted in the recently liberated Balkan countries of Southeastern Europe, but the UNRRA chief had a problem. Even though the new organization was designed to be supported and operated by its member governments—two thirds of its initial $2 billion budget coming from the United States—Lehman explained that governmental contributions alone would not be sufficient for the massive task ahead. In fact, they would fall far short of what was needed. Lehman implored the leaders of the American voluntary war relief societies in the room to begin "recruiting," as he tellingly phrased it, personnel from their agencies to serve as the operational backbone of the new behemoth intergovernmental organization. Lehman's belief that the voluntary agencies represented in that room possessed not just the potential resources but the organizational sophistication in early 1944 to take on such a great and complex responsibility was a stunning acknowledgement of just how much America's voluntary war relief sector had been transformed in the previous several years. Only a year and a half earlier, the sector seemed chaotic to many observers, disorganized, decentralized, and certainly incapable of serving as a major partner in the largest civilian war relief initiative ever attempted.[7]

What happened in the intervening and following months not only metamorphosed America's organized field of international philanthropy, but also significantly reconfigured the working relationship between that sector and the U.S. government, as both took the lead in managing a humanitarian crisis that dwarfed even that caused by World War I. As the United States emerged during World War II and its aftermath as an undisputed global hegemon, it partly but significantly justified its ascension by highlighting how it would be a new type of world power, one committed to making the world a more secure and prosperous place through humanitarian action aimed at protecting and nurturing the most vulnerable. It was a role the United States had also assumed in World War I, but now it did so at the pinnacle of world power with not only a far more robust and sustained commitment by the American state, but also a more sophisticated suite of civil society organizations, one that collaborated with that state.

This chapter explores these developments, first examining the U.S. government's attempts to assume an unprecedented degree of regulatory authority over war philanthropies. Next, it traces how a refashioned, government-molded private war relief sector joined its governmental counterparts in overseeing enormous humanitarian aid operations on multiple continents in what was, and, in many ways, remains the largest such project in history. Finally, the chapter concludes with an episode involving an American philanthropy in the Soviet Union shortly after the war's end. It offers a focused examination of the ways that the public-private network of humanitarian aid constructed during the war would both endure in ways that it had not after World War I but would see its operational canvas tightly framed by both the emerging Cold War and the American state that simultaneously helped to foster it.

Nongovernmental Organizations in the Nation-State's Image

The U.S. Neutrality Act of November 1939 is commonly remembered for the prohibitions it placed on American commercial enterprises looking to do business in countries actively engaged in the budding war. The law was intended to curb the possibility that the actions of private American enterprises could draw the U.S. government into conflict with one or more belligerent countries and, eventually, into the war. Less recalled is the fact that Section 8(b) of the law contained exceptions for organizations wanting to conduct humanitarian relief work of a purely non-profit and non-political nature in belligerent countries. Prior to this provision of the Neutrality Act nearly all internationally active American charities were subject to similar regulations as other American charities.[8] The Act required those American charities aiding belligerent countries to register with the State Department's Division of Controls. Licensed agencies could operate solely as nonprofit organizations, were only allowed to provide foreign populations with "humanitarian relief" (for example, not weaponry), and were prohibited from directly supporting the government or a particular political organization within the country receiving the aid. The president periodically added new nations to the list of belligerents, requiring all the previously unlicensed agencies operating in those countries to register. Few provisions, however, were included in the act for how the State Department would actually investigate the merits of an application, or monitor agencies' compliance with the law after licensing. It accepted the affidavits of the voluntary agencies at face value and effectively rubber stamped their licensing applications. With rare exceptions, agencies were permitted to operate mostly unsupervised thereafter. Within a year of the law's passage approximately four hundred agencies organized around the country had so registered.[9]

Although an impressive figure, these four hundred licensed agencies represented only a portion of the war charities that emerged in the first year or so of World War II. They did not include the scores of American voluntary agencies that had formed to help the populations of countries not yet listed as belligerents, nor did they include refugee relief agencies that aided displaced populations who had fled from their homes in the war zones to still-neutral countries.[10] Owing to its long, unique, and intimate relationship with the federal government, the American Red Cross was also exempt from licensing requirements of the Neutrality Act. Already considered a "quasi-official" agency of the federal government by many observers, the Red Cross would remain exempt from all new regulations the federal government developed to manage the rest of the field of war relief throughout World War II.[11]

With dozens of new relief agencies often emerging each month from late 1939 to early 1941 the field of American war relief was thriving. Not unlike what had happened during the First World War, it sparked a phenomenal burst of energy within the country's civil society. Even at a time when powerful government officials and large pockets of the American public insisted that the United States remain distanced from the mounting chaos in the world abroad, the vibrant activities of these war charities represented a counter, internationalist trajectory within American public life.[12] Americans gazed at suffering populations overseas with whom they identified and sympathized, and reached out to them. The organizations that they founded, supported, and directed fostered a renaissance in American public culture through which they could express a range of philanthropic identities, typically along ethnic, national, religious, and political registers.[13] The activities were not limited to white Americans. The country's black communities were similarly urged to contribute to humanitarian causes that aided their "darker brothers and sisters in war-torn colonies of Africa," as well as to the Soviet Union, which, as a

National Urban League official proclaimed, had "succeeded in stamping out racial prejudice from its national life."[14] Even before the United States officially entered the war, and Americans were regularly reminded by both governmental and nongovernmental personnel of their patriotic duty to buy U.S. War Bonds and support war relief charities in the service of the overall American war cause, these more specific group-oriented motivations to aid war victims overseas prompted many thousands to contribute to a burgeoning field of international humanitarianism.

War relief agencies became the reason for many people to attend rallies, meetings, benefit concerts, and religious services to contribute their capital, property, and labors. Social workers left their jobs at both public and private domestic welfare agencies, and traveled abroad to provide counsel and material assistance to the exploding populations of refugees who had found temporary safety in areas not yet affected by hostilities. New York mayor Fiorello La Guardia and William Hodson hung an "honor roll" in their city's Department of Public Welfare recognizing the importance of welfare workers to the American war cause.[15] Even during the period of American neutrality, sewing centers appeared around the country, from small Midwestern towns to New York City's Garment District, churning out textiles for war victims overseas, including coats, hats, sweaters, mittens, blankets, sleeping bags, socks, babies' bootees, and even dresses for young girls. In an Ohio village, the local chapter of the Women's Christian Temperance Union canned vegetables from area fields, which they then sold to purchase more sewing materials for eventual export to the Soviet Union. People throughout the nation lined up to donate cash, clothes, razor blades, soap, watches, books, canned goods, and the like at an array of sites, including churches, synagogues, Lions Clubs, Masonic temples, banks, city halls, and sports venues. The contributions were then typically transported to the scores of warehouses that were cropping up across the Eastern seaboard—mostly in New York City—to await shipment overseas.[16]

This thriving philanthropic sector also presented some significant problems. To an increasing number of people the rapid appearance of war charities created confusion, inefficiency, and distrust. Columnist Jonathan Daniels of the *Nation* warned in spring 1941 that the proliferation of "war charities has the home folks confused in the home towns, where there is a real and increasing desire to give. . . . in the enthusiastic confusion there is a real possibility that both the home folks and the essential foreign war charities may suffer together."[17] People were being bombarded by a constant slew of fundraising appeals, many of which seemed indistinguishable from one another. Some ninety agencies, for example, had emerged to provide aid to the people of Britain alone.[18] Many different agencies also concentrated on providing aid to the growing populations of refugees overseas.[19] With the imposition of the country's first peacetime draft, in October 1940, dozens more agencies had emerged to provide material relief to the families of American service personnel and recreational services to the soldiers themselves.[20] Business executives complained of feeling excessively pressured to donate to one agency over another, lest they suffer commercial backlash from the supporters of a jilted agency. Charges of fraud began proliferating, with Jonathan Daniels noting the growing feeling that "sometimes it is hard to tell whether the multiplicity of the good-intentioned or the ubiquitousness of the racketeers" threatened the viability of American war relief initiatives more.[21] While still director of New York City's public welfare bureau, William Hodson led an investigation into the fraudulent United States Friends of Greece, asking city police to arrest anyone caught fundraising for the organization.[22] What is more, funds were being raised and goods collected to send to territories for which there were no available inland transportation routes or overseas shipping space through which to deliver them.[23] With so many agencies emerging, there also developed a shortage of available personnel to work for them. A *Chicago Daily Tribune* reporter noted, "There is a real danger that essential and worthwhile activities may receive less support than they deserve because the multiplicity of campaigns makes it impossible for them to obtain an adequate staff of volunteer workers."[24]

By the spring of 1941 Secretary of State Cordell Hull urged President Roosevelt to address the situation. Hull warned that although "the finest human instincts" were typically responsible for the incredible recent growth of war charities, they had also spurred a level of charitable activity which threatened to collapse on itself without federal intervention. Whereas the secretary may well have sympathized with the specific goals of American war charities, his actions should still be understood as part of a broader narrative, one wherein, for the war aims of the federal government, the wartime state deployed a nearly endless array of techniques for marshalling, with effectiveness, the various resources of the country's civil society and commercial sectors. As part of this emergent, wider trend, Hull recommended that the federal government establish the "proper coordination" over a field of civil society activity that was fast becoming a national dilemma.[25] Roosevelt's response was the appointment of the three-man President's Committee on War Relief Agencies. All were well connected to the American philanthropic sector, and collectively boasted experience in foreign diplomacy, private law, commerce, and university administration. None, however, had prior experience in government regulation. Led by former U.S. ambassador to the Soviet Union Joseph E. Davies, the committee had an advantage over the State Department's Division of Controls before it, in that its members could concentrate solely on war relief issues. But its regulatory authority was limited, with the Davies Committee relying mostly on the voluntary cooperation of private agencies to consolidate with one another and generally to police their own sector with the committee's urging. Nevertheless, the committee helped to consolidate more than seven hundred agencies involved in foreign relief down to approximately three hundred between the spring of 1941 and the following summer, reducing substantial administrative overhead costs for many.[26]

Feeling that too many war charities were still beyond its reach "because of lack of authority," the Davies Committee convinced Roosevelt to grant it additional powers. In July 1942, the president reorganized the committee under the President's War Relief Control Board that would extend its authority not only over agencies engaged with relief in belligerent countries but to all American war relief organizations. Even agencies providing war-related services solely within the United States—primarily for soldiers and their families—had to receive a Control Board license.[27] A privately operated GI recreation center near Birmingham, Alabama, for instance, fell under the Control Board's jurisdiction just as a medical facility did in Cairo, Egypt, which was run by another American philanthropy to aid Moroccan refugees displaced by military fighting.[28] The authority of the Board expanded in other ways as well. This growth included transferring it from the State Department, where members of the Davies Committee had felt constrained in their work, to the wartime Office for Emergency Management, where the War Production Board, Foreign Economic Administration, War Manpower Commission, and most other wartime governing bodies resided.[29] As with the other federal war agencies, the New Control Board derived additional authority from the War Powers acts and the fact that the dramatic wartime increase in federal income taxes meant that nonprofit organizations were more concerned with adhering to federal regulations in order to enjoy increasingly important tax exemptions.[30]

Publicly minimizing its actual authority over America's voluntary sector, the Board insisted that it served as merely a "focal point" for the private agencies, gently "guiding and facilitating" them to maximize the efficiency of democratic philanthropy in the midst of wartime crisis. While it acknowledged that the exigencies of war behooved extra governmental oversight, the Board insisted that it would remain answerable to American civil society, not the other way around. Its supporters lauded it as the embodiment of responsive democratic governance.[31]

Yet the Control Board did possess a much broader legal authority and a greater political mandate than its predecessor committee, one with the potential ability to ignore the wishes of the voluntary agencies, to be unresponsive to civil society, and to be undemocratic. After the Board was disbanded in mid-1946, its members acknowledged in hindsight that certain of the regulations it enforced must have seemed "nightmarish" to voluntary agency personnel.[32] The most extreme and often controversial directive the Board could issue was an order forcing a voluntary agency to cease operations. During its tenure from July 1942 through May 1946, the Control Board reduced the number of agencies involved in war relief to under one hundred, a mere fraction of the many hundreds of others unable to secure or maintain an operating license from the Board. Sometimes the Board refused to grant or renew an operating license outright, but more commonly it urged an agency to consolidate operations with another agency—usually larger, more efficient, and better established—which the Board believed was performing a similar service.[33]

In its quest to reduce the number of voluntary relief agencies to what it considered a more manageable and "efficient" number, the Board determined that, ideally, only one agency should exist for each type of relief "task."[34] The Board, for instance, persuaded several refugee aid organizations to consolidate under one organizational umbrella, Refugee Relief Trustees, which the Board then licensed to provide assistance to growing populations of refugees abroad.[35] Similarly, dozens of agencies providing recreational services and supplementary material provisions to American military personnel were folded into the United Services Organization, known colloquially as "the USO."[36]

The vast majority of organizations that the Board licensed, however, were required to organize themselves along the lines of the particular nation-state they sought to aid, with typically only one agency allowed per nation-state. The policy had begun even before the Board's appointment, with the Davies Committee having persuaded, for instance, seventy British agencies to consolidate into one. While such initiatives were welcomed by the members of some agencies, and appear to have drawn little to no resistance from others, the government's interference with the philanthropic sector nevertheless could strongly conflict with the wishes of agency supporters who frequently operated along dramatically different, multifaceted, and fiercely embraced registers of identification than a nation-state label afforded. In claiming to refuse to make a distinction between various sections of any national group—meaning nation-state—the Board brought under the same organizational umbrellas groups of sometimes antithetical political positions and cultural perspectives. To continue helping fellow Serbians overseas, for instance, the Serbian National Defense League, was made to join ranks with America's Croatian and Slovenian communities under the new organization American Friends of Yugoslavia.[37] American Relief for France was similarly the consolidation of different agencies supporting Charles de Gaulle's Free France movement, on the one hand, with earlier supporters of the Nazi-controlled Vichy regime on the other.[38]

The controversy over Italian relief grew particularly heated when the Control Board refused to recognize a popular Italian American war philanthropy, American Committee for Italian Democracy (ACID), because certain of its leaders had previously been public supporters of Benito Mussolini. In February 1944, the Board instead created another organization, American Relief for Italy, as the country's sole war philanthropy for that country and appointed allies of the Roosevelt administration to the new agency's board of directors. Even staunch anti-fascist U.S. Representative Samuel Dickstein opposed the perceived federal overreach, calling the Board "absolutely impotent" for appointing people to the new organization who did not "enjoy that confidence among people in Italy which is so essential for the success" of America's humanitarian endeavors overseas. An editorial in an Italian-American newspaper, one aligned with ACID's leaders, asked derisively, "By what authority does anyone arrogate to himself the right to deny free American citizens an opportunity to engage in humanitarian endeavors?"[39]

In lionizing the primacy of national identity, the Board muted the types of group distinctions fiercely embraced by the diverse communities that formed the American nation, exposing a tension between more capacious and particular conceptions of wartime benevolence. In this, it narrowed the scope of political pluralism in the field of war philanthropy in favor of the politics embraced by the federal government's foreign policy apparatus, a politics fundamentally informed by the twentieth century's dominant political institution: the nation-state. In many instances, of course, the framework of the nation-state proved perfectly concordant with Americans' motivations to contribute. Giving to the Red Cross or purchasing U.S. War Bonds, after all, provided millions with a sense of contributing to the national war cause, of performing their patriotic duties. Support of one of the licensed voluntary agencies also offered that, to be sure, but it additionally allowed someone to support a more particular cause overseas, often a means to embrace other modes of identity beyond just "American." While popular memories of the war have long emphasized the degree to which home-front Americans sacrificed their labors, comforts, and property to a highly uniform national war cause, much of the impetus for these commitments also spawned from narrower sets of loyalties that in critical ways, expressed themselves through the licensed war relief charities.[40]

As the war drew on, the federal government increasingly molded war philanthropies in its own image. In October 1943 the Control Board began pressuring agencies to adopt the word "American" or "United States" in their names to "clearly reflect the fact that this relief is of American origin." Such a practice, the Board indicated, would create "good will between the United States and the countries which are being helped by the generosity of our people." The Board, after all, had been appointed not only to facilitate the efforts of private war relief but also to ensure that those efforts promoted the U.S. government's foreign policies: policies that engaged with a global system dominated by nation-states. For the supporters of the scores of closed or consolidated voluntary agencies who were motivated by other registers of group identification beyond a nation-state, the Board's approach circumscribed their spectrum of political and philanthropic expression.[41] It served as a powerful declaration that although American philanthropy stood poised as never before to extend its considerable reach overseas, it would do so under the close supervision and direction of the U.S. government. If the partial takeover by the U.S. government of America's voluntary war relief sector was not completely hostile, it was not always friendly either.

Hybrid Humanitarianism and International Hegemony

Though these regulatory interventions ruffled many feathers, the Board's strict regulatory policies also helped to produce a profoundly more effective and rationalized field of international relief than had existed in the early stages of World War II. Between 1939 and 1942, many hundreds of voluntary war agencies had operated around the country, often running inefficiently and in relative isolation from one another. From 1943 through mid-1946 the Board whittled that field down dramatically through agency closures and consolidations. In this rush of regulatory Darwinism those voluntary agencies that were able to survive often did so by transforming themselves into the kind of professionally organized and large scale organizations with which government and intergovernmental officials believed they could work in the field of humanitarian aid.[42]

This was certainly how Herbert Lehman, director general of the new United Nations Relief and Rehabilitation Administration, saw it in that February meeting in 1944 as he met to "recruit" the leaders of this philanthropic sector into the emerging "relief" arena of the American war cause. Where he, Secretary of State Cordell Hull, and other state officials once saw a civil society sector desperately in need of "proper coordination," they now saw some viable, if not equal, partners for the monumental task that lay ahead for UNRRA. The same went for other aid endeavors that the U.S. government was preparing to lead to bring humanitarian relief and geopolitical stability back to a world that was destroying itself on an order beyond that seen in the Great War two and a half decades earlier.[43] The stage appeared set for a hybrid blend of humanitarian initiatives performed through the collaboration of the American state with the non-state agencies it had regulated into more suitable associates.

The leaders of American war philanthropy whom Lehman consulted in that meeting had recently seen their agencies' institutional capacities expand through two other developments fostered by the federal government. At the beginning of the previous year, the Control Board created the National War Fund, its membership limited to the country's most robust and sophisticated war philanthropies. War Fund members had a distinct financial advantage afforded to two other state-related entities. As with War Bonds (U.S. Treasury) and the American Red Cross (Congressional Charter), one month annually was set aside for National War Fund agencies to fill their coffers through a massive and highly promoted fund drive when no other war relief agencies were permitted to collect donations.[44] In the fall of 1943, Lehman himself was partly responsible for the second development. In June 1943, he had explained to the directors of the leading voluntary agencies that, for the government to be able to collaborate with them, they must establish some kind of unity in their communications and operations, not unlike a single state agency, something they did by that fall under the name, the American Council of Voluntary Agencies for Foreign Service. The voluntary agencies of the War Fund and ACVAFS, largely boasting the same members, were to serve as the U.S. government's civil society junior partners in the looming humanitarian initiatives.[45]

Lehman understood that the increasingly well-coordinated philanthropies whose resources he sought to corral benefited from a uniquely rich reservoir of support among the American public. America's humming wartime economy and insulation from the ravages of the war upon its home front had helped to produce a nonprofit sector that dwarfed those of other industrialized countries. Tens of millions of Americans had contributed hundreds of millions of dollars in cash and kind to hundreds of different war relief charities since the beginning of the war in 1939.

Lehman's recognition of the potential of the country's philanthropic sector likely spawned less from innate skills of perception and administration (skills which his biographer has suggested were rather modest) than it did from his years of experience with American organizations that worked on behalf of Jewish refugees and other dispossessed civilians. (That recognition was promised for the war aims of the state.) Since the First World War, Lehman had leveraged the wealth and connections, afforded him through his family's banking empire, to support the American Joint Distribution committee, the National Refugee Service, and similar organizations. Consequently, beginning in late 1942—when NRS executive and member of President Roosevelt's advisory committee on refugees Joseph Chamberlain sought to convince federal war administrators that American philanthropies should be granted a meaningful role in war relief—he was able to make his case directly to Lehman. Thus began a series of communications between Lehman and his colleagues at the State Department and War Relief Control Board, on the one hand, and representatives of the voluntary agencies, such as Chamberlain, on the other.[46]

At his meeting with the voluntary agency leaders in February 1944, Lehman prepared to draw from this well, explaining that the fifteen hundred "voluntary workers" initially needed on the ground in a forthcoming relief campaign in the Balkans included first and foremost the many social workers and other welfare experts that typically formed the leadership and paid personnel of the private agencies. Also needed were refugee experts, doctors, nurses, translators, hygienists, accountants, mechanics, lab technicians, nutritionists, and caterers. The voluntary agencies would not merely be supplementing UNRRA official staff, however. They would constitute a full 80 percent of the manpower needed in the first phase of relief operations in the Balkans. Although paid by their individual private agencies, they would wear UNRRA "military type uniforms," Lehman explained. Additionally, while both UNRRA and the Allied militaries planned to supply most of the needed medical equipment and basic foodstuffs for the suffering populations, such as wheat and milk, UNRRA would need voluntary agencies to contribute other important items, such as clothing, blankets, certain medical supplies, and canned food.[47] The largest governmentally directed civilian relief organization the world had ever known would thus need to operate with the considerable contributions of America's nongovernmental philanthropies.

The pending Balkans campaign foretold of two significant dimensions of the emerging field of war relief. First, it would be a much larger endeavor than those recently begun by the Americans and British, whose militaries and foreign ministries initiated in 1943 some limited programs of relief in Allied-liberated North Africa and the Middle East.[48] Millions of displaced Greeks, Romanians, and Albanians were languishing in makeshift military camps, and the region's agricultural and industrial sectors were in ruins. When Allied militaries took more territory, the levels of human catastrophe promised to grow exponentially.[49]

As for the second factor, these first large operations conducted by UNRRA initiated a globally conspicuous test over whether the ravaged world that would eventually emerge from the war could be pieced back together through the collaborative efforts of a community of nations. In the two years of diplomatic negotiations between representatives of the "Big Four" Allies of the U.S. Britain, the Soviet Union, and China that ultimately created UNRRA in November 1943, it was taken almost as an axiomatic assumption that the League of Nations and humanitarian efforts that followed the First World War had failed to create a stable and ultimately peaceful Europe in large part because the United States had refused to become a full and sustaining participant in them.[50]

Things had clearly changed. While the three other big powers and even the forty other founding UNRRA nation-states exercised various degrees of authority in UNRRA, the intergovernmental organization was influenced disproportionately by one country. American diplomats had held the heaviest sway in the negotiations that produced UNRRA. The U.S. government had committed itself to funding two thirds of UNRRA's budget. The U.S. military was heavily involved in many operations affecting (and sometimes challenging) UNRRA. The American voluntary sector was disproportionately represented among civil societies from UNRRA member countries, and Americans boasted most of the administrative authority in the organization, from Lehman on down. Nursing the wartorn region back to health was not simply a matter of selfless humanitarianism for the Americans. As Lehman explained to those at the 1944 meeting, it was also critical for the war and postwar aims of both the United States and its allies. Devastated civilian populations presented a major distraction for Allied militaries as they took control of more and more territory from the enemy, and unstable economies might provide fertile ground for extreme politics of the right or left to take root.[51] As the UNRRA director put it on another occasion: since "shattered economies, pestilence, starvation and death breed riot and anarchy," the United States "must use food, clothing, shelter and the necessities of life as a real weapon to win complete and overwhelming victory and to secure the peace which must follow."[52]

The U.S. commitment to UNRRA was, until it ultimately waned with the waxing of the Cold War, nurtured by a cautious and dedicated campaign by

Figure 4. Office of War Information, Overseas Picture Division. "Mejex-El-Bab, Tunisia. A market operated by the Allied civilian relief groups to sell at cost food, clothing, kerosene, etc., supplied by the U.S. Office of Foreign Relief and Rehabilitation Operations to natives and Europeans, victims of war deprivation." 1943. Records of the Office of War Information. RG 208-LU, NARA, B 39, F N.

its supporters, especially those in the State Department. Secretary of State Dean Acheson and his subordinates, for instance, worked vigilantly to avoid the perceived mistakes of World War I, when President Woodrow Wilson's proposed League of Nations was deprived of U.S. support by the Senate. During the months in which the plans for the organization were being negotiated by diplomats from the Big Four, Acheson regularly sought counsel from members of Congress to the point where Republican senator Arthur Vandenberg, a recent and tenuous convert to American internationalism, acknowledged that "the State Department was amazingly cooperative, almost without precedent."[53] Congress passed seven funding laws for the organization between March 1944 and July 1946 to the tune of more than $2.6 billion.[54] The public buoyed Congress's support, with 82 percent of respondents to a poll in late 1945 approving of Congress committing more funds to UNRRA.[55]

Beyond the Roosevelt administration's savvy maneuvering, the willingness of Congress and the American public to support UNRRA for a critical period can be explained by a broader and deeper embrace of internationalism and federal power than that witnessed during the First World War. Historian Elizabeth Borgwardt has shown persuasively how the robust federal welfare programs of the New Deal helped condition Americans to their government assuming responsibility for the social security of wide swaths of the world outside American borders both during and, in particular, after World War II. James Sparrow has additionally demonstrated that the federal government proved remarkably adept at convincing the American people to accept far greater levels of state activity during the era than had been previously witnessed.[56]

The intergovernmental organization that relied so heavily on the United States proved to be an audacious, vast, and deeply imperfect endeavor, responding to a humanitarian crisis that far outmatched it. The forty-eight member states it eventually claimed represented 80 percent of the world's people. Its twenty thousand employees hailed from fifty countries. It spent almost $4 billion during its operational tenure between 1944 and 1947 to provide assistance to twenty million war victims in sixteen countries formerly controlled by Axis powers in East Asia, Africa, and across much of Europe. While UNRRA received strong criticisms on a number of grounds that have been well-documented by its contemporaries and subsequent historians, its operations nevertheless often made the difference between destitution and relative comfort for recipients of UNRRA aid, and for many, between life and death.[57]

These statistics do not count the human labor and material resources provided by the civil society organizations that worked underneath the institution's umbrella and the populations of the various member countries that supported them. Resolution 9, Section 2 of UNRRA's charter document stipulated that the organization enlist the support of non-state voluntary agencies whenever possible.[58] Thousands of voluntary personnel accordingly labored for UNRRA while officially affiliated with private agencies that had been licensed by the intergovernmental organization. For Americans, this primarily meant the American Council of Voluntary Agencies that Herbert Lehman had helped nudge into existence in 1943. Its British counterpart, accounting for the second largest faction of UNRRA's voluntary army, was the Council of British Societies for Relief Abroad.[59] The officials and voluntary organizations maintained constant contact with one another, perpetually negotiating countless matters pertaining to UNRRA's operations. These included major policy debates over, for example, stopping the forcible repatriation of refugees, allowing refugees to self-govern their camps, and permitting the free circulation of Western newspapers in the refugee camps even when the Soviets vigorously opposed such things.[60]

And even though its budget derived overwhelmingly from state coffers, the organizational support given to the UNRRA by American voluntary agencies alone was echoed by the $150 million in cash and goods directly given to the intergovernmental agency. The practice was part and parcel of the ways many people donated to their nongovernmental war relief agencies of choice. In addition to cash contributions, people regularly dropped off canned goods at their neighborhood church for transfer to one of the national war philanthropies in one month and delivered used clothing to the same church to be delivered to UNRRA the next month. From the millions of individual Americans who supported international aid initiatives to the operations of governmental and nongovernmental agencies themselves, the myriad elements constituting American war relief had become almost organically fused into a massive field of hybrid governance by war's end.[61]

UNRRA refugee aid was the one area where voluntary agency contributions were anything but supplementary, instead accounting for the bulk of such operations. UNRRA claimed responsibility for only a portion of the world's unprecedented refugee populations—albeit a significant one—but the crisis it confronted was almost unfathomable. Of the fifty-five million Europeans forcibly moved from their homes during the war and its early aftermath, between ten and eleven million Europeans remained outside their countries of original residence. The large majority of them resided in Germany, usually brought there as forced laborers or concentration camp inmates (the latter, numbering seven hundred thousand survivors). Most of the remainder were scattered elsewhere in Europe and the eastern Mediterranean, usually having fled the advances of various belligerent ground forces. UNRRA officials and military authorities coined the term "displaced persons" to categorize these eleven million refugees, a definition mainly limited to civilians outside their countries of origin at the end of the hostilities. While most of UNRRA's refugee aid initiatives concentrated on assisting these European displaced persons, it also boasted significant refugee aid operations in other war-torn regions. Voluntary agencies provided most of the personnel and much of the material aid to UNRRA's hundreds of displaced persons camps, most of them located in Germany. This provision permitted much more ambitious operations than would have otherwise been possible. As a measure of these initiatives, the three Western zones of occupied Germany alone housed seven hundred fifteen thousand persons at a time, with thousands more residing in similar camps in China, North Africa, the Levant, Austria, Italy, and beyond.[62] Such refugee aid operations were but a prominent example of the way in which American philanthropies seemed poised to make their mark as never before as they looked across a devastated postwar landscape, and committed themselves to helping masses of humanity made vulnerable by the actions of nation-states.

Fleeting Attempts at Nongovernmental Diplomacy

The prospects for America's voluntary sector offering a more benevolent alternative to the cold logic of states were confronted with a sobering reality, however, as one type of war morphed into another. In late summer 1945, with the European theater of the war officially concluded and the Pacific war on the verge of ending, Allied nations engaged in the ritual process of celebrating each other's role in the victory. America's voluntary relief agencies were lauded in commemorations both at home and abroad for the important roles that they had played in protecting tens of millions of refugees and other civilians from the worst fates of war.

One such ceremony occurred in Moscow, in the Kremlin's Council Room of the Supreme Soviet, where Soviet President Mikhail I. Kalinin presented the Order of the Red Banner of Labor award to Edward C. Carter, president of the voluntary agency Russian War Relief (RWR). Among the Allied powers, no country's citizens had suffered more than those of the Soviet Union.

Carter's philanthropy had given over $80 million worth of medical supplies, clothing, food, and other relief materials to the Soviet people, making RWR then the largest contributor of America's state-licensed war philanthropies. Carter's long résumé in international philanthropy reached back to his turn-of-the-century work with the YMCA in India. Since 1926, he had served as a leading official in the Institute of Pacific Relations, working through the organization to promote knowledge of the Eastern hemisphere in the West, a charge he continued when he joined other prominent professionals, business-men, clergy, and welfare officials in 1941 to found Russian War Relief. President Kalinin's presentation to Carter was designed to thank the ordinary persons of the United States for their help in both alleviating the suffering of Soviet civilians and sustaining the health of Soviet soldiers to repulse German armies on the Eastern Front. The ceremony was not intended as a coming-together of two governments, but of two peoples: Soviet and American. Kalinin explained that the award represented "friendship between our two countries and acknowledgement of material aid from private citizens of the United States to the workers and peasants of the U.S.S.R."[63] Indeed, thousands of American volunteers had given their cash, goods, and labor to Soviet citizens through the four hundred RWR committees represented in forty states across the United States, with the donated items marked by a small U.S. flag and a message that the contribution was intended for "the heroic people of the Soviet Union from the people of the United States of America."[64]

Having spent three weeks before the ceremony surveying postwar relief needs in the Soviet Union, Carter and his colleagues hoped to use their visit to parlay the group's humanitarian activities into a kind of postwar nongovernmental diplomacy that might help to mitigate the intensifying tensions between the American and Soviet states. While neither Carter nor his fellow RWR officials likely harbored any illusions that philanthropy could bridge the growing chasm between the two governments, they still betrayed a genuine confidence that comradery between the Soviet and American people could nonetheless endure. The sense of optimism of Carter and the RWR had been conditioned, after all, not by a cold war to come, but by a world war that the two countries had collectively fought and won over the previous several years. The year before the Kremlin ceremony, Carter had opined that "the Russian relief program has been largely instrumental in opening a Russian window on the United States and an American window on Russia which would have amazed that great Russian champion of window-openers, Peter the Great."[65] RWR official Fred Meyers echoed Carter's optimism upon return stateside from the Kremlin ceremony in 1945, suggesting that the gifts that his agency had given to the Soviet people represented "good-will that is doing more to cement friendly relations between the two nations than all the formal treaties and negotiations of State."[66] The 1946 final report of the President's War Relief Control Board made a similar case, albeit a broader one extending the confines of U.S.-Soviet relations, declaring that the "American relief enterprise will promote direct human relationships between the American people and the people of the war-stricken countries." As "these sufferers look to America," they will know that they are being helped not only with "the public funds of the United States" but also by ordinary Americans "as a direct expression of their sympathy and as a form of personal aid."[67]

As another group of American social ambassadors arrived in the Soviet Union the next summer, they traveled in a decidedly chillier environment between the Soviet and American governments. Their mission marked a fleeting effort at narrowing the growing rift in East-West relations through nongovernmental diplomacy.[68] Over the previous year, Russian War Relief leaders had grown critical of the Truman administration's hardening line toward the Soviet

Figure 5. Russian War Relief clothing drive operated by students of Carl Shurz High School in Chicago in the era of the Second World War. Office of War Information. Untitled. Records of the Office of War Information. RG 208-LU. NARA, B 22, F B.

Union, accusing the president of "betraying" FDR's policies that had treated the Soviets as valuable allies. Although there were still some liberals within the administration and Congress who similarly continued to promote friendly relations with the Soviet Union, the political momentum of the country had begun to shift notably in the other direction.[69] The delegation hoped to maneuver on a level below the high politics of government to salvage a degree of cordial relations between the two countries. This visit also differed from that of the previous year in that most members of the seven-person group were not RWR officials, even though their mission bore that agency's name. They were instead representatives from the New York State Chamber of Commerce, the General Federation of Women's Clubs, a medical foundation, the World Jewish Congress, and two Protestant ministries: the delegation's diversity was clearly intended to symbolize the open pluralism of American civil society.[70] The group accordingly used its five thousand-mile trip through the Soviet Union to publicize parallels between what it presented as the shared "freedoms" existing in both American and Soviet societies, liberties that the group believed would resonate particularly well at that time with the American public.[71]

Prominent among the ideals they emphasized was one long entrenched in the American psyche and conscripted for war aims in FDR's Four Freedoms address of 1941: freedom of worship. As the group's visit coincided with the tail end of a temporary Soviet wartime policy promoting organized religion— a policy established to mollify beleaguered and disgruntled masses[72]—the Americans could report with confidence that the church services they attended in Moscow, Leningrad, and Minsk were, in the assessment of Fred Meyers, "just like any service back home." In front of a two thousand-strong congregation at the Moscow Baptist Church, a minister from Atlanta, Louis D. Newton, drew his sermon from the New Testament's John 10:16, "One Flesh and One Spirit," stressing the importance of understanding the interconnectedness of all God's people. After the singing of familiar hymns, Newton reported that the service was "just as free and open a meeting as you would see in any Baptist church in the world."[73] The American delegation's Jewish representative later joined in the spirit of the moment, praising the Soviets for being "free of anti-Semitism."[74]

Applauding a more secular liberty, another RWR delegate echoed the sentiments of other persons on the trip, noting that "from the moment of our arrival in the Soviet Union . . . we had full freedom of travel," with little supervision from police or military authorities, and "no contacts with political leaders."[75] While freedom of worship was an old and well-articulated principle in

America, the freedom of movement boasted a shorter lineage, at least as an explicitly enshrined right. This was due in no small measure to growing attention to the confluence of two overseas developments making American headlines in recent months: a tremendous refugee crisis and a rising "Iron Curtain." The issue of volitional mobility, as with freedom of religion, had been used by Soviet and American officials to ratchet up tensions between the two new superpowers in the war's aftermath, and Americans traveling the RWR had clearly hoped to siphon away some of its corrosive power by exposing it as a norm that both cultures valued.

The debate focused especially on UNRRA's displaced persons camps in Germany, many of them operated by agencies that had been granted similar licenses from the U.S. government for overseas relief work as had Russian War Relief. Millions of citizens of the Soviet Union and its emerging cluster of satellite states, persons who had found themselves in the U.S. Zone of Occupation in Germany at war's end, had already been placed on cramped train cars and repatriated back East. Many Soviets returned against their will, having heard rumors that Siberian work prisons and systematic executions awaited those who had supposedly abandoned their homelands for the arms of the German enemy. Bowing to mounting pressures by some of the thousands of American voluntary agency personnel who had been laboring in UNRRA's displaced persons camps, U.S. government officials had begun refusing to repatriate Soviet Bloc "DPs" forcibly. Hundreds of thousands of DPs were instead permitted to remain in the refugee camps, creating a looming refugee crisis for the West. On the floor of the newly created United Nations American diplomats defended the U.S. practice against indignant Soviet protests. They claimed that the Soviet governments did not respect basic human freedoms, including the right to worship and to travel where one pleased, and thus, its displaced citizens had a right to refuse repatriation. Soviet officials countered by pointing to America's own shortcomings in protecting the rights of its more marginalized citizens—particularly women and African Americans—claiming that the U.S. government's blatant hypocrisy weakened its justifications for holding on to the Soviet DPs.[76]

If the American good will ambassadors in the Soviet Union tried to give an alternate spin to issues that were elsewhere inflaming U.S.-Soviet relations, two events that occurred during their trip must have dampened their hopes. One was triggered by a member of the American delegation, while the other happened in the American South. Both events revealed the pitfalls in the new geopolitical climate of deploying a strategy designed to alleviate East-West tensions—tensions dominated by high politics—by appealing to the ideological principles allegedly shared by each side's domestic culture. In the new international climate, the customs and ideologies of *the people* could be nearly as prone to fueling international discord as the strategic differences between states. Little was off limits in a Cold War that thrived on ideological differences, including matters behind national borders.

On the last day of July, several American representatives of the good-will mission held a press conference with Soviet reporters in Leningrad. Praising the country she was visiting, the president of the General Federation of Women's Clubs, Lucy Jennings Dickinson, observed that "in the Soviet Union women are regarded as equals and enjoy rights with men." By itself this statement constituted the type of innocuous praise of Soviet society that the American delegates had hoped to parlay into a warmer sense of trust between the two countries. Dickinson, however, continued with a thinly veiled jab at her home country, lamenting, "We American women do not enjoy these rights."[77] In less caustic times such a statement might have simply been understood as a polite gesture intended to win the favor of her hosts. But in the current environment it was ripe for divisive political manipulation as it suggested that American gender politics and attendant domestic norms in fact lagged behind those of the Soviet Union.[78]

Making Dickinson's comment more vulnerable to the political atmosphere of the moment, another event had occurred only several days prior that also served to indict the poor treatment of a marginalized group in the United States, albeit a different group and in far more dramatic fashion. On a backwoods road in Georgia four black cotton pickers (two married couples) suffered one of the most brutal lynchings in the American South's recent history. After an altercation between one of the men and his boss, a white plantation owner, a mob of twenty to thirty white men ambushed the four, bound them, broke their limbs, and repeatedly riddled their bodies with shotgun pellets, to almost beyond the point of recognition. With the help of the FBI, Georgia's state police were seeking the assailants, but the local residents and police had generally refused to cooperate. Expressing the enraged fatigue of America's black community with such incidents, the African American editorial board of the *Chicago Defender* threatened to use its influence to embarrass the U.S. government on the UN floor if a federal anti-lynching law were not passed soon.[79]

In an emerging pattern that would help define the propaganda battles of the Cold War, the Soviet newspaper *Pravda* and Soviet diplomats at the UN were soon invoking the two stories to embarrass the U.S. government to both

Soviet and international audiences alike. The U.S. government was charged with hypocrisy in its demand that displaced persons from the Soviet sphere be kept in the West—kept allegedly because they feared persecution should they return—while simultaneously discriminating against its own female and minority citizens at home. Reverend Louis Newton acknowledged to an American reporter that he had learned of the Georgia lynching committed in his own home state from a *Pravda* article during his good-will mission in the Soviet Union, which unlike many American papers, "had the full story."[80]

These events and, more precisely, the reactions to them, suggested that nongovernmental diplomacy across the Iron Curtain had little chance of offering an alternative to that of traditional state relations as the latter turned increasingly adversarial. The good will that American relief organizations had fostered in the Soviet Union, and in fact, across the Soviet sphere, quickly found precious few arenas for expression. The controversies in the summer of 1946 proved fatal to Russian War Relief. Throughout the organization's tenure, its officials had mobilized public relations campaigns to counter persistent charges that RWR was actually a communist front organization. That a minority of RWR support came from leftist labor unions with high levels of Jewish membership fueled the claim. As a more fervent politics of anticommunism took hold in the United States, the efforts of the philanthropy's officials proved overmatched.[81] Accused of being a "Russian relief racket," and losing key supporters within the Truman administration, the voluntary agency stopped soliciting donations by the end of 1946.[82]

Other American voluntary agencies that had been licensed by the President's War Relief Board to provide relief in countries such as Czechoslovakia, Hungary, Poland, Yugoslavia, Lithuania, Latvia, and Estonia similarly saw their overseas relief operations fade over the rest of the decade. The sources of their collective demise came from a variety of sources, including the U.S. government, the American public, and recipient states. In the spring of 1947, for example, the State Department crippled the operations of the American Committee for Yugoslav Relief by forbidding the distribution of American grain in the communist country even though it remained more buffered from Soviet influence than did other states in the region. As Honorary Chairman of the relief agency, Eleanor Roosevelt lamented in her near-daily column "My Day" that the U.S. government's growing "refusal to render aid to other nations which will keep their people alive and help them reestablish themselves on a healthy economic basis" seemed to her "a very short-sighted policy." By the end of the year, U.S. attorney general and future Supreme Court justice Tom Clark placed the philanthropy on a list of "subversive" organizations, a practice that similarly doomed the operations of other private organizations attempting to assist the people of countries communist governments ruled after the war. At the beginning of 1948, a House subcommittee released a study that strongly urged voluntary agencies to cease operations in those countries in which political interference from governments unfriendly to the United States was likely. This recommendation was made less necessary in part because of waning support among the American public for these operations, and in part because of the barring of American philanthropies by a growing array of governments in the communist world. The Polish government announced in March 1948 that it would begin a process of removing all foreign relief organizations. The next spring, the head of American Relief for Czechoslovakia was jailed in Prague, prompting the agency to announce that it would cease operations in short order.[83] In a development that further crystallized the degree to which America's non-state organizations were aligning themselves with the Cold War imperatives of the U.S. government, many reorganized themselves, joining their operations with the voluntary agencies providing humanitarian assistance to the U.S.-allied nations of Western Europe and Asia.[84]

New geopolitical realities did indeed circumscribe the geographical scope of American philanthropy. Nevertheless, U.S. philanthropic activities maintained a remarkable presence after the war in both the territories of America's Cold War allies and in unaligned countries. The country's voluntary agencies sent nearly $200 million abroad in 1946, mostly to Europe, with President Truman declaring in early 1947 that "a large need" continued for private American aid abroad. The emergency relief operations so common during the fighting and its immediate aftermath were joined increasingly by longer-term reconstruction initiatives, the latter serving as precursors to American modernization programs deployed across the globe as part of the country's Cold War battles against communism.[85]

The ties forged between the voluntary sector and the American state endured and evolved. Whereas the Advisory Committee on Voluntary Foreign Aid, the body that in mid-1946 replaced the President's War Relief Control Board, possessed less overt regulatory authority than did its predecessor, American voluntary agencies still had to abide by federal rules if they wanted to be a part of the expansive humanitarian and rebuilding efforts directed by the government after the war.[86] Beyond the well-known Marshal Plan was the International Refugee Organization, emerging in 1946 to offer the United

States and its allies a more Western-friendly conduit for refugee assistance outside the more broadly represented UNRRA which withered in 1947 as another victim of Cold War tensions.[87] The U.S. government also created the Government and Relief in Occupied Areas program to offer medical supplies, food, clothing, and other provisions to the citizens of Japan, Germany, and Austria. The voluntary agencies played an important role in these and related ventures, working through such new umbrella organizations as Licensed Agencies for Relief in Asia, the Council of Relief Agencies Licensed to Operate in Germany, and the Cooperative for American Remittances to Europe, with the Cooperative dispensing a seemingly endless stream of CARE packages from private Americans. It is significant that CARE soon changed its name to the Cooperative for Assistance and Relief Everywhere, as it was in the decades following the war that the aspirations of the country's voluntary sector echoed the growing international reach of the U.S. government.[88]

The American nongovernmental relief organizations that emerged and matured during World War II and its aftermath would form an important humanitarian-based core of what has been called an international "NGO revolution" in the second half of the twentieth century. Nongovernmental organizations have been heralded in recent years for their willingness and ability to challenge the self-serving and sometimes inhumane policies of national governments across the globe, standing as independent checks on a global system of nation-states that can betray a callous disregard for human rights. American-based NGOs, in particular, have been lionized by both broad international publics and scholars alike for their critical distance from the American state.[89] The mid-century history of American war relief charities, however, reveals a more complex picture. Certain voluntary organizations did indeed resent and even resist state intervention. But the U.S. government ultimately had the final say over whether those organizations persisted, and if so, in what fashion. Those entities that survived into the postwar order tended to do so with more vibrancy than they otherwise would have likely enjoyed. Their institutional capacities often owed much to the tight connections they forged with the U.S. government, both of a regulatory and a more collaborative nature. The legacy of these developments might be defensibly seen today as somewhat ironic and, depending on one's perspective on the proper role of nongovernmental organizations in the contemporary world, even disquieting. Many of the organizational ancestors of the modern NGO emerged and matured under the close supervision of the American state, not as independent opponents of it, but rather in the state's regulatory incubator.

CHAPTER 4

Benevolent or Fair Superpower?

During 1949 and 1950, groups of sharecroppers in Mississippi sent letters to newspapers, families, and friends chronicling their extreme hardships living amid the cotton fields of the Delta. The tone of their letters ranged from despondent to frantic. No matter how long and hard they labored, they complained, it proved impossible to free themselves of their debt to the plantation owners. Rather than run up larger bills at their plantation commissaries, some went hungry and worked barefoot in the fields, as decent food and new shoes were luxuries they could not afford if they ever hoped to leave sharecropping legally. They charged that their plantation bosses were "trying very hard . . . to push us into debt and slavery." "From early morning until late at night," one complained, "we pick cotton and pull heavy sacks on our stooped backs, our feet sinking deeply in mud. We have not had a bath for six months." Cardboard sometimes served as their roof. "Where is justice?" one sharecropper asked. "Have we been punished by God?" Another explained that to stay warm on cold winter nights, her family of four slept on the floor with their lone mattress lying on top of them. "We don't have any furniture," she lamented. "This is the life that we live, in an old Negro hut where water drips on our heads." This sharecropper described her abode as a "Negro hut" because she, her family, and in fact the other letter writers were all political refugees from Latvia.[1]

How did they arrive in such a seemingly improbable situation, moving from their Baltic homeland through refugee camps in Germany to the steamy cotton fields of Mississippi? Their plight was no accident. Rather, these Latvians had been brought to their sharecropper shacks through the U.S. Displaced Persons Program, America's first major immigration program aimed specifically at those persons deemed political refugees. As a result of Congressional legislation, from late 1948 through 1952 four hundred thousand Europeans who had been displaced from their homes by war, oppression, and regime change were specially admitted into the United States and then systematically resettled into scores of communities across the country through the "DP" Program. The planned resettlement component of the DP Act was officially a first for U.S. immigration law, though in a less overt and de facto manner, the admissions of many Jewish refugees from Nazism had been conditional upon private welfare organizations promising to facilitate, when needed, their adjustment to life in the United States without any immigrants becoming public charges.[2] The organized manner in which Mississippi Latvians were placed in the Delta was mirrored in the stories of nearly half a million other refugees who came to live in the United States in the late 1940s and early 1950s. A vast hybrid resettlement network of governmental, nongovernmental, and intergovernmental organizations helped to care for refugees abroad, transport them to pre-chosen communities in the United States, and then provide them with jobs, housing, and often, many other necessities of life in their new American homeland.

This chapter explores one aspect of the U.S. Displaced Persons Program—labor exploitation—to investigate how mid-twentieth century motivations of humanitarianism, geopolitics, and rights protection collided with some of the harshest dynamics of the American labor market. It argues that attempts by American refugee advocates to present the United States as the postwar world's benevolent, rights-protecting superpower were complicated as the DP Program came to look more like a massive, and at times, highly exploitative international employment service than the humanitarian-based endeavor that they originally envisioned. The DP Program was implemented on a world stage at a moment when both the U.S. government and the country's civil society institutions were beginning to define the content and styles of America's new position of global leadership. In actively resettling refugees from overseas in the United States, American people and institutions effectively extended the reach of American sovereignty by assuming responsibility for vast groups of destitute persons whose former national governments had either disappeared or posed a possible threat to their security. At this formative moment of the Cold War, the DP Program was heralded by its American supporters, both within and outside of government, as powerful evidence for a watchful world that the merits of the American way of life vastly outweighed those of the Soviet system. The extension of American sovereignty that the DP Program represented was manifest in efforts on behalf of the refugees both abroad and at home. Echoing the sentiments of many American liberals, internationalists, humanitarian activists, and most directly, secretary of state Dean Acheson, DP Program administrator Harry Rosenfield predicted that refugee resettlement in the United States would represent a "fundamental link" between the domestic and international dimensions of America's "strategy of freedom." It would provide humanitarian ammunition for the country's "arsenal of peace," the federal bureaucrat opined, in the struggle against international communism. American refugee policies promised to offer a softer side of American foreign relations after the war.[3]

Many thousands of displaced persons did indeed contribute to this "arsenal" by quickly establishing comfortable lives in the United States as "new Americans." Their success often owed a debt to a trio of resources that refugee advocates boasted would await them in the United States: resettlement assistance given to the immigrants by American philanthropy; a robust American economy that could richly reward hard work, skills, and autonomy; and a political and legal system that would provide refugees with a wide array of civil rights protections. But as this chapter shows, thousands of others languished in the United States. Included among them were cotton sharecroppers throughout the Deep South, indebted sugar cane workers in the bayous of Louisiana, fruit and sugar beet stoop laborers from California to the Dakotas, and sweatshop workers and strikebreakers in the Midwest and Northeast.[4] The lot of some of these less fortunate immigrants more closely resembled the portrayals of downtrodden workers in John Steinbeck's *The Grapes of Wrath* and Dorothea Lange's haunting Depression-era photographs than Norman Rockwell's images of the American Dream. This happened in part because they fell through cracks of an idealized resettlement system. Yet it also happened precisely because these refugees had in fact become a part of the system. They discovered that the American labor market could exploit as well as reward, and that mid-century American discourses of both human and civil rights could embrace notions of formal equality at the expense of social justice. The responses that federal officials and some prominent philanthropic leaders made to charges of refugees' poor treatment not only set an important precedent for future U.S. refugee initiatives, but also revealed a profound set of tensions between mid-century American liberal ideals of formal legal equality, an economic system often structured by inequality, and American attempts to promote a vision for the postwar world based on social justice and human rights.

Unlike most of the African Americans whose mistreatment in the United

States other historians have compellingly considered in an international Cold War context, these refugees were not American citizens.⁵ Instead, officials of the Soviet Union and its growing cluster of satellite states vehemently claimed these new immigrants as their own countries' citizens, stolen by the United States to exploit their labor. Their appeal as diplomatic and ideological weapons thus possessed an even more potentially combustible ingredient in the affairs between the two ascendant superpowers. The plight that befell exploited refugee workers through the DP Program was furthermore not typically the result of prejudicial discrimination and subversion of constitutional legal guarantees of equal protection, as was the main source of international and domestic controversies over the treatment of blacks in America during the era. Rather, these refugees suffered in their new homeland precisely because they *were* being treated in the same way as other poor laborers doing similar work. These episodes threatened to produce a particularly damning indictment of the American system of law and respect for individual rights, not because this system was failing to be applied to some, but rather because it *was* being applied to these admitted refugees in a way that propagated the dramatic exploitation of their labor and circumscribed their ability to find better opportunities in the United States.

Opportunity from Crisis

U.S. army lieutenant colonel and large Mississippi cotton plantation owner, Albert Callicott, played a seminal role in these developments, albeit one wholly unanticipated by the architects of the DP Act. By late 1948 Callicott would begin bringing hundreds of Eastern and Central European displaced persons to work on both his and others' cotton plantations in the Delta. But several years previously, at the war's end, he was serving as the U.S. army governor of the city of Nuremberg in the U.S. Zone of occupied Germany. At this post he was charged with repatriating tens of thousands of displaced persons back to their homelands, mostly in the Soviet Union and the countries of Central and Eastern Europe, which were falling under increasing Soviet control.⁶

The repatriations Callicott facilitated were part of a much larger repatriation project involving nearly ten million refugees who found themselves in Germany after the war, "displaced persons" whose fate was charged to the Western Allies and the UN Relief and Rehabilitation Administration (UNRRA).

Some had fled their homelands in Eastern and Central Europe during the war for Germany to avoid invading Soviet armies, while others had been lured or forced by the Nazis to work in German factories and fields in the service of the German war effort. The United States and Britain had committed themselves to helping with these repatriations through agreements they had made with the Soviet Union with the founding of UNRRA in late 1943, the Yalta Conference in early 1945, and the Potsdam Conference in the summer of 1945. Government officials of the emerging Eastern Bloc insisted that most of the displaced persons were citizens of their countries, and should thus be repatriated. Many of these refugees were vehement anti-communists, and resisted repatriation after the war because the Soviets now controlled their homelands. Contributing to their desire not to return, rumors circulated around the camps that repatriated displaced persons were being exiled to Siberian labor prisons, often being worked to death, or else killed outright for having supported the Nazis during the war, willingly or not. The agreement to forcibly return the Soviet Bloc citizens openly defied a principle of non-return (or *non-refoulement*) that had been gaining increasing currency in international law since the massive refugee crises of the World War I era, but, for a time at least, the Americans and British honored their wartime commitments.[7]

By 1947 the vast majority of the refugees had been placed on trains and sent back to their homelands, most of them to the Soviet East. The one million refugees still remaining, however, had grown more hostile to the idea of repatriation. With relations between the two new superpowers growing increasingly contentious, high-level U.S. military commanders accordingly became gradually less willing to force the resistant displaced persons onto trains bound for the East.[8] Members of the Truman administration and the U.S. Congress were now expressing growing resistance to forced repatriation and took their growing frustrations out on the UNRRA. Believing that the Soviets possessed too much influence over the massive intergovernmental war relief organization, including repatriation policies, Congress let American financial support for the agency die. In its place emerged the U.S. and British controlled International Refugee Organization with a mandate not only for the remaining refugees' protection and care, but also for resettling them to new homelands rather than repatriating them to their old.[9] All this infuriated Soviet officials, who vehemently protested the existence of the new IRO and its emphasis on resettlement over repatriation.[10] Soviet bloc delegates at the United Nations lambasted the West's growing insistence that the remaining refugees be allowed to emigrate instead of being coerced back to their Soviet-controlled homelands. They charged that the United States and its allies were only interested in exploiting the labor of the displaced persons for the benefit of their own economies. In late 1947 at the United Nations they further accused the United States of spreading anti-Soviet propaganda to the refugees, a violation of an international agreement between the two countries in April of that year.[11]

With a "residual" population refusing repatriation and the new UN-affiliated IRO charged with helping those displaced persons to resettle in new homelands, the governments of Western Europe, Australia, and North and South America began considering in earnest passing laws to admit large numbers of them to their countries as immigrants. Nearly all these countries, including the United States, boasted considerable legal barriers to large-scale immigration dating back to the World War I era and earlier, barriers strengthened even further during the Great Depression. To resettle the remaining refugees to permanent new homes, foreign policy officials and other refugee advocates considered special measures that would be needed to liberalize or circumvent existing immigration laws.[12]

While the forces allayed against liberalized immigration in the United States remained strong, the political, cultural, and economic climate after the war had turned more favorable for the advocates of reform than had been the case during the 1920s and 1930s. The Truman administration and Congress received considerable political pressure on both the international and domestic fronts to pass a special immigration law for the refugees. Government officials viewed the refugees as a "surplus" population that threatened to destabilize the economies and political climates of the countries where the displaced were predominantly located: Germany and, to a much lesser degree, Austria and Italy. At home a broad array of groups, collectively representing a significant part of a Democratic coalition, lobbied vigorously in support of a law. Organized especially through an umbrella organization—the Citizens Committee for Displaced Persons—they were represented by Catholic and Protestant groups, ethnic and nationality societies, and most importantly, Jewish Americans, who had been mobilizing for years to liberalize U.S. immigration law. With the elections of 1948 on the horizon, the diverse representation of the Citizens Committee lent the lobbying campaign added force. So too did the fact that currents of cultural pluralism flowed more forcefully in the postwar years than they had previously, the recent war against fascist states having helped to make more appealing the idea that ethnic and religious diversity would strengthen rather than weaken American society. A revived

American economy furthermore neutralized some of the power behind warnings by immigration opponents—concentrated especially in the American South and West—that refugees would take jobs away from veterans. Refugee advocates even managed ultimately to persuade the vehemently anti-immigration American Legion to support a limited refugee law. The support was, however, granted only on the condition that it would be designed as just a temporary measure, instigated to alleviate the European refugee crisis, and not instead a larger legislative opening for the long-term liberalization of U.S. immigration law more generally.[13]

Albert Callicott watched these developments with interest, growing determined to use the Displaced Persons Program, once operational, for his own economic benefit and that of other Mississippi Delta cotton planters more generally. After repatriating thousands of displaced persons back to the East, the Lieutenant Colonel retired his military commission in 1946. He returned briefly to the Delta to find that the supply of cotton workers in the region had dwindled considerably since the wartime economy had lured scores of thousands of them away to the factories and ports in southern and northern cities alike.[14] The reduction of the American cotton labor force had been occurring in earnest since the 1930s, driven largely by mechanization and federal New Deal policies that paid planters to reduce their productive acreage. Mississippi and nearby states had lost nearly 40 percent of their tenant farmers during the Depression. While the Delta did not require as many laborers to work the fields as it once did, many aspects of cotton production, such as chopping and thinning picked cotton, were not yet mechanized.[15]

Planters had furthermore grown concerned over the ascendance of the Southern Tenant Farmers Union and understood that a glut in the pool of available laborers would reduce the STFU's leverage in demanding higher wages and better working conditions. The activities of the STFU were echoed by attempts of the Congress of Industrial Organizations in various parts of the American South to organize black workers. Through such confederations as the American Farm Bureau and the Delta Council, for example, wealthy planters had begun to address the problem by persuading the U.S. Employment Service and the federal Farm Security Administration from advertising jobs available in other parts of the country in the Delta until the cotton planting and picking seasons had ended. The planters also attempted, not always successfully, to keep the region's labor supply sedentary and bloated by employing older techniques of labor supply management, such as debt peonage and physical coercion, particularly on African American laborers whose extreme subordination had become customary and whose practical recourse to the law was often scant.[16]

Believing he had a solution to his region's labor shortage, at least as he and other planters defined it, Callicott returned to the Nuremberg area in 1947 as a private insurance contractor for the U.S. military. This strategic professional move afforded him the opportunity to develop further relationships with key American and IRO officials in charge of caring for the remaining DP populations. It also gave him access to survey a group of Latvian refugees whose industriousness and tidy garden plots in and nearby the camps had caught Callicott's attention while serving as the army's governor of the area. As it became more evident that the U.S. Congress would soon agree to admit large numbers of the European refugees, Callicott grew determined to secure an inside track toward bringing "his Latvians," as he would later call them, back to his Mississippi plantations to work as cotton sharecroppers. He believed that they might even offer a broader solution to the labor shortages of the entire Delta. Other employers of sharecroppers and other types of stoop laborers across the country would also soon look to the DP Program as a welcome source of labor that had been drained during the war.[17]

Although there is no available evidence that Callicott lobbied Congress for a DP law, several provisions of the DP Act that went into effect in late June of 1948 nonetheless suited his designs beautifully. All of them were products of compromise between refugee advocates and wary Congress members who were only willing to support the bill if certain conditions were met. First, at least 30 percent of the first two hundred two thousand admitted refugees had to be farmers.[18] (A 1950 amendment to the law would extend its tenure to 1952, adding another two hundred three thousand immigration slots.[19]) Second, at least 40 percent of the admitted displaced persons had to hail from nation-states that had ceased to exist as a result of being conquered by another country. This meant the Baltic states of Latvia, Lithuania, and Estonia, which were now part of the Soviet Union. It was not lost on America's Jewish community and other immigration liberals that such provisions had the effect—clearly intended by some persons—to limit the number of Jews who might enter through the program.[20]

Most importantly for Callicott's plans, however, were provisions that helped to determine how refugees would be resettled under the DP Program. These resettlement provisions were forced into the law by those persons who were either lukewarm to the prospect of refugee admissions or outright hostile to them. They were designed to produce a cumbersome, nearly unworkable admissions process and make it unlikely that all the refugees eligible to enter the United States under the act would be able to do so before it expired. The supporters of refugee admissions both within and outside government had little choice but to resign themselves to working with the resettlement requirements. They soon even began embracing them as their own. Organized resettlement came to be marketed by supporters of the DP Program as evidence that the governmental and philanthropic institutions in the United States would guard the admitted refugees' rights under U.S. laws and lend them a helping hand, proving that the "land of the free" was also the home of the protected and nurtured. The federal Displaced Persons Commission, created to administer the program, the American voluntary agencies involved in refugee aid, and the International Refugee Organization actively forged close relationships with one another to deal with the DP Act's resettlement provisions. Whereas the cast of people and institutions involved in the U.S. DP Program represented a diverse array of interests and goals, they nevertheless very self-consciously created a hybrid resettlement network composed of governmental, nongovernmental, and intergovernmental actors.[21]

Callicott, however—and soon, many other American employers of stoop labor—also wanted to be part of this network even if most American refugee advocates had not originally envisioned them as a part of it. These employers saw the DP Act resettlement provisions as a serendipitous opportunity to secure refugee labor from Europe. They would surprise both the original supporters and opponents of refugee admissions by using resettlement provisions to grease the wheels the DP Program, not through commitments to rights protection, managed social security, and benevolence, but through recruitment of plentiful, cheap, vulnerable workers.

The DP Act required that refugees enter the United States with a resettlement plan pre-approved by the new federal DP Commission, appointed by the President, and charged with overseeing the DP Program. Supporters of refugee admissions heralded this federally monitored resettlement provision as a dramatic departure from what they called traditional "laissez-faire" immigrant resettlement practices where admitted newcomers had been permitted to settle virtually wherever they wanted with little or no government oversight. Organized resettlement appealed to a broad range of observers in the United States for its promise to control not only the type of immigrant admitted to the country—that was not new—but also where that immigrant lived and worked after admission. Thus, while the three former New Deal bureaucrats who headed the federal DP Commission could herald the DP Program as a shining example of how government regulation could improve the country, economist and free market champion Milton Friedman could simultaneously laud it as "this country's first large-scale experiment in selective immigration," something that promised to offer the American economy the types of laborers it really needed.[22]

The DP Act dictated that each resettlement plan originate with an American sponsor willing to provide the family with adequate housing and a self-sustaining job for the head of the family (virtually always the father and husband) so that the refugees would not become charges on public resources. Neither of these could be provided to the DP family by displacing any American citizens, which presented no problem for Callicott, whose sharecroppers had been fleeing his lands. The federal DP Commission was also required to ensure that admitted refugees were evenly distributed around the country. The Commission was not permitted to accept disproportionately large numbers of assurance applications for refugees looking to settle in the traditional immigrant-receiving cities of the industrialized Midwest and Northeast. American critics of refugee admissions managed to include the demographic distribution provision in the act to reduce the chances that large numbers of refugees would compete for top manufacturing jobs and place strains on the social welfare systems of overburdened localities.[23] For Callicott and other employers of stoop labor around the country, this situation meant that far larger numbers of refugees would be pressured to settle in rural regions of the country, places where, if given a choice, most of the newcomers would never have moved.

In discussing his plans to bring European refugees to the Delta, Callicott regularly insisted that he was not initiating a humanitarian "experiment" but simply believed that the newcomers would "prove an answer to the labor problems which the exodus of Negroes from the South has caused."[24] In the first half year of the DP Program's immigration operations, from late 1948 through mid-1949, Callicott carved out for himself the position of a de facto official of the program, helping bring more than two thousand refugees to the Delta to work on his and others' cotton plantations.[25] He accomplished this feat without holding any official post in the federal government, the state of Mississippi, the International Refugee Organization, or any of the voluntary agencies licensed by the DP Commission in the fall of 1948 to submit "blanket assurances" for large numbers of refugees on behalf of individual American sponsors.[26] Soon, however, he would grab their collective attention as reports of the harsh living conditions and poor treatment of the Mississippi Latvians

Figure 6. Eugen Bulabash served as a general in the White Russian Army during the Russian Civil War, after which he and his family lived in exile in Bulgaria. When Soviet forces entered Bulgaria during World War II, the Bulabash family fled to refugee camps in Germany. After the war, they were sponsored by the Lutheran World Federation to be resettled in Des Moines, Iowa, through the U.S. Displaced Persons Program. U.S. Displaced Persons Commission, "General Bulabash points to the state that will soon be his home." Records of the Displaced Persons Commission, 1948–1952, RG 278. NARA, B80, F Home-Towners.

spread across the country and globe, forcing those at the apex of the American resettlement network to determine what kind of resettlement arrangements they were willing to stomach to bring as many refugees as possible into the United States before the DP Program came to an end.

Worse Lives Than Sharecropping?

When the DP Act was passed in June 1948, Callicott set his plan in motion, submitting his resettlement applications for eighty-nine handpicked Latvians to the DP Commission. Whereas most Americans applying to sponsor DP families were encouraged to initiate their appeals through one of the licensed voluntary agencies who served as organizational liaisons between the American

public and governmental officials, Callicott needed no such intermediary. Pulling strings where possible with American and IRO officials in Europe, he managed to get "his Latvians," as he called them, on the second DP ship sailing for
the United States.[27] As they disembarked in Boston in mid-November, Callicott
had two private train cars waiting to whisk them away to their new homes on
his fifteen-hundred-acre cotton plantation.[28] The Latvian refugees arrived in
Senatobia, Mississippi, to gray skies and raucous fanfare. Nearly all the town's
twenty-five hundred curious residents greeted them at the train station, some
bearing small American flags, Cracker Jacks, and cookies for the "new Americans," as they were frequently called. Before being taken to what one of them
would later call their "Negro huts," they were treated to a "welcome home" meal
of stew in a large barn.[29]

A spattering of news articles appeared around the country to report on the
"oddity," some ringing what must have been a most welcome note to the ears
of the DP Program's supporters. Not only were these refugees thrilled to be in
the United States, but the United States should also be thrilled to have them.
Whereas most refugees were unable to "express their thanks in English, the
joy that lighted their faces" spoke clearly enough. Americans should lose their
apprehensions over the types of immigrants they were "being asked to welcome these days. They are not the dregs of a European society. Rather they are
idealists," ones who risked their lives by refusing to live under a communist
system. Yet the pieces also sounded a tone of bittersweet irony over the situation that might have served as a warning bell for the Displaced Persons Commissioners who had approved Callicott's assurances. The men, women, and
children of this group would "follow the traditional pattern of farming in the
south," one explained. With more precision perhaps, a journalist from Beaumont, Texas remarked that while "share-cropping in Mississippi has never
been considered the good life," at least "there are worse lives than sharecropping on a rich Delta farm."[30] Before long, the eighty-nine Latvians and thousands more European refugees resettled as sharecroppers, stoop laborers, and
migratory and day workers across the country would be able to judge the
veracity of this statement for themselves.

The fact that the Latvians were fair-complexioned and Protestant Europeans raises an interesting range of issues related to the intersection of race and
labor relations that must be addressed somewhat speculatively since the available historical record remains muffled on the issue. On the one hand, public
and private accounts of the Latvians tended to both racialize them as white
and spin that in a positive manner. The Louisville *Courier-Journal*, for exam-

ple, noted that, on first seeing a group of Latvian refugees at the Senatobia train station, a local white resident remarked reassuringly that "those people look just about like we do." In Callicott's statements to the press and in private correspondence with federal officials, he implied that the Latvians' racial composition and cultural background would make them harder workers than the mostly African American workforce remaining in the Delta. He did not use explicitly racist rhetoric, but rather employed racially coded language that, for example, contrasted the Delta's existing "slothful" workforce with the "industriousness" of the Latvians.[31] In the letters that the Latvians themselves wrote to complain about their plight, they distinguished themselves on the basis of race from the African Americans, in whose former homes they now resided, as well from other black field workers still in the area. Whereas the Latvians did not tend to emphasize explicitly a white identity for themselves, they nevertheless did insist on the fact that they were not "Negroes," and as such, should not be made to inhabit their dilapidated huts and work their backbreaking jobs.[32] They had, in other words, learned the racial hierarchy of America's cotton labor system quickly, and consequently now attempted to exploit it for their benefit.

On the other hand, the Latvians were not simply racialized along a neatly demarcated racial binary wherein one racial category was deemed desirable and the other not. The Louisville *Courier-Journal*, for example, favorably compared the Latvians with the "more intelligent and ambitious Negroes" who had managed to flee the region for better jobs in wartime and postwar industry.[33] Recent history had further shown that importation of laborers into the Deep South who did not easily fit into the region's black-white racial schema could accordingly create considerable tension. The region had in fact witnessed such a phenomenon during World War II, when federally interned Japanese nationals and Japanese Americans in nearby Arkansas insisted that they should fall on the white side of the Jim Crow color line when it came to working arrangements and access to public social spaces.[34] Similar controversies arose in the early twentieth century on a Mississippi Delta cotton plantation when laborers were recruited from Italy to work the fields.[35] Finally, managers and owners of cotton fields had long appreciated the benefits of employing black over white workers since the customs, politics, and legal traditions embedded in the Jim Crow system typically allowed them to pay blacks less and coerce them more than whites.[36] The European newcomers shared with their black counterparts a high degree of exploitability. Whereas the displaced persons were not subject to same vagaries of structural and cultural racism as the region's African Americans, it was nevertheless the case that the agricultural system in which they had been placed was foreign to them, thereby leaving them particularly vulnerable to it.

News of Callicott's activities did indeed attract the attention of both other Deep South plantation owners as well as the DP commissioners in Washington, D.C. Callicott began serving as a self-appointed refugee labor agent of sorts for dozens of Delta planters, pledging to bring in thousands more people from Europe to work in the cotton fields. Callicott secretly charged the planters a thirty-dollar fee for each DP family he brought to the United States for them. Although this type of finder's fee was prohibited by the DP Act, none of the Mississippi plantation owners appear to have brought it to the attention of the federal DP commissioners. They likely had little reason to feel resentful, after all, since the sharecropper agreements that Callicott had the refugees sign before they disembarked from Europe immediately passed the thirty-dollar fee onto the refugees, becoming a part of the debt that they owed to their new employers before ever stepping foot on American soil.[37] One newspaper betrayed a sanguine attitude about Callicott's endeavors, claiming that an influx of European refugees would add "new, vital blood" for a southern labor force that had recently been "weakened severely by the exodus of vast numbers" of "Negroes" who left to work in wartime northern industry. This was "an event of immense import to the South," and hopefully, the reporter opined, a sign of things to come.[38]

Meanwhile, Callicott's unofficial status with the DP Program became increasingly official, or at least quasi-official. He began negotiations with the DP commissioners in Washington, D.C. allowing him the type of authority in the program that only personnel of the International Refugee Organization, federal government, and licensed voluntary agencies were supposed to possess under the law. He soon gained nearly unfettered access to the refugee camps to sponsor, he explained, "the best of the available persons" before they were taken by "other countries."[39] Callicott further acquired from the federal government the special authority to submit assurances for large groups of refugees on behalf of other plantation owners directly to the federal DP Commission much like the licensed voluntary agencies were authorized to do. As with voluntary agency "blanket assurances," Callicott's sponsorships were scrutinized much less rigorously by the DP Commission for job, housing, and public charge guarantees than were applications made by individual sponsors sent directly to the federal commission. The rationale given for allowing the voluntary agencies—and increasingly, reputable state DP Committees—to submit such assurances was that their motivations were presumed to be "enlightened," in the refugees' best interest, and respectful of their rights. Considering that the federal commission did not have nearly the staff to audit closely every sponsorship application, ceding this authority to the voluntary agencies and select state Displaced Person committees that were emerging around the country was viewed as a necessary and largely risk-free administrative policy decision. A similar choice was made for Callicott.[40]

Whatever reservations the DP commissioners may have felt about Callicott's scheme were quickly outweighed by their delight at the number of refugees who would be able to enter the United States through such arrangements. In the program's early weeks, Commission staff and the voluntary agencies with whom they worked fretted about not being able to spark sufficient positive interest in the program throughout the country to manufacture enough sponsorship applications to make the program a success. They particularly worried about encouraging enough sponsorships outside traditional urban immigration centers in the Northeast and Midwest, which the law required through its demographic distribution provisions. The only way to obtain sufficient assurances, they came to believe, was through active participation of people like Callicott who sought to fill some of the least desirable jobs the United States had to offer.[41]

Before long, however, early concerns about a lack of interest or outright hostility to refugee resettlement in such places as the Deep South and southwest were replaced by new concerns about overzealous interest, perhaps the wrong kind of interest. To many in the resettlement network, these refugees were not guest worker migrants from Mexico or the Caribbean, or racial minority citizens whose exploitation had long been the accepted norm. These were "new Americans" from Europe, "future citizens," and symbolic "weapons" in the budding Cold War. Their plight in European refugee camps was unacceptable. Would their misfortunes in the United States be similarly problematic?

The geopolitical stakes involved in this issue were informed by coterminous developments in the field of international human rights. The United States had notoriously opted out of the Minority Rights Treaties after the First World War when the Senate refused membership in the League of Nations even though Woodrow Wilson, Herbert Hoover, and other prominent Americans had worked to advance their particular visions of international humanitarian norms for vulnerable groups of people. With the United States adopting a strikingly more internationalist stance in the aftermath of World War II, certain American leaders looked to enhance their country's global influence by supporting a newly configured discourse that emphasized the rights of all individuals over earlier guarantees for certain groups. United Nations representatives had been working on a Declaration of Human Rights since mid-1946, and, under the leadership of Eleanor Roosevelt, had approved a draft of the Declaration less than two weeks before the passage of the U.S. Displaced Persons Act in June 1948. In December 1948, as Albert Callicott secured for himself a special status with the federal DP Commission to recruit more refugees to work as cotton sharecroppers, the UN General Assembly passed the landmark Universal Declaration of Human Rights. It was an instrument famously championed by Eleanor Roosevelt, and significantly, though not exclusively, modeled on U.S. legal protections.[42]

The emergence of the two legal documents at such overlapping intervals was more than coincidental. Although the drafters of the Declaration aimed to create a lofty instrument that transcended specific circumstances and moments in time, a common, concrete point of reference for them was the mass of refugees suffering around the world as a result of World War II and subsequent upheavals. Similarly, the American champions of a DP law regularly argued that the United States had a responsibility to help its "fair share" of the European refugees because the United States had not only long been a symbol to the world as a place of sanctuary and freedom, but also because, in the atmosphere of an emerging Cold War, it was positioning itself as the world's conscience. Along with many other American refugee advocates, the federal DP commissioners believed that the DP Program offered a critical opportunity to demonstrate their country's resolve on these matters. Callicott's recruitment plans and similar schemes beginning to percolate around the country gave the commissioners an early boost of optimism that the DP Program just might be able to garner the necessary amount of interest from American sponsors to bring as many refugees to the United States as the law allowed.

In the early spring of 1949, however, as Callicott readied a new, much larger group of six hundred fifty displaced persons for passage to Mississippi, the DP commissioners were forced to question actively the wisdom of their previous enthusiasm. The State Department received word from its Paris office that three Mississippi planters were requesting clearance to enter several DP camps in the U.S. Zone of Germany. They were clients of Callicott's scheme and wanted a hand in selecting their refugees themselves. While this was expressly against official regulations, the commissioners decided to allow them access after some tense internal debate. Weighing heavily upon their decision was the fact that the planters had the backing of prominent Mississippi politicians, including the governor and three normally staunchly anti-immigration U.S. legislators: Senator James O. Eastland, Senator John C. Stennis, and Representative William M. Whittington.[43] A particularly vigorous opponent of the DP Act, Eastland had managed to get himself appointed Chair of the Senate Judiciary Subcommittee on Displaced Persons so he could keep a close eye on a program of which he was skeptical.[44] Generally speaking, this meant thwarting DP Commission activities wherever possible, but the senator's mood had been changed for the moment by a group of wealthy, plantation-owning constituents. As the DP Commission's director of European operations in Frankfurt, Alexander Squadrilli, put it, "we had much to lose and little to gain by turning down the request."[45]

It was the type of Faustian bargain with which DP Program officials were becoming quite familiar. Reports sprang from the camps that likely made them struggle with their acquiescence to such requests. One American observer reported that refugees were "crowded into small rooms, stripped and thumbed over in examinations reminding me of the old slave-market examinations." The inspectors did not, allegedly, seem interested so much in a refugee's character or needs, but instead simply looked only at "the physical, the muscles and such."[46] To one voluntary agency worker, the treatment of the refugees made them look as if they were "for sale."[47] A representative of California's fruit industry freely admitted that he gained entrance to the camps to determine which refugees met the "strict requirements in dexterity" required in the orchards.[48] When a European correspondent with the African-American newspaper the *Chicago Defender* noted in February 1949 that "a three-man delegation from Mississippi is touring the U.S. zone" looking for fifty-six DP families to select as sharecroppers, black sharecroppers who had fled the Delta for better, freer lives must have raised an eyebrow.[49]

While Callicott's labor recruitment plan had a jump on the competition, other employers also found ways to squeeze into the quasi-official openings of the DP Program to "order" their own refugee stoop laborers. In addition to the cotton planters of the Deep South many hundreds of blanket sponsorship applications for large groups of refugees began to be submitted in the first months of the DP Program from owners of sugar cane marshes in Louisiana, fruit orchards in southern California, sugar beet fields of the northern plains and upper Midwest, and beyond. When employers were unable to secure the privileges that Albert Callicott had received directly with the federal DP

Commission for submitting blanket assurances on their own, they often forged intermediary relationships with representatives of voluntary agencies that had been licensed by the federal government to do just that: voluntary agencies that had actively cultivated the role of the DP Program's conscience.[50] Three priests, for instance, used their affiliations with the DP Commission-licensed National Catholic Welfare Conference to gain access to refugee camps in Germany in order to assess the situation there, much as Callicott and the "delegation from Mississippi" had done. The priest from Louisiana returned home promising that he could immediately place fifty-five DP families with employers in his sugar-producing parish as soon as possible.[51] The sugar cane belt of southern Louisiana, like the Mississippi cotton region, had been suffering labor shortages as many black laborers moved to industrial cities in the North and Southeast. Fueling their exodus further, the U.S. Department of Agriculture's Sugar Division had been setting the wages for the region's sugar cane workers—never a well-paid field—particularly low in recent years. Their mass migration northward made the displaced persons in Europe seem like a panacea for leaders of the sugar industry. In the type of mutually beneficial arrangement that would be mirrored elsewhere, the New Orleans Archdiocese soon helped to alleviate these labor shortages by resettling several thousand Catholic refugees (mostly Poles) with some of the state's largest sugar industry employers.[52]

As with events in the cotton industry government officials in other areas also helped to move stoop labor resettlements along. Louisiana senator Guy Antonio and representatives of the U.S. Department of Agriculture's Sugar Division, for instance, regularly worked with the New Orleans Archdiocese and sugar industry employers to make sure that a good share of ships departing from Bremerhaven, Germany, landed in the New Orleans port, and that the refugees who disembarked there were pre-assigned to be resettled with area sugar employers. The conditions that these refugees encountered were at times even more impoverished and isolated than those of refugees simultaneously resettled three hundred miles up the Mississippi River in the Delta cotton country. While not officially sharecroppers, as most of the Mississippi Latvians had been, most of the sugar workers incurred an immediate and binding debt for food, furniture, and other basic living items at the company commissaries, which charged notoriously higher prices than other stores too far away for most refugees to travel. As with the Mississippi sharecroppers, these refugee sugar workers accrued debt that was similarly difficult to escape.[53]

This governing matrix of public officials, employers of stoop labor, and

sectarian institutions took on an interesting and perhaps ironic hue in California when Governor Earl Warren—future Supreme Court Justice and champion of civil rights—ordered all relevant state agencies to cooperate fully with
his state's newly appointed DP Committee, fruit orchard owners, and licensed
voluntary agencies in resettling European refugees in his state. Negotiations
with the Mexican government over the terms of the Bracero migrant worker
program that year (1949) had been difficult. Further influenced by growing
calls to deport undocumented laborers back to Mexico, Warren and the state's
fruit industry saw the resettlement of oft-heralded "new Americans" from
Europe as a good way to ensure that enough workers would be in the fields.[54]
Like Bracero and earlier migrant labor programs, the DP Program offered
Warren's constituents the cheap and abundant labor they sought. Also like
these other programs, early rhetoric promising workers a certain standard of
treatment was sometimes proving similarly hollow.[55]

The U.S. DP Program was beginning to look like a massive labor recruitment scheme, but of course in important ways, nothing was new about the
recruitment of the most desperate and easily exploitable workers available for
the least appealing American jobs. Minority citizens and various groups of
immigrants knew this well from many years of experience, as did economic
refugees displaced from their homes by the ravages of the Great Depression
and Dust Bowl in the previous decade. What provided the impoverished
stoop labor resettlements with an almost irreconcilable conundrum, however,
was the unique promise that refugee advocates made for the U.S. program
over those of other countries accepting displaced persons. While countries
such as Belgium and Canada admitted single men to perform backbreaking
work in coal mines and lumber mills,[56] advocates of America's refugee program bragged that the U.S. DP Program typically brought in its refugees in
family units. The newcomers were provided a five-year path to citizenship,
just as any other immigrant entering the United States as permanent resident
aliens. The program was hailed as the latest chapter in the country's long history as a welcoming haven for the world's immigrants, perhaps made even
better by the fact that a range of governmental authorities and voluntary agencies presumably watched over the refugees' rights and welfare.[57] Half a century
later, Latvia's president, and a former displaced person herself, handed down
a historic verdict that grouped the American program together with others in
a way that might have made the U.S. DP commissioners uneasy. She recalled
that labor recruiters in the IRO camps treated the refugees as "cattle or slaves
at a market, saying we need cotton pickers in Mississippi and coffee pickers in

Brazil and quarry workers in Australia." She added sarcastically, "Wonderful offers!"[58]

Beginning in the late winter of 1949 a series of events unfolded to expose just how wide the gulf was between the early rhetoric and emerging reality of the U.S. DP Program. Rumors that had been circulating about refugee mistreatment in the overseas camps were joined by a growing crescendo of complaints over the poor treatment of refugees resettled within American borders. After visiting Albert Callicott's Senatobia plantation in February, a New Orleans Baptist minister released a report indicating that the lives of the resettled refugees there were no longer as "bright" as the newspapers had reported three months prior. Conditions and morale on the plantation were extremely poor and showed few signs of improving. The DP commissioners decided to keep a closer eye on both the Callicott situation specifically and the growing mass of assurance applications he had sparked among planters around the Delta. The number of assurances being submitted was so surprisingly welcome to the federal commissioners, however, and the pressure from area planters and powerful Mississippi politicians to accept them so great, that they entrusted the recently formed Mississippi state DP committee to monitor the situation and report any egregious resettlements or questionable sponsorship applications. In a spirit of federalism blended with bureaucratic constraints and political prerogatives, the commissioners ceded a piece of their legal authority to a state committee. But that committee was directed, as it happened, by leading cotton planters who concerned themselves far more with expediting the movement of refugees from overseas camps to Delta plantations than with policing abuse.[59]

It took a report in the U.S. military's *Stars and Stripes* newspaper in April 1949 to begin exposing the harsher resettlements to broader domestic and international audiences and to force the federal DP commissioners to confront the issue more seriously. With thousands of refugees in Europe awaiting resettlement in sharecropper huts, sugar shanties, and mobile orchard camps in late April 1949, *Stars and Stripes* reported that Latvian refugees in the IRO-administered camps had been receiving disturbing letters from relatives resettled as sharecroppers in Mississippi complaining of mistreatment, exploitation, malnourishment, and dilapidated housing. Foreign language newspapers, both in Europe and the United States, had also begun to report the stories. The State Department immediately contacted the DP Commission for an explanation. The Soviet Union and its allies, the State Department worried, would likely use the information at the current session of the UN General Assembly in Lake Success, New York, to discredit the American refugee program and the system of American capitalism more generally. The U.S. delegation should be armed with a response. The Commission replied by providing the State Department with the report Mississippi's state DP committee had recently made.[60] The report claimed that the vast majority of the resettlement arrangements were completely legitimate, "decent," and "humane." After all, they explained somewhat tautologically, two of the planters served on the state's displaced persons committee. This last assertion was accepted as evidence of the Mississippi officials' concern for the admitted refugees' well-being, rather than heeded as a warning bell that the state report's conclusions may have been motivated by an overriding interest in keeping the Delta's labor force from leaving the area, as had occurred with previous waves of black cotton planters. Any problems were isolated, the report asserted, due more to an ill-tempered field manager or temperamental DP laborer than to anything systematic about the sharecropping arrangement. Although DP Commission personnel privately acknowledged that the problems in Mississippi "constitute a most unfortunate situation," they began to publicly assert that, "as far as we are concerned the charges are unfounded."[61] Satisfied that it had adequately rebuffed the charges, the DP Commission allowed for six hundred fifty of the Mississippi-bound refugees that Callicott had selected to set sail from Germany a week later. Their ship's destination was even changed from New York to New Orleans after IRO officials finally gave in to pressure from Mississippi's U.S. Representative Wittington and Senator Eastland, acting on Callicott's and other planters' behalves.[62]

As the refugees moved across the Atlantic Ocean for the port of New Orleans, the Associated Press and United Press agencies broke a story indicating that the problems of Mississippi were not "isolated," but part of a growing pattern in the DP Program that commonly placed refugees in exploitative living and working arrangements. This time the reported problems emanated from Louisiana, where recently arrived refugees had similarly written to friends and families in the refugee camps, as well as from foreign language newspapers in Europe and the United States. On hearing these reports, a priest from the National Catholic Welfare Conference New York headquarters flew to New Orleans, rented a car, and spent the next several days visiting sugar plantations along a hundred-mile stretch of Bayou Lafourche. The priest, the Reverend Carl Schutten, presented a scathing report of the situation to the New Orleans Archdiocese, through which many of the resettlements had been originally arranged on behalf of the area's plantation owners.

Schutten was "shocked beyond words" that the refugees were living in "semi-servitude" while the plantation owners lived in opulent mansions. The refugees were being paid next to nothing, he complained, and received literally nothing on the days the weather kept them from working. During rainy spells, he suspected that "some women went without food, so that their children could eat." Their isolation and lack of transportation meant that most refugees were forced to buy their goods at the "overpriced" plantation stores, also the only places where they could cash their checks. Many were already in debt for between one hundred and two hundred dollars, a seemingly impossible sum to repay for most.[63]

The May 3, 1949, press release of the report spawned related articles around the country and hit the pages of the *Evening Moscow* three days later. Referencing the earlier publicity surrounding the Mississippi controversy, the TASS News Agency claimed that recent reports from Louisiana were in fact part of a much wider trend. At least twenty thousand "so-called European Displaced Persons" across the United States, it charged, were "virtually working in conditions of slavery." They were being used as a source of "cheap labor for agriculture, tending to replace Mexican, Puerto Rican and other agricultural workers in the U.S." An alarmed State Department once again urged the DP Commission to help mollify the situation one way or another. The commission was in a fix. American diplomats regularly accused the Soviet press of outright lies, but as a native-born American priest had himself referred to the refugees' situation as "bondage," it was more difficult to call the *Evening Moscow* charges of "slavery" mere hyperbole.[64]

Coming to the federal government's rescue were the New Orleans Archdiocese, Louisiana senator Guy Antonio, and the Department of Agriculture's regional chief of sugar production, William Grayson. Since Louisiana governor Earl Long had not yet appointed a DP Commission, they represented the core of the state DP resettlement network, along with the powerful sugar interests. Their response to the negative publicity spoke as much to an emerging discourse of American liberalism as to the particularities of the Deep South's political economy and labor culture. They launched a vigorous campaign in the press acknowledging that the state's sugar workers were indeed paid very low wages, but—foreshadowing the language of civil rights opponents in the years soon to come—most had been content until "outsiders" arrived and "stirred things up." USDA Sugar Division representative William Grayson further argued that the low wages paid to the refugees were not the result of manipulative or xenophobic plantation owners but rather a designated wage-scale agreed on between the U.S. Agricultural Department and the American sugar industry every year. The Department's Sugar Division, he explained, closely regulated the plantations operations, ensuring that all workers received an officially established pay rate for their job without any discrimination based on race or citizenship.[65]

The crux of their point was that refugees were paid no less than "native citizen" workers. In fact, this same defense had been and would continue to be made by the cotton planters of Mississippi, the citrus growers of California, and others when charged with exploiting their new refugee laborers. Employing an argument that would soon grow into a common refrain for many in the DP Program's resettlement network, all insisted that there was no exploitation because there was no discrimination. This rationale became reified through these and similar episodes as the measuring stick for defining "acceptable resettlement standards" for thousands of other refugees across the country over the next three years.

For the three federal DP commissioners there was an alluring logic to this explanation even if the stories swirling around the various problem resettlements continued to dog them as unsettling. Each commissioner—a Jew, a Catholic, and a Protestant—were racial liberals, or at least ethnic pluralists, for their time. They were rather young former New Deal progressives, who, now in the prime of their professional lives, stood at the bureaucratic vanguard of President Harry S. Truman's Fair Deal.[66] Among the core liberal mantras to which they subscribed was *equal opportunity for all*. This principle lay behind the Truman administration's baby steps toward civil rights, fair employment practices enforcement, and a (failed) national health care system. It was also the central theme that the U.S. delegation promoted during the drafting of and deliberation over the Universal Declaration of Human Rights, passed in December 1948. The DP commissioners were intent on making the norm of equal opportunity the ethical cornerstone of the DP Program. Yet the growing news of problem resettlements in places like Louisiana, Mississippi, and California challenged the "humanitarian decency," as they often called it, of their program's operating philosophy. It furthermore laid bare the shortcomings of an emerging rights-based liberalism buttressed by formal doctrines of equality but which operated within an economic system often based on inequality.

Unlike the federal commissioners, Father Schutten held an unequivocal opinion of the "nondiscrimination" explanations coming from Louisiana's powerful elite: he was outraged. The fact that the federal government sanctioned the same paltry pay scale for all, "without discrimination," made the situation that much less defensible, not more so. "My going to see the DPs merely opened my eyes" to the suffering that had been occurring in the area for years, lamented the priest. The conditions were unacceptable for anyone, he railed, "American or DP, white or black." When confronted with the Agricultural Department's explanation that the low wages were based on the perpetually narrow profit margins of the weak American sugar industry, Schutten countered that most of Louisiana's sugar producers made the vast bulk of their profits not from domestic operations, where the sugar was cut, but from their refineries in the Caribbean. The returns from the American operations were skewed, and thus, as a direct result of a federal directive, the common sugar workers lived in "conditions worse than many under Communism."[67]

Among the most common charges made by Schutten and many other critics of such resettlements over the next three years was the inability of the refugees to escape their plight without outside assistance. In the case of the citrus workers, they had signed a ten-and-a-half month contract almost as soon as they stepped off their IRO ship and before many of them fully understood what lay ahead. While they could leave without fear of legal recourse, to encourage their compliance with the contract, much of their pay would be held back until the agreement expired. For the sugar workers in Louisiana, as well as the sharecroppers of Mississippi and places such as Arkansas, Texas, Alabama, and Kentucky, their immobility was secured more tightly: through rigid debt laws, punishable, as generations of native-born sharecroppers had learned before them, by intimidation and imprisonment.[68] European refugees could indeed enjoy the benefit over many black and Mexican stoop laborers of being generally racialized as white in the United States. They also enjoyed the legal status of "permanent resident alien," and hence were on the road to U.S. citizenship. But on the other hand, they were newcomers to such labor arrangements, and in this critical sense, they were particularly vulnerable as bottom-rung workers.

Faced with the various charges along with the publicity surrounding them, in July 1949 the DP commissioners considered once again whether to discontinue the practice of allowing such resettlement plans. And once again, they decided to continue the practice, though they promised to keep their ears open for any particularly egregious reports.[69] By November that year, refugees who had been recently resettled in Mississippi began sending letters to the head of a well-established Latvian cultural organization in Milwaukee, Lauma Kasak, complaining of the harsh conditions that they were enduring living as

indebted cotton sharecroppers. Unsatisfied with the response that she received from the DP Commission in Washington, Kasak raised $1,500 from
friends, and traveled to the Delta. At a kitchen table of one of the largest plantation owners in the state, she bought the debt of a handful of his Latvian
sharecroppers while "tears rolled down their cheeks." Continuing the practice
whenever she could raise more money and secure pre-arranged jobs for the
refugees in Wisconsin, Kasak freed many more refugees from their debt
bondage in this way, escorting them by bus to her Milwaukee home before
they could get settled elsewhere. The hundreds of displaced persons Kasak
ultimately helped to leave troubling resettlement arrangements had also been
living beyond the Deep South, in Tennessee, Missouri, New York State, Minnesota, and South Dakota. While the record suggests that more of the refugee
sharecroppers also managed to leave through similar means within a decade
or less, it is also clear that others did not. A cemetery near the old Callicott
cotton plantation in Senatobia, for instance, boasts upward of twenty grave-
stones bearing Latvian names of people who likely learned firsthand whether
indeed "there are worse lives than sharecropping on a rich Delta farm."[70]

It should not be surprising that groups of immigrants came to the United
States and found themselves exploited and trapped, at least for a while, in
exceptionally difficult circumstances. Such a phenomenon had been previously, was at that time, and would continue to be a staple of the immigrant
experience for a certain portion of America's newcomers. But the experiences
of those displaced persons recruited into peonage, sometimes in a condition
of virtual bondage, is noteworthy for the phenomena they expose about that
time and place.

The United States emerged from the Second World War as not just an
arguably unprecedented world power, but one whose influence was commonly justified by the way of life it offered its people and, by theoretical extension, other people around the globe. It shared this simultaneous
opportunity and burden with its new superpower rival, the Soviet Union.
Millions of immigrants had previously buoyed America's global reputation by
finding their version of the American Dream while others tarnished it because
they had not. But with the Displaced Persons program, the stakes were higher
not only because an ideologically charged Cold War put the immigrants' fortunes under a geopolitical spotlight. The very logic of the country's first full-
fledged refugee program created a set of expectations the United States was
not fully capable of meeting at midcentury, if ever. In the rendering of its

supporters, the Displaced Persons Program offered a wider array of American resources than most other immigrants had been promised upon arrival: namely, that their "adjustment" to American life would be guaranteed by a federal government and network of voluntary organizations that had both grown remarkably more adept at meeting the social needs of people in recent years, not just in the United States, but abroad. Added to this component was the promise of an American economy that had left the Great Depression well behind and a growing embrace of rights discourses that pledged equal treatment under the law. The DP Program, then, appeared ready to bestow the full spectrum of American resources to immigrants whose experience in their new homeland was framed as an early litmus test of the benefits of American systems of government and society relative to those of the Soviet Union.

That the federal commissioners continued to accept most resettlement plans of the sort that had led to the problems was more the result of pressures they faced and norms they continued to hold than any callousness on their respective parts. Seemingly the résumé of the group's most liberal member, Harry Rosenfield, painted him as someone highly sympathetic to the plight of the less fortunate, a person who believed that the state had a responsibility to address such plight. After seven years as head of New York City's public school system, he moved to Washington in 1942 to work for the federal government's welfare bureau, the Federal Security Agency. In a direct embodiment of the connections between the refugee program and the postwar project of human rights promotion, in 1946, he became an advisor to the U.S. delegation to the UN Economic and Social Council, which housed both the UN Committee on Refugees and Displaced Persons and the Commission on Human Rights. In that capacity, Rosenfield not only joined his American colleagues in promoting the "right to freedom of movement and residence within the borders of each State"—the right to mobility eventually enshrined in Article 13 of the Universal Declaration of Human Rights—but also another right that some other members of the American delegation had rejected. That is, Rosenfield lobbied for the U.S. team to support the inclusion of social and economic rights in the hallmark document, in addition to the various civil and political rights the United States more heartily endorsed. These social and economic rights became enshrined in Article 25 of the Declaration as the "right to a standard of living adequate for the health and well-being of [a man] himself and of his family, including food, clothing, housing and medical care." Rosenfield's embrace of economic rights represented a vision of social security that Rosenfield and many other government administrators had come to embrace during the New Deal and war years, although a new political climate was beginning to make such a vision increasingly difficult to realize.[71]

It likely was not lost on Rosenfield and the other commissioners that a troubling number of the refugees resettled by their federal program effectively possessed none of these rights. Ultimately, however, they determined that other factors carried heavier weight. These other considerations included intense pressures, for both geopolitical and humanitarian reasons, to bring as many of the refugees caught in limbo abroad to the United States before only the "more difficult to place" remained or the DP program reached its end date before the program's quota was reached. This was a goal especially supported by the three commissioners, all supporters of liberalized U.S. immigration policies more generally. Also included was an apparent calculation that, unfortunate as the national and international publicity about the problem cases was, it did not outweigh the perceived propaganda benefits of the overall program.

A final element in their calculations, however, revealed a vexing tension between the way that the United States was attempting to present its particular way of life to a watchful world in the early Cold War and a more complicated reality within American borders. The idealized trope of an America vigorously marketed to an early Cold War world as the land of freedom, security, and comfort was said to rest considerably on burgeoning liberal norms of formal equality, of a growing commitment to policing discrimination. But as the plight of European refugees recruited into bonded peonage demonstrated, even the firm application of the principle of formal equality left ample room for substantive injustice.

CHAPTER 5

State of Voluntarism for Hungarians?

As columns of Soviet tanks barreled toward Budapest to crush a nationwide Hungarian rebellion in the fall of 1956, the U.S. refugee aid network had reasons to be both confident and wary about its ability to handle the mounting flood of persons escaping across the Austrian border. In its favor was a decade and a half of recent experience in building organizational capacity, soliciting financial and political support from across the American landscape, developing working relationships among the network's state and voluntary components, and learning to confront the unique problems faced by political refugees. It had managed large humanitarian crises abroad and refugee resettlement programs at home. As for the former, the War Relief Control Board had been replaced by the government's Advisory Committee on Voluntary Foreign Aid to maintain a degree of federal control over the internationally active non-state agencies. The most important of these operated under the coordinating umbrella of the American Council of Voluntary Agencies for Foreign Service. Through these institutional arrangements, American state and non-state organizations had expanded from an overwhelming focus on crisis response into the field of longer term development assistance in Europe and beyond through such programs as the Marshall Plan, CARE, and the Agricultural Trade Development Assistance Program, later known as Food for Peace.[1] As for refugee aid initiatives in the United States, since resettling over four hundred thousand refugees into thousands of American communities during the Displaced Persons Program of 1948 to 1952, the hybrid network had resettled another two hundred fourteen thousand Europeans hailing from communist lands in the three years since through the DP Program's successor, the Refugee Relief Program.[2] Whether abroad or at home, the hybrid aid network had become a perpetual feature of American geopolitics, domestic policies, and civil society activities, something not witnessed after World War I.

Yet the emerging crisis in Hungary also provided the United States refugee aid network reason for concern. The numbers of refugees fleeing into Austria—nearly two hundred thousand in only a matter of weeks—promised to lay harrying pressure on the efforts of aid organizations from the West, the most important being those from the United States. The size and chronologically condensed nature of the crisis would test the very logic of the refugee regime's foundation. This included the belief that the state and civil society institutions could collaborate effectively in initiatives simultaneously designed to demonstrate a humanitarian-based responsibility for persons who felt that their communist home state would no longer protect them, strike diplomatic blows against a Soviet adversary, and promote forms of international stability beneficial to the United States and its allies. The relationship between the public and private arms of the network would be particularly tested.

While America's hybrid network of refugee aid had matured enough by 1956 to address quickly a sudden refugee crisis of major proportions, it ultimately proved too diffuse and inefficient, prompting calls for a dramatic reassessment of its balance between state and non-state contributors. An array of experts in refugee affairs, including an elderly but still vibrant Herbert Hoover, charged that the role played by America's private voluntary organizations had grown too large and independent from government control in the field of international humanitarian aid. These persons demanded a vigorous assertion of federal authority over the voluntary agencies in international refugee aid initiatives. Though international humanitarian aid initiatives were widely considered to be an important part of the U.S. government's geopolitical strategy at this moment of the Cold War, the state would continue to cede large realms of those endeavors to America's private aid agencies much as it had in the past. The Hungarian crisis produced considerable new pressure for altering this dynamic, but the time for radical change had not yet arrived.

"We Shamelessly Failed Them"

As summer turned to fall in 1956, the mood on Hungary's university campuses was growing insubordinate, a response to recent worker riots in Poznan, Poland. Just as the Polish reformers began to ease the pressure of hardline Stalinist policies, however, anxious Soviet officials pushed back. Since Josef

Stalin's death in March 1953, Soviet satellite states had grown bolder in demanding political reforms away from hardline communism and a larger degree of autonomy from the Soviet Union. Although Nikita Khrushchev would not solidify his power until spring 1958, the process of de-Stalinization was underway by the time of the Poznan protests. News of Khrushchev's "secret speech" to a closed session of the Soviet Party Congress in early 1956 criticizing Stalin's "cult of personality" and ruthless governing style further emboldened reform movements in the satellites. The anti-Stalinist "Bread and Freedom" movement, centered in Poznan, succeeded in loosening Moscow's grip on Poland to a degree, but the violent suppression of some rioters by Soviet-backed Polish police, a build-up of Soviet tanks on Poland's border, and a surprise visit to Warsaw by Khrushchev made it clear that Polish reformers would be given a very short leash.[3]

By later October, student protests in Budapest grew to eighty thousand strong, with thousands of laborers soon joining the students. Matters became violent, as street skirmishes between protestors and police prompted Soviet forces to flood the streets of Budapest. Soviet jets rained down munitions from above on the fast-emerging militias of anti-Soviet rebels.[4] The Soviets briefly tried to quell the situation by replacing the Stalinist Hungarian leader, Ernő Gerő, with reform-minded communist Imre Nagy as Prime Minister. The attempt at placating a rising tide of resentment failed, as Nagy withdrew Hungary from the Warsaw Pact on November 1 and, at the United Nations, called on the Western governments—especially the United States and Britain—to recognize an independent, neutral Hungary while opposing Soviet aggression.[5] As had happened with the far less violent insubordination in Poland, the Soviets had had enough. Within days, scores of Soviet tanks had taken Budapest. The rebellion would be effectively crushed country-wide a week later even though skirmishes and acts of civil disobedience would continue for a time. Not only would Hungary remain under the yoke of Soviet power for the foreseeable future, but the country was in tatters as well. Much of its population was ailing and in danger of starvation.[6] A group of Scandinavian news correspondents, who managed to flee Hungary for Vienna several days after the arrival of Soviet tanks, estimated that twenty thousand Hungarians had been killed by the onslaught.[7]

American leaders arguably shared a portion of the blame for the bloodshed. When the protests began, the U.S. government's approach to the dissidents was, at least in hindsight, clumsy and quite likely counterproductive. Cold War architect and former Truman advisor George Kennan urged the federal government to support the type of reform movements that might work to loosen the Soviet grip on the satellites—akin to what Josip Broz Tito had accomplished in Yugoslavia—warning that anything bolder would prompt the Soviets to reassert their authority violently. The Eisenhower administration went in an entirely different direction, largely because of the influence of Secretary of State John Foster Dulles and his brother and CIA director Allen Dulles, both hawkish Cold Warriors. The CIA flew helium balloons over Hungary carrying cartoons that equated leading Hungarian reform-minded socialists with Stalin, suggesting that no room existed for gradualist reform, only radical regime change. Though the Hungarian reform movement had largely adopted, before the outbreak of violence, a more gradualist orientation along the lines of Kennan's model, Radio Free Europe consistently urged the Hungarian rebels not to stand down until the Soviet Union completely vacated Hungary, leaving it a Western-style capitalist democracy. With hints of the possibility of American military assistance, the protest movement had grown considerably more strident and Western in its orientation. The reforms had quickly come to include a move away from a one-party communist state, free elections, civil and political rights protections, a renewed embrace of Hungarian nationalism, the dissolution of the dreaded Soviet-supported Hungarian Secret Police, the withdrawal of Soviet troops from Hungary, and greater overall political autonomy from the Soviets. The widely anticipated U.S. support of the rebellion, however, never materialized.[8] Hardline anti-communist senator Joseph McCarthy later lamented, "We shamelessly failed them when they looked to us for help as the Russian troops and tanks ruthlessly bore down upon them." The Hungarian rebels were on their own, vastly outgunned by the militaries of the Soviet Union and the Soviet-backed Hungarian government.[9]

In the two weeks between the start of hostilities on October 23 and the Soviet offensive on November 4, four thousand Hungarians fled across the border to neutral Austria. The pace dramatically accelerated as the chances of a rebel victory dimmed. Over the following week another sixteen thousand refugees fled, with double that number leaving the next week.[10] By mid-February 1957, when the Soviet-dominated Hungarian government all but sealed the borders with mines, wire, and disciplined guards, two hundred thousand refugees had escaped Hungary. Most of them—that is, approximately one hundred eighty thousand—crossed into Austria. When that border closed, an additional twenty thousand crossed into Tito's Yugoslavia instead.[11] The general consensus, both then and subsequently, held that a minority of the refugees—perhaps twenty-five thousand—had a genuine fear of political persecution from the Hungarian and Soviet governments for their efforts in the rebellion. Among these persons, many were university students or at least of college age. The vast majority, however, consisted of professionals, tradespeople, and skilled industrialists, most of whom never actively battled the Soviets.[12] After visiting the Austrian refugee camps, American novelist James A. Michener referred to this largest group of refugees as "fine clean, healthy, middle-class people who hated communism and saw a good chance to escape."[13] As the makeshift camps became flooded with tens of thousands of these Hungarians, American refugee advocates cultivated another term for them, one designed to convince the American public that the Hungarians deserved U.S. support: "freedom fighters."

Reaching Through the Iron Curtain

If U.S. government support for the uprising was mostly rhetorical, a tremendous wave of financial and material aid began gathering to address the humanitarian fallout of the crackdown nearly as soon as the flood of refugees started fleeing across Hungarian borders. The initial challenge for sending aid successfully to suffering persons within Hungarian borders proved less about raising funds for aid efforts—with Congress almost immediately appropriating $20 million for the overall aid effort with another $51 million shortly to follow—than convincing communist authorities to let aid supplies through. Soviet and Soviet-backed Hungarian authorities were frustratingly inconsistent throughout the months-long crisis regarding their policies of allowing Western aid into Hungary. This was true even when materials were channeled through the Congressionally chartered American Red Cross and other national Red Cross societies, which communist officials considered closely linked with the American and other NATO governments, and thus potential spies. The same logic was occasionally applied to the International Red Cross and the organization's national branch in neutral Austria; the UN High Commissioner for Refugees, which channeled the resources it raised through the International and Austrian Red Cross; and the Intergovernmental Committee of European Migration, the interstate organization that ultimately resettled most of the Hungarian refugees around the world, its budget mostly funded by the U.S. government.[14]

Beyond the Red Cross, other American relief organizations found their work similarly difficult to perform in Hungary during the crisis, with their licensing for overseas aid operations and the regulatory relationship with the U.S. State Department that came with that not helping to alleviate communist suspicions. Among these organizations were the Church World Service, Catholic Relief Services, United HIAS Service, Lutheran Immigration and Refugee Service, the nonsectarian International Rescue Committee, and the pan-agency federation focused on feeding the hungry internationally, CARE (Cooperative for American Relief Everywhere). Each of these organizations, and several others, had the official approval of the U.S. government, the UN, and the Austrian government to perform relief activities abroad during the Hungarian crisis. Circumventing the various relief embargos imposed by communist officials, some of the American agencies, along with ones from other Western states, responded by initiating and nurturing existing ties with philanthropies already operating within Hungarian borders. Catholic relief agencies had Caritas operating in Hungary, for instance, Protestants had Hilfswerk, and the Jewish Joint Distribution Committee (New York headquarters) had a number of Jewish agency contacts behind state lines.[15] A new philanthropy led by Hungarian Americans, First Aid for Hungary, used both its special knowledge of the language and culture, and its Hungarian contacts, to move relief supplies into the country when others could not, sometimes through smuggling and bribery. First Aid was also able to set up refugee relief operations immediately on the Austrian side of the border by early November 1956, nearly a month before almost any other organization developed a presence there. Providing critical initial relief to the first groups of asylees making their way into Austria were First Aid's four field kitchens, three mobile pharmacies, and seventeen first aid stations.[16]

The first outpouring of public support for the victims of the failed uprising was led by ethnic Hungarians and Hungarian ex-patriots, many of whom had fled westward as refugees across the Iron Curtain after World War II. Mass rallies and protests occurred in cities all over Western Europe. Their counterparts in the United States sometimes numbered more than ten thousand participants and included events held outside the White House, in front of the Soviet delegation at the United Nations in New York, and at Madison Square Garden.[17] The Eisenhower administration led a vigorous propaganda campaign to "sell," in the words of historian Carl Bon Tempo, the Hungarian refugees to the American public as valiant freedom fighters worthy of America's embrace. The White House even employed the efforts of two advertising firms to manage the messaging in the press and other venues.[18] Interest in the

situation correspondingly spread among non-Hungarians. The narrative of
the freedom fighters bravely fighting the Soviet invaders for liberty and independence had tremendous appeal in an ideological and political environment
so colored by Cold War rivalry. Fundraising campaigns sprang up all over the
country. Eighty-two-year-old Herbert Hoover, former U.S. president and the
country's most recognized expert on refugee crises since World War I, was
brought back into the field by First Aid for Hungary, agreeing to be the organization's honorary chairman and unofficial fundraiser. Receiving letters and
unsolicited contributions for the cause at his Waldorf-Astoria penthouse from
scores of Americans with diverse surnames that indicated the issue's broad
appeal, Hoover held a fundraising gala at Madison Square Garden and
reached out to wealthy contacts in commerce and industry, urging them to
give personally and to initiate employee and shareholder giving programs
through their businesses.[19]

As had happened in the World War II, Americans' intense desires to support the aid effort produced confusion and duplication with fundraising appeals. These included charges of fraudulent telephone solicitations for "the
starving Hungarians" that, along with other scams run by "professional pro-
moters," raised eyebrows in Congress and the administration. Unlike a decade
and a half prior, however, the solution was easier, owing to an American overseas philanthropic sector whose close ties to the state could be pointed to as a
way of directing contributors either toward the long established Red Cross or
one of the "recognized" voluntary agencies, as they were commonly called.[20]

Beyond providing an important supplement to the larger contributions of
the federal government, these funding campaigns, and the publicity behind
them, did something rather unique at a moment of Cold War intensity not
three years removed from the Army-McCarthy hearings: they provided an
avenue in the midst of the Cold War for many ordinary people and the civil
society organizations they supported to engage with populations hailing from
behind the Iron Curtain. In this, the campaigns and their publicity were similar to America's two major refugee programs since World War II, the Displaced Persons Program and the subsequent Refugee Relief Program, both of
which had allowed American families and employers to interact with two
thirds of a million persons hailing from behind Europe's Iron Curtain since
late 1948. They tapped into a common vein that had prompted Americans to
send thirty-four million letters to people around the world, including communist countries, as part of the State Department "Letters from America
Week." The initiative was designed to, in President Eisenhower's words,

"strengthen bonds of international understanding and unity" and "establish in the world a new basis for hope and freedom."[21] The Hungarian crisis offered Americans more than the feeling of personally connecting with ordinary people in the communist sphere. It also gave them the opportunity to feel that they were genuinely helping these persons.

"Playing Canasta with a Dozen Well Meaning Eels"

Though the formal connections between state and interstate institutions abounded by the time the Hungarian refugee crisis exploded in November 1956, the management of the refugee aid operations in Austria was anything but strong or centralized. This situation was especially true regarding the United States: the nation-state that, besides Austria itself, contributed by far the most resources from its public and civil society sectors to the cause.[22] The humanitarian relief efforts in Austria, where the vast majority of the refugees first fled, served as evidence for some observers that, despite a well-developed field of American voluntary agencies and a degree of state regulation over them, the response of American institutions to the crisis was too diffuse and diverse to produce an organized, rational, and efficient refugee aid operation abroad.

With myriad Western voluntary agencies vying to establish and expand their aid activities in Austria, the International Red Cross was, in November 1956, placed officially in charge of operating the refugee camps. Worked out in a detailed agreement with the Austrian government and given sanction by the UN, the Red Cross leadership of the camps was often more nominal than de facto. The actual management of the refugee camps was often decentralized, shared among voluntary and governmental institutions from an array of Western nation-states, none with as great a presence as those from the United States. Though some observers believed that the Austrian government might have been better equipped to direct the camps, it was in a particularly delicate situation with regard to Hungarian relief activities generally. The thousands of refugees flooding the country each week—sometimes each day—greatly taxed Austria. The government needed outside help. Yet, not wanting to compromise its official neutrality or its precarious proximity to the Soviet bloc, Austrian officials needed to tread carefully over how exactly to allow foreign elements to help. Making the matter seem even more tenuous, Soviet troops had left Austria only the year before, having been stationed there since the end of World War II. Soviet officials occasionally decried Austria's role in the refugee relief operations, warning "shortsighted politicians" not to forget "the instructive lessons of history," and ominously charging that "some elements in Vienna do not prize Austria's reputation as a neutral state." Putting the International Red Cross officially in charge of the refugee camps gave the Austrian government a degree of cover, the Geneva-based organization headquartered, as it was, in another neutral country, and officially unaffiliated with any nation-state. The Austrian government, out of necessity, allowed the militaries and civilian agencies of Western states, including the United States, to function in Austria during the crisis, but under strict guidelines that their activities would remain of a purely humanitarian nature, and that explicit Cold War political maneuvering be minimized, lest the hostilities spread across the Iron Curtain.[23]

Only weeks after the exodus from Hungary exploded across Austria's borders some basic working arrangements over how to begin handling the refugee populations had been worked out between the various governmental, nongovernmental, and intergovernmental organizations involved, but matters were not running so smoothly. Complaints abounded that the camps were poorly run, the conditions for the refugees, "deplorable."[24] The large refugee reception center in Eisenstadt, Austria, near the Hungarian border was said to be perpetually muddy, like a "barnyard." The situation became barely better for the refugees as many were, after initial processing at Eisenstadt, transported via train to a holding camp in Traiskirchen that had been hastily transformed from an abandoned cadet training school used during Austria's imperial era. Although that camp was at least warm and well-stocked with food, the refugees were nevertheless "jammed in" undersized bunkers.[25] There was a perpetual call for greater financial and material contributions to ease the problems to be sure, but considerable blame was aimed at the overall lack of coordination among the many different organizations responsible for managing various components of refugee aid in Austria, including registration, sustenance, health care, pre-processing for potential migration to countries of resettlement, and transportation. The former head of the massive, if short-lived, International Refugee Organization, W. Hallam Tuck, lamented that there was "a first class mess building up" in Austria.[26]

The early operations of the American voluntary agencies in Austrian refugee camps drew particular concern from U.S. government officials and a cadre of unofficial advisors with experience in refugee affairs. Since the end of the U.S. Displaced Persons Program in 1952, the voluntary agencies had been undeniably busy helping refugees who had either found themselves on the

western side of the zones of occupation after World War II or who had escaped from behind the Iron Curtain subsequently. But the approximately two
hundred thousand refugees who were eventually admitted to the United States
through the Refugee Relief Program of 1953 to 1956 were mostly able to be
counseled and processed for American immigration in places like West Ber-
lin, Munich, and Paris, where the voluntary agencies had well-established
offices and clear lines of responsibility between themselves and relevant government institutions.[27]

The suddenness and scope of the Hungarian uprising and the refugee crisis it spawned had the voluntary agencies scrambling to establish makeshift
operations in the ever-expanding array of camps. The agencies waged periodic
turf battles with one another over areas of authority, available resources, and
priority of command.[28] Herbert Hoover lamented to his son, Acting Secretary
of State Herbert Hoover, Jr., that he had received reports from Austria of
"great wastes, duplications and confusion" among the voluntary agencies. If
concerns over the confusion of fundraising appeals were addressed in a relatively short time, the actual coordination of relief operations proved to be a
different matter. Drawing on his decades of experience, Hoover opined that
the voluntary agencies served critical functions, but they were not always so
adept at handling such "practical business problems" as "purchasing, shipping, distributing of [sic] supplies on the ground" and transporting refugees
throughout Austria and, eventually, to countries of resettlement.[29]

The operations in Austria revealed tensions between the American state
and its close longtime philanthropic partner, the American Red Cross, on the
one hand, and the various voluntary agencies licensed with the State Department's postwar Advisory Committee on Voluntary Foreign Aid on the other.
Government and ARC officials in Washington and the refugee camps in
Austria recognized that the array of voluntary agencies, as one federal official
put it, certainly "help in many important ways: registration, processing in
general, spiritual guidance, amenities, etc., etc." But Red Cross personnel were
supposed to be directing them in these activities, something the voluntary
agencies were loath to accept. In a dispute partly between the values of centralized uniformity versus pluralistic expressions of heterodox philanthropic
identities, the voluntary agencies that operated under their federated umbrella
of the American Council of Voluntary Agencies for Foreign Service tended to
believe that they had a more organic connection with the refugees with regard
to religious, cultural, or political affinities. Furthermore, since the American
Red Cross did not participate, as a matter of policy, in resettling refugees

admitted to the United States, voluntary agency personnel were genuinely better equipped to match refugees in the Austrian camps with potential sponsors, jobs, and communities in the United States once an anticipated large-scale immigration program materialized. As had been the case since the 1930s, American voluntary agencies would again play a critical role in the admissions process through such efforts, linking refugees in the overseas camps to sponsors in the United States. The admissions-resettlement nexus remained a defining feature of American refugee affairs during the Hungarian Refugee Program, with the private agencies continuing to serve as the most important element binding the two together.[30]

Much as formal agreements between the Red Cross, Austrian government, and UN stated otherwise, the reality on the ground showed that the American voluntary agencies, in particular, were running significant portions of camp activities independent from much oversight. The quasi-official American Red Cross, with its tight connections to the U.S. state, represented one of the federal government's best conduits for staying on top of developments in the Austrian camps. It was one of rather few levers federal officials had for asserting a greater degree of control over a chaotic situation that was not only fraught with geopolitical risks, but also, once the immigration program for the Hungarians eventually ramped up, with high domestic stakes as well. While the licensing authority of the State Department's Advisory Committee might indeed have been adequate during ordinary times, an emerging opinion existed in some quarters that a way must be found to exercise "adequate authority," as expressed by a government official, over the private agencies in such a harried environment.[31]

Reports filtered back to the White House by mid-November that efforts were being duplicated in the Austrian camps among the various governmental and nongovernmental relief organizations, with a major source of the problem being inadequate coordination of the American voluntary agencies. President Eisenhower responded by asking his friend Tracy Voorhees to take leave from his New York law practice, look into the matter, and propose a solution. Voorhees had a distinguished history of periodically stepping away from his lucrative legal career to coordinate refugee relief both in the United States and abroad. During World War II and its aftermath Voorhees coordinated international relief efforts on behalf of displaced and starving victims of hostilities in Europe. He performed these efforts both as a private citizen and as a high-ranking military official before resigning as under-secretary of the army in 1950.[32] From November 1956 through the following spring, Voorhees served as Eisenhower's "special refugee chief," traveling frequently between the United States and Europe in an attempt to establish a higher degree of federal coordination over the private relief agencies than existed in the crisis's early stages. Voorhees began his work by seeking the counsel of several other experts in the field of international refugee aid. As with Voorhees himself, some had previously served under Hoover in various humanitarian aid projects over the decades.[33]

One of them was Paul Comly French, a former top official in the nongovernmental relief-package agency, CARE. French stressed to Voorhees how politically delicate he would need to be in dealing with the American voluntary agencies. The leaders of the private agencies could grow easily offended, French warned, if they felt that their organizational authority was being impeded by the state or Red Cross, as they most certainly did in Austria. "Make clear," French advised, "that private agencies are not being brushed aside" by the government or Red Cross. "This always worries them." French encouraged Voorhees to massage media accounts to laud the job the agencies were doing, mentioning that "if they see in the papers that you actually mention them by name"—which began occurring with regularity—then Voorhees' job of coordinating their activities would go much more smoothly.[34]

For certain other refugee aid experts, concerns about the voluntary agencies extended beyond the issues of fragile egos and public relations strategies to questions about whether the agencies' diverse institutional personalities and resources could be coordinated sufficiently for the complex task at hand. Sharing Hoover's alarm about the "great wastes, duplications and confusion" produced by the voluntary agencies in Austria were two men who had worked closely with him for several decades on various projects of international humanitarianism. Perrin C. Galpin and William Hallam Tuck had helped the "Chief," as both still affectionately called him, manage humanitarian crises from the relief missions of World War I through Hoover's famine committee in the aftermath of World War II. After Galpin and Tuck were asked by Voorhees in late 1956 to help obtain control over the voluntary agencies in Austria, the two former "Hoover boys" regularly consulted with each other and their former boss about how best to manage a refugee aid operation they agreed was too reliant on "a very autonomous minded group" of private aid organizations. They determined that the associations had grown too independent from government control since they emerged from the aftermath of World War II with expanded institutional capacities and attendant public support.[35]

The situation was made more difficult by the fact that the private agencies were, in Galpin's assessment, so distinct from one another in "policy, different in religion and varying greatly in the where withal [*sic*] they can apply in the field."[36] An editorial in the *Washington Post and Times Herald* concurred, noting the discomfort among American voluntary personnel themselves in being charged with "giving the initial stop and go light to homeless Hungarians" regarding immigration decisions. Whereas other nations were more likely to use government officials for this task, thus applying more uniform procedures, the American "voluntary agency workers' first loyalty must necessarily go to the religious groups they represent." The situation lent itself to refugees falling through the cracks, wherein, for instance, workers with the National Catholic Welfare Conference "have had to make an uneasy decision when confronted with a divorced vs. an undivorced applicant." Representatives from each religious voluntary agency, furthermore, "have had to think twice about giving the green light to an atheist."[37] Referencing a popular card game at the time, Galpin lamented the lack of centralized governance in the Austrian camps, observing that "to find out all about [the voluntary agencies] and coordinate their efforts is somewhat like playing Canasta with a dozen well-meaning eels."[38]

By the time that Voorhees began visiting Hoover's home in the last weeks of 1956, seeking advice on the crisis at Eisenhower's behest, Hoover, Galpin, and Tuck had arrived at a consensus that a stronger, more centralized approach must be taken by federal officials.[39] It was not a stretch for any of the men to come to such a conclusion. Even though Hoover was well known as a believer in utilizing the resources of the voluntary and commercial sectors to solve public problems, he also had long insisted on managing humanitarian crises firmly, whatever that entailed. His conservatism, in other words, included a high degree of comfort with liberally exploiting the vast reservoirs of state power when he deemed the situation demanded it. He had done this during and after World War I, for instance, first as the U.S. Food Administrator, controlling a massive sector of the American economy through public powers granted to him by the president, and then as head of the American Relief Administration, having the commissions of many hundreds of U.S. soldiers transferred to his civilian command. Hoover maintained this philosophy in the aftermath of World War II when, in 1946, he sought to create a permanent international relief agency to manage humanitarian crises. By the end of the year, a circumscribed form of his vision emerged when the UN General Assembly formed the United Nations International Children's Emergency Fund, which Hoover actively supported until shortly before his death in 1964.

Hoover's concern with fostering efficient, centralized government continued from his mid-seventies through his early eighties when he was appointed by Presidents Truman and Eisenhower respectively to lead two commissions tasked with reorganizing the executive branch of the federal government. Tuck had worked with Hoover on the second of these commissions, with the group completing its work only the year before the Hungarian uprising of 1956.[40]

Voorhees visited Hoover's Waldorf-Astoria penthouse several times shortly after his appointment seeking the former President's counsel on the Hungarian crisis, one of a growing stream of people do so. With the type of warm reverence that many of Hoover's former subordinates in the field of humanitarian aid displayed toward their old boss, Voorhees affirmed, "with devotion as always," that "we need to lean heavily upon your wisdom." Acknowledging that while the dilemma in Central Europe was considerably smaller than the humanitarian crises that Hoover had tackled while a younger and more active man, it would nevertheless "appear insurmountable without your [Hoover's] help."[41]

It is difficult to assess whether Voorhees sought Hoover's counsel on managing the Hungarian situation out of a genuine desire to tap into Hoover's expertise or if Voorhees and Eisenhower were merely paying the aging former president a courtesy. Having worked with Hoover on humanitarian projects himself, Voorhees' affection for the Chief appeared genuine. And indeed, Hoover remained an active presence in refugee affairs and other arenas of public life. Regardless of the intent, Hoover took the request seriously. In the process, he articulated to Voorhees and Eisenhower in the coming weeks a vision of refugee-crisis governance that he, Galpin, Tuck, and an array of other observers shared.[42]

Although Voorhees asked Hoover to provide some of his thoughts on the situation in a simple "memo," the former president sent him in early December a multifaceted, detailed proposal for Eisenhower's consideration, some of which he had already shared with his son. The centerpiece of Hoover's plan was the creation of a bold new federal administrative agency for refugee affairs fashioned in the spirit of the massive federal American Relief Administration (ARA) that Hoover reigned over after World War I. Hoover recommended that the new "strong central organization" be called the "American Refugees Administration," so as to share the acronym and associated reputational heft of its predecessor. The new ARA should be, in Hoover's estimation, "headed by a strong, full-time administrator, and he should establish an organization in Washington and in Vienna, each under experienced men of his choice."

Echoing a suggestion that Tuck had made to Hoover the day before, Hoover recommended that the new organization derive its staff primarily from the U.S. Army, as had the first ARA, in order to guarantee uniform discipline among the aid workers.[43]

While Hoover acknowledged that "the voluntary agencies have a vital spiritual part and an important administrative function in the solution of this whole problem," it was time for the president to secure the proper funds and executive authority from Congress and elsewhere to provide resources well "beyond the capacity of the voluntary agencies." The new ARA should be granted authority over particular operations of the military and the Departments of State, Agriculture, Labor, and Justice to ensure not only that more effective relief was provided, but also that the country's foreign policy stances be consistently controlled and that the eventual absorption of large numbers of the refugees into the United States be appropriately initiated overseas. The new ARA should furthermore be given enough authority to review "the character" of the voluntary agencies in Austria when it deemed fit. The voluntary agency officials, for their part, should be made to understand "that they will coordinate their activities in Austria through the Refugee Administration officials in Austria." The former president concluded his memorandum with the bold assertion that "inefficient agencies" should be eliminated by the federal government.[44]

President Eisenhower responded ambivalently on December 12, announcing the appointment of the President's Committee for Hungarian Refugee Relief with Voorhees as chairman. The Committee was charged with coordinating both government and voluntary agencies responding to the crisis. On the one hand, the Committee signaled a greater federal commitment and ultimately showed some success in gaining some control over a hectic environment. Over the next half year of the Committee's short life Voorhees would periodically assure both President Eisenhower and Hoover that he and the many "business men" helping him were slowly making the Committee "function smoothly" on a "business basis." Voorhees assumed greater authority to coordinate the voluntary agencies. By the end of December he had, partly through the power of the committee, made significant headway in ascertaining what operations the various voluntary agencies were undertaking, coordinating their efforts in order to reduce duplication and achieve a greater overall degree of government oversight. Established institutions of the federal government, as Hoover and others advised, also developed a more robust presence in Austria. The U.S. military became very active in and around the

Austrian refugee camps, providing the Red Cross, voluntary agencies, and Austrian government with food, medical supplies, clothing, personnel to help dispense them, and transportation services for the refugees. The Departments of Agriculture, State, Labor, and Justice also became well represented, especially after large numbers of refugees began to be granted U.S. visas and needed to be processed for resettlement.[45]

The new "Committee," however, was a far cry from what Hoover had recommended. It did not boast the authoritative "Administration" name, nor did it possess nearly the federal powers that Hoover deemed critical. Gently chiding the president with a tone approaching officious deference, in December 1956, Hoover responded to Eisenhower's recent moves by acknowledging that whereas "it is not my business to be determining your policies in Hungarian relief matters," nevertheless, "as officials of the Government do me the honor to seek my advice, I will expand a suggestion which I previously made to you." The government officials that Hoover referred to in this reiteration of his previous proposal had been appearing at his residence quite frustrated with what they considered to be still a fairly clunky operation. By this time Hoover had come to the opinion that, if Eisenhower were not willing to give Voorhees a powerful enough administrative apparatus, then at least a more powerful official should take over the reins: Vice President Richard Nixon. While Eisenhower did agree to have Nixon make a conspicuous fact-finding trip to Austria to assess how many refugees could be absorbed ultimately into the American economy and society, Voorhees remained in charge of the President's Committee until it was disbanded the next spring.[46]

It was clear that, even had Eisenhower and Voorhees been interested in the counsel of Hoover, and by extension, other refugee aid experts like Galpin and Tuck, the administration was not keen to put the Hungarian Refugee Program through a major overhaul. The fact was the Hungarians began to be resettled at a much faster rate than they had during any other time since World War II, partly as a result of a purposely expedited screening and sponsorship process managed to a considerable degree by the voluntary agencies. This was ultimately the primary objective of the Eisenhower administration: to resettle the refugees from the camps in Austria to new homelands, demonstrating to a global audience that the non-communist world offered a far superior and welcoming alternative to the lands behind the Iron Curtain.[47]

Nevertheless, by the late winter of 1957, criticisms still abounded about the efforts to aid the Hungarian refugees overseas, the vast majority who would ultimately flee Hungary having already done so. Approximately one hundred ten thousand refugees had been resettled in other countries already, led by the United States (twenty-six thousand by then) and Britain (sixteen thousand). But approximately eighty thousand refugees continued to languish in camps. Sixty to seventy thousand remained in Austria. Since Hungarian and Soviet forces had successfully sealed the Austrian border, seventeen thousand persons had crossed into Yugoslavia. Not part of the Warsaw Pact, Tito's communist government in Yugoslavia was nevertheless perpetually aware of the tightrope it walked with the Kremlin.[48] While Yugoslavia agreed to harbor the Hungarian asylees, it forbade them from resettling in any new country. Members of the press, voluntary agency personnel, and others with first-hand knowledge of the camps voiced their disgust publicly over the conditions in which the refugees were forced to live. Moses Leavitt of the Joint Distribution Committee complained to Voorhees that "at best, the conditions in the camps are horrible beyond words. . . . The massing together of men, women and children—sixty, seventy, and eighty in a room—breaks down normal inhibitions which human beings have absorbed in their upbringing and which we take for granted." Referring to the horrific conditions under which most devastated European refugees lived after World War II, Leavitt warned that the Hungarians would adopt a " 'DP psychology,' " at risk of finding "their readjustment in a normal society" nearly impossible.[49] The Catholic Relief Services' Father Fabian Flynn called the overcrowded conditions that Leavitt referenced "immoral and obscene." In a prediction possibly designed to unnerve State Department personnel and other government officials engaged in Cold War propaganda and jockeying, Flynn predicted that "if the Government does not correct these evils of camp life, I'm sure hundreds will go back."[50]

It seemed that the U.S. operation in Europe had hit a tipping point. Tens of thousands of Hungarians had been resettled from the camps to new countries of residence—including thirty thousand to the United States by this point—but tens of thousands more remained. They existed amid a bleak present environment that, if little changed in the U.S. government's commitment to the refugee camps, threatened to become a perpetually bleak future.

Throwing in the Cards

Faced with mounting pressure to make a bold new commitment to the refugee aid initiatives abroad, the Eisenhower administration instead turned in the opposite direction, allowing the endeavor only a few remaining breaths. In early April, the American ambassador to Austria announced that the United States would be withdrawing its support of the Hungarian Refugee Program shortly. Voorhees' committee ceased most operations immediately.[51] Although the United States would, over the next few months, continue to support Hungarian refugees through a few thousand more immigration admissions and periodic State Department grants to the Austrian and Yugoslav governments, the enterprise had all but ended. Beyond the fact that a great many refugees had indeed been resettled in the United States and elsewhere by that point, there were two other reasons why the administration decided largely to close shop. The first related to what had become a controversial refugee admissions program (as considered in the next chapter). The second spawned from fiscal conservatives in Congress who believed that the United States had overextended itself financially on international humanitarian affairs that could not quickly boast tangible results for American geopolitical aims.

U.S. representative and longtime chairman of the House's subcommittee on immigration, Francis E. Walter, and Senate Minority Leader William F. Knowland led the charge on this second front in what became a heated battle between supporters and opponents of a robust federal commitment to the Hungarian refugees abroad. Both promised to use their influence with the American public and in Congress to place a stranglehold on continued governmental support of the Hungarians. Walter charged that spending federal resources on the Hungarian refugees amounted to a wasteful welfare program for unworthy foreigners. Acknowledging that some of those persons who had fled Hungary were genuine freedom fighters, others, he asserted, were communists who left when they believed the revolutionaries might still oust the Soviets. Still others—the majority, in Walter's opinion—were merely economic refugees: "opportunists who decided to leave when they found that business was bad in Hungary." The Pennsylvania Democrat claimed that American taxpayers, in response to their disillusionment with the character of the refugees, had begun demanding en masse that the federal government stop wasting money on the Hungarian program.[52] Doubting that the chorus of complaints was as rousing as Walter claimed, nationally prominent Episcopalian leader James Pike echoed the opinion of other religious leaders committed to strong, public-private initiatives providing American humanitarian aid abroad. Calling Walter's fiscally conservative approach "penny-wise and pound-foolish," Pike argued that the good will that the United States was earning through the relief efforts would be returned many-fold in the international arenas of the future.[53]

Senator William Knowland's critique of the refugee program was, if anything, more far-reaching than Walter's, presenting America's response to the Hungarian crisis as symptomatic of a widespread foreign policy epidemic. Speaking to an annual meeting of forty-five hundred Masons, Knowland argued that the very idea of international humanitarian aid was suspect, and called for dramatic cuts to the entire U.S. foreign aid budget, including for Hungarian relief initiatives.[54] Such threats unsurprisingly sparked the ire of those persons affiliated with America's humanitarian-based voluntary agencies. American members of the World Council of Churches demanded that its government respect the important role that humanitarian interaction had to play on the world stage. A reader of the *Washington Post* warned that if the advice of such people as Walter and Knowland was followed the United States would risk "throwing away altogether the large measure of good will it has won" through Hungarian aid initiatives. "This is America in an exceedingly unbecoming role," the observer asserted, laying blame on both the executive and legislative branches for the imminent end of federal support of the program.[55] Knowland dismissed such positions out of hand, lecturing that "we cannot buy international friendship any more than personal friendship can be purchased . . . Nor should we attempt to remake the world in our economic or political image."[56]

This position flew directly in the face of the approach that such Cold Warriors in Knowland's own party as Secretary of State John Foster Dulles and CIA Director Allen Dulles had espoused for Hungary and throughout the Soviet empire. Yet the reality was that many persons in the Republican Party had never been terribly enthusiastic about fighting the Cold War through humanitarianism. The same response held true to varying degrees for conservative Democratic members of Congress in the South and Midwest, not to mention the president. There had certainly been pressure on the U.S. government throughout the Hungarian crisis to commit massive federal resources to the endeavor, but the most ardent supporters for such a policy tended not to hold positions of high state office. They were instead the voluntary relief organizations; the immigrant, nationality, and religious societies affiliated with them; the millions of Americans who supported them all; and, of course, longtime experts in the field of international refugee affairs, such as Herbert Hoover and Hallam Tuck. These supporters of an increased federal commitment to alleviating the Hungarian refugee crisis may have proven occasionally persuasive, but ultimately not enough to push the federal cart over the humanitarian hill. And though the Eisenhower administration could have mustered enough resources from the State Department, military, and other corners of the executive branch to maintain a considerable hold on refugee camp operations, its most influential members never developed a sufficiently unified or sustained faith that either the domestic political or geopolitical payoff was worth it. What had been for a short period a strong consensus both within and outside government to help Hungary's revolutionaries faded over the course of 1957. The Soviet Union had undeniably crushed the rebellion along with viable signs of future resistance. If the Hungarian exiles remaining in the squalid refugee camps maintained any symbolic power to remind the world that Soviet oppression could be resisted from within, such potency was fast fading behind the reality that the Soviets had won the more concrete battle of raw force. In a telling sign of this transformation, only one year after *Time* magazine had named the Hungarian "Freedom Fighter" the "Man of the Year" the same periodical gave Nikita Khrushchev—labeled "the Butcher of Budapest" by Hungarians—the same honor.[57]

As the federal government withdrew financing, transportation services, and civilian and military personnel from the refugee camps of Austria, it soon became clear that the policy of retreat came with a price as well, both in the field of Cold War propaganda and, especially, for the well-being of the remaining Hungarian refugees. At the time of the announcement in early April, Austria still harbored over forty thousand Hungarians. Yugoslavia held approximately fifteen thousand, though Tito's communist government had not allowed either the U.S. government or American voluntary agencies to play much of a role in refugee aid operations there.[58] With the levels of material and transportation support from the U.S. government waning, the voluntary agencies in Austria were forced to scale back their activities as well.[59] The International Red Cross announced that it would continue to operate the refugee camps in conjunction with the Austrian government only through June, at which point it would hand off responsibilities to Austria's chapter of the organization, a much smaller entity.[60] American officials had claimed that between twenty and thirty thousand of the remaining refugees would be absorbed by Austria's economy and society, thereby easing the situation. Such hopes, however, were soon dampened as reports surfaced that bad blood created between Austrian employers and the refugees placed such a plan on shaky ground. Hungarian refugees complained widely that Austrian employers treated and paid them unfairly, while the employers charged the Hungarians with being lazy, unwilling to work.[61] With camp conditions promising to grow only more squalid, and chances of migrating to the United States or

Figure 7. This poster was produced by the USIA to be used as anti-communist propaganda in the Philippines under the auspices of the Federation of Free Farmers, a Filipino cooperative of agricultural workers. U.S. Information Agency. "Communism Gives You Security," April 9, 1957. Records of the U.S. Information Agency, 1900–2003. Series, Propaganda Posters Distributed in Asia, Latin America and the Middle East, ca. 1950–ca. 1965. RG 306-PPB-119. NARA, No. 6948991.

other appealing countries of resettlement dwindling, the situation grew hopeless for many refugees.

The plight of the remaining refugees deepened, becoming in some ways
even more grafted to Cold War geopolitics. Particularly for those whose
chances of immigrating somewhere acceptable to them were growing slim,
the refugees had limited options through which to demonstrate their anguish,
voice their protest, or improve their lot. The few ways in which the Hungarians could exercise some form of control over their lives betrayed a profound
sense of desperation, an anguish blamed on a betrayal by the United States.
Shortly after the announcement of the federal scale-back of the refugee program, reports surfaced of many Hungarians attempting suicide throughout
Austria, sometimes successfully. Refugee camps across the country were put
on suicide watch.[62] Dr. Charlotte Teuber, the chief social worker at Camp
Traiskirchen near Vienna, painted a grim picture of the situation, laying the
lion's share of the blame on the United States:

> Our offices are being stormed by boys with tears in their eyes, most of
> them in complete despair about their future. . . . These boys were
> praised as heroes when they were fighting Russian tanks with bottles of
> gasoline. Now the West has forgotten about them. The greatest western
> power, in which they had tremendous confidence, is turning its back.[63]

Thousands of Hungarians also chose another form of corporal self-abuse to
protest the U.S. decision, hunger strikes. Echoing Teuber's account, an Austrian
official reported that "Hungarian men and women broke into tears" upon hearing news that the U.S. government was winding down its refugee program.
"Many feel that they have been betrayed by America for the second time," he
reported, "first when they received no arms to fight off the Russians during the
revolution and now again."[64] Not only were the doors for immigration around
the world closing on the Hungarians, but also a cloud of uncertainty settled
over how they would be able to survive in Austria without significant U.S. aid.
Declaring that the recent decision by the U.S. government "means nothing less
than depriving these people of their last bit of confidence," Teuber ominously
warned that, "it may drive them back to the Communists."[65]

She was right. Though some Hungarian refugees crossed back over the
border to their homeland when relief operations were at their height, the pace
accelerated after the U.S. government's announcement in early April 1957. By
fall that year, Western observers estimated that ten thousand Hungarians had

returned, a number called too low by the Soviet and Hungarian govern-ments.[66] Whatever the actual figure, the fact that such a volume of people was willing to repatriate is remarkable considering two factors in particular. First, on April 1—only five days before the U.S. announcement—a period of am-nesty the Soviets had created for any returning refugees expired. Anyone going back after that could expect punishment from the authorities.[67] Second, in early April, the first public trial of Hungarian revolutionaries concluded in Budapest, signaling that retribution for suspected rebels and other dissidents could be harsh. Three people were sentenced to death with several others set to serve long terms for their roles in the revolt. The most prominent defendant receiving the death penalty was a twenty-five year-old female medical student who was convicted of injecting gasoline in the neck of a suspected secret po-liceman at a hospital. Western critics charged this and subsequent proceed-ings as being "show trials," short on legal fairness and high on political propaganda. The Hungarians who crossed the border back into their home-land were undoubtedly aware of the risks.[68] Even though communist author-ities periodically created new periods of amnesty for any refugees willing to return, over time reports leaked back to the western camps that some of the repatriated citizens had been "liquidated." Voluntary agency officials grew in-creasingly frustrated that "the Red bosses of Budapest" were occasionally suc-cessful in their hopes "to snare some unwary émigrés."[69]

This was not the script that Hoover, Galpin, Tuck, Eisenhower, American vol-untary agency leaders, U.S. foreign policy officials, or a host of other advocates for Hungarian refugees had intended to write when they decided that address-ing the Hungarian crisis was in the best interests of both the United States and humanity. With the benefit of historical hindsight, however, how might we ultimately assess the American response? Judging by both humanitarian and geopolitical criteria, America's international relief operations on behalf of the Hungarians produced mixed results.

    On the one hand nearly two hundred thousand persons were fed, shel-tered, and provided medical care as a result of U.S.-led efforts. The majority of them were aided in migrating to new countries of resettlement, with almost forty thousand refugees—as the next chapter explores—going to the United States. As with American aid efforts during the First and Second World Wars, the initiatives sent a message to the displaced and dispossessed that the United States of America valued their well-being, even from thousands of miles away. During the Cold War, such a message carried extra weight, as the contest between East and West was fought in part both over people's hearts and minds as well as the votes they cast with their feet through international migration.

One the other hand, the U.S.-led relief operations left much to be desired, drawing widespread and scathing critiques not only from the advocates and opponents of refugee aid, but also from the refugees themselves. From the perspective of Cold War propaganda battles, the specter of thousands of refugees conducting hunger strikes and attempting suicide in reaction to U.S. government policy was a significant embarrassment. But even more damning to America's image as a beacon of hope to disaffected populations in the Soviet East were the ten thousand or more Hungarians who crossed back over the border to their homeland. On the floor of the UN and in their state-run media, Soviet-bloc officials regularly attempted to discredit the West's efforts on behalf of the refugees on the grounds that it was only "a few crime-sullied émigrés," in the words of a Moscow radio report, who refused to return to their homeland on political or economic grounds. Many others, the script went, had simply fled the violence for temporary safety, and if the West let them, they would one day return willingly. Though the bulk of the evidence proves such claims to have been overwhelmingly specious, the return of so many Hungarians at least bolstered the Soviets' ability to make such a case.[70] However spun by government officials and the media, the repatriations sent a powerful message on their own. If, as American refugee advocates perpetually boasted, the Hungarians who fled into Austria, and eventually Yugoslavia, "voted with their feet" against authoritarian communism and for the principle of democratic freedom and the comforts of market economies, their return home signaled that they had grown even more disenchanted with the Western candidate. Their actions signaled to the world a belief that Western relief operations in Austria led by the United States offered disaffected Hungarians a bleaker existence than the prospect of returning to a Soviet-controlled Hungary.

To be fair, the scale and suddenness of the humanitarian crisis sparked by the Hungarian revolt presented an extraordinarily difficult challenge to those persons charged with alleviating the situation. Creating orderly comfort from the painful chaos of such violence and mass human exodus would have been, arguably, an impossible task. Yet the U.S.-led relief operations in Austria were undeniably disorganized even considering the obstacles they confronted. This dynamic was exacerbated—at least according to a wide range of critics—by a relatively meager commitment by the U.S. government. Not only did federal officials fail to more tightly coordinate the diverse and often overlapping activities of the many American voluntary agencies, but they also balked at committing the levels of federal resources directly to the refugees that Herbert Hoover and others insisted was necessary for a more successful venture. Though the management of the post-World War II displaced persons camps had come under considerable criticism as well, the presence of the U.S. military and U.S. civilian personnel in administering those earlier camps had been exponentially larger. This occurred largely by default, however, since the U.S. military and American-led civilian agencies had been executing significant humanitarian relief operations in Europe well before hostilities had ended. As the smoke lifted from the World War II battlefields, and the scope of the refugee crisis became clear, the U.S. government's presence on the ground was already large. The question of whether the U.S. government should dedicate unparalleled resources to a humanitarian endeavor, thus, had been relatively moot with these earlier initiatives. The situation was different with the Hungarian crisis, meaning that the question of what role the U.S. government should play in such a geopolitically charged humanitarian crisis vis-à-vis nongovernmental organizations was more of an open question.[71]

In the end the Hungarian crisis demonstrated that the practice begun after World War II of aiding Soviet Bloc refugees abroad would continue as a conspicuous component of U.S. foreign policy. After the experiences of World War II had proved, however, how important strategically deployed, international humanitarian assistance could be for American geopolitical interests, one might have expected the U.S. government to have taken a more robust role in the Hungarian crisis. Yet instead, even before the April 1957 decision to begin winding down government support of the Hungarian Refugee Program, America's nongovernmental foreign relief agencies were left with an enormous share of the burden in managing the refugee camps. They ultimately assumed a major portion of the responsibility for crafting the environment in which the United States would be judged in handling the humanitarian challenge even though it was typically the state which bore the brunt of the criticisms against America's treatment of the refugees.

Herbert Hoover and others had tried to coax a stronger and more sustained commitment from the federal government in this field of international humanitarianism that resided where Cold War geopolitics and ethical humanitarianism met, where state and non-state actors eyed each other with suspicion even while collaborating on matters of life and death. The eighty-two-year-old humanitarian had hoped the American state would take a bolder stand on behalf of the world's dispossessed. Instead, it returned to its seat at the Canasta table with the dozen well-meaning eels.

CHAPTER 6

Freedom Fighters on the
American Home Front

At twenty-two, Andre Toth's professional dreams seemed dashed, at least for the moment. It was the middle of 1956, and the artistic Hungarian had been seeking an outlet for his creative energies in the field of motion pictures. Working as a lighting designer at a production studio in Budapest, Toth applied to Hungary's premier film school with the hopes of moving his career up a couple of notches to the level of cinematographer. Although he excelled in the technical aspects of the institution's entrance exam, he failed the dramatic performance segment. The young man was no actor. As it happened, however, even had Toth been admitted to the school, he would have completed no more than a few weeks of instruction. The great revolt against Hungary's Soviet-puppet government that October brought normal life in the country to a violent halt. Yet that uprising ultimately afforded Toth the opportunity to earn an education in the visual arts after all, but in the United States, not Hungary. Within the next whirlwind of a year, Andre Toth would avoid Soviet tanks in the streets of Budapest, escape death while detained by Hungarian security forces, sneak out of Hungary for dismal refugee camps in Austria, sail into New York Harbor just before the New Year's Ball dropped in Times Square, and, perhaps most notably for posterity, cause a racial uproar by becoming the first identified white student to enroll at a historically black university in South Carolina.[1]

This chapter explores the experiences of Andre Toth and the thirty-eight thousand other Hungarians who fled their homeland for the United States in reaction to the Soviets' swift defeat of the rebels in November 1956. As the second of two chapters on Hungary, it invites us to gaze more deeply at mid-century American refugee affairs in two ways, both involving compari-sons. One perspective emphasizes transnational dynamics, while the other is more chronological in nature.

With the first perspective, the chapter serves as the domestic counterpart to the previous chapter's focus on international developments. The discord produced from the management of the camps in Austria over finding the proper balance of responsibility among state and voluntary actors echoed on the American home front, but the resulting journey somewhat altered its res-onance. Whereas seasoned refugee aid experts such as Herbert Hoover, Perrin Galpin, and Hallam Tuck grew frustrated at the Eisenhower administration's resistance to expending more federal resources on overseas operations, the government's support for domestic resettlement initiatives did, in fact, expand in significant if still limited ways during the Hungarian program. This expan-sion included the repurposing of a U.S. military base in New Jersey where most refugees from Hungary resided—for varying amounts of time—while their sponsorship offers were fine-tuned, they recuperated from recent trauma, and for some of them, also prepared for life in America through lan-guage, vocational, and cultural training. The voluntary agencies remained critical to the resettlement process, continuing their responsibility of linking sponsors with immigrating refugees. Through this process, the agencies main-tained the link created in the 1930s for Jewish refugees, one that made the government's approval of refugee admissions contingent on a system of insti-tutional resettlement support for those refugees after arrival. As in the past, this admissions-resettlement nexus produced by a grand bargain of sorts be-tween refugee advocates and the government's gate keepers was a key feature differentiating U.S. refugee affairs from mainstream immigration policy. But the state played an expanded part in resettlement during the Hungarian pro-gram. This occurred not only through the federal processing center, but also in limited forms of public welfare being made available to the refugees by local governments as well as with the federal government reimbursing the volun-tary agencies a modest sum for their resettlement services. More importantly, federal officials actively developed resettlement schemes for certain refugees, particularly those college-aged such as Andre Toth. The officials did this in an effort to expedite the absorption of the Hungarians into American society, thereby signaling not only America's benevolence to the victims of the coun-try's geopolitical adversaries, but also the superiority of American democracy and market capitalism.

Moving more squarely to the chronological comparisons invited by this chapter, in some ways, little was new about the Cold War-inflected messaging propagated by American refugee advocates. A concerted effort had also been marshaled, for instance, during the DP Program to prove to international audiences that refugees would live better lives in the United States than from behind the Iron Curtain. Yet the Hungarian program did differ from its predecessor in a number of ways. This included having the benefit of resettling a population of admitted refugees that was younger, more homogeneous, and better positioned to succeed economically in the United States than the diverse groups who had entered through the DP Program.[2] And whereas the U.S. economy was certainly expanding during the DP Program, the mid-1950s nonetheless sat squarely in the middle of the American economic boom. If an opportunity ever existed, in other words, to pitch the American Way of Life while demonstrating the country's benevolence through a refugee program, it was through the successful resettlement of the Hungarians. When additionally considering the more modest and thus more manageable number of Hungarians to be resettled, the stage seemed set for success. In many ways success was indeed achieved, but as the first part of this chapter demonstrates, not without considerable failures that exposed a range of challenges inherent in the cycles of American capitalism, the country's social safety nets, and a refugee resettlement matrix that appeared to have forgotten about the Hungarians almost as quickly as it had become enamored of them. Some Hungarians came to believe that if this was what America had to offer at its best, perhaps they would take their chances by returning home.

The chapter next revisits another issue explored with the DP Program—race in America—by following Andre Toth's journey from Hungary to South Carolina. As with the displaced persons exploited in peonage across the Deep South and elsewhere, it was a resettlement system fueled by geopolitics and humanitarianism that ironically placed this particular refugee in a situation where contradictions were embarrassingly exposed between an idealized narrative of American freedom and a racialized one rooted in its absence. In both instances, the highly institutionalized and politicized nature of refugee resettlement fashioned a warped mirror against which Americans were faced with troubling images of themselves, images that at other times were easier to overlook. Unlike the circumstances of the displaced persons, however, the controversy sparked by Toth's introduction to his new homeland emerged as the Civil Rights Movement began saturating American public life. It occurred at a moment when another group of young people carrying the moniker "freedom fighters" also challenged Jim Crow segregation, but from the other side of the color line. It proved an odd hero's welcome for the Hungarian refugee.[3]

New Scripts, Old Scripts

The flood of American donations for philanthropies supporting suffering Hungarians overseas during the crisis spawned by the 1956 uprising translated into significant support among the general public for their admission into the United States as political refugees deserving special consideration. Its political ear to the ground, the Eisenhower administration, in the words of one historian, "wanted a refugee program quickly, both to help the Refugees in Austria and to reap the public relations and diplomatic advantages it sought."[4] From its own experience with the passage and implantation of the Refugee Relief Act of 1953, and from watching the Truman administration go through something similar with the Displaced Persons Acts of 1948 and 1950, Eisenhower and his advisors understood well that shepherding a Hungarian refugee admissions program through Congress would be neither quick nor provide the administration the authority it wanted over implementation.[5]

It settled on two interrelated solutions that would allow the executive branch overwhelming, if not quite total, authority over operations. Beginning in mid-November, less than two weeks after the first refugees began crossing the border into Austria, the administration began issuing to Hungarians lining up at the U.S. consulate in Vienna immigration visas that had been originally slated for other European refugees from the Communist bloc through the U.S. Refugee Relief Program (RRP), set to expire at the end of 1956. Sixty-five hundred Hungarians immigrated in this fashion. The intensive security screening required for others coming with RRP visas was considerably eased to expedite their travel, a sign of the remarkable hold that the freedom fighters had over the American imagination for the moment. Over thirty thousand additional visas were granted to Hungarians using the attorney general's "parole" authority. Written into immigration law to allow a presidential administration to admit an alien, or perhaps a handful of them, for exceptional circumstances when deemed to meet the public interest, the Eisenhower administration remolded the parole authority into something utterly unrecognizable from its original Congressional intention. But at least during the height of the nation's frenzy over the Hungarians in late 1956, neither Congress nor the public seemed to mind much. Even traditionally stalwart opponents of liberalized immigration like representative Francis Walter, also sensing the political winds, urged the administration to admit as many Hungarian refugees as reasonably possible.[6]

As a result of these developments, the large majority of the approximately thirty-eight thousand Hungarians arrived in the United States in just over three months, between mid-November of 1956 and late winter of the following year, with several thousand more entering over the rest of the year. The United States ultimately admitted more of the refugees than any other country, although most countries in Western Europe also received thousands combined, along with Canada, Australia, Israel, and several countries of Latin

Figure 8. U.S. Information Agency. "Refugees from the Failed Hungarian Revolution on an Airplane to the United States, 1957." Records of the U.S. Information Agency, 1900-2003, Series, Master File Photographs of U.S. and Foreign Personalities, World Events, and American Economic, Social, and Cultural Life, ca. 1953–ca. 1994. RG 306-PS-57-787. NARA, No. 7452311.

America.[7] Though the "parolees" did not arrive with permanent resident status, they were placed on a pathway to legal citizenship in 1958.[8]

Admissions decisions remained tied to resettlement in the Hungarian Refugee Program, a critical factor that continued to differentiate the governance of refugee matters from those for other immigrants. Pre-arranged resettlement plans were required before the refugees were admitted into the country, following what had become a tradition through the DP Program, RRP, and, less officially, with the arrival of Jewish refugees fleeing Nazism in the 1930s and 1940s. Though the voluntary agencies retained their important place in the resettlement process, different levels of government took on larger roles. Nearly all Hungarians first passed through a federal reception center on U.S. soil before being released to the scattered American communities to join their resettlement sponsors. A converted old military base in New Brunswick, New Jersey, Camp Kilmer in many ways resembled the better-run refugee camps overseas from later World War II and the Cold War, including those operating in Austria on behalf of the refugees from the Hungarian uprising. The refugees arriving at Kilmer might encounter up to twenty-two voluntary and government agencies with operations there. Among the fifteen voluntary agencies licensed by the state to work at Kilmer, those with the largest presence and most established résumés in the field of refugee relief and resettlement were the National Catholic Welfare Conference, Church World Service, Hebrew Immigrant Aid Society, Lutheran World Federation, and the nonsectarian International Rescue Committee. Beyond the U.S. military personnel who were ultimately in charge of camp operations, the federal government's presence at Kilmer included officials from the Departments of State (Visa Division), Justice (Immigration), Labor (U.S. Employment Service), and Health, Education, and Welfare.[9] The responsibility the government assumed in resettlement would extend beyond the confines of Kilmer. Voluntary agencies received a total of $1.5 million to help defray their costs in resettling the Hungarians, though the agencies were informed that the practice should not be considered as establishing a precedent.[10] Some municipal governments additionally gave the refugees access to various forms of public welfare, with the commissioner of the Federal Housing Authority even asking states and cities to ease residency requirements for the refugees so they could find affordable homes more easily.[11]

During a typical stay at Kilmer—lasting generally from several days to several weeks—refugees were screened on matters of health, security, vocational skills, language abilities, and religion and other cultural attributes that might help match them with an appropriate sponsor, job, and resettlement community. In a relatively streamlined process, the order of a refugee's experience after arriving at Kilmer consisted of being examined by the U.S. Public Health Service and then interviewed by U.S. Customs and the Immigration and Naturalization Service. After this the refugee would receive any necessary medical care. The U.S. Employment Service would next interview the refugees who were of working age and ability. As had been the case with earlier refugee programs, male refugees received most of the employment-related attention since they were presumed to be either capable of financial independence (if single) or the primary breadwinners for their families. Women were often interviewed about their employment prospects as well, particularly if they were single or would need to work to supplement their husbands' incomes. All relevant information was stored on small data management cards designed by experts at IBM specifically for the Hungarian resettlement operation. These procedures, as well as security screening, had also often occurred in the camps overseas, but given the speed with which the refugees were being moved through Austria, as well as the chaotic situation in that country, additional procedures were instituted at Kilmer to secure more reliable information.[12]

Kilmer also offered an array of material comforts that must have been a welcome change for the Hungarians after languishing in such challenging conditions in the Austrian camps and, for some refugees, life outside of them amid an Austrian public that proved sometimes less than welcoming. Beyond ample food, the camp offered the benefits of recreation halls, theaters, and a library stocked with periodicals in Hungarian, the latter sponsored by First Aid for Hungary.[13] Upon arrival, the voluntary agencies provided the adults with gift packages filled with slippers, safety razors, combs, chewing gum, and tooth brushes. Children received yo-yos, crayons, and other items to play with. On St. Nick's Day in early December, a significant children's holiday in Hungary, Red Cross volunteers delivered gifts, such as dolls, games and candy, to Hungarian parents at Kilmer late at night, with which to greet their children in the morning.[14] Stories such as these appeared around the country, serving to provide some reassurance to elected officials and their constituencies that the newcomers arriving in the United States were being well cared for, and perhaps more implicitly, would not be released into American communities until they were ready to care for themselves.

And care for themselves many refugees did. The demographics of the refugees fleeing Hungary were fairly well suited for comfortable, if not perfect, absorption into the U.S. economy. Begun primarily by students, and joined by

laborers, the failed Hungarian uprising produced a refugee population disproportionately young and male compared to other refugee crises that the United
States responded to with immigration resettlement programs. After studying
the refugee populations overseas and at Kilmer, Vice President Nixon judged
that "the large majority are young people—students, technicians, craftsmen
and professional people."[15] While a greater proportion of the skilled laborers
and professionals were men, Americans interested in sponsoring girls and
women as domestic workers learned that relatively few of the Hungarian arrivals fit this bill, instead often sharing the job training experience of their
male counterparts.[16] By April 1957, when nearly all refugees had processed
into and out of Kilmer, 65 percent had at least a high school education, 15
percent had an undergraduate college degree, and 25 percent were either scientific personnel or had been enrolled as college students in Hungary. The
National Academy of Science called the refugees in the United States a "Who's
Who of Hungarian professional life," predicting that they "will play an important part in relieving the U.S. of its serious scientific manpower shortage."[17] A
great many of the refugees were placed in resettlement arrangements in industrial areas along the northeastern seaboard and such steel and auto-centric
cities as Detroit, Cleveland, Akron, and Pittsburgh in a period when the
American economy was expanding the country's middle class through just
such jobs.[18]

The private refugee aid agencies and the Eisenhower administration
worked diligently to highlight successful cases of Hungarians' integration into
the American economy, recognizing that the general enthusiasm which welcomed the newcomers in the immediate wake of the anti-Soviet uprising was
bound to fade. Tracy Voorhees, Eisenhower's appointee to lead the government's Hungarian operations in Austria and in the United States, hired two
public relations firms to help make the case that the Hungarians would be
ideal Americans in the making. In the months following the Hungarian uprising, both because of the work done by Voorhees's agencies and because of
significant pockets of support for the refugees in the American press, print
and broadcast media burst with the message that the newcomers were both
politically and culturally similar to most Americans, or at least, capable of
becoming so. The refugees received favorable coverage in a range of publications that included *Reader's Digest*, *Look*, *Life*, *Newsweek*, the *Saturday Evening
Post*, and *Sports Illustrated*. Perhaps most influential of all was *Time*'s decision
to make the Hungarian "Freedom Fighter" its "Man of the Year" in 1956.
Television programs like *Meet the Press*, the *Tonight* show, *The Ed Sullivan*

Show, and *What's My Line?* joined the action too.[19] Originally part of a *Reader's Digest* series, James Michener's award-winning *The Bridge at Andau* offered heroic, if presumably somewhat selective, portrayals of the types of brave, typically anti-communist Hungarians he encountered during the his six weeks at the Austrian refugee camps.[20]

The portrayals especially tapped into the purported ease with which the refugees acclimated to American norms regarding gender, family, and domestic consumption after having experienced such different lives behind the Iron Curtain. The *New York Times*, for instance, ran a story on Ildiko Rath, a twenty-three-year-old "heroine" who was said to have killed five Soviet soldiers during the uprising. But the article reassured its readers that Ildiko had "become a model housewife" after settling calmly into her new life in Harrisburg, Pennsylvania, with her husband Karl.[21] A voluntary agency official, Martin Bursten, wrote a book-length account about the assimilability of the Hungarians into American culture that relied on a range of press pieces and voluntary agency case studies. Flipping through the pages of *Escape from Fear* from beginning to end, the reader was invited to witness the materialization of the American Dream. Pictures of modestly dressed rebels still in Hungary graced the early pages of the book. Smiling, smartly attired Hungarian families appeared in photographs near the end, enjoying the comforts of their new American homes. In one photo, a father enjoys a game of chess with his son, a pack of Marlborough cigarettes lying neatly on the table. On the other side of the living room, the mother presents a new doll to her daughter, the caption explaining that while not all Hungarians had yet "acquired more than the minimal amount of furniture, their apartments were immaculately clean." In another photograph a newly arrived family, the Frankels, celebrate their first Thanksgiving Day. Their clothes appear simple but clean, their expressions pleasant yet weary. The father carves a turkey, but with no other food on the table. An American flag frames the scene on the wall behind them. The photo below shows the same family exactly one year later. They all wear nicer clothes. The young boy even sports a suit. In a Norman Rockwellian image, everyone's face is bright, and the father appears confident and casual as he prepares to carve another turkey. This time a bounty of side dishes also appears in the frame, while the mother holds the picture from the year before. The caption articulates the visually obvious: "the Frankels had much for which to be thankful."[22]

Not every Hungarian did, however. Even though the Kilmer facility theoretically gave refugee aid personnel a better opportunity to find the Hungarians good resettlement matches, there was considerable pressure to move the immigrants into their new American communities as quickly as possible, where their examples could be publicized for the country and world to see. In his role as director of the President's Committee for Hungarian Refugee Relief, Tracy Voorhees worked to increase the speed with which the voluntary agencies found refugees sponsors for resettlement. He arranged contests to produce "friendly competition" among the agencies. Whichever agency met their sponsorship "quotas" first, won.[23] A study conducted nearly a half year after the first Hungarians arrived concluded that such competition may have served to send refugees unnecessarily into jobs and communities poorly prepared and ill matched to their needs and abilities. With another year's perspective, in mid-1958 director of the Catholic Relief Services Monsignor Aloysius Wysislo judged that "the pressure to get refugees out of Kilmer was bad."[24]

Though Kilmer's presence on American soil surely improved the chances of finding good resettlement matches for some refugees, as was the intention, it had the opposite effect for others. Only the well-placed and highly committed prospective employers of cheap and exploitable refugee labor had managed to gain access to the displaced persons camps of Germany, but breaching the grounds of Kilmer proved a far easier endeavor. One voluntary agency worker reported that "hijackers" had "raided Camp Kilmer for cheap labor and bamboozled some of the bewildered Hungarians into going with them and discarding carefully arranged agency sponsorships." Another observer noted that the "best refugees often fell into the hands of sharks," recruited with big promises only to be put to work as poorly paid farm hands, textile sweatshop workers, and the like. Causing particular alarm among the refugee aid workers at Kilmer were the occasional reports of young, single Hungarian women being lured away to cities (usually New York) by people promising them a career in show business or modeling, only to discover that they were expected to work as prostitutes. The women sometimes went missing, out of contact with their families, friends, and voluntary agency personnel.[25]

As had happened with the Displaced Persons Program, American refugee advocates appear to have underestimated the surprising challenges that the American labor market could throw at workers, particularly at a population of aliens with little knowledge of the United States The advocates also failed to predict how insufficient the normal public and private safety nets in the United States would prove to be for the Hungarians if, as periodically happened, the country entered an economic recession. Certainly, many of the labor problems faced by Hungarians were the same in many respects as those experienced by both other immigrant and long established American communities. But the Hungarians' roles as Cold War freedom fighters who had escaped the grip of the Soviets to enjoy a safe and prosperous life in the United States gave their plight an added political dimension, and ultimately garnered them an extra degree of attention and institutional support.

By mid-1957, industrial production in the steel, auto, and similar industries was beginning to be hit hard by a recession, precisely in the areas of the northeastern seaboard and northeastern Midwest where most of the refugee laborers and their families had settled. Although most employable Hungarians had managed to land jobs shortly after leaving Camp Kilmer many suffered the "last in, first out" syndrome as the recession grew and layoffs began. The *Washington Post* estimated that between 25 and 30 percent of Hungarian industrial workers were out of work by mid-1957. Making matters, worse two thirds were said to be ineligible for unemployment insurance since they had not been employed long enough.[26] In certain communities that had attracted scores of Hungarians with carefully arranged resettlement plans just the year before, unemployment reached as high as 90 percent for the refugees. The situation was especially bad in those cities dependent on the auto industry, where an especially large proportion of Hungarians had settled. By mid-1958 in Detroit, 70 to 80 percent of Hungarian refugees were unemployed.[27]

With so many of the immigrants being young men, voluntary agency personnel grew especially concerned over the psychological and moral effects unemployment might have on people who had arrived in America while still maturing into adults. Andrew Jacobs, a Detroit priest with the National Catholic Welfare Conference, was "alarmed" by the fact that many of the refugees in his city "have had only five or six months' work in their eighteen months here. . . . The situation is pretty bad." While certain male refugees had joined the U.S. Army to hold a steady job, one which might in turn secure a meaningful living, many of them were soon discharged because of their poor English language skills. "Now they are on the street with nothing," Father Jacobs lamented. "No job. No unemployment compensation."[28] Cecilia Cox, director of Lutheran Relief Services, predicted that many refugees would become "wanderers" since so many of the teenagers and young adults who fled after battling the Soviets left their parents behind either in Hungary or the refugee camps in Europe. In what surely would not have seemed a problem to the young Hungarians themselves, the director of Church World Service, Roland Elliot, lamented that young Hungarians with too much time on their hands had been seen performing the jitter-bug and other popular American dances that would be frowned upon in their homeland. Catholic Relief Services' Monsignor Wysislo warned of an even more troubling development: the "sudden exposure" of the Hungarian youth "to American rock 'n' roll."[29] Temptation of American pop culture aside, the problems were real. Complaints circulated that young refugees would "drift about the country from job to job, often getting into trouble." A young unemployed and homeless Hungarian in Detroit smashed the window of a jewelry store and waited for the police to arrive and arrest him so that he could at least have a place to sleep."[30]

At the same time, while Hungarian exiles in Austria and Yugoslavia were voluntarily returning to Hungary by the thousands in reaction to the bleak conditions of the refugee camps overseas, their counterparts in the United States began threatening the same action in response to their seemingly hopeless plight. If the mass repatriations originating in the European camps were dealing an embarrassing blow to the international reputation of American refugee initiatives, the prospect of so many Hungarians leaving what was supposed to be their *American* oasis for communist Hungary threatened even darker implications for U.S. propaganda amid the tense, competitive publicity environment of the Cold War.[31] The economic recession in the United States had left many Hungarians without hope for self-sufficiency, and whatever social safety nets some had been able to fall back on were disappearing quickly. Certain cities, such as Detroit, offered limited public relief to newly arrived resident aliens, but others did not. Privately run soup kitchens that had been opened to help struggling Hungarians began to close under the ongoing and increasing demands from the unemployed and hungry refugees. With seemingly little outside help, Hungarians began filing applications for repatriation to Hungary, and at a rate that some American refugee advocates found alarming. Some fifty refugees had already returned to Hungary from the Detroit area alone by July 1957 with, as Father Jacobs assessed, "a whole slew of people ready to go back." Jacobs recalled a conversation with one young man who explained that he would prefer to return to Hungary than beg in the United States, even if it meant that he would sit in prison for six months upon arrival. Another refugee complained, "at home we had other troubles but not trouble to find work. I haven't been out of work for such a long time in my whole life as in the last 18 months."[32] In an act disturbingly reminiscent of the mass suicide attempts being reported from the Hungarian refugee camps abroad, twenty year-old Ferenc Kish dealt with his disillusionment in the United States by shooting himself in the stomach with a 22-gauge rifle. In trying to explain the refugee's attempted suicide, Kish's Washington, D.C., sponsor opined that "life here was not the golden dream Ferenc thought it was" when he arrived in the United States half a year prior.[33] When three Hungarian refugees were jailed in western Minnesota on vagrancy charges, one of them—a forty-five-year-old former machinist—begged authorities to arrange his deportation back to Hungary. When asked why, he responded, "no working, no working." Having traveled through central Canada and the northern U.S. plains states for the previous two months in search of work, they had enjoyed a roof over their heads for only three nights.[34]

The federal government was largely AWOL through the crises and publicity surrounding them, as the President's Committee for Hungarian Refugee Relief had disbanded in mid-May 1957, a year before the worst of the recession hit the Hungarians and only a half year after the first refugees had begun arriving.[35] The eighteen voluntary agency members of the American Council of Voluntary Agencies for Foreign Service grew committed to revitalizing their efforts to find some unemployed Hungarians new resettlement sponsors, acknowledging that "the wave of sentiment that greeted the Hungarian refugees has subsided and now the newcomers are facing the long, difficult ordeal of integrating into a strange culture." Many of the new opportunities found for the unemployed refugees, however, were in agriculture, menial labor, and other areas less well-suited for them than industry.[36]

Though the threats of mass repatriation eventually subsided, the voluntary agencies were right: the initial wave of excitement over the freedom fighters had indeed waned, in the American public as well as in high politics. An early proponent of the Hungarians' arrival, Representative Francis Walter had since returned to his traditional anti-immigration stance, charging that lax security screening had allowed a great many communists to enter the United States from Hungary. Joined by Congressional colleagues, Walter orchestrated a vigorous campaign during 1956 and 1957 to oppose the Eisenhower administration's simultaneous efforts to have Congress sanction the future parole of up to 62,000 refugees from behind the Iron Curtain into the country per year, and normalize the status of the Hungarians already paroled into the country. The political climate had turned decidedly in the favor of Walter and other opponents of the refugees. A poll conducted in the spring of 1957 revealed that more Americans believed refugees would have a negative rather than a positive effect on the country. Another poll conducted that year, this time in the summer, showed respondents evenly split on whether the paroled Hungarians should be permitted to become permanent residents or remain in legal limbo without visas. While the paroled refugees eventually had their legal status normalized the next July, it had occurred only after a bitter public battle made clear that their cultural status as "freedom fighters" had been tarnished. Each paroled refugee submitted to new screening tests for subversive political beliefs and histories. Whereas only a relatively small number were deported—between several dozen and several hundred depending on the source—the honeymoon was clearly over. As a further indication that the political climate had shifted, Congress refused the administration's request for more parole authority. Congress's patience with the White House acting with near autonomy on refugee matters had run out, at least for the moment.[37]

Even if the political milieu had turned worse for the Hungarians, the economic circumstances eventually improved with the passing of the recession. A study released by the INS in 1960 assessed, perhaps with a degree of sanguinity that some refugees would have questioned, that "The vast majority of the Hungarian parolees have been assimilated into the population of the United States without difficulty." This said, 630 of them had returned by their will as a result of economic, cultural, and other hardships.[38] As with many of the Displaced Persons who preceded them, the Hungarian refugees of the middle and later 1950s experienced an ambivalent welcome from the Free World's superpower.

What a Long, Strange Resettlement It's Been

Andre Toth had his first glimpse of the Statue of Liberty just hours before throngs of revelers cheered in the new year of 1957 several miles to the north in Times Square. His experiences over his first couple of years in the United States were in some senses atypical of other Hungarian refugees. Most notably, he was the first white-identified student to enroll in a historically all-black college or university in South Carolina and one of the few white persons to do so throughout the entire U.S. South. In this sense, not only was his particular precedence unique, but so too were both the controversy he sparked and the notoriety he gained. In a broader sense, however, Toth's experiences conformed to those of many Hungarian refugees in the United States in several ways. His political currency as a freedom fighter earned him admission, along with a suite of resources designed to offer him a relatively fluid transition to American life. And as had happened with many of his fellow refugees, that resettlement system perpetuated unintended and ultimately disruptive consequences for the young man.

Fresh from failing the entrance exam at Budapest's Academy for Theater and Film Art, twenty-two year-old Toth found in the Hungarian uprising of late October 1956 a change of direction, a new focus for his energies. Although he did not participate in the initial protest that sparked the uprising, Toth quickly joined the insurgency. As with many of the rebels, especially students and other young people, he supported the type of reformed socialism that the government of Imre Nagy had embraced from 1953 through mid-1955 before the Soviets replaced the leader with the hardline communist government of Mátyás Rákosi. Toth was particularly typical of the rebels in his distaste for Soviet influence over his homeland. Though he participated in some of the street battles against Soviet and Soviet-backed Hungarian troops in the streets of Budapest, Toth did not play a significant role in the rebellion. After several days of fighting, he found himself walking the streets of Budapest looking for a makeshift rebel unit to join for the day. Spying several young men wearing civilian-looking clothes and carrying weapons, he approached them and asked if he could join them in fighting the communist forces. It proved an unfortunate judgment, as Toth quickly found himself thrown in a holding cell. The young men that Toth had approached were not rebels but instead the widely feared Hungarian secret police, charged by the Soviets with helping to crush the rebellion, often by tortuous means. Toth spent the next few days being intensely interrogated. Charging him with being a leader in a well-organized student battalion, which he was not, Toth had pistols pressed periodically against his head, and threatened with death unless he admitted to their accusations. Eventually Toth's fortunes turned. Apparently believing that he was not a major operative in the uprising, the police released him.[39]

After his release, Toth briefly joined the newly formed "National Guard," one of the military factions fighting the Soviets and Soviet-backed Hungarian forces. The Soviet invasion of Budapest on November 4, however, proved too much for him and many of his comrades-in-arms. The tide had clearly turned, and the Soviets were not going to tolerate the uprising any longer. Toth spent about a week and a half in the middle of November lying low in his parents' Budapest home. Joining him were several friends from the film studio where he had previously worked. They used their artistic skill and photographic equipment to fashion in-country travel visas as well as specious documents indicating that the group was traveling to Hungary's western border to film a documentary. As thousands of Hungarians were trying to flee to Hungary's western border with Austria, one might have suspected that Toth and company's forged travel documents would have been denied for the fakes they were by soldiers at roadside checkpoints. Yet they were allowed to pass. Toth believed the Hungarian soldiers understood perfectly well that they were accepting false papers, perturbed as they seemed to be with the influx of Soviet forces throughout their country. His suspicions were reinforced by the fact that the Hungarian guards steered him and his companions away from roads with a heavy Soviet military presence.[40]

Crossing into Austria in late November he was processed at the large and unpleasant reception center at Eisenstadt before being sent by train to a refugee camp in Salzburg.[41] Because he was a practicing Catholic, Toth's case was picked up by the American voluntary agency Catholic Relief Services, the international counterpart to the National Catholic Welfare Conference, the latter of which was scheduled to manage his resettlement arrangements after arriving in the United States. From the Salzburg refugee camp, he was transported to the port city of Bremerhaven, Germany, where he sailed on the U.S.S. *General LeRoy Eldridge* toward New York Harbor in late December. Spending his first night in the United States on the ship, he disembarked for Camp Kilmer the first day of 1957.[42]

During a reasonably pleasant week and a half stay at Kilmer, Toth and some forty other young adult refugees were approached by voluntary agency officials to participate in a new intensive English-language program being offered to former Hungarian university students or those of college age.[43] The program Toth and the others were invited to join was developed by Robert W. Hartle, the French-language professor at Princeton who had initiated and directed the far less intensive—and maligned—English-language program at Kilmer. As it became clear that the environment at Kilmer was not ideal for teaching the refugees good English skills, Hartle and a handful of others worked to establish programs off-camp. These intensive programs were meant to serve as a way station of sorts for academically inclined refugees to obtain their linguistic footing between their hastened processing at Kilmer and hopeful enrollment at American universities. They were, in effect, an acknowledgment that the harried systems of processing—including English training—in the refugee camps both overseas and in the United States were leaving refugees unprepared for life in America. Those chosen for the special language programs generally had to be persons of university age who had either been students in Hungary or were deemed academically inclined. The same held true for those pegged to be awarded the hundreds of scholarships being funded around the country specifically for the Hungarians.[44] Andre

Toth fit the bill, providing him with a rather more privileged resettlement platform than were most other Hungarian refugees processed through Kilmer.

From February to mid-May 1957, Toth immersed himself in an English-language crash course at St. Michael's College near Burlington Vermont, along with forty-two other young Hungarian men and women.[45] The Hungarians' schooling, room, and board at St. Michael's were paid for by the Ford and Rockefeller Foundations and the National Catholic Welfare Conference. Area residents supplemented the Hungarian students' needs by contributing clothing and spending money. While learning English at the school Toth and other refugees had occasion to observe American-style politics as well, attending meetings of both the Burlington municipality and the Vermont state legislature.[46]

While Toth attended St. Michael's, a representative from the Institute of International Education informed him that he had been offered a scholarship to an American university. The funds for the scholarship—which included tuition, board, and a small stipend—were composed of joint contributions from the school and the Institute of International Education. The history of the New York-based IIE—an institution most known after World War II for its Fulbright scholarships—dated back to 1919, when prominent academics and former secretary of state Elihu Root established it with a $30,000 grant from the Carnegie Corporation. Conceived in reaction to the vagaries of the First World War, the IIE was designed to promote peace by fostering international connections between international students and American universities, as well as between American students and academic institutions abroad. Though it always had some connections with the federal government's foreign policy apparatus, those connections proliferated during World War II in an effort to produce and disseminate anti-Axis propaganda. The Hungarian Refugee Program provided an ideal opportunity for the mutual agendas of the IIE and the State Department to coalesce in both the field of international academic exchange and geopolitical imperatives. With its close institutional connections to the State Department, the President's Committee for Hungarian Refugee Relief asked both the IIE and State Department to drum up scholarships from university and other funding sources around the country. Taking the lead was Dr. John A. Krout, a member of the President's Committee and provost of Columbia University. Tracy Voorhees reported that Krout had effectively acted "as a sub-committee of one . . . to assure appropriate educational opportunities for" Hungarian students. Although Krout was not responsible for all the scholarships awarded to the Hungarians, his efforts helped match over seven hundred refugees with "the many generous offers of scholarships which have been received from educational institutions throughout the country."[47]

Along with scholarships offered to four other Hungarians whom Toth did not know, Toth's offer came from Allen University. Located in Columbia, South Carolina, Allen was one of the nation's oldest historically all-black academic institutions, dating to 1870. If the working connections between the State Department and the IIE were intended to create a seamless connection between the more humanitarian-based goals of international academic exchange and the foreign policy prerogatives of the federal government, persons apparently had failed to do their homework with the scholarship that Toth and the four others were offered. With so many scholarship offers arriving— and the desire of the State Department, IIE, and others to showcase as quickly as possible the strides that the refugee freedom fighters would make—it is unsurprising that the racial composition of Allen's student body was missed.[48]

Though a fan of big-city cosmopolitan life, Toth was intrigued by the offer to move to the relatively sleepy town of Columbia after learning that Allen had an art education program. It was something that the young Hungarian had wanted to pursue ever since being turned down for the cinematography program at Budapest's Academy for Theater and Film Art the previous fall. After a representative of a Hungarian American organization had somehow figured out the controversy that Toth was unwittingly poised to enter, he strongly urged him to back out. Soon thereafter, a family friend of Toth's parents, a friend who taught medieval history at the University of Notre Dame, echoed the point, insisting that the young man should instead set his sights on an Ivy League university. It was a reasonable proposition considering that the Ivies and other elite universities had been particularly active in admitting and funding other Hungarian refugee students.[49]

In the face of pressure to change his mind Toth stuck with his initial decision. Certain contemporary accounts of the situation claimed that Toth had no idea that his enrollment at Allen would stir the controversy it did. Such an assessment, however, rings dubious, considering both other evidence and the clear attempt on the part of some American journalists to paint Toth as an innocent foreigner unable to comprehend the type of extreme racial injustice surrounding him in South Carolina.[50]

It seems considerably more likely that Toth understood well that his enrollment would rattle the foundations of Jim Crow segregation, though he probably did not predict the intensity of the situation. Looking back on the events with a half-century's perspective, Toth recalled that he probably chose to enroll in Allen based on a mixture of the idealism and the contrarianism of youth. Common in curricula throughout the Soviet Block in the 1950s, Toth had learned in his Budapest high school about American race problems, including the South's system of Jim Crow segregation in schools. Furthermore, well before Toth had any inkling that he would migrate to the United States, his ethical and political worldviews had been shaped by Jean-Paul Sartre's *The Respectful Prostitute* (*La putain respecteuse*). On its publication in 1946, Toth's French mother gave a copy of the short play to her son, an early adolescent then. Chronicling an incident of racial injustice in the United States—and less explicitly, gender injustice—the plot traced the aftermath of a violent incident perpetrated by a white man on a train. The only witness was a white female prostitute who was pressured by the authorities to lie and testify that an innocent black man was the culprit, all in the name of preserving a social and legal system of racial hierarchy. For Toth—a young teen maturing as the Soviet empire removed many traces of his country's independence—the story initially read to him like a parable for Hungary's woes: a powerful system keeping down the powerless. On arriving in the United States, and being offered a scholarship to an all-black university in the Jim Crow South, Toth found in Sartre's play a more literal, more immediate meaning.[51]

Affected as he may have been by a social conscience, perhaps other motivations prompted Toth to enroll at Allen as well. Toth later recalled that just as his participation in the Hungarian uprising of 1956 was probably as much about the restlessness of youth as it was the idealism of political reform, something similar had likely been at play in his decision to eschew the sober advice of those older adults in the United States who implored him to seek his American education elsewhere. Looking back on the various events, he believed that part of him just wanted to do "something rebellious. . . . Maybe in a funny way, I didn't want to be categorized."[52]

A desire to avoid categorization, however, could also represent or even become far more than a youthful whim. It could be, fully consciously or not, a highly politicized choice. Slated to arrive at a place that elders had told him his type was not meant to go, Toth had had experience with being categorized. To the Hungarian Secret Police, Toth played the role of "usurper" initially, and eventually just "menace." For many in the U.S. government and American public, Toth became one of many "freedom fighters." For others, he embodied the category of "culturally unassimilable alien" or "communist infiltrator." And as he prepared for his journey to the Jim Crow South, Toth was set to be transformed into a cluster of highly charged categories never particularly relevant to his life before: "white," "civil rights hero," and "racial instigator."

In May 1957, shortly after Toth was awarded the scholarship to Allen and just as he was leaving St. Michaels with a better, though still limited grasp of English, three Allen University professors were fired after being called "reds" and "communistic" by South Carolina governor and unreconstructed segregationist George Bell Timmerman, Jr. The president of the eighty-seven-year-old African Methodist Episcopal (AME) university, Frank R. Veal, was placed under great public pressure after evidence surfaced that the three philosophy professors (two white, one black) had been encouraging non-black students to enroll at Allen. Though not part of the public controversy at the time, the three were suspected of obtaining scholarships for the five Hungarians invited to Allen. By most accounts, Veal was a supporter of integration, but he also had the viability of his institution to worry about. As a private school, Allen was legally immune from South Carolina's segregation requirements for state-funded institutions of higher learning, but Veal also surely understood that public power could extend beyond the stated law in the Deep South, especially in racial matters. Veal recommended to the Allen Board of Trustees that the three professors be released, preferring to sacrifice them than the school.[53]

Several members on Allen's board opposed the firings, and launched an investigation. The investigation, rather cleverly, did not focus on whether the three professors were encouraging integration at Allen, which was the underlying though unstated cause for Governor Timmerman's demand. Instead, the investigation sought evidence for the governor's explicit charge: that the three had ties to the Communist Party or related political organizations. Finding no such evidence, Allen's board reinstated the three professors in August 1957, just weeks before the school year was set to begin.[54]

Jim Crow Through the Looking Glass

Andre Toth arrived in Columbia on Saturday, September 7, and by the following Monday morning he had registered for classes in Allen's College of Fine Arts. The other four Hungarians who were offered Allen scholarships never showed, possibly having followed the counsel of others more familiar with the contentious issue of educational desegregation in the U.S. South than they. News of Toth's presence spread quickly.[55] Likely exacerbating an already tense racial environment, Arkansas Governor Orval Faubus had only a week prior ordered his state's National Guard to block the entrance of Little Rock Central High School to prevent nine African-American teenagers from entering the previously all-white school. Three years after the *Brown v. Board of Education* ruling made school desegregation more of a legal promise than a governed reality, the "Little Rock Nine" incidents gave the issue a sense of immediacy: exciting for integrationists, alarming for segregationists.[56]

Amid this heightened atmosphere, South Carolina Governor Timmerman convened a secret meeting on the very Monday that Toth had registered for classes with the State Board of Education to address the developments at Allen. Knowing that two thirds of Allen students were pursuing their teaching certificates, the state officials decided to land what amounted to a paralyzing blow to the small university. While Allen's private status forbade the state to close the school down outright, the Board of Education issued a statement that "approval of Allen university for teacher training is withheld until such time as the board may determine that it is in the public interest to grant approval." The Board of Education further reminded all schools in South Carolina that only state-certified instructors were allowed to teach their pupils. It specifically explained to them that Allen University graduates would not be certified for the foreseeable future. With the short proclamation, the majority of Allen's students suddenly had no immediate professional basis for continuing to pursue their degrees at the university. South Carolina attorney general T. C. Callison acknowledged that since Allen was private, "there is no law in South Carolina that can prevent the action." But he added that since "it's against public policy" the state had to sanction Allen somehow. The state's decision to intervene in such a heavy-handed way with a church-based private university was considered unprecedented.[57]

Toth became a minor celebrity overnight. While it had long been common to see a spattering of white students enrolled at such historically black colleges and universities in the north as Wilberforce (Ohio) and Lincoln (Pennsylvania), such occurrences in the south were far rarer. It was not unheard of for white faculty at certain black schools in the south, motivated by pragmatism or sometimes religious ethics, to enroll their own children, but the involved parties tended to stay sequestered on campus for fear of reprisals from the outside community.[58] Since the *Brown* decision in 1954, school desegregation had become a more contentious issue on both sides of the debate. Begun even before the *Brown* decision, institutions of higher learning that had previously excluded black students began reversing policy after World War II. A few white students with no familial connection to a particular university had even begun crossing the traditional color barrier at historically black schools. Talladega College of Alabama and Philander Smith of Arkansas had enrolled a handful of white students for several years by the time that Toth arrived at Allen, with Philander Smith graduating its first white student in 1954.[59] That same year Mary G. Howard became the first white student to receive a degree from Fisk University in Nashville, specifically a master's degree in sociology.[60]

Southern state governments generally kept a close watch on black colleges and universities regarding the issue of racial integration, although perhaps not uniformly as close as with white schools. Until South Carolina's governor and State Board of Education intervened so forcefully over Toth's enrollment, only Alabama, Mississippi, and Georgia had been completely vigilant in policing the color line at black colleges when transgressions occurred, holding the revocation of the school's tax exempt status as a potential weapon against them. Other state governments had permitted school administrators to tread upon a razor-thin gray line of segregation only lightly and infrequently. As one school official who hosted an annual interracial sporting tournament opined, "most of us know from experience what will and what will not be tolerated" by public officials. The key was not drawing too much attention.[61] So while Toth's enrollment was not completely unprecedented, the spotlight that followed him at nearly every step was unusual.

Newspaper, journal, and broadcast media reporters sympathetic to educational desegregation, especially from the African American press, immediately flocked to Allen to interview the "naturally shy and quiet" "freedom fighter." How accurately the media covered Toth remains a legitimate question. It seems likely that reporters variously employed objective journalistic practices, embellished to reflect what they may have honestly perceived as an accurate picture of reality, and fabricated quotations and stories to conform to a normative conception of what this European refugee from the Soviet Bloc should represent in such a novel situation. He was occasionally quoted at length, and in suspiciously good English, as opposing segregation in the name of "freedom." Toth was generally portrayed as surprised by all the attention, as someone whose intensely held politics were confined to his hatred of Soviet communism. At Allen, the implication went, he could carry a powerful message simply by being present and offering common sense comments that betrayed a love of freedom with a general bemusement about what all the fuss over him could be about. The *Philadelphia Afro-American* reported that Toth "shrugs off most questions concerning race and integration. 'I want to get on with learning. . . . to paint and study art.' "[62]

In discussing his new classmates Toth was made to seem like just another student, "given a hearty welcome on campus by Allen officials and student body."[63] Toth was said to interrupt his interviews regularly to say "hello" to familiar student faces. He reportedly ended one interview early to meet his new roommate, quoted as telling the journalists in anything but "halting English," "'I hope you don't mind making the interview short,' he adds pleasantly, 'My roommate arrived late last night. I was asleep and didn't get a chance to know him well. I don't even remember his name and I'm anxious to get to my room and see what kind of fellow I'll have to put up with for the next nine months.'"[64] Toth later recalled that most faculty and staff at Allen were indeed exceptionally polite to him, but that the students in particular generally kept their distance. All seemed to understand well the damage his presence had already caused to the school, potentially to many of their careers in teaching, and possibly to their personal safety. The three "communistic" professors who had previously drawn the ire of state officials for their support of desegregation proved an exception to this cautious approach. They seemed, in fact, so eager to befriend Toth that the young Hungarian opted to keep a respectful distance from them, lest the controversy he carried around with him be exacerbated.[65]

Even beyond the reaction of the state government, Toth attracted plenty of negative attention along with the positive and merely curious. Shortly after the initial media circus died down, he was visited by FBI agents who travelled to Columbia to assess whether Toth might be a spy sent to the United States through the Hungarian Refugee Program by the Kremlin.[66] Beyond FBI director J. Edgar Hoover's penchant for suspecting a communist subversive behind every civil rights activist, the visit may have been additionally prompted by the campaign that Francis Walter, Senator James Eastland, and other powerful anti-immigration voices had begun waging earlier in 1957 to kill the refugee admissions program with claims that communist subversives were roaming the country as a result of it.[67] In such an environment of vigilant suspicion, Toth was subjected to three straight days of questioning in a Columbia motel. The process would have been shorter, but the federal agents decided to fly in a Hungarian translator from Washington, D.C., since Toth's training at St. Michaels had not been able to overcome the language barrier between him and his interrogators. Not finding cause to detain him further, they released the young man from intense police interrogations for the second time in roughly a year. Though allowed to return to Allen, Toth was intimidated by another group. White townspeople began standing at the gates of Allen, sometimes shouting racial epithets and even hanging Toth in effigy just beyond the campus property line.[68]

The Institute of International Education, which had arranged for his scholarship, viewed these developments with alarm. It then arranged for Toth to receive scholarships to any of a number of different schools outside the South (and certainly not in historically black institutions), and strongly encouraged him to accept one. Toth's mother wrote to him from her job in the French Embassy in Hungary urging him to leave, believing that she might be fired for the controversy that her son was causing. Although a member of NATO, France had maintained a relatively limited role among the larger Western nation-states in addressing the Hungarian refugee crisis. Catching wind of Andre's exploits in South Carolina, the French ambassador feared that publicity over the events could cause a rift between Budapest and Paris, considering that Toth's mother worked in the embassy. It was one thing for Soviet-backed propaganda to point out the hypocrisies of the United States lambasting the communist governments for committing injustices on their citizens while racial discrimination ran rampant in the United States. But in the American media's coverage, Toth conflated the injustices he battled in Hungary with the ones he was opposing in the United States. Toth assured his mother that he would keep a lower profile in the future, a decision the troubling actions of the South Carolina state government, the FBI, and disgruntled townspeople likely influenced. But he also told her and the Institute of International Education that he planned to stay despite intense pressure to leave.[69]

Though Allen students may have kept a polite distance from Toth, his enrollment sparked acts of solidarity for him and the cause they saw him championing as well. Allen officials feared that the state's sanctions would immediately cause students majoring in education to drop out. Instead, during the few weeks after Toth's arrival new students continued to enroll, causing the student body to "surge above 800 . . . the largest in college history." Many students were even turned away due "to crowded conditions and lack of facilities."[70] An op-ed writer to the *Norfolk Journal and Guide* decried the state's dis-accreditation, calling it "an invasion of institutional privacy" and "an attack on academic freedom." Allen "had a legal and moral right to admit the young European." The school's "officers and students know intimately the trials and tribulations of freedom fighters," as they faced similar challenges every day. As such, the piece continued, they displayed "an act of kindness, understanding, and courage to welcome this refuge [*sic*] from a nation bloodily dominated by the Soviet Union." The writer called on "the many associations of teachers, colleges, university professors, [and] university graduates" to protest the sanctions, and urged other state boards of education to welcome Allen grads to teach in their schools.[71]

Over the next months, South Carolina and Allen University officials sparred and negotiated over the tenuous situation with neither side budging. Meanwhile Andre Toth spent the fall term developing his skills as a painter and studying the history of art at Allen. He also took his challenge to racial segregation beyond the classroom, sometimes in what would have been seen as reckless, even masochistic exercises in civil disobedience to many born and raised in the United States, black or white. He befriended some fellow Hungarian refugees who had enrolled and successfully stayed in the army, and were stationed at the Fort Jackson Army base near Columbia. On several occasions Toth convinced the Hungarian-born soldiers to attend dances at Allen where they, for the first time in their lives, danced with black women, students from the university. When a Ku Klux Klan rally was scheduled in Columbia to protest the interracial activities at Allen, Toth set off to attend. Fortunately, he recounted in retrospect, he became lost, never found the event, and wound up at an ice cream shop instead.[72]

At the beginning of 1958, Governor Timmerman sought to break the impasse telling AME prelate for South Carolina, Bishop Isaiah H. Bonner, in a meeting that Allen could have its accreditation reinstated if it fired the three subversive professors once and for all. The solution would allow Toth to stay at the school, and was possibly appealing to Timmerman because the young Hungarian had proven a difficult foe, at least in an indirect sense. "Toth the freedom fighter" had a broad appeal in the midst of the Cold War even if "Toth the outside instigator" was a menace to the regional racial order. The media had painted him as an unassuming, polite young man who had transplanted his objections to Soviet oppression onto the Jim Crow system of segregation. After much internal debate, Allen's board of directors refused to bow to Timmerman's demand. The governor responded by having the state legislature launch its own investigation into the professors' ties to communism. Allen made regular protests to the Southern Association of Colleges and Secondary Schools as well as the American Association of University Professors. While charges were laid at the state for infringing on the academic freedom of a private institution, the state continued. In the end, the legislature could find no more proof that the professors were communists than had Allen's own investigation the previous year. They were reinstated. On July 10, a month and a half after Andre Toth completed his first year at Allen, the university's accreditation was restored.[73]

Though the three professors who recruited Toth to Allen were not sacrificed for the school's overall well-being, a sacrifice was made nonetheless. Toth's first year at Allen would prove to be his last, a decision made by the school, not Toth. The young Hungarian was deemed too much of a political risk for an institution still reeling from a year and a half of controversial publicity and profound legal sanction. When the spotlight shone squarely on the three professors, Toth was able recede somewhat into the background, providing both him and Allen with a modicum of relief. Though he often believed himself somewhat isolated throughout his academic year, the faculty and students were kind, with even some white townspeople warming to him. He made a number of good friends, and found the art instruction to his liking as well. As he left Columbia, South Carolina, at the end of his spring term for a summer job at a Long Island resort, he looked forward to returning the next fall. When he did return, an Allen official politely and sympathetically refused him access to a dorm, instead buying him a night's stay in a nearby motel and a train ticket back to New York the following day. Toth was told that his presence there was simply too costly for the hundreds of other students seeking their teaching degrees. It remains unclear whether representatives from Allen and the state came to an explicit agreement that the school's reaccreditation would stand only if Toth were expelled, or if university administrators were making calculations on their own. Either way, Allen officials had determined that, whereas Toth's enrollment the previous year might indeed have made a noble point, it was now time to think pragmatically and move on. With media attention focused elsewhere, the young Hungarian was asked to go away quietly, which he did, at least to a degree.[74]

Toth spent much of the next year making ends meet as an elevator operator and bus boy in New York City. He also, at times, laboriously avoided a newspaper reporter trying to track down why exactly he never returned to Allen. He later recalled that after the previous year's attention he just "wanted to be ignored." He eventually received a letter at the midtown YMCA where he lived from a minister of the AME church. The minister apologized to Toth for being treated as he had by Allen, and offered to make amends by giving him a scholarship to another historically black educational institution, but one less likely to stir such controversy. In the fall of 1959, Toth enrolled in Wilberforce University near Dayton, Ohio, an institution with ties to the Underground Railroad and a long history of admitting handfuls of white students to its predominantly African American student body. It had been three years since Toth had had a pistol pointed at his head for his suspected role in the great Hungarian uprising of 1956. Two years had passed since he first arrived at Allen University with ambitions to challenge an unjust system of oppression and shake the rattle of rebellious youth a bit. By the time Toth entered Wilberforce the refugee had found a way to exercise the political ideals he had cultivated in Hungary, but in the comfortable shade of relative anonymity his newly adopted country could also provide.[75]

The experiences of Toth and others presented here demonstrate that the actual engagement of Hungarian refugees with American society sometimes produced a strikingly different set of narratives about American refugee aid initiatives than those scripted by refugee advocates. Amid an environment largely hostile to liberalized immigration, the "freedom fighter" image crafted for the Hungarians earned Cold War currency that in turn opened the doors of admission to them. The American resettlement network that matured in World War II's aftermath retooled itself to offer, for the first time, all admitted refugee adjustment services on U.S. soil in a centralized location: services provided by both voluntary and federal agencies. Yet the speed and haphazard manner with which the refugees were moved through Camp Kilmer left many in poorly matched resettlement arrangements and unprepared to weather an economic recession. And Toth's saga at Allen University showed that the unique opportunities made available to these Cold War European refugees had the potential to shake up American society on multiple sides of the racial divide.

Looming over these developments, often implicitly, were questions over what role the U.S. government should play in domestic refugee aid initiatives relative to the voluntary agencies. The operations at Camp Kilmer produced a significant change on this front, but the voluntary agencies still ran more of the show when it came to helping refugees adjust (or sometimes, not adjust) to life in the United States. The difficulties that many of the refugees faced in the United States, and the controversies they sometimes sparked embarrassed the diverse regime of American refugee resettlement aid. The more highly publicized of these problems also served, by extension, as a globally conspicuous indictment of American society, the country's economic system, and the ability of American institutions to provide a better social safety net than those behind the Iron Curtain. Even with a greater federal commitment to helping with resettlement during the Hungarian Program than before, these dilemmas echoed those from previous years.

As Andre Toth began his classes at Wilberforce in the fall of 1959, the traces of federal support he had received on first entering the United States had long since disappeared. The private scholarship he enjoyed at this second school had not, unlike the one for Allen University, been offered through the encouragement of the U.S. State Department. The question whether the U.S. government should play a more robust and less fleeting role in the resettlement of future political refugees admitted to the United States was put to rest for the moment. Yet events were brewing just several hundred miles to the south of Toth—led by a charismatic revolutionary named Castro—that would revive the issue, and produce a profoundly new set of answers for the future of American refugee affairs.

CHAPTER 7

Revolutions in Cuba and Refugee Welfare

Miami mayor Robert High beamed with pride when considering the promise that the new Cubans exiles in his city held for the intertwined futures of the United States, Cuba, and the rest of Latin America. "Think of it!" the mayor exclaimed to a *Reader's Digest* reporter in late 1962. "We are privileged to have as our guests what may well be the future governing group of another nation."[1] High made his remarks as Fidel Castro was nearing his fourth year in power on the Caribbean island only ninety miles to the south. As the Cuban leader moved increasingly toward the Soviet Union and communist left over that span, what had begun as a rather modest exodus of people fleeing Cuba for the United States had subsequently ballooned to two hundred thousand, with more refugees on the way.[2] Most of the exiles had concentrated themselves in and around Miami, poised to return at a moment's notice.[3] Even though the Bay of Pigs invasion, assassination plots, and other American efforts to unseat the fiery Cuban prime minister had failed thus far, Mayor High echoed a sentiment commonly held by Americans engaged in the refugee situation: Castro's days were numbered. When he fell, the mayor predicted that the members of the Cuban exile community would return to their homeland to institute an enlightened democratic government that would one day forge "a model to the rest of Latin America." High warned, however, that the United States bore a heavy burden in ensuring that those future leaders would return to their homeland both friendly to their host country and instilled with the best principles their temporary host nation had to offer. If the United States failed its charge, the government the refugees ultimately forged might be neither enlightened nor friendly. "It would be a sad thing," High warned, "if we missed the opportunity they offer us."[4]

What was it that Mayor High believed the United States could offer these

Cuban refugees to help ensure that they eventually would return to their homeland with favorable impressions of the American government and the country's way of life before establishing a post-Castro Cuba? We now know, of course, that the mayor's goal was moot in terms of creating a new Cuba in the wake of Castro's predicted demise, but the context of his remarks can nevertheless offer a window onto the development of American refugee affairs in this period and perhaps a gloss on our understanding of American Cold War political ideologies during the era of the New Frontier. If we are to take cues from the conventional wisdom about America's Cuban exile community over its first decades in the United States, then we might assume that Mayor High was referring to an enhanced respect for such traditionally conservative ideals as free markets, individualism, and small government. After all, for a half century after the first refugees from Castro's regime arrived in the United States, the Cuban American community leaned heavily toward the Republican Party, positioning itself as an especially potent political force in Florida.[5] In fact, America's prior history with organized refugee resettlement might further bolster such a prediction. Beginning in the 1930s, the central model for absorbing admitted political refugees into America's economic, political, and cultural fabrics relied, with occasional exceptions, on relatively little direct government support. Instead, the country's voluntary agencies were primarily enlisted to find admitted refugees jobs, housing, and the cultural, material, and legal support they would require in their new communities. Yet both the traditional thinking about the political culture of America's Cuban exile community and the legacies of earlier American refugee resettlement initiatives provide, as it happens, rather poor indicators for understanding what Mayor High and a wide range of other interested parties had in mind when promoting a particular vision for how the Cuban refugees should be treated in the United States before returning home to start anew.

A metamorphosis had begun. Far from highlighting how two separate political cultures might forge an ideological synergy based on a mutual respect for small government, free market capitalism, and individual initiative, Mayor High's remarks were embedded in a larger defense of a major federally subsidized welfare program for the Cuban exiles that had been in place for nearly two years by that point. What explains this fact? Providing such large numbers of political refugees—or any new immigrants, for that matter—with such substantial federal social welfare support was utterly unprecedented in American history. Referred to as the Cubans' "New Deal," for decades after Castro's assumption of power, Cuban immigrants received tens of millions of dollars per year in federal welfare support directed toward such benefits as cash payments, health care, food, housing, job and language training, education, child services, and relocation to other parts of the country.[6]

This chapter explores the emergence and maturation of the Cuban Refugee Program, for roughly the first half of the 1960s, to trace the contours of this sea change in the governance of American refugee affairs, the ripples from which would be felt for decades to come. It traces two interrelated sets of developments. First, the Cuban Program altered radically the respective working relationships between American state and non-state actors involved with resettling admitted political refugees in the United States. The most obvious change was the dramatic growth in the federal government's overt commitment to organized resettlement, a phenomenon that Miami's Mayor Robert High and others believed would make the Cuban Refugee Program a success. Despite some halting and fleeting moves of this sort during the Hungarian Refugee Program, the American state's role in Cuban refugee affairs represented something significantly new. The change was sparked by a number of factors. Most important, these contributors included a fundamentally different sort of refugee crisis than the country had experienced over the previous thirty years: the arrival of massive numbers of *asylees* seeking political refuge in the United States as their first country of exile, asylees that, for geopolitical imperatives, America's foreign policy establishment did not want to send back. The new federal commitment to resettling refugees, however, would not ultimately displace the centrality of the voluntary agencies in the resettlement network. For decades to come, the voluntary agencies would remain, for the Cubans and other refugees, in many ways as relevant as they had long been. Yet their role in the resettlement process would indeed change as their relationship to the federal government became largely defined on a fiscal basis. The voluntary agencies were effectively transformed through the Cuban Refugee Program into subcontractors for the state.

If the first set of developments described above relates to shifting dynamics between institutions, the second set addresses a transformation in the relationships between those institutions and the exiles themselves. The Cuban Refugee Program fundamentally reordered the federal government's legal, material, and symbolic relationships with political refugees admitted to the United States. It ushered forth a significantly greater assumption of federal responsibility for that particular category of alien. While in previous decades, the United States government often assumed a sizeable role in providing for the welfare of political refugees while they were overseas, it commonly ratcheted down its levels of commitment to some of those same persons once they were welcomed onto American soil, relying on a sometimes faulty assumption that American civil society, market capitalism, and the country's legal system would provide the refugees with sufficient resources to achieve the American Dream. The arrival of thousands of Cold War refugees directly on American shores, however, required some kind of deviation from this precedent. A roughly thirty-year-old federal welfare system that was beginning to enter its second generation of policy innovations offered an appealing solution. The confluence of these two events helped to write a new script for the resettlement of refugees in the United States, one where newly arrived aliens invested with valuable geopolitical capital were offered levels of federal support that sometimes exceeded those provided to needy American citizens. These dynamics simultaneously nurtured and threatened the viability of American refugee affairs.

Critically, however, the tight connection remained during the Cuban program between the government's willingness to admit political refugees—or, more accurately in this case, to allow them to be present—and guarantees that the needy among them would enjoy access to institutional support. The difference between this transformed admissions-resettlement nexus and that which had helped define American refugee affairs since the 1930s was that the federal government assumed a dramatically larger role for the Cubans' welfare than it had for early groups of refugees. The new arrangement would largely endure for future populations of refugees arriving in the United States for decades to follow, with the link between admissions and the promise of organized welfare support continuing to differentiate those persons entering as refugees from most other immigrants.

New Developments, Old Habits

Between January 1959 and fall 1960, increasing numbers of Cubans arrived in the Miami area, eventually taxing local and state resources to the breaking point. Although anti-Castro refugees began arriving on American soil in large numbers immediately after the Commandante wrested power from Fulgencio Batista in January 1959, it took nearly two years before the situation in Miami deteriorated enough for federal officials to feel compelled to address refugees' welfare needs in any significant way. Initially, the main role of the federal government was that of gatekeeper, not caregiver. America's immigration

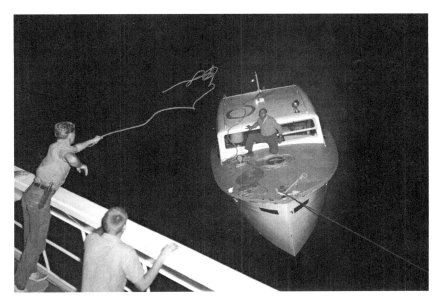

Figure 9. U.S. Coast Guard Official Photo. "Coast Guard Tows Stranded Boat to Key West," November 5, 1965. Records of the United States Coast Guard. RG 26-G. NARA, B 99, No. 6122.

bureaucracy held the door wide open for this particular group of people, a first for large groups of non-Europeans admitted explicitly on political grounds as refugees.[7]

As elaborated in Carl Bon Tempo's study of U.S. refugee admissions policies during the Cold War, these and later groups of Cubans were allowed to enter the country without much serious opposition from or regulation by the government. Especially in the early years of the exodus, the refugees and U.S. government officials alike generally assumed that their stay would be temporary and would last only until Castro was overthrown. The executive branch's central immigration arms—that is, the State Department's Visa Division and the Justice Department's Immigration and Naturalization Service—permitted refugees already in the United States with temporary visitor visas to stay indefinitely and allowed other Cubans to enter with no documents. Normal screening procedures were liberalized considerably as compared with those previously admitted as political refugees. This change was true even with regard to the Hungarian freedom fighters, whose symbolic power as oppressed opponents of communism had similarly captured large parts of the American

public's attention, at least in the early aftermath of the failed Hungarian uprising. Critically, gone were the trio of resettlement requirements—de facto with
Jewish victims of Nazism in the 1930s, and de jure with most other political
refugees thereafter—that before being granted legal exile in the United States,
a system would be in place to prevent the refugee from becoming a charge on
public resources and to provide him or her with housing and a job. Additionally, the Cubans had effectively the same legal benefits as did most documented aliens, both at that time and previously; the major exception was their
not holding permanent resident alien (PRA) status until 1966. After that, Cubans boasted a pathway to citizenship along with those entering the through
mainstream immigration law as PRAs.[8]

Unlike with previous refugee resettlement programs, the situation did not
lend itself to federal officials and voluntary agency personnel developing a
pipeline of sponsorship offers while refugees waited in overseas camps or, in
the case of the Hungarians, in a sequestered military base on U.S. soil. These
refugees were fleeing an emerging enemy of the United States, an enemy that
was not across an entire ocean, but only ninety miles from American soil. That
proximity helped create an environment where, for the first time in recent
history, the United States would be the country of first asylum for massive
numbers of persons specially admitted to the country because they were
deemed to be fleeing political persecution. Federal immigration officials had
various options: detaining the many thousands of Cubans arriving on southern Florida's shores until it was determined what to do with them, sending
them back home and dissuading others from fleeing, or allowing them to remain in the United States legally. The first option was nearly impossible logistically. The second option, whereas more practically feasible, also confronted
powerful Cold War calculations that placed significant political value in the
specter of people fleeing a neighboring regime that increasingly associated
itself with socialism and the Soviets. It was therefore decided that the first
waves of refugees would indeed be permitted to remain in the United States.
Intermittently over the coming years, many thousands more would take the
cue of this U.S. immigration policy and join them.[9]

Without a national resettlement network of voluntary and federal agencies
in place to greet the initial flood of asylees, the task was handled by local private welfare agencies around Miami, particularly those agencies that operated
through the regional Catholic Diocese.[10] By and large, however, little institutional support was needed by the wave of exiles that arrived in approximately
the first year of Castro's rule. The first twenty-five thousand Cubans to flee for

the southern tip of Florida were the Batistianos, generally wealthy supporters of the deposed right-wing dictator, Fulgencio Batista, and members of his government. Most of these refugees were educated and able to arrive in the U.S. with considerable capital and other assets. Approximately twenty thousand Cubans moreover were already established in the area, further easing the economic and cultural absorption of the newcomers.[11]

Beginning in mid-1959, Castro began moving increasingly to the left, nationalizing land and major industry, and increasingly aligning his government with the Soviet Union. A second, larger wave of Cubans responded by leaving Cuba for the United States, again mostly for the Miami area. Composed mainly of middle- and upper-class educated people, this second group did not generally include Batistianos. Some of them were, in fact, former supporters of Castro's revolution who had grown disillusioned by his turn toward communism. Anxious that their relatively comfortable social and economic positions in Cuba would be jeopardized if they stayed, in some cases these refugees believed themselves pushed out by the Castro regime.[12] During 1960, sixty thousand of these Cubans fled to the United States, but unlike the first wave of exiles, many were prohibited from leaving with more than a pittance of their possessions.[13]

By the middle of 1960 the newcomers were taking a major toll on the area's resources. Governmental and philanthropic leaders began calling the situation "critical" and "explosive."[14] Miami proper had a population of only three hundred thousand and the greater metropolitan area barely numbered one million.[15] The new influx of increasingly impoverished Cubans not only significantly expanded the population, but the immigrants were difficult to absorb into the local economy. Miami was suffering from fairly high unemployment: 7.3 percent compared with 5.5 percent nationally.[16] The new arrivals had been principally professionals, small business owners, and tradespeople, while what the area's economy then needed was agriculture workers. The number of children arriving both as orphans and with family was growing from the hundreds into the thousands, and Miami's public schools were being taxed accordingly with the sharply increased enrollments.[17]

What had begun as a sizeable but manageable influx was threatening to balloon into the type of large-scale humanitarian crisis that America's hybrid refugee aid network had previously committed itself to alleviating in other countries. By October 1960, there were reports of near starvation among the refugees. The local Catholic charities were stretched to the breaking point. Public welfare was not an option since Florida had a strict five-year residency requirement before someone could apply for assistance, whether citizen or alien. The situation took on the geopolitical hues of the Cold War, much as had occurred with controversial, embarrassing, or otherwise troubling developments in previous U.S. refugee admission programs. As with, for instance, the Latvians resettled as cotton sharecroppers in Mississippi or the "freedom fighters" demanding repatriation to communist Hungary for want of jobs in their new American homeland, the specter of the newly arrived Cubans languishing so dramatically could be read by observers in both the United States and beyond as a failure of the American economic, political, and cultural systems. The number of Cubans facing destitution was far greater, however, than anything witnessed in the previous resettlement programs. Exacerbated by the Cubans' concentration in a single locality, the situation seemed fraught with dangers unparalleled in postwar American refugee resettlement initiatives, both in a more strictly humanitarian sense and in the field of Cold War propaganda.[18]

The growing crisis attracted the attention of the national coordinating arms of the country's sectarian-based immigrant aid societies and private welfare agencies. Most important among them were the National Catholic Welfare Conference, the Church World Service, and the United HIAS Service; the second society, it should be noted, was pan-Protestant and Eastern Orthodox, and the third, as noted earlier in the book, Jewish. Joining them in addressing the problem was the non-sectarian International Rescue Committee. The IRC had, since Hitler came to power in 1933, focused its efforts primarily on helping victims of fascist and communist aggression abroad, but since the United States had, for the first time in the modern era, become a country of first asylum for tens of thousands, its leadership decided to shift more of its resources to addressing the needs of Cuban refugees in the United States. Foreshadowing the increased role that the federal government would soon play in the resettlement of the Cubans, the domestic soil of the United States had in this sense become like international terrain for IRC officials, who were accustomed to working with refugees in (foreign) countries of first asylum.[19]

The leaders of these voluntary agencies met in late September 1960 with the representatives of local charities and public welfare officials representing Miami and the state of Florida. Tom Wintersteen of the Dade Welfare Planning Council echoed the consensus of alarm by stating, "We've tried to do our best with this problem, but it has thorns all over it."[20] Agreeing that the problem had grown "national," the group petitioned President Dwight Eisenhower to provide federal relief for both the voluntary organizations and the variety of public services that had thus far borne the cost of managing the influx. Florida's public officials demanded that the federal government assume responsibility for the plight of the Cubans since federal immigration officials were permitting their presence, not the state and municipal governments. The voluntary agency representatives justified their request for federal intervention because, unlike previous programs that aided refugees within the United States, these Cubans were not initially residing in another country of first asylum where concerns such as jobs, housing, and American family support could begin to be arranged for the exiles before embarking for the United States. The voluntary agencies were expected to perform all of these tasks for great numbers of people immediately on American soil, and critically, in a locality that had simply run out of each of those necessary resources.[21]

The president's response appears timid in hindsight. In a setting befitting the rather casual approach he would soon take to the mounting crisis, Eisenhower received the plea for federal help at his vacation home on the lush Augusta National golf course in Georgia. Having visited there nearly thirty times since assuming office in 1953, the federalist-style structure acquired the nickname "the temporary White House." As he had several years prior with the Hungarian refugee crisis, the President asked his friend and former army colleague Tracy Voorhees to look into the situation and see what could be done.[22]

Voorhees' experience with refugee aid efforts reflected the approach that the United States had taken with refugee crisis management in the past: while international relief initiatives typically employed the robust engagement—if not always sufficiently or deftly deployed—of both governmental and nongovernmental agencies, domestic assistance to refugees admitted to the United States relied overwhelmingly on the voluntary agencies, typically with only minimal governmental support. With the Hungarian situation, Voorhees had been in charge of committing significant state resources to managing the camps in Austria. This task included struggling to achieve some semblance of state coordinating authority over the independent-minded and heterodox array of voluntary agencies in the camps. But even with the federal government being nominally in charge of the Camp Kilmer reception facility in New Jersey and indeed having representatives from seven federal agencies working there, Kilmer nonetheless had remained largely a voluntary agency operation. The domestic resettlement component of refugee affairs had been, under Voorhees' watch and well beyond it, the primary purview of private philanthropy.

Voorhees' approach to the Cuban crisis remained consistent with these precedents of public-private governance even though the circumstances—the sudden arrival of tens of thousands of poor, first-country asylees on U.S. soil—were unprecedented and radically different. He reassembled much of the same team of administrators who worked for him during the Hungarian program to assist him with the Cuban situation.[23] In late 1960, when Voorhees called a meeting with representatives of the various entities that had been addressing the influx of Cubans over the prior two years, the Eisenhower administration was entering its twilight, waiting to hand over power to the vigorous young Senator from Massachusetts who had defeated Vice President Nixon only a week and a half earlier. The panoply of personnel at the meeting included welfare officials from the state of Florida, Dade County, and the city of Miami; representatives of the national voluntary agencies; and local charity leaders who had been involved with the Cuban situation since its inception nearly two years prior. A voluntary agency official echoed the frustration of others at the meeting, reporting that "it was quite obvious that [Voorhees] was anxious that the private agencies accept full responsibility for the problem, and that the Federal Government not be involved." Voorhees opined optimistically that the situation "could be solved in thirty to sixty days."[24]

Not only did Voorhees' experience with domestic refugee affairs condition him for a minimalist federal response, but the president also took a similar line, noting that the issue should "continue to be dealt with locally."[25] At Voorhees' recommendation, Eisenhower allocated $1 million from an executive contingency fund to deal with the issue. A paltry sum considering the scope of the problem, the figure underscored the administration's determination to minimize the federal government's role by giving the funds to Voorhees personally instead of channeling them through an existing government office.[26] The federal allocation went primarily to a new Cuban Refugee Emergency Center in Miami that served as a clearinghouse where refugees would be pointed to an appropriate voluntary agency. Committed to finding private solutions to the crisis, Voorhees also personally raised tens of thousands of dollars from the Rockefeller Foundation, New York Cardinal Francis Spellman, and the Texas Oil Company, most of which he diverted to the voluntary agencies to help alleviate a modicum of their major financial problems.[27]

In the month and a half between Eisenhower's $1 million allocation and the inauguration of John F. Kennedy as president, the situation in Miami continued to deteriorate.[28] Through the efforts of the newly established refugee center, several dozen Cubans were placed in jobs away from the overburdened Miami economy, but hundreds more, sometimes thousands more, were arriving in the area each week from Cuba. Voorhees downplayed the scope of the problem, insisting that the "extraordinary generosity" of Miami's citizens was keeping the growing refugee population in good living conditions.[29]

With the benefit of hindsight, the sheer scope of the blooming crisis makes it difficult to imagine that Eisenhower, Voorhees, and colleagues could have continued on such a minimalist path if Eisenhower, hypothetically, had been able to continue onto a third term. At the end of Ike's second term, however, it may have been difficult to foresee either the scope of the future Cuban influx or the demands it would place on the federal government to assume responsibility for it. And while Herbert Hoover, Perrin Galpin, Hallam Tuck, and others had urged Eisenhower administration officials to build a more substantial federal apparatus for handling the Hungarian refugee crisis just a few years prior, the president and Voorhees had deflected the pressure then and, with a new administration about to take office, they chose to proceed similarly. Reading the writing on the wall, government officials in Florida and the voluntary agency representatives shifted their sights to ensuring that the incoming Kennedy administration took a more active role in the situation than the Eisenhower administration had been willing to do.[30]

The Revolution Ninety Miles to the North

Before examining the policy that the Kennedy administration adopted regarding the Cuban refugee situation, it is useful to pause and consider some major options that were plausibly available to it as officials addressed the situation. Some echoed those faced by the Eisenhower administration when the Cubans first began arriving en masse in 1959 while others were colored by evolving developments. First, the new administration could continue its predecessor's decision of allowing nearly all Cubans who could make it to the United States to remain legally present while providing them only scant federal assistance. With hundreds and sometimes thousands of new refugees arriving each week, however, many observers believed this solution was untenable and would spell doom for an economic and social environment in Miami often called "explosive."[31] Second, the administration could deport the refugees already in the United States and refuse entry to any new arrivals, both of which carried problematic repercussions. While forcibly deporting refugees back to their homeland when there was a justifiable fear of political persecution would violate the international law of *non-refoulement* (non-return), U.S. immigration authorities had done this in the past, and would do so again in the future, especially with Haitians and other refugees from oppressive right-wing regimes in the Western Hemisphere. The American political environment at the time, however, continued to mitigate against either deporting the Cubans or refusing entry to any more. Castro's alliance with the Kremlin had solidified both politically and economically, and the Kennedy administration seemed poised to receive substantial political capital by receiving and sheltering the refugees. The administration also had the option of permitting continued immigration but at the same time providing considerable federal resources for resettling many refugees away from southern Florida to other parts of the country, where available jobs and housing would then give them the opportunity to be self-sustaining. The Kennedy administration chose none of these options immediately, instead adopting a policy that concentrated on continuing to admit the Cubans, but initiating a federally funded welfare program for the refugees where they already were: in the Miami area.

A month after his inauguration the new president asked Abraham Ribicoff, secretary of the Department of Health, Education, and Welfare (HEW), to take charge of the problem. Ribicoff was assigned to coordinate the activities of his department with the Departments of State, Defense, Labor, and Agriculture.[32] Whereas Voorhees boasted a long history of promoting solutions to humanitarian problems that relied heavily on the private sector, Ribicoff's professional résumé suggested a greater faith in governmental solutions to welfare needs. Serving as a state legislator, a U.S. representative, and governor of Connecticut from the 1930s through the early 1960s, he regularly pushed for increased public funding of welfare services.[33]

As secretary of HEW, Ribicoff could not concentrate full-time on the Cuban situation, so he assigned Dillon S. Meyer to spearhead the new federal efforts. As with Ribicoff, Meyer's appointment signaled that a new willingness for federal involvement was imminent. Meyer had considerable experience with two federal entities that were responsible for some of the most ambitious—and at times, notorious—population management schemes in American history. As former commissioner in the Bureau of Indian Affairs, Meyer oversaw the country's large reservation system, serving as the federal government's chief liaison with the American Indian community. Meyer had also served as director of the War Relocation Authority during World War II. Responsible for forcibly moving one hundred twenty thousand persons of Japanese descent in the western United States to ten internment camps inland in the war's early stages, his offices then worked to resettle many of them into new communities at the war's end. He had thus worked to manage large groups of people—composed of both U.S. citizens and otherwise— who occupied culturally and often legally liminal positions vis-à-vis the American nation state. His duties had implications for American domestic policies, as they occurred on U.S. soil, and yet possessed significant elements of foreign policy, destabilizing, as they did, traditional lines of territorial sovereignty.[34] In these ways, Meyer's professional journey mapped quite neatly onto his newly assigned task of managing a growing population of Cuban nationals on Florida's southern tip.

By the end of February, President Kennedy had approved a program of Ribicoff's and Meyer's design for dealing with the refugee problem. Kennedy forecast a change in approach in a letter to Voorhees, thanking him for his previous work. "I believe," Kennedy explained, that "this problem can now best be augmented by bringing to bear the vast welfare, health and other skills available, in the Department of Health, Education and Welfare," as well as "the activities of other Federal agencies in this field."[35] Most notably, the federal government almost immediately began giving Cuban refugee families in Miami a monthly welfare check. It also agreed to fund other initiatives that included reimbursing Miami public schools to deal with the increased enrollment of Cuban children, paying area medical facilities for the refugees' health care needs, providing money to social agencies caring for the thousands of unaccompanied Cuban children whose parents were forced to remain in Cuba, and undertaking free food distribution derived from federal surpluses. The initial $4 million allocation came from the State Department's International Cooperation Administration—predecessor to today's Agency for International Development, or AID—but for many years thereafter, a sympathetic Congress would regularly earmark exponentially higher amounts for the Cuban program, to be channeled directly through HEW, and upon its creation in 1979, the Department of Health and Human Services.[36] Between fiscal years 1961 and 1966 alone, the Kennedy administration spent $214 million to help Cuban refugees adjust to life in America.[37]

With the pressure upon Florida's and Miami's public education and health services now considerably eased, attention turned to how the direct welfare payments to the Cuban refugees should be handled. The central issues included deciding how to determine who qualified as sufficiently needy to receive checks, how much the refugees should receive, and who would distribute the checks. These matters extended well beyond issues of finances and the incidental details of bureaucratic management. They raised fundamentally new questions about the parameters of both U.S. foreign policy and citizenship, and whether the responsibility for non-citizens in the United States ultimately lay with the institutions of official government or civil society. In the past, refugee immigrants received welfare payments from the private voluntary agencies. This had been the practice with the first waves of incoming Cubans until the charitable funds began drying up in 1960. Such private support was a well-established practice dating far back in American immigration history, and was generally intended as a nongovernmental means of helping newcomers establish themselves in the United States until they could become self-supporting. Although public welfare had been occasionally given to aliens at local, state, and federal levels, the public charge clause in immigration law held that receiving various types of public aid could be grounds for deportation if occurring within five years of admission and if it was found that the conditions causing reliance on the aid existed before admission but were not reported to immigration officials. As a conspicuously symbolic subset of the broader immigrant population infused with considerable political capital, sympathetic government officials and voluntary agency personnel alike worked especially hard to keep refugees off of the government rolls. The consensus view held that an alternative course would reflect poorly to domestic and international audiences on the refugees themselves and the capacity of America's vaunted private sector to take care of its most vulnerable people.[38]

Within weeks of Kennedy's inauguration, Ribicoff, Meyer, and other federal officials decided to leave precedent behind by claiming for the federal government a dramatically larger role in the welfare of a refugee immigrant population than had ever been the case previously. As German Porto awoke very early on a Monday morning in late February 1961, he had reason to believe that he would be the first recipient of the American state's path breaking refugee welfare program. Even though it was only 5 a.m. when Porto arrived at the Cuban Refugee Emergency Center in downtown Miami, however, he nevertheless found forty-four people ahead of him in line. The fifty-one year-old former Havana restaurant owner had been unemployed since arriving in Miami, scraping by on a few groceries given to him by a local Catholic charity, which had also been providing him a bunk. While his first semi-weekly federal check of fifty dollars certainly would not solve all of his economic challenges, receiving the same amount every two weeks promised to offer him some much needed help.[39] By the end of the day, a thousand more Cubans joined Porto and the other forty-four in that queue, forcing the anxious refugees to wind themselves around the block in the bright sun.[40] In short order, another twenty-three thousand Cubans received their welfare checks, forty thousand had their medical care paid for by the federal government, and throngs more lined up at the Florida State Welfare Department's Miami distribution center to receive federal food surpluses.[41] These numbers grew considerably in the coming years. Dillon Meyer even managed to convince myriad federal agencies to begin hiring unemployed refugees with professional skills in such fields as medicine, economics, engineering, and agri-science.[42]

A popular image of Florida's Cuban community has been crafted—both by members of the community and those outside—over the years to distinguish Cubans from other immigrant groups in America, particularly other Latinos. One of the purported distinguishing characteristics of the Cubans was their proud disdain for aid outside their particular community, especially public assistance. Such a bootstrap ideal, however, seems to have been trumped—understandably so—for people like German Porto by a desperate need to accept federal aid to survive in Miami. Posing gleefully with his check for a news photographer, Porto explained that the new federal payments would enable him to purchase his own food and find his own place to rent. A former high-school teacher from Cuba, Humberto Lamas, echoed Porto's pleasure, sending a message to the American people through an interpreter that "we will never forget the kindness they have shown to me."[43]

While voluntary agency leaders almost uniformly recognized the need of the federal government to claim the primary financial responsibility for the refugees, not all were thrilled with some of the ramifications. Most concerned were officials of the National Catholic Welfare Conference who resented being moved to the edge of the refugee welfare process so dramatically. They argued that federal welfare cash should be channeled through the voluntary agencies and their affiliated local charities on the ground, not through existing public welfare bureaus in Florida, which regularly faced charges of being understaffed and generally inept. The Catholic leaders had another, unstated reason for their position. The majority of the Cubans in the Miami area—numbering near one hundred thousand at this point—had been relying on Catholic charities for support.[44] As many of those clients received cash assistance from public welfare offices, it might cut the church organization out of the loop, reducing its connections with and influence over the community. The federal welfare payments made directly to individuals and families were not alone in drawing Catholic criticism. Cardinal Francis Spellman and other prominent American Catholics, for instance, claimed that the Kennedy administration's refusal to reimburse Miami's Catholic schools for their swollen enrollments from the influx of Cuban children amounted to an abandonment of the Church.[45]

Other voluntary agency officials by and large accepted the new federal role, but still voiced certain misgivings. The federal government was, after all, taking over what had traditionally been a significant part of their raison d'être. In a mark of this ambivalence, even though leaders of the International Rescue Committee were among those bodies regularly lobbying for continued federal funding of welfare programs, they simultaneously worried that it would serve to reduce contributions from the American public to the private organizations.[46] Bonnie Steiner, a case worker for the Jewish-run United HIAS Service (UHS), noted that the massive crowds lining up for government welfare checks at the Cuban Refugee Emergency Center blocked her Cuban clients from reaching the on-site UHS offices, where they had appointments for counseling. She lamented that they physically "could not break through" what she described as a "mad race for money." In a bit of ironic symbolism, the voluntary agency was able to remain active with the Cuban Refugee Program only because of federal intervention, but that same federal intervention created a situation where the link between the voluntary agency and its refugee clients was in danger of suddenly being severed.[47]

Literally overnight, the arrangement for providing the most critical sources of domestic refugee aid was turned on its head. Since the New Deal, public welfare bureaus regularly referred needy refugees to the private welfare offices affiliated with the national voluntary agencies. Now the opposite occurred. Newly arrived Cubans would be pointed toward the federally funded Emergency Center by family, former community members, churches, and synagogues. Once there, the new Cubans would be referred to the offices of one of the resident voluntary agencies, typically according to the refugees' religion. Voluntary agency personnel would then determine if they were eligible for various forms of government assistance, which increasingly, most were. Paperwork would be completed so that the refugees could then be directed toward the state of Florida's public welfare office, located in the same building, to receive their first federal relief check. The voluntary agencies continued to perform some services for the refugees such as counseling, but a core part of their responsibility had become that of a simple link—a liaison—between the refugees and the government.[48] A large part of the business of refugee welfare was now assumed by the federal government.

Echoes of the Past, Visions of the Future

While the Cuban refugees would not be put on a path to juridical U.S. citizenship until 1966, in ways not typically considered, this switch from mostly private to largely public support prefigured that more formal transition of status while immediately imbuing the newcomers with some significant benefits of *social* citizenship in their host country.[49] It offered important symbolic recognition, in other words, that the Cubans might be nascent members of American society, and not only temporary visitors awaiting their imminent return home ninety miles to the south. The role of the voluntary agencies and state in this process was complex too. Leaders of the voluntary agencies had long heralded their ability to care for political refugees in the United States privately instead of with government funds. Not only did this allegedly promote self-sufficiency among the refugees, but it also built important cultural connections between the agencies and the new immigrant populations. But there had also long been minority voices in the voluntary agencies arguing that direct government aid to the refugees would be a welcome acknowledgement of the immigrants' partial inclusion in their new homeland. Such policy innovation would not only facilitate, as Jewish refugee case workers opined at the end of World War II, "the integration of the refugee into American democracy." It would also provide counter-evidence to America's international critics of the U.S. government's "commitment to anti-discrimination at home." Public welfare support for newly admitted political refugees had the potential of signaling to all that the United States respected the diversity of its inhabitants, whether one was a legal citizen or alien, in the population's cultural majority or minority. The material and political benefits of such a public welfare program could be considered as the first rung in the refugees' climb toward full inclusion in the economy, culture, legal system, and polity of the United States.[50]

Further contributing to the sense that federal support for Cuban refugees' welfare represented a partial step toward social citizenship was the fact that the guidelines used for determining eligibility and aid levels for American citizens who requested federally subsidized welfare were used as a rough template in the new Cuban program. True, the Cubans differed significantly from citizens and many other immigrant aliens in that foreign policy imperatives both paved the way for the Cubans' admission into the country and helped to fuel a federal welfare program for them. But the welfare program for the refugees would in many ways run parallel to those for citizens, with the latter having provided a readily available blueprint for the former.[51]

If the new federal welfare program for Cubans offered exiles a sense of entitlement and welcome in their host country, it also bred resentment from Americans who believed that the Cubans were being treated too well by their host country. This had also occurred with the arrival of previous refugees, but now, as a considerable amount of taxpayers' dollars were being given to the latest group of exiles, the federal government could be seen as more directly and broadly culpable. As such, questions over U.S. citizenship were brought into sharper relief. Some of the first voices to cry foul emanated from the African-American community, historically accustomed to receiving the short end of the public welfare stick, particularly in the South. Florida's state welfare bureau had become more equitable by the 1960s in its grants to black citizens than had previously been the case (including for federally subsidized programs), but this phenomenon was only a recent one. A reader of the *Chicago Defender* chastised the paper's editorial staff for endorsing the Kennedy ticket in the 1960 election, noting that, while Kennedy had given millions in "relief for the Cuban refugees . . . what has been appropriated by the Democrat administration for the Negroes in Fayette County, Tenn.?" For about a year by that point, many of the blacks in Fayette County had become refugees themselves, living in a squalid tent city after having been forced from their homes by area white landowners in retribution for a voter registration drive.[52] Discontent in Miami's black community with the Cuban situation was growing as well. African Americans questioned the fairness of Cuban aliens receiving publicly subsidized health care, good public education, and special federal loans for college, while many blacks still had little practical access to such things.[53]

Such complaints were joined by a wider chorus. In the fall of 1961, with one hundred thousand Cubans in Miami relying on some form of federal aid, members of Congress balked at the largesse of the Cuban Refugee Program.[54] Legislators with liberal records on immigration affairs, such as Senator Phillip Hart, grew alarmed that the rising tensions in Miami over public welfare allowed the Cubans to become "a convenient scapegoat for Miami's ills."[55] The bold and unprecedented federal welfare program for the Cubans in Miami had assuaged their unacceptable material plight, but that same program fomented untenable social and political resentment. The welfare program initially designed to sustain the policy of large-scale Cuban admissions was now challenging that policy's continued viability.[56]

Was there an answer to this vexing riddle? Since the Cold War fervor against Castro and his Soviet allies remained strong, neither a cessation of admissions nor the mass deportation of the Cubans was deemed an acceptable option. Abraham Ribicoff advocated for more federal resources to be funneled into Miami. The Health, Education, and Welfare secretary believed it was the most efficient way to manage the situation.[57] The Senate Judiciary Committee on immigration affairs, however, represented the more widespread position that the federal government should foster the dispersal of many of the Cubans across the country and away from the powder keg of Miami.[58] Only a better commitment to resettling Cubans outside Miami, it was argued, would alleviate the situation.[59] Although Ribicoff was "cool to the idea," the dispersal plan ultimately won out.[60]

In certain ways the consensus solution that arose echoed the precedent set for post-World War II refugee resettlement by the Displaced Persons Program a decade and a half earlier. If successful, the dispersal approach would expose Cubans to far greater employment and housing opportunities than existed in and around "Little Havana." It held the promise that a possibly much larger portion of the exile population could become self-sufficient than if nearly all remained in Miami. This had also been a core rationale for the earlier attempts of America's hybrid refugee aid networks to resettle the displaced persons and other postwar refugees away from the cities where the immigrants would have otherwise chosen to settle. In fact, since the early twentieth century, observers of refugee affairs throughout the West had frequently advocated sending the displaced to more sparsely populated areas around specific countries, and even around the globe, as a viable solution to "overpopulation." The specter of needy newcomers congregating in already densely occupied locales had commonly exacerbated charges that the refugees were unfairly taxing an area's available pool of jobs, housing, and other community resources. The sheer numbers of Cuban refugees concentrated in a single metropolitan area made the Cuban situation particularly challenging, especially when compared with earlier influxes of refugees into the United States since the 1930s.[61]

If the impetus for dispersing earlier groups of refugees reverberated with the Cuban situation, there was considerably less resonance between past and present when it came to actually implementing a plan. Before being granted an immigration visa, the displaced persons had had to promise to abide by the resettlement plan arranged for them by one of the licensed voluntary agencies or the federal committee overseeing the program. The Poles working in Louisiana sugar cane fields would have, we can assume, preferred to have landed in Chicago, but they were not given that option. The Hungarians at Camp Kilmer were typically required to accept similar arrangements before being permitted to leave that military base. But the Cuban asylees were already living in their American city of choice. How could they be convinced to leave Miami for other American communities? It was patently clear that the vast majority of Cubans were vigorously resistant to leaving Miami, with its familiar climate and close proximity to a Cuba that many continued to believe would rid itself of Castro before long.

The plan that ultimately emerged for implementing the program of refugee dispersal took strong cues both from earlier refugee programs that relied so heavily on the voluntary agencies and the more recent model begun with the federal government's foray into the field of refugee welfare support. It offered another piece of evidence that, while the decades-old link would remain between the federal government's acquiescence to refugees' presence in the United States and an institutional guarantee for their welfare, this admissions-resettlement connection took on a new look with the Cuban crisis. In the fall of 1961, the Department of Health, Education, and Welfare announced that it would begin systematically giving cash inducements to refugees willing to leave Miami. It expanded the program considerably the following May. As with the emergence of the federal welfare program in Miami the previous February, this was an unprecedented step. Yet the voluntary agencies would not be left out of the picture. Having been pushed somewhat to the side of refugee aid efforts in Miami, the voluntary agencies entered the center of the frame once again, as they had so regularly over the previous decades. The agencies, it was announced, would be responsible for locating suitable jobs, for housing, and for overall commitments from their affiliated local congregations and charities for the willing refugees before they would be asked to embark for their new communities. This arrangement not only revived the hybrid approach to governing refugee affairs developed in previous decades. It was itself a hybrid product of the recent program in Miami and the older tradition of refugee resettlement in the United States. While the federal government would, as it had in Miami, earmark specific funds to help the refugees adjust to life in their host country, unlike the situation in Miami, those funds would not be channeled through the local and state *public* welfare bureaus. Instead, they would be given to the voluntary agencies as intermediary institutions, which would then pass the funds on to the refugees as a part of their new resettlement assistance packages.[62]

Why did HEW not follow more closely the model it had implemented in

Miami for the rest of the country? The answer lay less with high political ideals or a noble sense of obligation to the federal government's longtime private partners in refugee resettlement programs than it did with limited governing options. No public institution possessed the capacity and the connections to perform this task, one national in scope and requiring tight relationships with myriad localities. The voluntary agencies, on the other hand, boasted nearly countless chains of connections from their national headquarters, and even international headquarters, to the many thousands of local churches, synagogues, private social service agencies, and nationality services scattered across the country. Those local organizations, in turn, claimed many further associations with their respective community's employers, co-religionists, and other individuals and families interested in helping the Cuban refugees make a life for themselves—whether temporary or longer term—away from the gathering maelstrom in Miami.

What had been a trickle of Cubans leaving Miami for other parts of the country soon grew to hundreds, and sometimes even thousands, leaving each month. While Miami remained the epicenter of America's Cuban community, this development critically eased the pressure on the city by dispersing tens of thousands of Cuban refugees around the country. It also made the voluntary agencies centrally relevant once again to the governance of refugee resettlement in what was fast becoming the largest domestic refugee program the United States had yet seen.[63] These developments not only signaled well ahead of the 1966 status adjustment law that the Cubans were beginning to be considered more as a settled immigrant population than a temporary group of asylees ready to return home upon Castro's fall.[64] They represented as well a wider sea change in American refugee affairs, a dramatic departure from the relationship between what had long been the operational heart and soul of America's diffuse resettlement network, the voluntary agencies, and a state largely willing to commit only relatively limited resources to refugees' adjustment in the United States. As a significant portion of the relationship between the two sectors began running along fiscal lines, the voluntary agencies effectively became contractors for the state, a dynamic that would come to increasingly define the nature of American refugee resettlement policies in the future. Whereas previous groups of refugees had been allowed to enter and remain in the United States because no or few public resources would be required to sustain them, the large influx of Cubans was ultimately sustained by the federal government stepping forward to guarantee their welfare.

*   *   *

Figure 10. U.S. Coast Guard Official Photo. "A Cuban Woman, Carrying a statue of Christ, is helped aboard by a Coast Guard [official]," November 26, 1965. Records of the United States Coast Guard. RG 26-G. NARA, B 101, F AA.

The decision by U.S. authorities shortly after Castro's rise to power to begin providing legal sanctuary to thousands of Cubans has come to be understood in both popular memory and historical scholarship as not only a signal marker of Cold War gamesmanship, but also as a turning point in American immigration affairs. Building up steam beginning with the Displaced Persons Program, a logic emerged to make special room for large numbers of European immigrants on political grounds. If their persecutors or alleged would-be persecutors were America's adversaries—namely, communist—then they might be granted admission to the United States outside mainstream immigration law. If their persecutors were not the enemy of the U.S. government, on the other hand, then they were subject to the rigid immigration quotas of America's national origins system. As discriminatory as this system often was—so frequently divorced from the ideals of neutral, universal humanitarianism frequently employed to justify it—it nevertheless allowed hundreds of thousands of downtrodden Central, Eastern, and Southern Europeans to enter the United States when considerable cultural and legal forces would otherwise have often spelled their exclusion. Before the late 1950s the Cold War-driven logic of U.S. refugee admissions policies had been almost entirely a European affair. Whereas the Cuban Refugee Program broke that particular trend—a critically important development—the political rationales of American refugee admissions policies remained remarkably wedded to the past, informed by a Cold War framework until the conflict finally ended at the dawn of the 1990s. Even when, beginning in the 1970s, *human rights* emerged as a justification for why the country should or did admit certain refugees, the large majority of those admitted to the United States as persecuted refugees fled communist regimes. Only exceptionally did they gain legal entry as refugees when claiming persecution by American allies.[65]

The ways in which Cuban refugees were offered institutional assistance after gaining admission, however, reveals another part of the story, one defined more by an abrupt shift than by continuity. The Cuban Refugee Program, that is, bequeathed an even more original legacy to American refugee affairs than has been typically considered. The Cold War logic of refugee admissions to the United States did not, after all, emerge with the Cuban crisis, but rather in Europe shortly after World War II. The most significant and resilient innovation of the Cuban Program, then, might arguably be considered the reordering of the relationships between state and non-state institutions on the one hand, and between those institutions and the refugees on the other.

The massive arrival of Cuban asylees directly on U.S. soil joined with anti-communist geopolitics to produce an environment where the dramatic expansion of domestic public refugee assistance to the exiles seemed not only politically possible for the first time, but also critically important. That growth in domestic federal aid, in turn, allowed the foreign policy imperative of admitting large numbers of exiles from Castro's Cuba to proceed. Foreign and domestic policy developments fueled one another along a chain on which federal governing capacity grew, sometimes into the realms previously occupied by nongovernmental institutions. In the process the federal government assumed unprecedented degrees of responsibility for a large and internationally conspicuous group of aliens on its soil.

The story is more complicated, however, than the public co-option of responsibilities and endeavors previously claimed by non-state entities. Federal resettlement dollars allowed the voluntary agencies to induce far more

Cubans to move away from Miami than would have gone otherwise, thereby considerably increasing the agencies' opportunities to ply their trade. The private agencies furthermore retained a significant amount of on-the-ground contact with the exiles themselves, whether around the Miami area or beyond it. Instead of withering as it appeared they might before the federal government intervened in early 1961, they were able to grow and thrive in future decades, effectively lobbying the government for general immigration reform—which came in 1965—and various future political refugee programs. The policy of the federal government contracting through the voluntary agencies for domestic refugee support not only continued for years with Cuban refugee policy, but was also applied in the 1970s to other admitted refugee groups, most prominently hundreds of thousands of Indochinese in the wake of the U.S.-Vietnam War.[66] These ad hoc and scattered policies were enshrined in legislation in 1980 as the country's first unified and rationalized refugee law.[67] The emergence and maturation of the Cuban Refugee Program thus retained some decades-old elements of American refugee affairs while considerably altering others. Voluntary agencies and the state sustained an associational partnership wherein the old link endured between a refugee's right to be present and institutional guarantees for his or her welfare. The new balance struck in the 1960s between the responsibilities of the state and civil society organizations would vacillate in the coming decades, but the federal government remained central to the field of domestic refugee welfare into the twenty-first century. As elaborated in the Epilogue, the model set by the Cuban program continued in no small measure because many more Cubans continued to arrive in the United States into the 1980s. Their physical presence alone placed ample pressure on the state to continue its support of them. But so, too, did an ever more powerfully entrenched lobby, consisting not only of the Cuban American community itself, but also of various public officials, representing both Florida and Miami, who between them bristled at the prospect of losing the significant federal funds that had been flowing their way. As had been the case for decades, American refugee affairs continued to be informed at least as much by politics and institutional arrangements as they were by human need.

Epilogue

The end of the Vietnam War helped to usher in many innovations in the way the United States would address refugee crises and related episodes of human dispossession wrought by violence, persecution, and political upheaval, but the ensuing four decades also demonstrated that that new initiatives were commonly built on older foundations. One such area marked by both persistence and change was the fiscal role assumed by the federal government for refugee resettlement, a role begun in earnest during the early 1960s to address the Cuban exodus. By 1967, as Cuban immigration ramped up again after a lull, over one quarter of a billion dollars had been spent to help the refugees adjust to life in the United States.[1] Cubans occupied public welfare rolls at increasingly higher rates in the ensuing years until reaching a peak in 1973, triggering alarm bells in American politics along the way.[2] By the later 1970s, approximately one billion dollars in federal funds were being spent annually on refugee resettlement, primarily on Cubans, Soviet Jews, and Indochinese.[3]

Even though the state's fiscal role in domestic refugee welfare had proven durable, the terms of that commitment would nevertheless evolve over the coming decades according to shifting political currents, with the federal government at some times expanding its commitment to refugees in the country, and at other times reducing its support. Likewise, the tight if often strained collaboration between the state and non-state agencies in the management of humanitarian crises simultaneously endured and evolved, tracing thick roots to the two world wars for international projects, and to the Great Depression and post-World War II eras with regard to the fusion of refugee admissions and organized resettlement. And though human rights assumed a significant new role in American refugee affairs (and much else) beginning in the 1970s, human rights operated alongside and within well-established traditions of humanitarian duty *sans* rights, the latter having been long interwoven with diverse strands of geopolitics, domestic politics, and cultural solidarities to produce a tapestry of American-led aid initiatives on behalf of select groups of the world's vulnerable people.

Certain changes in the past few decades, however, have been less equivocal. Starting with the arrival of one third of one million Indochinese during the last half of the 1970s, persons boasting European ancestry and racialized as white would no longer dominate the demographic composition of refugees admitted to the United States.[4] In a related development, beginning in the 1990s and picking up steam in the 2000s, new refugee arrivals have been represented increasingly by persons hailing from a much wider array of regions and nation-states than previously. Eventually, no one or two groups comprised the majority of entrants. Helping to animate these developments, American refugee policy has in recent decades more firmly embraced international humanitarian norms and principles of cultural pluralism than it had before, albeit with a legion of inconsistencies. These changes have helped cause the United States to offer refuge to a far wider range of vulnerable persons than previously witnessed, a trend echoed in the diversification and broadening of immigration to the country since the 1965 Immigration and Nationality Act.

Yet the effects of these changes have not always been to the benefit of the refugee immigrants. In decades past, most refugees admitted to the United States regularly enjoyed the dual benefits of, on the one hand, Cold War imperatives that valued narratives of refugees leading better lives in the United States than under communism and, on the other hand, well-established American ethnic communities moved by cultural affinities to help the newcomers adjust to their new lives. With both phenomena no longer animating American refugee advocacy as they once did, a series of other contributors have filled the void, including human rights politics and norms, more formalized collaborations between the American government and UN refugee operations, and refigured American foreign policies. Much as refugees and their advocates have welcomed these changes, this latter cluster of imperatives may have produced a more diffuse and ultimately weaker network of support for refugees, as those refugees continue to struggle against considerable obstacles to resettle comfortably and prosperously in their new homeland. This dynamic has been made even more challenging by anti-public-welfare politics and the effects of the attacks of September 11, 2001.

As the U.S.-allied governments in South Vietnam, Cambodia, and Laos fell to communist adversaries in the spring of 1975, the Ford administration responded to the ensuing humanitarian crisis in late April by committing the American government to the evacuation of up to two hundred thousand persons fleeing the victorious regimes, promising that they would eventually be paroled into the United States The U.S. mission in Geneva worked concurrently with the UN High Commissioner for Refugees (UNHCR) and the Intergovernmental Committee for European Migration to solicit resettlement offers from other countries. While twenty nations eventually volunteered (in an acknowledgment of America's central role in the region's conflicts) the United States nevertheless assumed most of the responsibility for managing the crisis. This assumption included direct assistance for overseas relief and domestic resettlement, as well as financing UNHCR operations in the refugee camps abroad.[5]

On May 23, Congress created, through the passage of the Indochina Migration and Refugee Assistance Act, the first of many funding streams targeted specifically for Indochinese refugee aid. The legislation appropriated $305 million to the State Department for transporting the refugees to camps fast emerging to handle the exodus throughout the region, an exodus that would eventually include Thailand, Guam, Indonesia, the Philippines, Malaysia, Singapore, Japan, and China.[6] Government funds would also be used to take the refugees to the U.S. mainland where, in an arrangement reminiscent of Camp Kilmer during the Hungarian refugee program of the 1950s, the refugees would stay in four U.S. military bases before the bases closed at the end of 1975.[7]

After further resettlement processing, medical attention, and preparation for life in the United States, the refugees were taken from the camps to their pre-arranged communities of resettlement, represented in all fifty states. Echoed, in various forms, since the later 1940s—with less formal patterns beginning in the 1930s—the resettlement process was primarily coordinated by the voluntary agencies licensed through the federal government. The 1975 law also gave the Department of Health, Education, and Welfare $100 million to facilitate the resettlement activities, largely by contracting services from the voluntary agencies and reimbursing states for public welfare services that the refugees were entitled to receive. Mirroring the Cuban Refugee Program, states received 100 percent reimbursement from the federal government for costs incurred by those refugees eligible for major public welfare programs, with Medicaid and Aid to Families with Dependent Children (AFDC) being the primary programs. As with the roughly two thirds of one million Cubans who had continued arriving on American shores over the previous decade and a half, states were reimbursed for the Indochinese refugees at much higher rates than were U.S. citizens and other resident aliens. The policy rested on the logic that, because Washington had admitted large numbers of persons expected to require high levels of organized assistance before becoming self-supporting, the refugees were accordingly the responsibility of the national government. Also similar to Cuban refugee operations, separate and parallel federally funded cash and medical welfare programs were made available to those needy Indochinese refugees who, because of family composition or age, were not eligible for the mainstream public welfare programs.[8] Also echoing past challenges with resettlement, voluntary and government personnel continued to butt heads over divisions of responsibility, while unappealing and sometimes deeply exploitative resettlement arrangements prompted some refugees to threaten voluntary repatriation.[9]

Much like the Cuban refugee situation, the continued exodus of massive numbers of refugees from Indochina extended and expanded the U.S. response much longer than most observers initially imagined. Aside from a six-month lapse in funding for Indochinese resettlement in 1977 and 1978, the U.S. government committed significant resources through welfare support and ten separate executive-branch parole programs that, between them, admitted over three hundred fifty thousand Indochinese to the United States in the first five years after the war. By 1990, one million Indochinese lived in the United States, comprising six hundred fifty thousand Vietnamese, two hundred thousand Laotians (many of them Hmong minorities), and one hundred fifty thousand Cambodians. Most of the newcomers arrived outside mainstream immigration law, as refugees, but as the size and stability of Indochinese communities grew, increasing numbers entered through family reunification provisions in U.S. immigration law. Incorporation into the United States had been made smoother in 1977 when the refugees were—like the paroled Hungarians, Cubans, and others before them—made permanent resident aliens and put on a path to citizenship. The migrations continued into the twenty-first century, facilitated by special accommodations in those U.S. refugee admissions policies for persons hailing from an area where the United States had left in military defeat decades earlier.[10]

American efforts on behalf of Indochinese refugees borrowed much from the past, but significant differences were also in operation, differences that suggested the United States was in fact entering a new era of managing the world's dispossessed. Most notably, the conflicts of Southeast Asia served to stifle the triumphal message that had long linked American programs for the displaced and persecuted with justifications for the country's global exertions of power. In the words of one subsequent observer, "Indochinese refugees were the first allied aliens to arrive in the United States as the result of an American military defeat rather than an attempt by the United States to undermine an enemy state, [with] the refugee crises in Southeast Asia [being] burdens rather than benefits to the makers of U.S. foreign policy."[11] Even though realities emerging from their implementation complicated the intended political messages of previous American refugee programs, the goal among diverse groups of American refugee advocates since World War II had nevertheless been rather consistent: to prove to American and international audiences alike that the United States could, if only partially, nonetheless significantly justify its exertions of global power because it was a humane hegemon, a *benevolent* superpower. That is, the dispossessed falling under the country's philanthropic gaze were promised safer, freer, and more prosperous lives in the United States than they could have enjoyed in their former homelands ruled by America's adversaries. Even though America's international relief missions of the World War I era often lacked an immigration component to their accompanying message, those missions too had been heralded as evidence that the country's burgeoning international authority indeed rested on principles that the rest of the world would do well to emulate.

America's involvement in Vietnam, however, precluded any similar triumphalism, as hundreds of thousands of persons fled by land and sea for refuge across Southeast Asia. The war had served to shatter the anti-communist Cold War consensus that had dominated American politics since the later 1940s, leaving American refugee advocates in search of new and often ultimately less politically potent clusters of rationales to promote their cause. In this sense, a new era in the politics of American refugee governance emerged with the end of the Vietnam War even while the governance of aid programs pressed forward through many of the same grooves past endeavors had already carved.

Opposition to the refugee program emerged from a variety of sources. The deep controversy about the war itself produced something of a collective aversion to all things *Vietnam* across the political spectrum. This included traditional supporters of liberalized immigration like Democratic Senator George McGovern, who suggested that the refugees, "including the orphans and babies," would be "better off in Vietnam" despite warnings of retribution. A member of the general public asked why the United States would welcome the refugees when they had "made heroin addicts of our G.I.'s." Concerns over cultural diversity sometimes bled into blatant racism, as when one American complained that Indochinese women "breed like flies," adding "We have too many Orientals now. We are losing our national character."[12]

Garnering at least as much resentment toward the refugees as anything was the conviction that the newcomers put a strain on limited resources, especially jobs and public services. Again proving that opposition failed to cleave along normal political lines regarding immigration matters, civil rights leader Jesse Jackson betrayed a marked skepticism found in portions of American minority communities when he declared, "Keep them out—there are 9 million jobless in this nation." In California, where nearly one third of the refugees settled during the first five years of the program, Governor Jerry Brown lobbied Congress to ensure that the refugees would not take jobs from long-time residents, even refusing to send state officials to register the Vietnamese for employment. Challenged to land jobs, over half of the Indochinese refugees were dependent on public assistance in California by late 1975. By 1982, 80 percent of Indochinese refugees in the United States for one and a half years or less received public assistance, a dynamic that continued into future years. Writing in opposition to refugee admissions, one member of the general public echoed widespread resentment in warning that the refugees would "all wind up on relief, adding hundreds of millions to our tax burden." In 1980 alone, the Department of Justice's Community Relations Service reported thirty-two incidents of troubling clashes between the refugees and their American opponents, some turning violent.[13]

The refugees' popularity also suffered from their association with growing public discontentment with immigration more generally. The phenomenon was fueled especially by skyrocketing asylum claims beginning in the later 1970s (including thousands of Cubans arriving with the Mariel Boat Lift of 1980) and expanding populations of aliens in the United States without legal sanction (especially from Mexico). Also hurting the popularity of immigration was the fact that growing numbers of immigrants were arriving in the United States from non-European countries as a result of the immigration reforms of 1965. Representative Robert Sikes of Florida demonstrated that the country's historical experience with refugees could also inform Americans' resistance to newer immigrants, complaining that his state was already "stuffed full" of Cubans.[14]

If aid to the Indochinese refugees remained generally unpopular among the grassroots of American political culture, it found critical pockets of support among elites in both American civil society and government. Especially well represented among them were those who had played direct roles in the war, including journalists, members of the Ford and Carter White Houses, officials in the military and diplomatic wings of the federal government, and members of Congress. Carl Bon Tempo has observed that such supporters of Indochinese refugee aid were often motivated by "a keen sense of responsibility and guilt." The refugees were owed something from the United States, that is, because they had been America's allies, or at least victims of America's victorious enemies.[15]

Another important source of support for the refugee program came from those using an ascending discourse of human rights that, beginning in the earlier 1970s, had found increasing purchase among both the general public and government officials. This discourse demanded reforms to U.S. foreign policy that would place greater value than had previously been the case on the human effects of American actions around the world. Human rights rationales were often used differently by those persons on various parts of the political spectrum. Liberals tended to invoke human rights as a way to emphasize the need to reorient U.S. foreign policy away from a blind embrace of anti-communist regimes, no matter how oppressive those American allies were to their own people. Such a political formulation began to be mobilized in the earlier 1970s, for instance, to help secure the admission by 1977 of eleven hundred Chileans fleeing the oppressive regime of Augusto Pinochet after the U.S.-aided coup of 1973. The politics of human rights played a notable role in altering, slightly but significantly, the decades-old calculus of U.S. refugee admissions, a calculus that equated "admissible refugee" exclusively with someone fleeing communist regimes. Whereas human rights politics did not resonate as widely on the political right as they did on the left, such politics nonetheless found supporters there too. These supporters included a growing cadre of neoconservatives, who deployed a version of human rights politics intended to revivify and reorient Cold War rivalries through pointing the spotlight on the human rights abuses perpetrated by America's communist enemies. Human rights rationales were part of a range of tactics used to pressure the Soviet Union to allow thirty thousand Soviet Jews to enter the United States as refugees during the 1970s, with tens of thousands more Jews emigrating to Israel and other countries. And so, when Americans argued that the United States had a moral responsibility to assist Indochinese refugees because the latter had been victims of human rights abuses, they engaged in a broader, vibrant, and malleable discourse about refugee affairs and much else in the American political milieu of the 1970s.[16]

By 1980, such streams of support helped to secure the admission of roughly six hundred sixty-six thousand Indochinese refugees into the United States, the peak of Indochinese migration both before and since.[17] As it became clear that the Indochinese refugee program would indeed represent more than a one-time response to a short-term crisis, pressure mounted from various spots on the American political terrain to rationalize a disparate field of ad-hoc refugee programs under a single policy umbrella. After over a year of debate, in March 1980, Congress passed the country's first ever comprehensive refugee law. Shepherded through the process by a bipartisan group of legislators, one that included such prominent senators as Ted Kennedy and Robert Dole, the Refugee Act of 1980 aimed to address both the admissions and resettlement sides of U.S. refugee law. As for the former, the law was designed to give Congress a much larger role regarding which and how many refugees the country admitted each year. For nearly a quarter century, since the Hungarian refugee program of 1956 and 1957, refugees had been admitted overwhelmingly through the will of the executive branch, primarily via the Attorney General's parole authority. The new law required that the presidential administration collaborate with the judiciary committees of Congress to determine the goals for each coming year's admissions, in terms of those countries and regions from which admitted refugees should hail, as well as the numbers to be admitted. (The 1980 act capped the annual quota at fifty thousand persons, though the actual annual quota proved higher than that in many of the coming years.) This reform was also justified as allowing Congress to give its implicit consent to fund the refugees' resettlement based on admissions numbers that it helped to determine. Though the law articulated various preferences, ones that included persons for whom American foreign policy held a particular humanitarian interest, it also broke new ground in explicitly committing the United States to reserve a considerable portion of refugee admissions to those nationals who had a reasonable fear of persecution regardless of geographical origin or whether the country from which they fled was ruled by a communist government. This provision nominally placed U.S. refugee law much more in line with those international norms spawning especially from the UN 1951 Refugee Convention and its 1967 Protocol.[18]

Regarding resettlement, the law decreed that a single program replace the various separate ones for distinct refugee communities. During Congressional debates, much was made of the fact that different refugee groups were offered different levels of federal funding for resettlement. Soviet Jews, for instance, were eligible for $1,100 in federal funds per month if a voluntary agency matched the amount, which the well funded and professionally operated

Jewish resettlement network frequently did, bringing the possible total amount to $2,200. Indochinese refugees, on the other hand, were offered only $500 per month from the federal government, with no requirement for a voluntary agency to match it. As the strikingly differing levels of support given to refugees from different voluntary agencies created considerable resentment among refugees, such divergent federal funding policies only made matters worse. Indochinese refugees, for instance, had learned to seek out affiliation with certain voluntary agencies while avoiding others, as the amount of initial "pocket cash" each agency gave varied from $5 to $110. Additionally, certain members of Congress had grown alarmed at the granting of recurring extensions of federal aid for resettlement. Even though the Department of Health, Education and Welfare (HEW) began recommending in 1974 that the federal government stop fully reimbursing state welfare coffers (namely, Florida's) for Cubans on AFDC and Medicaid, vigorous pressure by Florida officials and certain politicians in Congress time and again thwarted the HEW request. With hundreds of millions of dollars having been spent on Cuban refugees since 1961, in 1976, HEW pressed its case further with statistics showing that, since 1970, the income gap between Cuban refugees and other Florida residents had been cut in half, with Cubans earning only 20 percent less per capita income than non-Cubans in Florida by the mid-1970s. HEW predicted that the number would be sharply reduced further in the following three to five years.[19]

Congress's persistent refusal to end or reduce federal support for the Cuban resettlement program, even two decades after the revolution and in the face of HEW's evidence, helped to convince many persons that limits on such support be formalized in law for all refugees admitted to the country. The Indochinese resettlement program looked similarly set to be extended in perpetuity, a concern exacerbated by the fact that a surprisingly high rate of Indochinese—often arriving in especially bad physical and emotional condition and with relatively few linguistic and cultural tools to help them adjust to life in America—were staying on public assistance for extended periods of time. The 1980 act accordingly tied federal resettlement funding (primarily flowing to the voluntary agencies and states, as before) to individual refugees, and thus no longer to a particular refugee group and its attendant refugee aid program. Funding ended three years after arrival in an attempt both to reduce federal costs and encourage refugees to become self-sufficient.[20]

In the decade following the passage of the 1980 Refugee Act, the law accomplished some of the goals behind it while straying from others. Most refugee admissions during the 1980s occurred, as the law dictated, through the annual quotas and demographic distributions determined through deliberations between Congress and the executive branch. This said, the law said relatively little about how the executive branch should handle asylum claims, the effects of which were felt almost immediately as the Carter White House admitted one hundred twenty-five thousand Cuban Marieletos in 1980 with little consultation with Congress. Similarly, though the Refugee Act dictated that admissions decisions respect international norms that defined refugees as persons with a genuine fear of persecution regardless whether the country from which they had fled was communist, the overwhelming portion of refugees and asylees admitted to the United States during the 1980s nevertheless fled the communist regimes of America's enemies. The largest portion of refugees hailed from Indochina with those from Cuba and the Soviet bloc trailing not far behind. Meanwhile, receiving much smaller quota allotments were many persecuted persons from non-communist states in Africa, the Middle East, the Caribbean, and Central and South America. Though Ted Kennedy and other liberals had hoped that the Refugee Act would help to move U.S. foreign policy past what they considered the debilitating constraints of the Cold War, the Reagan administration and Cold Warriors in Congress had other ideas.[21]

While the 1980 law made federal aid to refugees more consistently about individual and familial need than about the particular group to which a refugee belonged, the new resettlement policies still produced confusing variation among the resettlement support refugees received. As the law dictated, newly arrived refugees were indeed folded into the same resettlement scheme with regard to the amount of federal aid dedicated to each. But these levels depended on the rules governing welfare eligibility in the states and localities where refugees were initially resettled. Also important was the voluntary agency assigned to each refugee, especially the organization's particular resource base, level of professionalism, and overall approach to its work.[22]

However, the overall commitment of the federal government to refugees' welfare began a steady and determined retreat shortly after passage. The large proportions of refugees requiring institutional assistance—and more to the point, the attendant publicity surrounding this phenomenon—had the effect of refugees becoming linked, in political discourse, to the growing unpopularity of public welfare witnessed in America in the 1980s. The latter developments, in turn, were part of a broader assault on what many on the right perceived as among the fiscal and regulatory overreaches of the federal government, overreaches they contended had started with the New Deal. As poor refugees became increasingly stigmatized alongside U.S. citizens and other immigrants on welfare rolls, whatever advantages certain refugees may have once enjoyed through their identification with American geopolitical imperatives began to wane. In an early sign of a trend in Congress to tighten the government's fiscal belt while moving refugees more quickly to self-sufficiency, in 1982 Congress overturned a specific provision in the 1980 Refugee Act, one that allowed refugees a grace period during their first sixty days in the United States before having to register for work with a local employment agency. The same year, Congress passed another revision of the 1980 law, that cut in half the amount of time that refugees could receive medical and cash assistance—specifically, from three years to eighteen months, for those persons ineligible for similar mainstream welfare programs because of family composition or age. In 1991, the time permitted was further cut to eight months. By the mid-1980s, concern over the high rates of refugees on welfare threatened to stifle admissions. In 1986, Congress reduced the time period in which the government reimbursed states for those refugees who were on AFDC and Medicaid at a higher rate than other residents from the original thirty-six months to thirty-one. (That higher rate was 100 percent.) Such reimbursement would continue to be whittled down throughout the decade, with states receiving no additional reimbursement at all for refugees by the early 1990s.[23]

Not every person supported the changes. California representative Gary Condit called the cuts "unconscionable" because of the toll they would take on refugees in dire need of welfare assistance. Echoing frustration felt by officials and voluntary agency personnel across the country, California's director of the state's social services bureau accused the federal government of shirking the responsibility it assumed for admitted refugees in the 1980 act, predicting that the trend would "eat away public support for the refugee program."[24]

Properly historicizing American refugee affairs of the 1990s and early twenty-first century in the longer narrative arc of the twentieth century awaits deeper analysis accompanied by the critical historical distance the passage of time affords, but several preliminary observations can still be offered. Among them, from the 1990s through the early twenty-first century, the federal government has, generally speaking, continued to assume considerably less responsibility for refugees' welfare than the architects of the 1980 law had envisioned. Though the Office of Refugee Resettlement, housed within the Department of Health and Human Services, has funded a range of services for refugee immigrants—services that include English classes, job training, and preventative health—it has continued nevertheless to reimburse states for the country's primary public cash and medical welfare programs only at the rates of other residents.[25]

Such policies meant that refugee aid services were hit further by cuts to welfare programs across the board with the passage of the Personal Responsibility and Work Opportunity Act in 1996. The federal support funneled to the voluntary agencies by the Department of State's Reception and Placement Program, for helping refugees adjust to life in the United States, declined steadily versus inflation until the Obama administration reversed the decline in 2010. A 2008 study conducted by the Lutheran Immigration and Refugee Service (LIRS) showed that only 39 percent of the services required by RPP were included in federal reimbursements. The rest of the funding came from in-kind donations, voluntary work, and direct payment from the budget of LIRS. It was an arrangement that would likely not have seemed onerous before the federal government's relationship with the voluntary agencies became fixed along a regulatory and fiscal basis, a shift that had begun in the early 1960s during the Cuban Refugee Program. The across-the-board "sequestration" budget cuts of 2013 further reduced federal funding to voluntary agencies and state and local governments for refugee aid programs, forcing the closure of affiliated offices in communities across the country. The 2015 federal budget for resettling refugees in the United States was set at $1.6 billion, a figure that would have stunned Dwight Eisenhower and many others overseeing domestic refugee aid programs in earlier decades, but that number is in fact estimated to account for only about one-tenth of the amount spent by states, municipalities, and voluntary agencies on refugees in the United States.[26] And yet, a wide spectrum of voices, from those persons supporting and opposing restrictions on admissions, has continued to insist that many refugees fail to receive nearly the level of institutional assistance they need to help build prosperous, fulfilling, and independent lives for themselves in the United States. Poverty and dependence have been recurrent markers of some refugee communities even while others have successfully established themselves. The Great Recession that began in 2007 and 2008 caused unemployment among refugees to skyrocket, creating additional burdens on the already strained resources of their respective communities. In reaction, state and local governments threatened to put moratoria on refugee resettlement, while federal officials reduced the number of annual refugee admissions from earlier projections.[27]

This last point serves as a reminder that the viability of robust refugee admissions continues to rest considerably on the prospect that refugee immigrants should be able to adjust successfully to life in America without taxing the country's resources beyond what evolving political climates permit. In this sense, the move of U.S. refugee admissions policies away from Cold War rationales toward international humanitarian norms, based on more neutral calculations of need, may have ironically served to weaken support both for aid to refugee communities within the United States and for larger admissions. The development emerged slowly, as the first decade after the Cold War failed to revolutionize U.S. refugee admissions policies on a post-Cold-War basis. Approximately three-quarters of the refugees admitted to the United States during the 1990s hailed from the former Soviet sphere and Indochina, while relatively paltry proportions were allotted for those persons from other parts of the world who were also experiencing pronounced dislocations. By the later 1990s, however, the refugee admission recommendations, produced jointly by the State Department and Congress, began to draw significantly from the list of resettle-able refugees around the world as determined by the UNHCR each year. Even while U.S. foreign policy continues to color the national and regional composition of admitted refugees, the increased reliance on international recommendations has had a profoundly diversifying effect on the demographic composition of refugees resettling in the United States. In recent years, refugees legally arriving in the United States regularly hail from over sixty countries across the globe. Even though the terrorist attacks of September 11, 2001, reduced significantly admissions of refugees coming from predominantly Muslim countries—and for several years, reduced overall admissions as well—by the end of the decade over one quarter of admitted refugees arrived from such nation-states. What is more, although other countries shoulder the profound burden of harboring far more asylees from violent dislocation and persecution, the United States has nevertheless continued to accept far more refugees for permanent resettlement than has any other refugee-receiving country. Since 1994, for instance, it has accepted more refugees than the other thirty-three countries in the Organisation for Economic Co-Operation and Development combined.[28]

Such a phenomenon of course has been understandably welcomed by many refugee advocates, and more importantly, has served as a lifeline for many thousands of refugees, but it seems to have come at a cost as well. Though the climate of the Cold War long prompted the United States to ignore the plight of the dispossessed when the perpetrators of that plight were not communist, Cold War politics specifically also served to mobilize critical degrees of support for refugees when further admissions were threatened. Even with the country's turmoil over the Vietnam War, hundreds of thousands of Indochinese were still allowed entry rather than returned to countries ruled by communist governments. As a telling counterpoint from the first half of the 2010s, while camps overseas have swelled with refugees from the turmoil wrought by America's recent wars, comparatively small numbers of Iraqis and Afghanis have been welcomed to the United States. Similarly, while the geographical, racial, and religious diversity of recent refugee arrivals speaks well of modern American principles of democratic openness and cultural pluralism, most refugees lack influential, broad bases of support among American communities that ethnically European predecessors of today's refugees enjoyed. Refugee communities in the early twenty-first century rarely benefit from similar solidarity by large and well-established American groups to help sustain them over both the short and long terms. Exceptions do exist, certainly, and especially among groups of refugees admitted in larger numbers, for longer periods, or from more developed regions in the world. But overall, the political climate and demographics that inform American refugee affairs in recent times seem to have diluted the depth of advocacy that earlier generations of refugees often enjoyed.

This dynamic informed American public discourse beginning in late summer 2015 as hundreds of thousands of Syrians fleeing their country's four-year civil war moved steadily westward across the borders of European states. With European Union countries initially contemplating taking one hundred sixty thousand—and Germany, on its own, agreeing to an additional eight hundred thousand over the next year—Americans began debating what their nation should do about the crisis. When President Barak Obama announced that his administration would ask Congress to admit approximately ten thousand Syrians during the next fiscal year, the reaction varied widely. Conservative columnist Jonah Goldberg acknowledged that he owed his life in America—if not his very life—to the fact that his recent ancestors had been able to escape the Russian pogroms a century or more earlier. Additionally, his "wife's father was a refugee from the Communists. And yet," Goldberg wondered, echoing the sentiments of many American opponents of Syrian immigration, "where does it end?"[29]

While many opponents of Syrian admissions unsurprisingly raised concerns made commonplace since the attacks of 2001 that a liberalized policy for the Syrians would threaten national security, Goldberg and others argued that the situation must also be viewed through an economic lens. In response to the crisis, representative Brian Babin of Texas introduced a bill to halt all future refugee resettlement until the Government Accountability Office released the full costs of refugee aid to the country. Though Babin's bill had few initial prospects of passing, it also seemed clear that those favoring a more generous program for this latest group of refugees no longer possessed the political firepower their predecessors commanded in the aftermath of the Second World War and Cold War. While some public officials had responded to Obama's proposal by suggesting that the United States should take one hundred thousand of the Syrian refugees in the upcoming year, their chances of success seemed slim considering the political environment. After four years of war and countless atrocities visited upon the Syrian people, millions of whom had been fleeing for some time, the United States had resettled fewer than fifteen hundred Syrian refugees by the time of Obama's announcement in 2015.[30]

While proponents of more robust refugee admissions used often powerfully articulated human rights rationales to justify a policy change, various factors once again pushed against their goal. First, the would-be refugee immigrants from Syria boasted no significant group of national comrades in the United States to vigorously advocate on their behalf. Second, political imperatives that had once driven Americans to support refugee programs they believed would convince the world of the country's benevolence still existed, but seemingly in a less vigorous state. The prospects for increased admissions diminished further beginning in late 2015 when extremists tied to the group calling itself the Islamic State launched attacks in Paris and San Bernardino, California. The voices of support for some of the world's most desperate refugees sounded faint amid renewed cries to keep them out of the United States.[31]

Such observations surely do not suggest, however, that America's concern for the dispossessed should return to periods when geopolitics and domestic political culture meant that the overwhelming proportion of persons the country assisted suffered only at the hands of America's enemies and, until the Indochinese program, boasted European ancestry. Rather, the history of those developments, for all its problems, shows that America's interests were frequently best served when the country tapped into its genuinely benevolent impulses on behalf of the world's "tired . . . poor . . . huddled masses, yearning to breathe free."[32] If the American people still want to justify their country's enormous authority around the globe at least partially through a claim that they are genuinely interested in improving the lot of the world's most vulnerable, they might do well to deepen their feelings of solidarity even as they broaden them.

ACID   American Committee for Italian Democracy
ACNS   American Council for Nationalities Service
AFII   American Federation of International Institutes
AFDC   Aid to Families with Dependent Children
AFSC   American Friends Service Committee
AICC   American Immigration and Citizenship Conference
AME   African Methodist Episcopal
APD   American Political Development
ARA   American Relief Administration (as proposed American Refu-
           gees Administration)
ARC   American Red Cross
CARE   Cooperative for Assistance and Relief Everywhere
CRB   Commission for Relief in Belgium
CWS   Church World Service
DHEW   or HEW Department of Health, Education, and Welfare
DP   displaced person
DPC   Displaced Persons Commission
ECOSOC   Economic and Social Council (UN)
ERB   Emergency Relief Bureau
FRUS   Foreign Relations of the United States
IGCR   Intergovernmental Committee on Refugees
JDC   Joint Distribution Committee
HIAS   Hebrew Immigrant Aid Society
IATF   Interagency Task Force for Indochinese Refugees
IIE   Institute of International Education
IRC   International Rescue Committee
IRO   International Refugee Organization
JWB   Jewish Welfare Board

LRS	Lutheran Resettlement Service
MID	Military Intelligence Division
NARA	National Archives and Records Administration
NATO	North Atlantic Treaty Organization
NCC	National Coordinating Committee
NCJW	National Council of Jewish Women
NGO	nongovernmental organization
NRS	National Refugee Service
OFRRO	Office of Foreign Relief and Rehabilitation Operations
PCWRA	President's Committee on War Relief Agencies
PRA	permanent resident alien
RRP	Refugee Relief Program
RWR	Russian War Relief
STFU	Southern Tenant Farmers Union
TANF	Temporary Assistance to Needy Families
TASS	*Telegrafnoye Agentstvo Sovetskogo Soyuza*, or, in English, Telegraph Agency of the Soviet Union
UHS	United HIAS Service
UNHCR	United Nations High Commissioner for Refugees
UNRRA	United Nations Relief and Rehabilitation Administration
U.S. AID	Agency for International Development
USFA	U.S. Food Administration
WPA	Works Progress Administration
WRCB	War Relief Control Board
YIVO	Yidisher Visnshaftlekher Institut
YMCA	Young Men's Christian Association
YWCA	Young Women's Christian Association

N O T E S

Introduction

1. Joseph Conforti, "David Brainerd and the Nineteenth Century Missionary Movement," *Journal of the Early Republic* 5 (1985): 314; Merle Curti, *American Philanthropy Abroad* (Rutgers, N.J.: Rutgers University Press, 1963), 138–74; Ian Tyrrell, *Reforming the World: The Creation of America's Moral Empire* (Princeton, N.J.: Princeton University Press, 2010), 191–92; Daniel Walker Howe, "The Evangelical Movement and Political Culture in the North During the Second Party System," *Journal of American History* 77 (1991): 1222–23.

2. Michael Barnett, *Empire of Humanity: A History of Humanitarianism* (Ithaca, N.Y.: Cornell University Press, 2011), 57–75; Curti, *American Philanthropy Abroad*, 138–223; Julia Irwin, *Making the World Safe: The American Red Cross and a Nation's Humanitarian Awakening* (New York: Oxford University Press, 2013), 13–34; Emily Rosenberg, *Spreading the American Dream: American Economic and Cultural Expansion, 1890–1945* (New York: Hill and Wang, 1982), 28–35; Tyrrell, *Reforming the World*, 98–120.

3. Whereas a long, vigorous, and interesting debate does exist over the application of the term "empire" to the United States, it is nonetheless not the purpose of this book to engage with it directly. Rather, as with "benevolent," the use of "empire" in the title is intended to frame a perpetual tension between actions simultaneously motivated by altruism and self-interest as performed imperfectly by Americans, Americans who were often ambivalent about their country's tremendous power in the world. On the issue of the United States as an empire, see, for example, Andrew Bacevich, *American Empire: The Realities and Consequences of U.S. Diplomacy* (Cambridge, Mass.: Harvard University Press, 2003); Charles Beard, *American Foreign Policy in the Making, 1932–1940* (New Haven, Conn.: Yale University Press, 1946); Mary Ann Glendon, *A World Made New: Eleanor Roosevelt and the Universal Declaration of Human Rights* (New York: Random House, 2001); David Grondin, "Mistaking Hegemony for Empire: Neoconservatives, the Bush Doctrine, and the Democratic Empire," *International Journal* 61 (2005/06): 227–41; Paul A. Kramer, *Blood of Government: Race, Empire, the United States, and the Philippines* (Chapel Hill: University of North Carolina Press, 2006); Mary A. Renda, *Taking Haiti: Military Occupation and the Culture of U.S. Imperialism, 1915–1940* (Chapel Hill: University of North Carolina Press, 2001); Eric P. Roorda, *The Dictator Next Door: The Good*

Neighbor Policy and the Trujillo Regime in the Dominican Republic, 1930–1945 (Durham, N.C.: Duke University Press, 1998); William Appleman Williams, *The Tragedy of American Diplomacy* (Cleveland: World, 1959).

4. For the best overview of the field to date, see Brian Balogh, *The Associational State: American Governance in the Twentieth Century* (Philadelphia: University of Pennsylvania Press, 2015), 1–22. Other intelligent, critical surveys of the field include Meg Jacobs and Julian E. Zelizer, "The Democratic Experiment: New Directions in American Political History," in *The Democratic Experiment: New Directions in American Political History*, ed. Meg Jacobs, William J. Novak, and Julian E. Zelizer (Princeton, N.J.: Princeton University Press, 2003), 1–19; Karen Orren and Stephen Skowronek, *The Search for American Political Development* (Cambridge: Cambridge University Press, 2004). For examples of scholarship exploring the "associational," "hidden," or "public-private" nature of American governing arrangements, as those arrangements have been called, see Elisabeth Clemens, "Lineages of the Rube Goldberg State: Building and Blurring Public Programs: 1900–1940," in *The Art of the State: Rethinking Political Institutions*, ed. Ian Shapiro, Stephen Skowronek, and Daniel Galvin (New York: New York University Press, 2006); Jacob Hacker, *The Divided Welfare State: The Battle over Public and Private Social Benefits in the United States* (New York: Cambridge University Press, 2002); Ellis W. Hawley, "The Discovery and Study of a 'Corporate Liberalism,'" *Business History Review* 52 (1978): 309–20; Christopher Howard, *The Hidden Welfare State: Tax Expenditures and Social Policy in the United States* (Princeton, N.J.: Princeton University Press, 1997); Michael B. Katz, *The Price of Citizenship: Redefining the American Welfare State* (New York: Metropolitan, 2001); Jennifer Klein, *For All These Rights: Business, Labor, and the Shaping of America's Public-Private Welfare State* (Princeton, N.J.: Princeton University Press, 2003); Andrew Morris, *The Limits of Voluntarism: Charity and Welfare from the New Deal Through the Great Society* (New York: Cambridge University Press, 2009); William J. Novak, "Public-Private Governance: A Historical Introduction," in *Government by Contract: Outsourcing and American Democracy*, ed. Jody Freeman and Martha L. Minow (Cambridge, Mass.: Harvard University Press, 2009); Emily Rosenberg, *Spreading the American Dream: American Economic and Cultural Expansion: 1890–1945* (New York: Hill and Wang, 1982).

5. The intellectual genealogy of the U.S. in the World field is thoughtfully considered in Erez Manela, "The United States in the World," in *American History Now*, ed. Eric Foner and Lisa McGirr (Philadelphia: Temple University Press, 2011), 201–20 (quotation 203). On the similarities through which the fields of diplomatic history and policy history revived themselves partially through the appropriation of intellectual trends produced in other fields of history, see Robert J. McMahon, "Diplomatic History and Policy History: Finding Common Ground," *Journal of Policy History* 17 (2005): 93–109. For examples of scholarship that explicitly connects the international and domestic dimensions of U.S. history, see Carol Elaine Anderson, *Eyes off the Prize: The United Nations and the African American Struggle for Human Rights, 1944–1954* (New York: Cambridge University Press, 2003); Elizabeth Borgwardt, *New Deal for the World America's Vision*

for Human Rights (Cambridge, Mass.: Belknap Press for Harvard University Press, 2005); Mary Dudziak, *Cold War Civil Rights: Race and the Image of American Democracy* (Princeton, N.J.: Princeton University Press, 2000); Jeremi Suri, *Power and Protest: Global Revolution and the Rise of Détente* (Cambridge, Mass.: Harvard University Press, 2003); Penny M. Von Eschen, *Race against Empire: Black Americans and Anticolonialism, 1937–1957* (Ithaca, N.Y.: Cornell University Press, 1997).

6. Christopher Capozzola, *Uncle Sam Wants You: World War I and the Making of the Modern American Citizen* (Oxford: Oxford University Press, 2008); Curti, *American Philanthropy Abroad*, 244–300; Ellis W. Hawley, *The Great War and the Search for Modern Order: A History of the American People and Their Institutions, 1917–1933* (Prospect Heights, Ill.: Waveland, 1992); Michael J. Hogan, "Corporatism: A Positive Appraisal," *Diplomatic History* 10 (1986): 363–72; Hogan, *Informal Entente: The Private Structure of Cooperation in Anglo-American Economic Diplomacy, 1918–1928* (Columbia: University of Missouri Press, 1977); Irwin, *Making the World Safe*; William E. Leuchtenburg, *Herbert Hoover: The American President; The 31st President, 1929–1933* (New York: Times Books, 2009); Thomas J. McCormick, "Drift or Mastery? A Corporatist Synthesis for American Diplomatic History," *Reviews in American History* 10 (1982): 318–30; Bertrand M. Patenaude, *The Big Show in Bololand: The American Relief Expedition to Soviet Russia in the Famine of 1921* (Stanford, Calif.: Stanford University Press, 2002); Rosenberg, *Spreading the American Dream*, 3–160; Tyrrell, *Reforming the World*, 189–226.

7. For a foundational elaboration of the concept, see Joseph S. Nye, *Bound to Lead: The Changing Nature of American Power* (New York: Basic, 1990).

8. Barnett, *Empire of Humanity*; Seyla Benhabib, *The Rights of Others: Aliens, Residents and Citizens* (Cambridge: Cambridge University Press, 2004), 2; Thomas L. Haskell, "The Curious Persistence of Rights Talk in the Age of Interpretation," *Journal of American History* 74 (1987): 984–1012; Lynn Hunt, *Inventing Human Rights: A History* (New York: Norton, 2007); Samuel Moyn, *The Last Utopia: Human Rights in History* (Cambridge, Mass.: Belknap Press of Harvard University Press, 2010); Judith N. Shklar, *The Faces of Injustice* (New Haven, Conn.: Yale University Press, 1990). Among the works addressing the promotion of American international authority through humanitarian projects and rationales, see Borgwardt, *A New Deal for the World*; Curti, *American Philanthropy Abroad*; David Ekbladh, *The Great American Mission: Modernization and the Construction of a World Order* (Princeton, N.J.: Princeton University Press, 2011); Irwin, *Making the World Safe*; Paul Gordon Lauren, *Power and Prejudice: The Politics of Diplomacy and Racial Discrimination* (Boulder, Colo.: Westview, 1988); Amanda McVety, *Enlightened Aid: U.S. Development as Foreign Policy in Ethiopia* (New York: Oxford University Press, 2012); Moyn, *The Last Utopia*.

9. Examples of the historiography on U.S. immigration include Robert A. Divine, *American Immigration Policy: 1924–1952* (New Haven, Conn.: Yale University Press, 1957); Keith Fitzgerald, *The Face of the Nation: Immigration, the State, and the National Identity* (Stanford, Calif.: Stanford University Press, 1996); E. P. Hutchinson, *Legislative History of American Immigration Policy: 1798–1956* (Philadelphia: University of

Pennsylvania Press, 1981); Desmond S. King, *Making Americans: Immigration, Race, and the Origins of Diverse Democracy* (Cambridge, Mass.: Harvard University Press, 2000); Mae Ngai, *Impossible Subjects: Illegal Aliens and the Making of Modern America* (Princeton, N.J.: Princeton University Press, 2004).

10. Carl Bon Tempo, *Americans at the Gate: The United States and Refugees During the Cold War* (Princeton, N.J.: Princeton University Press, 2008); Gil Loescher and John A. Scanlan, *Calculated Kindness: Refugees and America's Half-Open Door: 1945 to the Present* (New York: Free Press, 1986). See also Richard Breitman and Alan M. Kraut, *American Refugee Policy and European Jewry, 1933–1945* (Bloomington: Indiana University Press, 1987); Leonard Dinnerstein, *America and the Survivors of the Holocaust* (New York: Columbia University Press, 1982); Henry L. Feingold, *The Politics of Rescue: The Roosevelt Administration and the Holocaust, 1938–1945* (New Brunswick, N.J.: Rutgers University Press, 1970); Haim Genizi, *America's Fair Share: The Admission and Resettlement of Displaced Persons: 1945–1952* (Detroit: Wayne State University Press, 1993); Michael R. Marrus, *The Unwanted: European Refugees in the Twentieth Century* (New York: Oxford University Press, 1985); David S. Wyman, *The Abandonment of the Jews: America and the Holocaust, 1941–1945* (New York: Pantheon, 1984); Arthur Morse, *While Six Million Died: A Chronicle of American Apathy* (New York: Random House, 1968); Wyman, *Paper Walls: America and the Refugee Crisis, 1938–1941* (Amherst: University of Massachusetts Press, 1968); Bat-Ami Zucker, *In Search of Refuge: Jews and US Consuls in Nazi Germany, 1933–1941* (Portland: Vallentine Mitchell, 2001); Norman L. Zucker, *The Guarded Gate: The Reality of American Refugee Policy* (New York: Harcourt Brace, 1987).

11. Ibid.

Chapter 1. A New Benevolent Empire?

1. A 1920 report and supporting documents of the events are published in Michael Beizer, "Who Murdered Friedlaender and Cantor: The Truth Rediscovered," *American Jewish Archives Journal* 55, 1 (2003): 63–114. Beizer also provides an analysis of both the events themselves, an account that largely accepts the conclusions of the initial report, and of the later accounts of the events, which Beizer argues persuasively have been prone to both purposeful and unintentional inaccuracies throughout the intervening years. "Report Prof. Israel Friedlander [*sic*] Killed with Rabbi Cantor, by Bandits in Ukraine," *New York Times*, July 11, 1920. Photographs of the uniforms worn by JDC personnel may be seen at http://images.archives.jdc.org/api/gallery-fallback.php?albumId=76, accessed March 20, 2015. The photograph of Cantor and Friedlaender, posing with Ukrainian Jews, would have been taken within weeks, if not days, of their July confrontation. Cantor is also pictured in the photograph of the "Overseas Unit No. 1," back row, fourth from right.

2. Julia Irwin, *Making the World Safe: The American Red Cross and a Nation's Humanitarian Awakening* (New York: Oxford University Press, 2013). Other literature that examines the connection between international humanitarianism and American power

during this period includes Merle Curti, *American Philanthropy Abroad* (Rutgers, N.J.: Rutgers University Press, 1963), 224–300; Bertrand M. Patenaude, *The Big Show in Bololand: The American Relief Expedition to Soviet Russia in the Famine of 1921* (Stanford, Calif.: Stanford University Press, 2002); Ian Tyrrell, *Reforming the World: The Creation of America's Moral Empire* (Princeton, N.J.: Princeton University Press, 2010), 189–226.

3. On home front voluntarism and its connection to obligation, coercion, and the American state, see Christopher Capozzola, *Uncle Sam Wants You: World War I and the Making of the Modern American Citizen* (Oxford: Oxford University Press, 2008).

4. Julia Irwin makes this persuasive argument for the American Red Cross in *Making the World Safe*. This chapter extends a related analysis both to Hoover's massive organizations and to smaller ones, the latter with more circumscribed institutional identities relative to Hoover's.

5. Though Friedlaender ultimately did not make the journey, the practice of such dual affiliation was not uncommon. Louis Marshall to Cornelius Bliss, Jr., March 8, 1918; Marshall to Bliss, March 9, 1918; Felix Warburg to "Whom it May Concern," March 7, 1918, all in the records of the New York Office of the American Jewish Joint Distribution Committee, 1914–1918, Georgette Bennett and Leonard Polonsky Digitized JDC Text Archive (hereafter JDC Dig., NY, 1914–1918).

6. Table 1 in Office of Immigration Statistics, U.S. Department of Homeland Security, *Yearbook of Immigration Statistics 2011* (Washington, D.C.: GPO, 2012), 5.

7. The JDC was a joint venture of philanthropic organizations representing a spectrum of American Jewry, including Orthodox and leftist Jewish communities that had typically arrived in the United States more recently as well as more assimilated, Reformed Jews, commonly of Western European background. The JDC drew most of its funding, leadership, and political clout from the latter group, though the rank-and-file workers in the organization represented a wider array of American Jews. Yehuda Bauer, *My Brother's Keeper: A History of the American Jewish Joint Distribution Committee, 1929–1939* (Philadelphia: Jewish Publication Society of America, 1974), 7–16, 25; Jaclyn Granick, "Humanitarian Responses to Jewish Suffering Abroad by American Jewish Organizations, 1914–1929" (PhD dissertation, Yale University, 2009), 9–17; Joseph C. Hyman, *Twenty-Five Years of American Aid to Jews Overseas: A Record of the Joint Distribution Committee* (New York: Jewish Publication Society of America, 1939), 7–26. Also contributing money, social ties, and labor to the JDC were America's *landsmanschaften*, societies organized around immigrants' former home towns to the east. See, for example, J. M. Naischtut to Boris Bogen, May 4, 1922, B3, F2, MSC 3, Boris D. Bogen Papers, American Jewish Archives (hereafter Bogen Papers).

8. Emma Lazarus, "The New Colossus" in *Emma Lazarus: Selected Poems and Other Writings* (New York: Library of America, 2005), 58.

9. Suda Lorena Bane and Ralph Haswell Lutz, eds., *Organization of American Relief in Europe: 1918–1919* (Stanford, Calif.: Stanford University Press, 1943), 1–25; Curti, *American Philanthropy Abroad*, 244–300; Herbert Hoover, *The Memoirs of Herbert Hoover: Years of Adventure, 1874–1920* (New York: Macmillan, 1951), 282–86; Hyman,

Twenty-Five Years of American Aid, 12–13; Walter Consuelo Langsam, *The World Since 1914* (New York: Macmillan, 1937), 87–88; Marrus, *The Unwanted*, 50–53; Samuel Mason, "Our Mission to the Far East," August 12, 1918, F5, B458, MSC 456, Jacob H. Schiff Papers, American Jewish Archives (hereafter Schiff Papers); J. M. Roberts, *Twentieth Century: The History of the World, 1901–2000* (New York: Penguin, 1999), 238–75; Frank M. Surface and Raymond L. Bland, *American Food in the World War and Reconstruction Period: Operations of Organization Under the Direction of Herbert Hoover, 1914–1924* (Stanford, Calif.: Stanford University Press), 3–44.

10. Peter Gatrell, *A Whole Empire Walking: Refugees in Russia During World War I* (Bloomington: University of Indiana Press, 1999), 3; Marrus, *The Unwanted*, 50–53.

11. Curti, *American Philanthropy Abroad*, 226–31, 240–41, 263–64. On anti-German sentiment and policies during this period, see Capozzola, *Uncle Sam*, 63, 107, 117, 183–205; Gary Gerstle, *American Crucible: Race and Nation in the Twentieth Century* (Princeton, N.J.: Princeton University Press, 2002), 83–94.

12. Curti, *American Philanthropy Abroad*, 226–41; Irwin, *Making the World Safe*, 55–66, 108.

13. Bane and Lutz, *Organization of American Relief*, 1–3; George H. Nash, *The Life of Herbert Hoover: The Humanitarian, 1914–1917* (New York: Norton, 1988), 362–65; Nash, *The Life of Herbert Hoover: Master of Emergencies, 1918–1919* (New York: Norton, 1996), 444–63; Surface and Bland, *American Food in the World War*, ix, 3–7.

14. Curti, *American Philanthropy Abroad*, 263–66; "Near East Relief Has Saved 1,000,000," *New York Times*, July 22, 1922.

15. Ibid., 226, 249–50.

16. Curti, *American Philanthropy Abroad*, 226; Julia F. Irwin, "Humanitarian Occupations: Foreign Relief and Assistance in the Formation of American International Identities" (PhD dissertation, Yale University, 2009), 7–18; Irwin, *Making the World Safe*, 55–66.

17. See, for instance, Brian Balogh, *The Associational State: American Governance in the Twentieth Century* (Philadelphia: University of Pennsylvania Press, 2015), 23–40; Louise W. Knight, *Jane Addams: Spirit in Action* (New York: Norton, 2010); Daniel T. Rodgers, *Atlantic Crossings: Social Politics in a Progressive Age* (Cambridge, Mass.: Belknap Press of Harvard University Press, 1992); Theda Skocpol, *Protecting Soldiers and Mothers: The Political Origins of Social Policy in the United States* (Cambridge, Mass.: Belknap Press, 1992); Michael Willrich, *City of Courts: Socializing Justice in Progressive Era Chicago* (Cambridge: Cambridge University Press).

18. Capozzola, *Uncle Sam*; Ellis Hawley, *The Great War and the Search for a Modern Order: A History of the American People and Their Institutions* (Prospect Heights, Ill.: Waveland, 1992), 1–46.

19. Irwin, *Making the World Safe*, 37.

20. The Great War Society, "The History of the Salvation Army in World War I," http://www.worldwar1.com/dbc/salvhist.htm (quotation), accessed April 2, 2015. Also "Agencies Coordinated by the Commissions," Committee on Public Information,

Bulletin 42, October 21, 1918; Curti, *American Philanthropy Abroad*, 254–57; Irwin, *Making the World Safe*, 119; Lester M. Jones, *Quakers in Action: Recent Humanitarian and Reform Activities of the American Quakers* (New York: Macmillan, 1929), 154–62; E. H. McKinley, *Marching to Glory: The History of the Salvation Army in the United States, 1880–1992* (Grand Rapids, Mich.: Eerdmans, 1995), 162; National Jewish Welfare Board, *The Jewish Welfare Board: Final Report of War-Emergency Activities* (New York: [n.p.], 1920); "Salvation Army's Methods with the Doughboy," *New York Times*, August 4, 1918; William H. Taft and Frederick M. Harris, eds., *Service with Fighting Men: An Account of the Work of the American Young Men's Christian Associations in the World War* (New York: Association Press, 1922), 148–49, 197, 206; YWCA, National War Council, *Report of the National War Work Council of the Young Women's Christian Associations of the United States of America, 1917–1919* (New York: War Work Council, 1919), 4–6.

21. U.S. Surgeon General's Office, *The Medical Department of the United States Army in the World War*, vol. 1 (Washington, D.C.: GPO, 1923), 4–7.

22. "Agencies Coordinated by the Commissions," Committee on Public Information, Bulletin No. 42, October 21, 1918; Blanchard, "History of the YMCA"; Catholic Research Center, "Historical Note"; Great War Society, "The Salvation Army"; McKinley, *Marching to Glory*, 162; National Jewish Welfare Board, *The Jewish Welfare Board*; "Salvation Army's Methods with the Doughboy"; Taft and Harris, *Service with Fighting Men*; YMCA, *Summary of World War Work of the American YMCA* (New York: YMCA, 1920), 148–49, 206; Young Women's Christian Association, National War Council, *Report of the National War Work Council of the Young Women's Christian Associations of the United States of America, 1917–1919* (New York: War Work Council, 1919), 4–6.

23. Irwin, *Making the World Safe*, 119; YMCA, *Summary of World War Work*, 197; McKinley, *Marching to Glory*, 163. A more detailed discussion of the use of uniforms by voluntary agency personnel, particularly those with the JDC, follows below.

24. Hoover, *Years of Adventure*, 240–309; Surface and Bland, *American Food in the World War*, 7, 18.

25. Curti, *American Philanthropy Abroad*, 270; Hoover, *Years of Adventure*, 276, 294–95, 383; Patenaude, *Big Show in Bololand*, 29–31; Surface and Bland, *American Food in the World War*.

26. Bruno Cabanes, *The Great War and the Origins of Humanitarianism, 1918–1924* (Cambridge: Cambridge University Press, 2014), 189–247.

27. Nash, *Hoover: The Humanitarian*, 374 (quotation). Also Curti, *American Philanthropy Abroad*, 270; Hoover, *Years of Adventure*, 276, 294–95, 383, Patenaude, *Big Show in Bololand*, 29–31. On Strauss's role in helping Hoover spearhead postwar relief operations, see Richard Pfau, *No Sacrifice Too Great: The Life of Lewis L. Strauss* (Charlottesville: University of Virginia Press, 1985), 7–22; Lewis Strauss, *Men and Decisions* (New York: Doubleday, 1962), 5–6.

28. Irwin, *Making the World Safe*, 175–76.

29. Edgar Siskin, "Chaim Weizmann and James Becker: The Story of a Friendship," *American Jewish Archives Journal* 27 (1975): 36.

30. Hortense Becker, "James Becker and East German Jewry After World War I," *American Jewish Archives Journal* 46 (1994): 286–89, 289. On James Becker's birth, see birth certificate for James H. Becker, December 11, 1894, in "Illinois, Cook County Birth Registers, 1871–1915," index, FamilySearch https://familysearch.org/pal:/MM9.1.1/N7MN-YJ6, citing vol. 30, p. 35, Chicago, Cook, Illinois, Cook County Courthouse, Chicago, FHL microfilm 1,287,740, accessed February 5, 2015. On the wave of Jews who emigrated to the United States from Germany and nearby areas during the nineteenth century, Hasia R. Diner, *A Time for Gathering: The Second Migration, 1820–1880* (Baltimore: Johns Hopkins University Press, 1992), 201–36.

31. "United States Passport Applications, 1795–1925," index and images, FamilySearch, https://familysearch.org/pal:/MM9.3.1/TH-1961-39693-43055-13?cc=2185145, accessed February 6, 2015 (M1490) Passport Applications, January 2, 1906–March 31, 1925, Roll 755, 1919 April, certificate no 77250-77499 > image 626 of 955; citing NARA microfilm publications M1490 and M1372 (Washington, D.C.: NARA, n.d.).

32. Abraham Becker was one of only two Jewish trustees of the Chicago Art Institute in the first three decades of the twentieth century, the other trustee being friend, business associate, and Sears and Roebuck retail magnate Julius Rosenwald. Abraham and Rosenwald were also leaders of Chicago's most prominent Reform synagogue, Sinai. For almost every year between 1903 and 1917, one of the two men served as president of Associated Jewish Charities, the federation of philanthropies supported by the city's established Reform Jewish community rather than by Chicago's ballooning population of Orthodox Jews from Eastern Europe. Tobias Brinkmann, *Sundays at Sinai: A Jewish Congregation in Chicago* (Chicago: University of Chicago Press), 227–28, 235. By 1920, A. G. Becker and Co. had offices on both coasts and in the Midwest, James Langland, ed., *Chicago Daily News Almanac and Yearbook for 1921* (Chicago: Chicago Daily News, 1920), 931. On James's interest in his father's philanthropic work, Hortense Becker, "James Becker," 286–87. On American Jewish philanthropy during this period more generally, Boris D. Bogen, *Jewish Philanthropy: An Exposition of Principles and Methods of Jewish Social Service in the United States* (Montclair, N.J.: Patterson Smith, 1969 [1917]).

33. Hortense Becker, "James Becker," 290–91.

34. On graduating with honors, James H. Becker, Personal Journal, and biographical data sheet on Becker, both in B1, F1, MSC 536, James H. Becker Papers, American Jewish Archives (hereafter Becker Papers). On Cornell scene, "Formal Exercises Only for 1917 Commencement" and "45 Percent of Male Students Gone," *Cornell Daily Sun*, both May 30, 1917.

35. Two years earlier, the parent company of Becker's direct employer, *N. E. Westinghouse,* had forged a contract with representatives of Czar Nicholas II to produce 1.8 million rifles and bayonets for the Russians. On Becker's employment, see Becker's June 5, 1917, draft card, "United States World War I Draft Registration Cards, 1917–1918," index and images, FamilySearch, https://familysearch.org/pal:/MM9.3.1/TH-1961-26302-277-52?cc=1968530, accessed February 7, 2015), Illinois > Chicago City no 13; A-O > image 354 of 4587, citing NARA microfilm publication M1509. On the correspon-

dence with his parents, see Hortense Becker, "James Becker," 291, 293. Alongside James Becker's draft card, the correspondence described by Hortense Becker indicates that James may have deceived his parents into believing that he worked at a furniture factory, presumably believing that his mother's opposition to the war would lead her to oppose him supporting America's new Russian ally. On the context surrounding the Selective Service Act of 1917, including the misgivings Becker's parents had, see Capozzola, *Uncle Sam*, 23–28.

36. James Becker to parents, July 20, 1917, F 1/3, Becker Papers (unless otherwise indicated, all letters from James Becker to his parents are from the single box that houses the Becker Papers) (quotation). Also Hortense Becker, "James Becker," 291, 293–94; War Trade Board, *Report of the War Trade Board* (Washington, D.C.: GPO, 1920), 443. Founded in October 1917, the War Trade Board was preceded by the Exports Administrative Board. Arthur E. Swanson, *Publications of the American Statistical Association* 16 (1919): 263. The buildings where James worked were located near "the Eclipse" lawn of the White House. Alfred Goldberg, *The Pentagon: The First Fifty Years* (Washington, D.C.: GPO, 1992), 5–9; "The New Home of the War Trade Board," *War Trade Board Journal* 9 (May 1, 1918); "Old War and Navy Offices Outgrown," *Washington Post*, October 13, 1918.

37. Becker to parents, November 12, 1919, F 1/3.

38. Becker Journal, January 3–6, 1919 ("job," January 4). On Strauss's role in helping Hoover spearhead postwar relief operations, see Granick, "Humanitarian Responses to Jewish Suffering Abroad," 103–4; Richard Pfau, *No Sacrifice Too Great: The Life of Lewis L. Strauss* (Charlottesville: University of Virginia Press, 1985), 7–22; Lewis Strauss, *Men and Decisions* (New York: Doubleday, 1962), 5–6. On Strauss and Oppenheimer, see Kai Bird and Martin J. Sherwin, *American Prometheus: The Triumph and Tragedy of J. Robert Oppenheimer* (New York: Knopf, 2005), 491–520.

39. Becker to parents, January 4, 1919, F 1/3.

40. Ibid., January 14–22, 1919.

41. Hoover, *Years of Adventure*, 294.

42. Becker Journal, January 24, 1919.

43. Hoover, *Years of Adventure*, 428.

44. Becker Journal, January 24, 1919.

45. Becker Journal, January 6, January 30, January 24.

46. Ibid., February 8, 10, and 15, 1919. In Lemberg, Poland, Becker and other members of the mission were regularly given the opera box used by the former Austrian Emperor. For example, see entries from February 16, 19, 22, and 26.

47. Ibid., February 23, 1919.

48. Ibid., January 24, 1919. On the poor conditions of the era's Jews in Europe and the Middle East generally, see Granick, "Humanitarian Responses to Jewish Suffering Abroad," 2–9.

49. Ibid., March 21, 1919; Curti, *American Philanthropy Abroad*, 271–72, 279–88; Hoover, *Years of Adventure*, 283.

50. Becker Journal, January 24, 1919.

51. On anti-Semitism in the U.S. military generally, and especially the MID, Joseph W. Bendersky, *The "Jewish Threat": Anti-Semitic Politics of the U.S. Army* (New York: Basic, 2000), 47–196; on concerns over the JDC specifically, 56–57, 101–4; on passport refusal lists, 110, 150–56; quotation 87. The official in Hoover's organizations was Anson Goodyear: "A. Conger Goodyear, 86, Dies," *New York Times*, April 24, 1964.

52. James Becker, "Address Delivered at the National Conference of Jewish Social Service," June 20, 1921, 7–9, Records of the New York Office of the American Jewish Joint Distribution Committee, 1921–1932, "JDC Dig., NY, 1921–1932." In the early stages of the Armistice period, before Hoover's relief operations were well underway, the JDC sometimes used U.S. consulates and embassies as government conduits for JDC funds, money which would ultimately be distributed by foreign authorities and local charities as aid. See, for example, "Letter from Secretary, Joint Distribution Committee to the Honorable, the Secretary of State," January 31, 1919, JDC Dig., NY, 1921–1932. On the tactics used generally by the JDC to funnel money to wartorn areas, see Granick, "Humanitarian Responses to Jewish Suffering Abroad," 39–102.

53. Pfau, *No Sacrifice Too Great*, 16–24.

54. "Speeches at a Dinner Given Friday Evening, April 30, 1920, at the Standard Club, Chicago, The Chicago Jewish War Relief Committee, in Honor of Lieutenant James Becker," 40–41, F1, Becker Papers (hereafter Becker Address, April 30, 1920).

55. Carole Fink, *Defending the Rights of Others: The Great Powers, the Jews, and International Minority Protection, 1878–1938* (Cambridge: Cambridge University Press, 2004), 69–170, 257–66.

56. Bauer, *My Brother's Keeper*, 10–12. For instances of this situation, ones in which an estimated 90 to 95 percent of the starving victims of a famine in Russia were Jewish, Boris Bogen to Lewis Strauss, April 13, 1922, JDC Dig., NY, 1921–1932; J. M. Naischtut to Boris Bogen, May 19, 1922, B3, F2, Bogen Papers.

57. See, for example, various telegrams and letters between Lansing and Warburg dated September 11, 1916, November 11, 1916, December 15, 1916, January 15, 1917, April 9, 1917, and August 18, 1917, all in JDC Dig., NY, 1914–1918; Mason, "Our Mission."

58. When, in 1916, the State Department finally authorized the first JDC commission to go to Europe, only two JDC officials were allowed to operate in the war zone. The direct presence of the organization increased throughout the war, but it did not in fact establish large-scale operations until the war's aftermath. Bauer, *My Brother's Keeper*, 8, 10–12, 24; Becker Address, June 20, 1921, 6–9; Hyman, *Twenty-Five Years of American Aid*, 8, 14–15.

59. Becker Journal, January 31, 1919. On Hoover's application of different principles in the dispensation of humanitarian aid, see Curti, *American Philanthropy Abroad*, 270–72, 279–88; Hoover, *Years of Adventure*, 283.

60. Becker Journal, February 15, 1919. Known as the Ukrainian city of Lviv today, Lemberg had long been part of the Hapsburg Empire until its collapse with the First

World War. Timothy Snyder, *The Reconstruction of Nations: Poland, Ukraine, Lithuania, Belarus, 1569–1999* (New Haven, Conn.: Yale University Press, 2003), 136.

61. Becker Journal, February 19, 1919 (quotations). The casualty figures relayed by Becker are within range of later estimates. The pogrom was in fact perpetrated by Polish troops who had recently captured the city from Ukrainians. David Engle, "Lwów: 1918, a Symbol and Its Legacy," in *Contested Memories: Poles and Jews during the Holocaust and its Aftermath*, ed. Joshua D. Zimmerman (Rutgers, N.J.: Rutgers University Press, 2003), 32–41.

62. Curti, *American Philanthropy Abroad*, 293; "Zionism and Israel Encyclopedic Dictionary: Russian Civil War Pogroms," http://www.zionism-israel.com/dic/Russsian_Civil_War_pogroms.htm, accessed March 4, 2015.

63. Becker Journal, February 21, 1919 (Becker quotations); Bendersky, *Jewish Threat*, 87 (Gibson quotation).

64. Capozzola, *Uncle Sam*, throughout, but especially 117–43, 190–97 (quotation 165).

65. On Americans' political positions regarding the preferred role of their country in the world and their consequent responsibility in the assumption of that role, see Irwin, *Making the World Safe*, 37–38; Thomas J. Knock, *To End All Wars: Woodrow Wilson and the Quest for a New World Order* (Princeton, N.J.: Princeton University Press, 1992), 48–69.

66. Becker Journal, March 14, 1919.

67. Ibid., March 3, 1919.

68. Ibid., March 6, 1919.

69. James Becker to Felix Warburg, April 14, 1920, 9, F 1/4, Becker Papers; Becker Address, June 20, 1921, 50.

70. Becker to parents, July 20, 1917, F 1/3.

71. Quoted from Hortense Becker, "James Becker," 286.

72. See Becker journal generally. See also, for example, Becker to Miss (Harriet) Lowenstein, August 12, 1919; F Correspondence '17–'20, 1/1; Becker to Felix Warburg, April 14, 1920, 8, F Misc., 1/4; James Becker to parents, August 24, 1919, F Correspondence '17–'20, 1/1; Julius Goldman to Felix Warburg, March 17, 1920, F Misc. 1/4, all in Becker Papers. Quotation from Becker journal, February 20, 1919. On the ways in which the various categories of dispossessed people were categorized by relief workers, see, for example, Becker, "Address Delivered at the National Conference of Jewish Social Service."

73. Quoted in Becker Address, April 30, 1920, 9. Becker was serving as acting director for European operations by early October 1920. Becker to Colonel H(erbert) Lehman, October 4, 1920, JDC Dig., NY, 1921–1932.

74. Meeting of the Joint Distribution Committee held at the hotel Pennsylvania, 2, JDC Dig., NY, 1921–1932 (hereafter JDC Meeting, December 12, 1920).

75. Hortense Becker, "James Becker," 286–87; Brinkmann, *Sundays at Sinai*, 227–28, 235.

76. The respective federations for Chicago's Orthodox and Reformed Jewish charities were separate until the early 1920s. Michael Rose, "New Interviews for the Rosenwald Schools: September 16, 2014," http://www.rosenwaldfilm.org/blog/?tag=associated-jewish-charities, accessed July 22, 2015.

77. Becker to parents, May 30, 1919, F 1/3.

78. Becker's speech consisted of over thirty typewritten pages. Becker address, April 30, 1920 (quotations 57).

79. Hortense Becker, "James Becker," 286–87.

80. On the phenomenon generally, especially in New York, see Hasia R. Diner, *In the Almost Promised Land: American Jews and Blacks, 1915–1935* (Westport, Conn.: Greenwood Press, 1977), 6–9; Gerald Sorin, *A Time for Building: The Third Migration, 1880–1920* (Baltimore: Johns Hopkins University Press, 1992), 38–68. On the racial dimensions of Jewish assimilation, Karen Brodkin, *How Jews Became White Folks, and What That Says About Race in America* (New Brunswick, N.J.: Rutgers University Press, 1998). For quotation, Bogen, *Jewish Philanthropy*, 90. On the number of immigrants, Rhoda G. Lewin, "Stereotype and Reality in the Jewish Immigrant Experience in Minneapolis," *Minnesota History* 46, 7 (1979): 259.

81. On the cultures and demographics of this earlier wave of immigrants, see Bogen, *Jewish Philanthropy*, 87–89; Diner, *Jews of the United States*, 79–88; Diner, *A Time for Gathering*; Sorin, *A Time for Building*, 1–2. On the foreignness attributed by assimilated American Jews to newer Jewish immigrants, see Bogen, *Jewish Philanthropy*, 2–4; Jules Chametzky, ed., *Jewish American Literature: A Norton Anthology* (New York: Norton, 2000), 110–11; Jack Glazier, *Dispersing the Ghetto: The Relocation of Jewish Immigrants Across America* (Ithaca, N.Y.: Cornell University Press, 1998), 5–26.

82. Bauer, *My Brother's Keeper*, 19.

83. Hortense Becker, "James Becker," 286–87 (quotations). On Jewish-led anti-Semitism directed toward Chicago's newer immigrants, see Melvin G. Holli and Peter d'A. Jones, eds., *Ethnic Chicago: A Multicultural Portrait* (Grand Rapids, Mich.: Eerdmans, 1977), 134–35, 142–44.

84. Becker to Lewis Strauss, June 23, 1919, JDC Dig., NY, 1921–1932. For another example of Becker directing ARA operations while officially affiliated with the JDC, see minutes of the Executive Committee of the JDC, January 26, 1920, F 1/4.

85. Becker Address, June 20, 1921 (quotation). After Becker's military commission ended, he began wearing civilian clothes when back in Paris and, quite likely, in the other, larger and more stable European cities where he traveled for his work with the JDC. See, for example, Becker to parents, August 24, 1919, F 1/1. On JDC field personnel wearing U.S. army uniforms or, at times, possibly replicas of them, Beizer, "Who Murdered Friedlaender and Cantor," 64.

86. Becker Address, June 20, 1921, 50; Newton Baker to Felix Warburg, September 24, 1920, both in JDC Dig., NY, 1921–1932.

87. Isidore Hirshfield to Hugh Gibson, April 18, 1921 (quotations). Also Becker Address, June 20, 1921, 50, both in JDC Dig., NY, 1921–1932. On the dispute between

the JDC and U.S. officials more generally, Becker Address, June 20, 1921, 50; James Becker to Felix Warburg, October 23, 1920; JDC to Colonel Harry Cutler, July 30, 1920; unknown JDC official to Louis Marshall, December 14, 1921, all in JDC Dig., NY, 1921–1932. On U.S. officials resenting Jews wearing uniforms, Bendersky, *Jewish Threat*, 103.

88. These persons were part of a larger contingent, eventually reaching 126 in total, of JDC field personnel sent to the broader region to ramp up relief operations for the organization. In the late spring, Podolia was occupied by an alliance of Polish and Ukrainian troops that had, in April, agreed to stop fighting each other to unify their forces against what each set of troops perceived as a more dangerous threat from the Russian Red Army. A civilian without military experience, Friedlaender may have followed the common practice among American relief personnel and procured his uniform from a veteran. Beizer, "Who Murdered Friedlaender and Cantor," 64–65, 71.

89. James Becker to parents, February 10 and 22, 1920, F 1/3.

90. Two other men were in the car as well, both Ukrainians: a chauffeur, whose life was spared, and an older Jewish leader from another town in the area, who was killed because—the Russian soldiers would soon tell the townspeople of Yarmolintsy—he was assumed to be a bourgeois landowner. Beizer, "Who Murdered Friedlaender and Cantor."

91. Becker to Warburg, October 23, 1920 (quotation). Also Becker to Warburg, September 24, 1920; Becker Address, June 20, 1921, 50; Isidore Hirshfield to Hugh Gibson, April 18, 1921; JDC to Colonel Harry Cutler, July 30, 1920; unknown JDC official to Louis Marshall, December 14, 1921, all in JDC Dig., NY, 1921–1932.

92. Becker to Miss Gonsolin, February 10, 1920 (first quotation); Becker to parents, January 18, 1920 (second quotation), both in F 1/1; Becker Address, April 30, 1920, 36–39. Also Hortense Becker, "James Becker," 281 (third and fourth quotations).

93. Becker to parents, January 18, 1920, F 1/1.

94. Ibid., November 12, 1919, F 1/3.

95. JDC Meeting, December 12, 1920, 112.

96. Ibid., 109–14, 122–23 (quotations 109, 110). For a fascinating report of HIAS's immigration operations that stretched as far east as China and Japan for Jews fleeing the Russian Civil War, see Samuel Mason, "Our Mission to the Far East," August 12, 1918, and Samuel Mason, confidential report "To the President and Board of Directors" of HIAS, September 30, 1918, both in F5, B458, MSC 456, Schiff Papers.

97. Bauer, *My Brother's Keeper*, 8–9.

98. Marrus, *The Unwanted*, 9, 27. For a chronological comparison, before 1880 and after 1910, Jews formed only 30 percent of the total Russian emigration. Greenberg, *Jews in Russia*.

99. Glazier, *Dispersing the Ghetto*, 28–29.

100. Some debate has occurred over the extent that the Russian state sanctioned, as opposed to just tolerated, the anti-Jewish violence in the empire throughout the late nineteenth and early twentieth centuries. John Klier, *Russians, Jews, and the Pogroms of 1881–1882* (Cambridge: Cambridge University Press, 2011), 384–414.

101. Diner, *In the Almost Promised Land*, 3–4; Granick, "Humanitarian Responses to Jewish Suffering Abroad," 2–9.

102. The classic treatments of the Nativist Movement and immigration restriction in this period are Roger Daniels, *Coming to America: A History of Immigration and Ethnicity in American Life*, 2nd ed. (New York: HarperPerennial, 2002); Robert A Divine, *American Immigration Policy, 1924–1952* (New Haven, Conn.: Yale University Press, 1957); Oscar Handlin, *The Uprooted: The Epic Story of the Great Migrations That Made the American People* (Boston: Little, Brown, 1951); John Higham, *Strangers in the Land: Patterns of American Nativism, 1860–1925* (New Brunswick, N.J.: Rutgers University Press, 1955). More recent studies include Keith Fitzgerald, *The Face of the Nation: Immigration, the State, and the National Identity* (Stanford, Calif.: Stanford University Press, 1996); E. P. Hutchinson, *Legislative History of American Immigration Policy, 1798–1956* (Philadelphia: University of Pennsylvania Press, 1981); Desmond S. King, *Making Americans: Immigration, Race, and the Origins of Diverse Democracy* (Cambridge, Mass.: Harvard University Press, 2000); Mae Ngai, *Impossible Subjects: Illegal Aliens and the Making of Modern America* (Princeton, N.J.: Princeton University Press, 2004).

103. Marrus, *The Unwanted*, 112–17, 65. See also Tony Kushner and Katharine Knox, *Refugees in an Age of Genocide: Global, National and Local Perspectives During the Twentieth Century* (New York: Routledge, 1999), 73–88.

104. James Becker to parents, January 18, 1920, F 1/1 (quotation). On Becker's return home and subsequent involvement with the JDC in the 1920s see, for example, telegram from James from Becker and B. Horwich to Albert Lucas, April 19, 1921; memorandum by James Becker, May 5, 1926; Becker to Colonel H. Lehman, October 8, 1920; Albert Lucas to J. J. Frieman, December 8, 1920; JDC Meeting, December 12, 1920; telegram from James Becker to Felix M. Warburg, May 7, 1928, all in JDC Dig., NY, 1921–1932. See also "The Chicago Relief Conference," *American Hebrew*, October 7, 1921; Constructive Relief Committee, "After Three Years: The Progress of the Jewish Farm Colonies in Russia," October 22–23, 1927, F 1/4, Becker Papers; "Seventeenth Annual Report of the American Jewish Committee," *American Jewish Year Book* 26 (1924/25): 603–72.

105. Irwin, *Making the World Safe*, 182, 185–99; Patenaude, *Big Show in Bololand*, 1–3, 7, 19–25, 96–102.

106. Bauer, *My Brother's Keeper*, 57–104.

107. Carl Bon Tempo, *Americans at the Gate: The United States and Refugees during the Cold War* (Princeton, N.J.: Princeton University Press, 2008), 11–33; Ngai, *Impossible Subjects*, 21–55.

108. Marrus, *The Unwanted*, 51–295; Mark Mazower, *Dark Continent: Europe's Twentieth Century* (New York: Knopf, 1999), 41–75, 138–81; Claudena M. Skran, *Refugees in Inter-War Europe: The Emergence of a Regime* (Oxford: Clarendon, 1995).

Chapter 2. Refugees in the Shadow of the New Deal

1. "Report of Proceedings of Conference Called by the National Coordinating Committee for Aid to Refugees and Emigrants Coming from Germany," September 17, 1938,

Records of the National Coordinating Committee, RG 247, F2, YIVO Archives, Center for Jewish History (hereafter NCC). The two main Jewish American organizations offering aid to Jews made vulnerable by Nazi persecution were the Joint Distribution Committee and the United Palestine Appeal. In 1939, the United Jewish Appeal was created as the central fundraising and allocating entity for the NCC and its two internationally focused counterparts. Henry L. Feingold, *The Politics of Rescue: The Roosevelt Administration and the Holocaust, 1938–1945* (New Brunswick, N.J.: Rutgers University Press, 1970), 14, 33, 73–74; "Proceedings: President's War Relief Control Board," April 26, 1945, Records of the President's War Relief Control Board, Administrative Files, 1941–1947, RG 469, Entry 671 (hereafter WRCB), B 13, NARA; Sir John Hope Simpson, *The Refugee Problem: Report of a Survey* (London: Oxford University Press, 1939), 186–87, 348; "3 Jewish Groups Unite for Refugees," *New York Times*, January 13, 1939; Lyman Cromwell White, *300,000 New Americans: The Epic of a Modern Immigrant-Aid Service* (New York: United HIAS Service, 1957), 161, 279–80. On weather, "First Australian Woman in U.S. Title Round: Rain Drenches 13,500," " 'Nation Is Warned of Foreign 'Isms,' " and "Rain Delays Field Events Until Today," all in *New York Times*, September 18, 1938.

2. NCC "Proceedings of Conference" (Razovsky quotation, interpreting the information she had received from her contact). Though the hospital caring for the refugees was public, the patients in question were not legally considered public charges as long as their bills were paid by a private entity. Jane Perry Clark, *Deportation of Aliens from the United States to Europe* (New York: Columbia University Press, 1931); *People of the State of New York ex rel. State Board of Charities via N.Y.S.P. C.*, 162 NY 430 (also 42 NY App. Div. 83).

3. Richard Breitman and Alan M. Kraut, *American Refugee Policy and European Jewry, 1933–1945* (Bloomington: Indiana University Press, 1987); Leonard Dinnerstein, *America and the Survivors of the Holocaust* (New York: Columbia University Press, 1982), 1–8; Feingold, *Politics of Rescue*; Michael, R. Marrus, *The Unwanted: European Refugees in the Twentieth Century* (New York: Oxford University Press, 1985); Arthur Morse, *While Six Million Died: A Chronicle of American Apathy* (New York: Random House, 1968); David S. Wyman, *The Abandonment of the Jews: America and the Holocaust, 1941–1945* (New York: Pantheon, 1984); Wyman, *Paper Walls: America and the Refugee Crisis, 1938–1941* (Amherst: University of Massachusetts Press, 1968); Bat-Ami Zucker, *In Search of Refuge: Jews and US Consuls in Nazi Germany, 1933–1941* (Portland, Ore.: Vallentine Mitchell, 2001); Sir John Hope Simpson, *The Refugee Problem: Report of a Survey* (London: Oxford University Press, 1939). Accounts in the early Cold War period were generally less critical of American policies and social climates than later ones, preferring instead to lionize the heroism of rescue efforts and condemn the postwar expansion of international Communism. See Lyman Cromwell White, *300,000 New Americans: The Epic of a Modern Immigrant-Aid Service* (New York: United HIAS Service, 1957), 29–76; Mark Wischnitzer, *To Dwell in Safety: The Story of Jewish Migration since 1800* (Philadelphia: Jewish Publication Society of America, 1948), 235–38. For an examination of American political, economic, and cultural climates affecting immigration and alien issues for non-Europeans, see Mae Ngai, *Impossible Subjects: Illegal Aliens and the*

Making of Modern America (Princeton, N.J.: Princeton University Press, 2004), 56–90, 129–38, 228.

4. Laura Fermi, *Illustrious Immigrants: The Intellectual Migration from Europe, 1930–41* (Chicago: University of Chicago Press, 1968); Donald Fleming and Bernard Bailyn, eds., *The Intellectual Migration: Europe and America, 1930–1960* (Cambridge, Mass.: Belknap Press of Harvard University Press, 1969); Jarrell C. Jackman, *The Muses Flee Hitler: Cultural Transfer and Adaptation, 1930–1945* (Washington, D.C.: Smithsonian Institution Press, 1983); Donald Peterson Kent, *The Refugee Intellectual: The Americanization of the Immigrants of 1933–1941* (New York: Columbia University Press, 1953); Claus-Dieter Krohn, *Intellectuals in Exile: Refugee Scholars and the New School for Social Research*, trans. Rita Kimber and Robert Kimber (Amherst: University of Massachusetts Press, 1993).

5. While just under one hundred thousand German-born Jews legally entered the United States during the Nazi era as quota immigrants—that is, as permanent resident aliens—it is nevertheless still generally believed that many more secured haven in the United States through other means, ones that included overstaying visas and undocumented entry. Herbert Strauss, "The Immigration and Acculturation of the German Jews in the United States of America," *Leo Baeck Institute Yearbook* 16 (1971): 69–70. For considerations on the number of Jewish refugees from Nazism who found refuge in the United States before the end of the war, see Maurice R. Davie, *Refugees in America: Report of the Committee for the Study of Recent Immigration from Europe* (New York: Harper and Brothers, 1947), xvi, 24, 27; Haim Genizi, "New York Is Big: America Is Bigger: The Resettlement of Refugees from Nazism, 1936–1945," *Jewish Social Studies* 46, 1 (1984): 61; National Refugee Service (hereafter NRS), *Annual Report, 1943* (New York: National Refugee Service, 1944), 3–4; Zosa Szajkowski, "The Attitude of American Jews to Refugees from Germany in the 1930s," *American Jewish Historical Quarterly* 61, 2 (1971): 101.

6. Philip C. Jessup to Cecilia Razovsky, November 9, 1939, Records of the NRS, RG 248, F 519, YIVO.

7. Gil Loescher and John A. Scanlan, *Calculated Kindness: Refugees and America's Half-Open Door, 1945 to the Present* (New York: Free Press, 1986). See also, for instance, Carl Bon Tempo, *Americans at the Gate: The United States and Refugees During the Cold War* (Princeton, N.J.: Princeton University Press, 2008); Dinnerstein, *America and the Survivors of the Holocaust*; Haim Genizi, *America's Fair Share: The Admission and Resettlement of Displaced Persons, 1945–1952* (Detroit: Wayne State University Press, 1993); Norman L. Zucker, *The Guarded Gate: The Reality of American Refugee Policy* (New York: Harcourt Brace, 1987).

8. These matters are considered extensively in Chapter 4 of this book.

9. The literature on xenophobia and anti-Semitism during the period is considerable. See, for instance, Steven M. Lowenstein, *Frankfurt on the Hudson: The German-Jewish Community of Washington Heights, 1933–1983: Its Structure and Culture* (Detroit: Wayne State University Press, 1989), 52, 256; Beth S. Wenger, *New York Jews and the Great Depression: Uncertain Promise* (New Haven, Conn.: Yale University Press, 1996); 1–3, 21–24, 31–32, 130–34, 188–90, 197–201.

10. Robert A Divine, *American Immigration Policy, 1924–1952* (New Haven, Conn.: Yale University Press, 1957), 97–99; Stephen H. Legomsky, *Immigration and Refugee Law and Policy*, 2nd ed. (Westbury, N.Y.: Foundation Press, 1997), 753–54.

11. E. P. Hutchinson, *Legislative History of American Immigration Policy, 1798–1956* (Philadelphia: University of Pennsylvania Press, 1981), 229–68.

12. Davie, *Refugees in America*, xvi–ii, 8, 20–29.

13. Hutchinson, *Legislative History*, 229–68.

14. Although the U.S. Constitution referenced asylum among "certain rights" to be protected, this had not been typically construed to mean a positive legal protection that individuals could claim in court against governmental authorities. Asylum claims were collapsed into the general field of immigrant admissions, over which the executive and legislative branches enjoyed plenary authority. Neither the 1951 UN Convention on Refugees nor the 1967 UN Refugee Protocol obligated participating nation-states, the United States among them, to grant asylum. The Justice Department instituted the country's first specialized standards and procedures for granting asylum in 1974 (39 Fed. Reg. 28439). Exceptional asylum protections first appeared in federal legislation in 1980 with the country's first comprehensive refugee law (Pub. L. 96-212, 201(b), 94 Stat. 102, 103, 105). Deborah E. Anker, *The Law of Asylum in the United States*, 3rd ed. (Boston: Refugee Law Center, 1999); Divine, *American Immigration*, 9, 18, 93, 96, 100, 104, 105, 116; Guy S. Goodwin-Gill, *The Refugee in International Law*, 2nd ed. (New York: Clarendon, 1996); Atle Grahl-Madsen, *The Status of Refugees in International Law* (Leyden: A. W. Sijthoff-Leyden, 1966), 24, 326–28; Legomsky, *Immigration and Refugee Law*, 769–71; Paul Weis, "The Development of Refugee Law," in *Transnational Legal Problems of Refugees*, Michigan Yearbook of International Legal Studies (New York: Clark Boardman Callaghan, 1982), 27–42.

15. Tony Kushner and Katharine Knox, *Refugees in an Age of Genocide: Global, National and Local Perspectives During the Twentieth Century* (New York: Routledge, 1999), 145–68; Vivian D. Lipman, "Anglo-Jewish Attitudes to the Refugees from Central Europe, 1933–1939," in Julius Carlebach, ed., *Second Chance: Two Centuries of German-Speaking Jews in the United Kingdom* (Tübingen: Mohr, 1991), 519–21; Marrus, *The Unwanted*, 128–58.

16. "For a Discussion of Possible Coordination of the Work of Various Organizations in the U.S. in Connection with the German Refugees," meeting minutes, March 9, 1934, Joseph Chamberlain Perkins Papers, RG 278, F 26, YIVO Archives (hereafter Chamberlain Papers); NRS, *Annual Report, 1943*; White, *300,000 New Americans*, 34–35.

17. "Discussion of Possible Coordination;" Szajkowski, "Attitude of American Jews."

18. Breitman and Kraut, *American Refugee Policy*, 15–16, 19–23.

19. "Discussion of Possible Coordination" (quotation). Also Szajkowski, "Attitude of American Jews."

20. Ibid.; *NRS, Annual Report, 1943*, 2; press release, December 29, 1938, NCC, F 5; Wenger, *New York Jews*, 7–8, 76; White, *300,000 New Americans*, 34–35.

21. Minutes of meeting of Board of Directors, December 31, 1934, NCC, F 1.

Beginning at this first meeting, representatives of HIAS complained that a new organization was not necessary to supplant the activities of existing immigration agencies. Szajkowski, "Attitude of American Jews," 119–20. Leaders of NCJW also periodically complained that the new refugee service unfairly encroached on the types of immigrant assistance that NCJW had been doing free from outside oversight for years. As a compromise, NCJW was allowed to continue certain activities autonomously during the Nazi era while others would be coordinated by the new agency. Bat-Ami Zucker, *Cecilia Razovsky and the American Jewish Women's Rescue Operations in the Second World War* (Portland, Ore.: Vallentine Mitchell, 2008), 20–23, 67.

22. NCC's institutional membership varied, but hovered around twenty groups. Erika Mann and Eric Estorick, "Private and Governmental Aid to Refugees," *Annals for the American Academy of Political and Social Sciences* 203, 1 (1939): 143; Haim Genizi, *American Apathy: The Plight of Christian Refugees from Nazism* (Jerusalem: Bar-Ilan University Press, 1983); Szajkowski, "Attitude of American Jews," 122–30; Zucker, *Razovsky*, 15, 18.

23. Genizi, *American Apathy*.

24. Davie, *Refugees in America*, xvi, 24, 27; Genizi, "New York Is Big," 61; National Refugee Service, NRS, *Annual Report, 1943*, 3–4; Szajkowski, "Attitude of American Jews," 101; White, *300,000 New Americans*, 76.

25. "German Immigration Far Under Quota," *New York Times*, June 26, 1938; Zucker, *Razovsky*, 25.

26. *NRS, Annual Report, 1939*, 1, 6, 8; *NRS, Annual Report, 1940*, 1, 3, 25, Table; *NRS, Annual Report, 1942*, 8.

27. Ibid., *1940*, 25; *1942*, 8. Whereas the State Department's Visa Division controlled the issuance of permanent residence visas, Francis Perkins's Labor Department, as it was more accepting of immigrants relative to the State Department, governed temporary visas. Breitman and Kraut, *American Refugee Policy*, 16–17.

28. The NRS operated on a $15 million budget from its inception through the war's early aftermath while its predecessor spent only one fifth of that over the previous five years. Genizi, "New York Is Big"; Violet Lutz, "Historical Note," *Guide to the Records of the National Refugee Service 1934–1952* (New York: Center for Jewish History, 2013); White, *300,000 New Americans*, 35–37. On funding specifically, "Proceedings: President's War Relief Control Board."

29. See, for example, "Minutes from a Meeting at the Home of William Rosenwald," June 26, 1938, NCC, F 2; "Minutes of Meeting of Private Agencies with Representatives of INS Regarding, 'European Project,'" February 6, 1946, Chamberlain Papers, F 53; "Meetings of the NRS with Representatives of the Émigré Group," Chamberlain Papers; memorandum "To All Cooperating Committees" from William Haber and Razovsky, August 2, 1939, NCC, F 16; Marrus, *The Unwanted*, 137; *NRS, Annual Report, 1943*, 2–3; White, *300,000 New Americans*, 34–39. The meetings between voluntary agency and federal immigration officials occurred primarily with officials of the State Department's Visa Division and the INS, the latter, housed in the Labor Department until 1940, when

it was moved to the Justice Department. Davie, *Refugees in America*, 7, 10, 87; "Statements Attesting the Sincerity of Affidavits of Support," June 22, 1938 memorandum from George L. Warren to Chamberlain, Chamberlain Papers, F 67.

30. Divine, *American Immigration Policy*; Hutchinson, *Legislative History*, 229–68; Legomsky, *Immigration and Refugee Law*; White, *300,000 New Americans*. Whereas it is an accepted fact that influential American immigration officials harbored bigotry against Jews, the degree to which this limited admissions has been debated. See, for instance, Breitman and Kraut, *American Refugee Policy*; Breitman and Kraut, "The State Department, the Labor Department, and German Jewish Immigration, 1930–1940," *Journal of American Ethnic History* 3, 2 (1985): 5–38; Feingold, *Politics of Rescue*; Wyman, *Paper Walls*.

31. "Selfhelp in Action: Report on the Activities of the Activities of the Selfhelp for German Émigrés, Inc., 1938–1939," Records of Selfhelp for Immigrants from Central Europe, RG 245.8, 10.4, F 339, YIVO; Wyman, *Paper Walls*, 28–29.

32. Cecilia Razovsky to Presidents and Chairmen of all Branches of the NCJW, October 17, 1934, NCC, F 3; "Statements Attesting the Sincerity of Affidavits of Support"; Zucker, *Cecilia Razovsky*, 64–68.

33. "George Lewis Warren, 90, is Dead," *New York Times*, March 27, 1981; Richard McKinzie, "Oral History Interview with George L. Warren," November 10, 1972, Harry S. Truman Library online, http://www.trumanlibrary.org/oralhist/warrengl.htm, accessed August 216, 2015.

34. NCC "Proceedings of Conference"; "Statements Attesting the Sincerity of Affidavits of Support"; Joseph Chamberlain to All Cooperating Committees, July 11, 1939, NCC, F 16; Chamberlain to Edward F. Pritchard (INS), March 19, 1941, Chamberlain Papers, F 47; Chamberlain to Razovsky, June 24, 1938, NCC, F 5; Harry Greenstein, "Experience with Refugee Services," *Public Welfare News*, 7 (1939): 7–11. On the Evian Conference, see Feingold, *Politics of Rescue*, 22–44.

35. NCC "Proceedings of Conference"; H. Ziegler memorandum, "Study of Affiant and Relative Contacts," August 5, 1940, NRS, F 745.

36. NCC "Proceedings of Conference" (quotation). See also Chamberlain to Edward F. Pritchard (INS), March 19, 1941, Chamberlain Papers, F 47. This folder also contains records of numerous communications between Chamberlain and federal officials.

37. Chamberlain to Pritchard, March 19, 1941.

38. NCC "Proceedings of Conference" (first and third quotations); "Meetings of the NRS with Representatives of the Émigré Group," Chamberlain Papers, F 43 (second quotation). On this issue, see also Chamberlain to Razovsky, June 25, 1938, NCC, RG 247, 3.1, F 5; "International Committee on Refugees: Report of the 4th Plenary Session, London," August 15–17, 1944, and "International Committee on Refugees: Report of the 5th Plenary Session, Paris," November 20–22, 1945, both in Chamberlain Papers, RG 278, F 22; "James G. McDonald to Chamberlain," October 10, 1935, Chamberlain Papers, RG 278, F 25.

39. Wenger, *New York Jews*, 148–51; 148. Mayoral administrations and urban political

machines across the country benefited from New Deal federal spending, becoming an increasingly important base of FDR's support. None benefited as much as La Guardia's Fusionist Party. Lyle W. Dorsett, *Franklin D. Roosevelt and the City Bosses* (Port Washington, N.Y.: Kennikat Press, 1977), 49–61; Steven P. Erie, *Rainbow's End: Irish-Americans and the Dilemmas of Urban Machine Politics* (Berkeley: University of California Press, 1988), 133. Amenta, Benoit, et al., "Bring Back the WPA: Work, Relief, and the Origins of American Social Policy in Welfare Reform," *Studies in American Political Development* 12, 1 (1998), 52–53; "The City," editorial, *New York Times*, March 24, 1935.

40. Andersen, Morris Ardoin, and Mararita Zilberman, eds., *120 HIAS Stories* (New York: HIAS, 2002); Gabriel Davidson, "The Jews in Agriculture in the United States," in *American Jewish Yearbook* 37 (1935): 99–134; Hasia R. Diner, *In the Almost Promised Land: American Jews and Blacks, 1915–1935* (Westport, Conn.: Greenwood, 1977), 6–9; Gerald Sorin, *A Time for Building: The Third Migration, 1880–1920* (Baltimore: Johns Hopkins University Press, 1992), 38–68; Wischnitzer, *To Dwell in Safety*, 67–141. On the commonly referenced "Stuyvesant Pledge" whereby Portuguese Jews promised New Amsterdam's governor in the seventeenth century to forever "care for our own," see Boris D. Bogen, *Jewish Philanthropy: An Exposition of Principles and Methods of Jewish Social Services in the United States* (New York: Macmillan, 1917), 4, 84–85.

41. Michael B. Katz, *In the Shadow of the Poorhouse: A Social History of Welfare in America* (New York: Basic, 1996), 214; Andrew Morris, *The Limits of Voluntarism: Charity and Welfare from the New Deal through the Great Society* (New York: Cambridge University Press, 2009), 1–78; Walter I. Trattner, *From Poor Law to Welfare State: A History of Social Welfare in America* (New York: Free Press, 1974), 274–75, 286. Gruber and Hungerman suggest further that Americans reduced their church donations as a conscious reaction to increased public relief services. Jonathan Gruber and Daniel M. Hungerman, "Does Government Crowd out Church? Evidence from the New Deal," paper presented at Social Science Research Council Program on Philanthropy and the Nonprofit Sector Capstone Conference (Florence, March 2005).

42. Wayne W. Parrish, "Report, New York, New York," November 17, 1934, Harry Hopkins Papers, Box 66, Franklin D. Roosevelt Library.

43. Wenger, *New York Jews*, 152.

44. Katz, *Price of Citizenship*, 2. According to Walter Trattner, as governor, Franklin Roosevelt made New York State's Public Welfare Law "the most progressive" in the country, foreshadowing much of the New Deal's early relief initiatives. Trattner, *From Poor Law*, 281–82.

45. The ERB position only applied to aliens in the country legally, however. "Relief Preference to Aliens Is Denied," *New York Times*, September 17, 1936.

46. "Aldermen Ask ERB to List Aliens Getting City Relief," May 6, 1936; "Alderman Wants WPA Aliens Listed," February 5, 1936; "Aliens on Relief not Known to ERB," May 20, 1936; "ERB Alien List Demanded," May 22, 1936, all in *New York Times*.

Funds derived from New York State's Temporary Emergency Relief Administration, the Federal Emergency Relief Administration, and the Works Progress Administration were not allowed to be used to discriminate based on race, color, religion, political affiliation or activities, and citizenship status. "Aldermen Imperil TERA Fund to City," *New York Times*, May 21, 1936. In practice, significant discrimination did occur, especially based on race. La Guardia's Democratic critics also provided evidence that the city discriminated based on political affiliation. Perhaps the most notorious form of discrimination within New Deal initiatives concerned the fact that certain sectors of the economy (esp. agriculture and domestic work) were not covered under the labor regulations of the National Labor Relations Act. Ngai, *Impossible Subjects*, 75, 136–37, 158–66.

47. In New York City and state, however, aliens remained eligible for home relief and medical payments. Additionally, many aliens were able to remain legally eligible to receive WPA jobs if they had filed their first papers by June 21, 1938, though they were more likely to be among the first cut from WPA rolls when federal funds proved insufficient to meet need. "Aliens Lose WPA Jobs," March 7, 1939; "Some Aliens in WPA Are to Be Deported," March 12, 1939; Thatcher, *Immigrants and the 1930s*; "WPA Begins Alien Check," February 21, 1939; "WPA Here to Drop 12,000 Next Week," June 23, 1937, all in *New York Times*.

48. "Relief Preference to Aliens Denied"; Oswald Garrison Villard, "Slumbering Fires in Harlem," *The Nation* 142 (January 22, 1936): 99–101; Richard Weiss, "Ethnicity and Reform: Minorities and the Ambience of the Depression Years," *Journal of American History* 79 (1979): 566–85. Arguments pitting the welfare rights of minority citizens against resident aliens had its counterpart in the "charity begins at home" movement designed to prioritize domestic charitable spending over international aid. Wyman, *Paper Walls*, 67–98.

49. "House Votes WPA $100,000,000 More, Bars Higher Grant," *New York Times*, April 1, 1939. On this issue generally, Thatcher, "Immigrants and the 1930s."

50. "Change Opposed in Alien Quotas," *New York Times*, March 4, 1934 (quotation). New York State applied this restriction until the early 1940s. "Considerations in the Use of Public Assistance for Jewish Aliens Residing in U.S. over Five Years," 1944 (exact date unclear), NRS, F 519.

51. Cohen, *Making a New Deal*, 270–71.

52. "Minutes of Meeting of the Migration and Alien Status Committee," October 26, 1943; "Preliminary Report of Study of N.R.S. Relief Cases to Determine Public Charge Risks," July 9, 1943; "Problems Arising out of Policy Regarding Referrals for Public Assistance," October 20, 1943, all in Chamberlain Papers, F 57.

53. Fiscal Year 1939 proved to be the first and only year when the immigration quota from Nazi controlled countries was filled, although it was considerably exhausted during the next two years as well. *NRS, Annual Report, 1939*, 1, 6, 8; *NRS, Annual Report, 1940*, 1, 3, 25, Table; *NRS, Annual Report, 1942*, 8; *NRS, Annual Report, 1943*, 25, Table 1.

54. *NRS, Annual Report, 1939*, 3–4, 7; *NRS, Annual Report, 1940*, 3–4, 21; *NRS,*

Annual Report, 1942, 8–12, 15; *NRS, Annual Report, 1943*, 4; White, *300,000 New Americans*, 44, 56.

55. *NRS, Annual Report, 1943*, 4; "Proceedings: President's War Relief Control Board."

56. "Minutes of the First Meeting of the Advisory Committee on Political Refugees," May 16, 1938, Chamberlain Papers, F 58; Cecelia Razovsky to Mr. Baerwald and Chamberlain of the International Conference in Evian, June 1, 1938, NCC, F 5.

57. "Displaced Persons in Germany," *Department of State Bulletin* 8, 317 (1945): 127–28; "Proceedings: President's War Relief Control Board"; Franklin Roosevelt, *First Report to Congress on U.S. Operations in UNRRA, March 28, 1944* (Washington, DC: GPO, 1944); UN Department of Public Information, Research Section, "Refugees," Background Paper No. 78, December 29, 1953, Records of the United Service for New Americans, RG 246, F 597, YIVO.

58. "'Urgent Cable'" to President of Cuba, June 7, 1939, Chamberlain Papers, F 100.

59. See, for example, "Minutes of the Technical Sub-Committee of the Intergovernmental Committee of Refugees," Evian, France, July 13, 1938; "Report of the 4th Plenary Session, London"; "Report of the 5th Plenary Session, Paris"; all in F 22, Chamberlain Papers, F 22.

60. *NRS, Annual Report, 1940*, 21–22.

61. According to Deborah Wenger, "both Jewish and non-Jewish social workers expressed great concern about the quality of service offered by state relief bureaus." Wenger, *New York Jews*, 152.

62. "Preliminary Report of Study."

63. "Minutes of Migration and Alien Status Committee."

64. Divine, *American Immigration Policy*, 124–28; Hutchinson, *Legislative History*, 280–81; "Minutes of Migration and Alien Status Committee"; "Preliminary Report of Study of N.R.S. Relief Cases"; "Problems Arising out of Policy." For broader discussions of the differences between American Zionist and non-Zionist Jewish leaders, see Breitman and Kraut, *American Refugee Policy*, 63, 83–5, 90–91, 103; Feingold, *Politics of Rescue*, 33, 218–19; Wyman, *Abandonment of the Jews*, 160, 169, 175, 200. On the mainstreaming of Jews and other Euro-American ethnic and religious groups during this period, see Karen Brodkin, *How Jews Became White Folks, and What That Says About Race in America* (New Brunswick, N.J.: Rutgers University Press, 1998), 1–102; Matthew Frye Jacobson, *Whiteness of a Different Color: European Immigrants and the Alchemy of Race* (Cambridge, Mass.: Harvard University Press, 1998), 171–200, 246–73.

65. "Minutes of Meeting of Migration and Alien Status Committee"; "Problems Arising Out of Policy"; Wenger, *New York Jews*, 140–45, 148–65.

66. "Considerations in the Use of Public Assistance for Jewish Aliens Residing in U.S. over Five Years," 1944 (exact date unclear) (quotations). Also "Statement of Suggested Practices and Procedures Regarding the Referral of Aliens to Public Agencies," undated, but written in late 1943 or early 1944, both in NRS, F 519.

Chapter 3. Recruiting Philanthropies for Battle

1. American-led Allied Armies took both Algeria and Morocco from Axis forces the previous November in the surprisingly swift "Operation Torch." Michael C. C. Adams, *The Best War Ever: America and World War II* (Baltimore: Johns Hopkins University Press, 1994), 49–50.

2. "Eric Knight Victim," January 22, 1943; "Hodson Is Killed in Plane Accident," January 21, 1943, both in *New York Times*. Also "List of Dead in Air Crash," January 22, 1943; "Worst Air Tragedy in Annals of U.S. Fatal to 35," January 22, 1943, both in *Washington Post*. Also "35 Die in Crash of U.S. Plane in South America," *Chicago Daily Tribune*, January 22, 1943.

3. "A Bill to Alleviate the Hazards of Old Age, Unemployment, Illness, and Dependency, to Establish a Social Insurance Board in the Department of Labor, To Raise Revenue, and for Other Purposes" (Washington, D.C.: GPO, 1935), 534–35; "Hodson Is Killed"; House Ways and Means Committee, "Economic Security Act: Hearings Before the Committee on Ways and Means House of Representatives, 74th Cong., 1st Sess., on H.R. 4120; Leslie Leighninger, "Social Workers as Politicians," *Journal of Progressive Human Services* 12 (2002): 71–76; Walter I. Trattner, *From Poor Law to Welfare State: A History of Social Welfare in America* (New York: Free Press, 1994), 262–63, 276.

4. Amenta, Benoit et al., "Bring Back the WPA: Work, Relief, and the Origins of American Social Policy in Welfare Reform," *Studies in American Political Development* 12, 1 (1988): 52–53; "The City," editorial, *New York Times*, March 24, 1935; City of New York, Department of Welfare Directory (Prepared by the U.S. WPA Bureau of Information and Inquiry), April 25, 1938, Records of the National Coordinating Committee, RG 247, F 2, YIVO Archives (hereafter NCC); "Hodson Is Killed"; Trattner, *From Poor Law*, 281–82.

5. "Hodson's Idealism Lauded by Lehman," February 17, 1943; "Struggle in Peace Is Seen by Hodson," January 10, 1943, both in *New York Times*; "Hodson Is Killed." On public welfare in New York during the New Deal, particularly as it affected aliens and minority citizens, see Chapter 2 of this book; see also Mary Anne Thatcher, *Immigrants and the 1930s: Ethnicity and Alienage in Depression and Oncoming War* (PhD dissertation, University of California at Los Angeles, 1973).

6. On the connections that Hodson and his public welfare bureau forged with private welfare agencies (particularly refugee relief societies) see, for example, Augusta Mayerson to Cecilia Razovsky, June 30, 1938, NCC F 26; Abraham J. Simon to Marcel Kovarsky, November 30, 1943, Records of the National Refugee Service, RG 248, YIVO (hereafter NRS). On the relationship between public and private welfare agencies more generally, including those in New York, see Andrew Morris, *The Limits of Voluntarism: Charity and Welfare from the New Deal Through the Great Society* (New York: Cambridge University Press, 2009), 1–78; Beth S. Wenger, *New York Jews and the Great Depression: Uncertain Promise* (New Haven, Conn.: Yale University Press, 1996), 148–55. On Lehman and Hodson, "Hodson's Idealism Lauded by Lehman."

7. "Minutes of Meeting Called by the President's War Relief Control Board," February 8, 1944, Records of the President's War Relief Control Board, Administrative Files, RG 469, Entry 671, B 13, NARA (hereafter WRCB); Report of "Team Directors' Conference," July 12, 1946, Records of the United Nations Relief and Rehabilitation Administration, S-0424-0023-07, United Nations Archives, New York City (hereafter UNRRA). On U.S. financial commitments to UNRRA, see Franklin Delano Roosevelt, Executive Order 9453, Providing for the Participation of the U.S. in the Work of UNRRA, *First Report to Congress on U.S. Participation in Operations of UNRRA, as of September 30, 1944* (Washington, D.C.: GPO, 1945), 14–15. While Roosevelt had begun funding UNRRA from an executive fund in late 1943 the U.S. Congress first appropriated American funds in March 1944. The Congressional appropriation of $1.35 billion represented two thirds of UNRRA's initial budget. P.L. 267, 78th Cong.

8. One notable exception to this practice had taken place. Charities providing relief to the people of Spain during the Spanish Civil War had, for several years, already been required to register with the U.S. State Department at the time that the Neutrality Act was passed. Merle Curti, *American Philanthropy Abroad: A History* (New Brunswick, N.J.: Rutgers University Press, 1963), 414.

9. U.S. Department of State, President's War Relief Control Board, *Voluntary War Relief During World War II: A Report to the President*, Department of State Publication 2566 (Washington, DC: GPO, 1946), 2–9; 54 Stat. 4.

10. "Begins Latin Relief Drive," August 3, 1940; "Benefit Is Planned for Russian Relief," October 11, 1941; "Bowl of Rice Ball Is First of Party Series Planned by Bureau of Medical Aid to China," October 13, 1940; "Labor Group Opens Refugee Fund Drive," November 10, 1939; "Nation-Wide Appeal To Aid Allies' Needy," September 18, 1939; "Stage Group Plans War Drive," August 14, 1940, all in *New York Times*. Also "Drive Set to Aid Child Refugees," *Washington Post*, July 1, 1940.

11. Since 1900 the American Red Cross had been the only American charity holding a Congressional Charter. For decades previously this charter had given the ARC a near-monopoly over American disaster relief operations abroad, particularly with medical aid to soldiers in the field. Although the ARC collected privately donated funds from its annual "Roll Call" campaigns, a large portion of the relief provisions that it had dispensed overseas during the previous several decades had been given to it through Congressional appropriations. Government officials had so closely supervised the operations of the ARC that further oversight seemed redundant. "Burden on Our Red Cross Expected to Rise Sharply," *New York Times*, May 5, 1940; Curti, *American Philanthropy*, 438–39; Foster Rhea Dulles, *The American Red Cross* (New York: Harper and Brothers, 1950); Patrick F. Gilbo, *The American Red Cross: The First Century* (New York: Harper and Row, 1981); Julia Irwin, *Making the World Safe: The American Red Cross and a Nation's Humanitarian Awakening* (New York: Oxford University Press, 2013); "Red Cross Opens Drive Against Misery," *Washington Post*, September 29, 1939.

12. Some isolationists recognized that sending private relief overseas in itself formed a powerful and, in their minds, dangerous international commitment for the United

States. As such they vehemently opposed such contributions. See, for example, "Fighting at Home," *Washington Post*, February 23, 1940.

13. See, for example, "Benefit Is Planned for Russian Relief," October 11, 1941; "Bowl of Rice," October 13, 1940; "Labor Group Opens Refugee Fund Drive," November 10, 1939; "Nation-Wide Appeal to Aid Allies' Needy," September 18, 1939, all in *New York Times*.

14. "Start of National War Fund of 16 Service Agencies," *Chicago Defender*, July 3, 1943 (quotation on "colonies of Africa"). Quotation on Soviet Union spoken by Lester B. Granger, "Urges Funds for Russian War Relief," *Chicago Defender*, September 18, 1943. Other examples include "Dr. Bethune Urges Negroes to Back Nat'l War Fund," November 6, 1943; "Honor Joe Louis in Defense Drive," March 14, 1942; "Million Negroes Visit USO Clubs Each Month," July 17, 1943; "Name Negro to Capital War Fund," September 19, 1942, all in *Chicago Defender*.

15. "593 Welfare Aides in War Honor Roll," *New York Times*, September 1, 1942.

16. "Garment Union Gives $305,000 War Relief," September 19, 1941; "Given to Fr. Walsh," December 23, 1939; Harold J. Seymour, *Design for Giving: The Story of the National War Fund, Inc., 1943–1947* (New York: Harper, 1947), 88; "Mrs. Morgenthau Heads Patroness List for Concert," June 16, 1940; "2,000,000 in Europe's War Zone Need Help," April 19, 1940, all in *Washington Post*. "All Gifts of Russian War Relief Labeled as 'From People of U.S.,'" January 4, 1944; "Asks Gifts to Send Supplies to Russia," August 20, 1941; "War Intensifies Refugee Problem," February 11, 1940, all in *New York Times*. "Proceedings of Arbitration Hearings for Russian War Relief," Russian War Relief, December 4, 1944, WRCB, B 13.

17. Jonathan Daniels, "A Native at Large," *Nation* 152 (April 12, 1941), 436.

18. The President's Committee on War Relief Agencies (PCWRA), "Minutes of Conference with Leading British War Relief Agencies," May 2, 1941, WRCB, B 3.

19. Curti, *American Philanthropy Abroad*, 434–38; *Relief for Starving Peoples: Hearings Before a Subcommittee of the Committee on Foreign Relations of the U.S. Senate* (Washington, D.C.: GPO, 1944).

20. "Proceedings of the President's Committee on War Relief Agencies Conference on Welfare Services and Gift Programs of the Armed Services," March 31, 1942, WRCB, B 13.

21. Daniels, "A Native at Large," 436.

22. "Conference on Welfare Services," WRCB; Curti, *American Philanthropy Abroad*, 428–29; "Park Avenue Canteen Loses its Charter," *New York Times*, November 24, 1942.

23. Memorandum to "all registered agencies disapproving advertising solicitation by or in the name of registered agencies," October 23, 1943, WRCB, B 3, in "Compilation of Documents"; "Conference with Leading British War Relief Agencies"; "Labor Group Opens"; "Park Avenue Canteen Loses its Charter," *New York Times*, November 24, 1942.

24. "War Relief Drives," *Chicago Daily Tribune*, May 2, 1942.

25. Cordell Hull to Franklin Delano Roosevelt, March 3, 1941, WRCB, B 3 (quotations). Also Malvin Morton, *The Development and Structure of the War Relief Agencies*, Social Research Monograph 6 (Pittsburgh: Federation of Social Agencies of Pittsburgh

and Allegheny County, 1945); Arthur C. Ringland, "The Organization of Voluntary Foreign Aid: 1939–1953," *Department of State Bulletin*, no. 5413, March 15, 1954 (Washington, D.C.: GPO, 1954); WRCB, *Voluntary War Relief*, 4, 53. On the appropriation and regulation of the resources of America's civil society and commercial sectors by the federal government during the war, see James T. Sparrow, *Warfare State: World War II Americans and the Age of Big Government* (New York: Oxford University Press, 2011); Bartholomew Sparrow, *From the Outside in: World War II and the American State* (Princeton, N.J.: Princeton University Press, 1996).

26. Joseph E. Davies to Franklin Delano Roosevelt, July 16, 1942; Cordell Hull to Roosevelt, July 16, 1942, Interim Report of the President's Committee on War Relief Agencies, October 4, 1941; U.S. Department of State Press Release, President's Committee on War Relief Activities Final Report, July 27, 1942, all in WRCB, B 3, "Compilation of Documents." Also Seymour, *Design for Giving*, 4; WRCB, *Voluntary War Relief*, 4–5, 56. Another member was Charles Phelps Taft, Cincinnati lawyer, philanthropic leader, son of former president and Supreme Court justice William Howard Taft, and brother of Senator Robert Taft of Ohio. The remaining member, Frederick P. Keppel, had previously been president of the Carnegie Corporation in Washington and dean of Columbia College. U.S. Department of State, Press Release, March 20, 1941, WRCB, B 3, F "Compilation of Documents."

27. PCWRA "Final Report," July 27, 1942, WRCB, B 3 (quotation). Also Executive Order 9205 establishing the President's War Relief Control Board; notice from Joseph E. Davies to "officers and governing boards of war-relief and welfare agencies concerning requirements for registration with the Board," August 7, 1942; press release announcing the creation of the President's War Relief Control Board, July 27, 1942, all in WRCB, B 3, in "Compilation of Documents."

28. Examples taken from "Conference on Welfare Services," WRCB, 86; "The Lehman OFRRO Blueprints its Task," *New York Times*, January 7, 1943; "Plans Being Made to Feed Italy When She Breaks with Nazis," *New York Times*, January 18, 1943; WRCB Meeting, February 8, 1944.

29. U.S. Division of Public Inquiries, Office of War Information, *Emergency War Agencies*, U.S. Government Manual (Washington, D.C.: GPO, 1945), 60–62, 84–87, 95–99, 152.

30. Steven Rathgeb Smith and Michael Lipsky, "The Political Economy of Nonprofit Revenues," in *Making the Nonprofit Sector in the United States*, ed. David C. Hammack (Bloomington: Indiana University Press, 1998); Ethan Stone, "Adhering the Old Line: Uncovering the History and Political Function of Unrelated Business Income Tax," University of Iowa Legal Studies Research Paper 04-06, March 2005; WRCB, *Voluntary War Relief During World War II*, 19. On importance of War Powers acts: Joseph E. Davies to Roosevelt, July 16, 1942; Hull to Roosevelt, July 16, 1942. On the role of taxes: Notice to "selected registrants concerning application to the Tax Exemption Division of the Bureau of Internal Revenue," June 23, 1944, WRCB, B 3, in "Compilation of Documents."

31. PCWRA, "Conference with Leading British"; Press Release, May 16, 1945;

PCWRA, "Final Report"; "Proceedings of Arbitration Hearings for Russian War Relief," WRCB; Statement from the President's War Relief Control Board to Appropriations Committee of House of Representatives, August 24, 1945, all in WRCB, B 3, in "Compilation of Documents." "Conference on Welfare Services," WRCB.

32. WRCB, *Voluntary War Relief*, 17.

33. It is difficult to determine the exact number of agencies which either ceased operations altogether or consolidated with others as a result of Control Board regulations and hearings. Approximately three hundred agencies were licensed with the State Department, through the Davies Committee, when the Committee disbanded in July 1942. Many more agencies came under the Control Board's purview as a result of its broadened jurisdiction, a jurisdiction over agencies giving aid in the United States and to non-belligerent countries. To estimate that the direct and indirect actions of the Control Board resulted in four to five hundred agencies closing or consolidating in its four-year tenure is likely conservative. PCWRA "Final Report"; "Registrations" file, WRCB, B 1; WRCB, *Voluntary War Relief*, 26–50, 73.

34. Though the Board did make some exceptions to this rule, it held in most cases. Executive Order No. 9205; Notice to "registrants not participating in the National War Fund concerning basis for continuation of their registrations," July 20, 1943, both in WRCB, B 3, in "Compilation of Documents."

35. The founding constitutive agencies of Refugee Relief Trustees were the nonsectarian International Rescue and Relief Committee, the American Committee for Christian Refugees, and the Unitarian Service Committee. "Red Unit Seeks to Gain Entry in War Relief," *Chicago Daily Tribune*, December 23, 1943; "War Fund Approves Refugee Committee," *New York Times*, September 1, 1944; WRCB, *Voluntary War Relief*, 45.

36. "Army-Navy Benefits Restricted by Board," *New York Times*, September 26, 1942; "Conference on Welfare Services," WRCB.

37. On the agencies for Britain and the Board's practices generally, see various files containing registration applications and correspondence between the Control Board and the voluntary agencies, WRCB, B 1; WRCB, *Voluntary War Relief*, 4–5, 56. On Yugoslavia, see "Serbia Eyes Future: Desires Ouster of Minorities," *Washington Post*, May 6, 1943. Also "Tea to Aid Yugoslavs," December 9, 1942; "Yugoslav Relief Seeks $2,000,000 for Prisoners, Children, Refugees," October 1, 1942, both in *New York Times*. .

38. "Fighting French to Raise Funds by Art Display," January 10, 1043; "French Relief Unified," July 15, 1944; "New French Relief Fund," March 31, 1943; "Three Sponsor French Relief 'Work' Tour," September 8, 1944, all in *New York Times*.

39. "Dickstein Criticizes our Relief in Italy," April 30, 1944 (first quotation); "Daily Here Scores Italian Relief Bar," May 3, 1944 (second quotation), both in *New York Times*. On the episode generally, see Stephen R. Porter, "Defining Public Responsibility in a Global Age: Refugees, NGOs, and the American State" (PhD dissertation, University of Chicago, 2009), 125–31.

40. As Julia Irwin has explained, the American Red Cross during World War II "played a far more limited role in aiding noncombatants" than it had during World War

I. Irwin, *Making the World Safe*, 199–207. See also Curti, *American Philanthropy Abroad*, 411, 438–39, 475, 483. On War Bond campaigns, Sparrow, *Warfare State*, 127–36. On complicating representations of the war as a phenomenon around which all Americans expressed patriotic fervor, Adams, *Best War Ever*.

41. Notice to "selected registrants."

42. Morton, *The Development and Structure of the War Relief Agencies*, 8; Ringland, "The Organization of Voluntary Foreign Aid, 384–45, 390; WRCB, *Voluntary War Relief*, 4–5, 56.

43. WRCB Meeting, February 8, 1944.

44. The three National War Fund campaigns raised $750 million, with nearly half the contributions distributed to the national war relief agencies, and the remainder to local welfare initiatives. The 1945 campaign covered every county in the U.S. Bureau of the Budget. "Community Chests Plan Joint Fund Drives"; "Private Relief Support Urged"; "Voluntary Aid Necessary," March 8, 1943, all in *New York Times*. Morton, *The Development and Structure of the War Relief Agencies*, 7–10; *The United States at War: Development and Administration of the War Program by the Federal Government* (Washington, D.C.: GPO, 1946), 18; WRCB, *Voluntary War Relief*, 10. .

45. Curti, *American Philanthropy Abroad*, 458–59; Reiss, *The American Council of Voluntary Agencies*, 1, 9–11, 15, 18, 20–22, 26–27, 38–39, Appendix IV; "Voluntary Aid Necessary." Before being appointed the UNRRA director shortly after the organization's founding in November 1944, Lehman had been serving as head of the government's Office of Foreign Relief and Rehabilitation Operations. "The Lehman OFRRO Blueprints Its Task," *New York Times*, January 7, 1943. OFRRO was established in November 1942, but was preceded by the Special Research Division of the U.S. State Department; the Division had begun formal studies of postwar issues in September 1941, two months before the bombing of Pearl Harbor. Bureau of the Budget, *The United States at War*, 409; Reiss, *The American Council of Voluntary Agencies*, 6; U.S. Department of State, *Foreign Relief and Rehabilitation Operations* (Washington, D.C.: GPO, 1943), 3, 31; *U.S. House of Representatives Hearings on UNRRA Participation*, December 1943 to January 1944 (Washington, D.C.: GPO, 1944), 8–10; "War Victim Relief Setup Is Drafted," *Washington Post*, January 11, 1943.

46. Allan Nevins, *Herbert H. Lehman and His Era* (New York: Scribner, 1963); Reiss, *The American Council of Voluntary Agencies*, 1–11, 22; Ben Shephard, " 'Becoming Planning Minded': The Theory and Practice of Relief, 1940-1945," *Journal of Contemporary History* 43 (2008): 411, 413; "Voluntary Aid Necessary." See also "Jewish Appeal Led by E. M. M. Warburg," March 13, 1940; "Praise New Hebrew Aid Group," April 27, 1941; "Relief Campaign Opened by Women," February 19, 1943, all in *New York Times*.

47. WRCB Meeting, February 8, 1944; Roosevelt, *Report to Congress on UNRRA*, September 30, 1944, 14–39.

48. On the existing relief campaigns of the U.S. and British governments see "Planning for Peace Seen Gaining in U.S.," *New York Times*, February 28, 1943; *U.S. Senate Hearings on H. J. Res. 192, UNRRA Participation*, February 1944 (Washington, D.C.:

GPO, 1944), 30. The Free French government had also begun dispensing relief supplies in North Africa that it had obtained through the U.S. Lend-Lease program. *U.S. House Hearings on UNRRA Participation*, December 1943 to January 1944 (Washington, D.C.: GPO, 1944), 22–23.

49. At this point, there were an estimated twenty million refugees in Europe and another forty million in Asia, mostly Chinese. *Senate Hearings on UNRRA*, February 1944, 22.

50. Stephen R. Porter, "Humanitarian Diplomacy After World War II: The United Nations Relief and Rehabilitation Administration," in *Foreign Policy Breakthroughs: Cases in Successful Diplomacy*, 27–37, ed. Robert Hutchings and Jeremi Suri (New York: Oxford University Press, 2015).

51. EO 9453; Roosevelt, *Report to Congress on UNRRA*, September 30, 1944, 14–15; P.L. 267, 78th Cong.; P.L. 382, 78th Cong., 2nd Sess.; Malcolm Proudfoot, *European Refugees, 1939–1952: A Study in Forced Population Movement* (Evanston, Ill.: Northwestern University Press, 1956), 106–8, 230–31; Roosevelt, *Report to Congress on UNRRA*, September 30, 1944, 5, 13–18; WRCB Meeting, February 8, 1944. On the total U.S. government financial contribution to UNRRA, George Woodbridge, *UNRRA: The History of the United Nations Relief and Rehabilitation Administration* (New York: Columbia University Press, 1950), 1:105, 112–18; 3:500. Though a civilian agency, UNRRA was ultimately subject to the authority of occupying militaries, something that at times caused considerable friction. "Agreement to Regularize Relations between UNRRA and Supreme Commander, Allied Expeditionary Force, During the Military Period," Archives Nationales du Luxembourg, Luxembourg. Relations Internationales. UNRRA, AE 8088, accessed on August 21, 2013, http://www.ena.lu/mce.cfm. These various issues are elaborated in Stephen R. Porter, "Humanitarian Politics and Governance: International Responses to World War II's Civilian Toll," in *The Cambridge History of the Second World War*, vol. 3, *Total War: Economy, Society and Culture*, ed. Michael Geyer and Adam Tooze (Cambridge: Cambridge University Press, 2015), 502–27.

52. "Lehman Discusses Food as a Weapon," *New York Times*, February 1, 1943.

53. Porter, "Humanitarian Diplomacy," 27–37; *Senate Hearings on UNRRA*, February 1944, 11–13 (quotation 13).

54. Woodbridge, *History of UNRRA*, 1:105, 112–18; 3:500.

55. National Opinion Research Center, University of Chicago, October, 1945, US-NORC.450135.R18A.

56. Borgwardt, *New Deal for the World*; Sparrow, *Warfare State*.

57. Woodbridge, *History of UNRRA*, vols. 1–3. Scholarship discussing criticisms leveled at UNRRA includes Sharif Gemie, Fiona Reid, and Laure Humbert, eds., *Outcast Europe: Refugees and Relief Workers in an Era of Total War, 1936–1948* (London: Continuum International, 2011), 321–23, 327, 332, 424, 488; Jessica Reinisch, "'Auntie UNRRA' at the Crossroads," *Past and Present* 218, supplement 8 (2013): 70–97. Also Gerard Daniel Cohen, "Between Relief and Politics: Refugee Humanitarianism in Occupied Germany"; Katerina Gardikas, "Relief Work and Malaria in Greece"; Jessica Reinisch, "Introduction:

Relief in the Aftermath of War"; and Frank Snowden, "Latina Province, 1944–1950," all *Journal of Contemporary History* 43 (2008): 365–66, 388. On refugee related matters that include UNRRA forcibly deporting displaced persons to Soviet controlled countries and the often poor treatment of uprooted German *Volksdeutsche*, see Gerard Daniel Cohen, *In War's Wake: Europe's Displaced Persons in the Postwar Order* (Oxford: Oxford University Press, 2011), 4–5, 18, 104; R. M. Douglas, *Orderly and Humane: The Expulsion of Germans After the First World War* (New Haven, Conn.: Yale University Press, 2012), 78, 187, 240, 243, 296; Anna Holian, *Between National Socialism and Soviet Communism: Displaced Persons in Postwar Germany* (Ann Arbor: University of Michigan Press, 2011), 81–119; Andrew Janco, "Soviet 'Displaced Persons' in Europe, 1941–1951" (PhD dissertation, University of Chicago, 2012); Porter, "Humanitarian Politics," 505–7; Jessica Reinisch and Elizabeth White, eds., *The Disentanglement of Populations: Migration, Expulsion and Displacement in Postwar Europe, 1944–1949* (New York: Palgrave, 2011), 51–70; Mark Wyman, *DP: Europe's Displaced Persons, 1945–1951* (Philadelphia: Balch Institute Press, 1989), 15–37. In addition to these operations were others performed outside UNRRA's official purview, and more unilaterally, by the U.S. government and American voluntary agencies, most notably in occupied Japan, Germany, and Austria under the Government and Relief in Occupied Areas program. Nicholas Balabkins, *Germany Under Direct Controls: Economic Aspects of Industrial Disarmament 1945–1948* (New Brunswick, N.J.: Rutgers University Press, 1964); FRUS, *The Far East*, vol. 8 (Washington, D.C.: GPO, 1946), 85–604; FRUS, *Foreign Economic Policy of the Historian, 1961–1963*, vol. 9, sec. 4 (Washington, D.C.: GPO, 1964); Eiji Takemae, *The Allied Occupation of Japan and Its Legacy*, trans. Robert Ricketts and Sebastian Swann (New York: Continuum, 2002); U.S. Senate Committee on Appropriations, *European Interim Aid and Government and Relief in Occupied Areas: Hearings Before the Committee on Appropriations, United States Senate, Eightieth Congress, First Session* (Washington, D.C.: GPO, 1947).

58. Agreement for the United Nations Relief and Rehabilitation Administration, November 9, 1943, in Woodbridge, *History of UNRRA*, vol. 3, Appendix III; *Senate Hearings on UNRRA*, February 1944, 21, 38.

59. Gemie, *Outcast Europe*, 362.

60. Erika Mann and Eric Estorick, "Private and Governmental Aid to Refugees," *Annals of the American Academy of Political and Social Sciences* 203, 1 (1939): 142–54; Michael R. Marrus, *The Unwanted: European Refugees in the Twentieth Century* (New York: Oxford University Press, 1985), 170–72; Malcom J. Proudfoot, *European Refugees*, 30–31.

61. "Ninth and Final Financial Report of the United Nations Relief and Rehabilitation Administration for the Entire Period of Operation," March 1949, UNRRA Publication, Records of the United Service for New Americans, RG 246, 2:12, F 596, YIVO Archives; "Text of Truman UNRRA Message," November 13, 1945, Speech to US Congress, F 1398, NRS; United Nations Department of Public Information, Research Section, "Refugees," Background Paper 78, December 29, 1953; UNRRA Press Release, "Remarks by Herbert H. Lehman, Director General, UNRRA, September 12, 1945." Late in its

operational tenure, it stopped the practice of receiving private donations. "UNRRA Shuts Door on Private Gifts," *New York Times*, September 9, 1946; "UNRRA Takes No More Aid from Private Groups," *Chicago Daily Tribune*, September 4, 1946.

62. One million Chinese, for instance, were internally displaced and, though not officially categorized as "displaced persons," were nonetheless given transportation assistance by the Chinese relief agency that UNRRA funded. Cohen, *In War's Wake*, 35–57; Holian, *Between National Socialism*, 3–4; Reinisch and White, *Disentanglement of Populations*; Woodbridge, *History of UNRRA*, 2:469–96. UNRRA's constitution forbade it from supporting enemy civilians in Germany and Japan, vast populations who were also in desperate conditions after the war. UNRRA Agreement, November 9, 1943.

63. The Soviet government honored four officials of Russian War Relief that summer, with two officials receiving less prestigious awards that same day at the Kremlin ceremony. The Russian relief organization was known by a variety of names during the war, "Russian War Relief" being the most common. On the ceremony and attendant quotation, see "All Gifts of Russian War Relief"; "Russian Aid Chief Gets Soviet Honor," August 29, 1945 (quotation); "Russian Relief to Continue," January 1, 1947; "U.S. Group Quits Russia," August 11, 1946, all in *New York Times*. On the importance of RWR among American voluntary agencies and on Carter's biography, see Edward C. Carter, "Russian War Relief," *Slavonic and East European Review* 3, 2 (1944), 61, 64–65; "Biography," Edward C. Carter Collection, University of Vermont Libraries and Special Collections, accessed July 21, 2015, http://cdi.uvm.edu/findingaids/collection/carter.ead.xml#Biography.

64. Carter, "Russian War Relief," 67–70, 74, quotation 62.

65. Ibid., 61.

66. "All Gifts of Russian War Relief."

67. WRCB, *Voluntary War Relief*, 14–15.

68. "Group to Survey Needs of Russians," *New York Times*, July 12, 1946.

69. Trying to maintain friendlier relations with the Soviets, for instance, were Commerce Secretary Henry A. Wallace and Senator Claude Pepper of Florida. "Contrasting Views on Russian Moves," March 20, 1946; "Russia Praised Here," June 3, 1946, both in *New York Times*. See also "'Patience Without Appeasement' Urged by Dr. Stockman as U.S. Policy on Russia," September 16, 1946, *New York Times*. Founded in 1941, the Russian relief organization had been typically headed by business leaders, diplomats, and retired military officers, often without any ancestral affiliation to the Soviet Union. Former U.S. ambassador to the Soviet Union and War Relief Control Board member Joseph Davies, for instance, had been centrally involved in the agency's founding. Curti, *American Philanthropy Abroad*, 463–65; "Gen. Haskell Is Elected," June 4, 1942, *New York Times*; Morton, *Development and Structure of the War Relief Agencies*, 34–35; Seymour, *Design for Giving*, 87–88. This said, RWR did periodically come under attack for alleged communist sympathies by some of its officials. These criticisms increased over time as relations between the United States and the USSR grew more hostile. "The Russian Relief Racket," *Chicago Daily-Tribune*, August 6, 1946; "Union Denies Gift to Russian Group," *New York Times*, November 9, 1941.

70. "Needs of Russians."

71. The main cities on the tour were Moscow, Leningrad, Minsk, and the Georgian capital, Tbilisi. "American Relief Workers Tell of Conditions in Russia," August 16, 1946; "Credit for Soviet Urged," August 12, 1946, both in *New York Times*.

72. From 1929 to the early 1940s, Soviet officials worked to destroy organized religion in the Soviet Union by extreme taxation, church closings, and persecution of clergy. This policy was reversed in 1943 when Joseph Stalin met with leading church officials in the Kremlin, agreeing to help revive organized religion. In 1946 and 1947, however, with the war over and the Cold War beginning, government policy became less hospitable toward organized religion once again. By the late 1950s, under the direction of Nikita Khrushchev, Soviet policy toward religion had once more become hostile. Tatiana A. Chumachenko, *Church and State in Soviet Russia: Russian Orthodoxy from World War II to the Khrushchev Years*, ed. and trans. Edward E. Roslof (Armonk, N.Y.: Sharpe, 2002); Heather Coleman, "Atheism Versus Secularization? Religion in Soviet Russia, 1917–1961," *Kritika: Explorations in Russian and Eurasian History* 1 (2000): 547–58.

73. "Baptist Tells Here of Tour of Missions," August 21, 1946; "Credit for Soviet Urged," August 12, 1946; "Find Baptist Rites in Moscow Like Ours," July 23, 1946; " 'Patience Without Appeasement' Urged"; "U.S. Group Quits Russia," August 11, 1946, all in *New York Times*; "Russia Baptist Population Set at 1,500,000," *Washington Post*, July 23, 1946. In autumn of the previous year a Russian archbishop spoke to a large New York congregation, at the invitation of Russian War Relief, assuring them that there was indeed a clean separation of church and state in the Soviet Union. "Freedom of Church in Russia Stressed," *New York Times*, November 28, 1945.

74. "Peace Held Desire of Soviet People," *New York Times*, August 15, 1946.

75. "Credit for Soviet Urged" (quotation). Also "Peace Held Desire"; "U.S. Delegation Finds No Soviet 'Curtain,' " August 2, 1946, all in *New York Times*.

76. See, for example, the many debates from 1946 to 1949 between U.S. and Soviet diplomats over the fate of Soviet Bloc refugees and the role of the International Refugee Organization in the files of the United Nations Economic and Social Council and the United Nations General Assembly, both found in General Records of the State Department, Records Relating to the International Refugee Organization and the Displaced Persons Commission, IRO Subject File, 1946–1952, NARA, RG 59, Bes, 1, 21, 23, and 26. These battles continued into the late 1940s. Louise W. Holborn, *The International Refugee Organization: A Specialized Agency of the United Nations, its History and Work, 1946–1952* (London: Oxford University Press, 1956), 22, 31–33, 44, 167, 339–64; Proudfoot, *European Refugees*, 131–33, 152–57, 207–20.

77. "Finds No Soviet 'Curtain' "; "Tell of Conditions in Russia."

78. On this issue generally, see Elaine Tyler May, *Homeward Bound: American Families in the Cold War Era* (New York: Basic, 1988).

79. "American Lidice," August 3, 1946; "Citizens Ask Truman Head Lynch Quiz," August, 1946; "Four Negroes Murdered by Georgia Mob," August 3, 1946; "Nation's Lynch Toll Nears 5,000," August 17, 1946, all in *Chicago Defender*.

80. "Atkinson vs. Zaslavsky," *New York Times*, July 14, 1946; "Mr. Zaslavsky Takes his Pen in Hand," *Chicago Daily Tribune*, July 28, 1946; "Finds No Soviet 'Curtain"; "Peace Held Desire"; "Tell of Conditions in Russia."

81. Carter, "Russian War Relief," 63–64; Murray Friedman, *Philadelphia Jewish Life: 1940–2000* (Philadelphia: Temple University Press, 2003), 5–8, 14, 61, 241–42; Joseph McBride, *Frank Capra: The Catastrophe of Success* (Jackson: University Press of Mississippi, 2011), 600.

82. "The Russian Relief Racket," *Chicago Daily-Tribune*; August 6, 1946. RWR would, however, continue to purchase and distribute goods for another six months. Carter, "Russian War Relief," 63–64; "Russian Relief to Continue," *New York Times*, January 1, 1947. A program RWR had run to provide clothing to Soviet orphans was passed on in a limited form to the newly organized Church World Service in 1947. "Clothing for Russians," March 7, 1947, *New York Times*. See also "Contrasting Views on Russian Moves," March 20, 1946; "Policies of Soviet Hit by Harriman," September 23, 1946; "Relief for Russia," August 6, 1946, all in *New York Times*.

83. "50 Leaders Endorse Yugoslavia Relief," April 21, 1947; "House Group Hails Voluntary Relief," February 1, 1948; "Poland Will Oust Third Relief Unit," November 4, 1949; "Yugoslav Aid Unit Plans to Disband," all in *New York Times*. See also Eleanor Roosevelt, "My Day," November 17, 1947, accessed July 28, 2015, https://www.gwu.edu/~erpapers/myday/, accessed July 14, 1948.

84. Much of the institutional energy behind those wartime agencies that had been organized along the lines of recipient nations became rechanneled after the war, especially through religious affiliation. Many postwar refugee aid initiatives were directed by such new entities as (pan-Protestant and Orthodox Christian) Church World Service, and the Department of Welfare in the National Lutheran Council, alongside older relief organizations supported by America's Jewish and Roman Catholic communities. Most of the agencies remained under the ACVAFS umbrella. "Catholics to Aid Post-War Europe," *New York Times*, March 12, 1943; Curti, *American Philanthropy Abroad*, 452, 477–526; Haim Genizi, *America's Fair Share: The Admission and Resettlement of Displaced Persons, 1945–1952* (Detroit: Wayne State University Press, 1993), 28–63; Akira Iriye, *Global Community: The Role of International Organizations in the Making of the Contemporary World* (Berkeley: University of California Press, 2004), 52–53; Reiss, *The American Council of Voluntary Agencies*, 52–64, Appendix III; Reiss and Eileen Egan, *Transfigured Night: The CRALOG Experience* (Philadelphia: Livingston, 1964), 22, 24, 65, 71, 95.

85. "Truman Backs Relief by Private Agencies," February 28, 1947 (quotation); "Voluntary Relief for Europeans in January Put at $14,084,653," March 15, 1947; both in *New York Times*. On projects variously referred to as "reconstruction," "modernization," or "development," see, for example, Dean Acheson, *Present at the Creation: My Years in the State Department* (New York: Norton, 1969), 133, 223, 226–35, 237, 261; David Ekbladh, *The Great American Mission: Modernization and the Construction of a World Order* (Princeton, N.J.: Princeton University Press, 2011); Amanda McVety, *Enlightened Aid:*

U.S. Development as Foreign Policy in Ethiopia (New York: Oxford University Press, 2012); Reiss, *The American Council of Voluntary Agencies*, 65–79; David F. Schmitz, *Thank God They're on Our Side: The United States and Right-Wing Dictatorships, 1921–1965* (Chapel Hill: University of North Carolina Press, 1999), 125–292; Takemae, *Allied Occupation of Japan*.

86. The new federal committee would not regulate *domestic* war relief charities, as had the Control Board. Nor were internationally-active voluntary agencies required to register with it. However, practically, an agency was behooved to register if it had any hope of playing a very significant role in the largest international relief initiatives, increasingly mobilized through the U.S. government and the UN agencies. Through agencies such as the U.S. Agency for International Development (USAID), the federal government has continued this realm of regulatory partnership into the twenty-first century. See, for example, the finding aid summary of the WRCB files: 220.5.6 WRCB, Case files, 1941–46; Reiss, *Voluntary War Relief*, 20, 54, 68–76.

87. Cohen, *In War's Wake*, 30–34, 61–67; Holborn, *The International Refugee Organization*; Jacques Vernant, *The Refugee in the Post-War World* (New Haven, Conn.: Yale University Press, 1953), 33–38.

88. Porter, "Humanitarian Politics," 525.

89. UN Secretary General Kofe Annan, for instance, remarked in 2000, "I see a United Nations which recognizes that the NGO revolution—the new global people-power—is the best thing that has happened to our Organization in a long time." Steve Charnovitz, "Nongovernmental Organizations and International Law," *The American Journal of International Law* 100 (2006), 363. Examples of scholarship suggesting that the post-World War II growth of NGOs has often challenged the primacy of the nation-state system include Kenneth Cmiel, "The Recent History of Human Rights," *American Historical Review* 109, 1 (2004): 117–35; Korey, *NGOs*; Iriye, *Global Community*; Paul Gordon Lauren, *The Evolution of International Human Rights: Visions Seen* (Philadelphia: University of Pennsylvania Press, 1998). Samuel Moyn is notable among those who have questioned the degree to which that nation-state system has actually been challenged by global transformations since World War II, particularly with regard to the politics of human rights. Moyn, *The Last Utopia: Human Rights in History* (Cambridge, Mass.: Belknap Press of Harvard University Press, 2010).

Chapter 4. Benevolent or Fair Superpower?

1. "Excerpts from a letter from a D.P. in Mississippi," signed "E.C.," undated, but prior to March 6, 1950, State Historical Society of Wisconsin, Governor's Committee on Resettlement of Displaced Persons, Series 2195, B 7, F Lauma Kasak (hereafter Wisconsin DP Committee); E. Celms to Kasak, January 6, 1950; Stanislavs Jermacans to Kasak, January 11, 1950; Paul Karklins to Lauma Kasak, November 29 (actual date December 29), 1949; Paul Karklins to "Madam" (Lauma Kasak), December 11, 1949; J. Kaulins to Kasak, April 18, 1950; Maria Silis to Kasak, June 17, 1950; Karlis Zemitans to Kasak, June 13, 1950; Kasak to Elliot M. Shirk, November 13, 1950; Kasak to Shirk,

November 30, 1950; Olga Velitis to Kasak, October 6, 1950, all in Records of the U.S. Displaced Persons Commission, Resettlement Division, RG 278, B 113, F Mississippi, NARA (hereafter DPC).

2. These matters are discussed in Chapter 2.

3. Quotations from Harry N. Rosenfield, "The DP Program—The Free World's Way" (speech given at the [Southern] Regional Conference of the Displaced Persons Commission, November 30, 1950), Harry N. Rosenfield Papers, 1945–1953, B 13, F New Orleans Conference, Harry S. Truman Presidential Library (hereafter Rosenfield Papers).

4. Generally, see boxes 108–18 in DPC. Beyond those documents cited later in this chapter, specific examples from the collection include Minutes of a Meeting of the California Displaced Persons Committee, November 10, 1948, B 108, F California; Harry Rosenfield to Leon Climenko, March 1950, B 115, F New York, day not recorded. See also Edward B. Marks, "First thoughts on resettlement of D.P.s in the U.S.," June 24, 1948, and Edward B. Marks, Jr., to Harry N. Rosenfield, August 19, 1948, both in Rosenfield Papers, B 2, F ECOSOC; "Union Asks DP Shifts," July 9, 1949; "Union Wins, DP Loses Job," August 3, 1949, both in *New York Times*.

5. Carol Elaine Anderson, *Eyes off the Prize: The United Nations and the African American Struggle for Human Rights, 1944–1954* (New York: Cambridge University Press, 2003); Thomas Borstelmann, *The Cold War and the Color Line: American Race Relations in the Global Arena* (Cambridge, Mass.: Harvard University Press, 2001); Mary Dudziak, *Cold War Civil Rights: Race and the Image of American Democracy* (Princeton, N.J.: Princeton University Press, 2000); Paul Gordon Lauren, *Power and Prejudice: The Politics of Diplomacy and Racial Discrimination* (Boulder, Colo.: Westview Press, 1988); Penny M. Von Eschen, *Race Against Empire: Black Americans and Anticolonialism, 1937–1957* (Ithaca, N.Y.: Cornell University Press, 1997).

6. "Bright New World Is Opened for Latvians in Mississippi," *Commercial Appeal* (Memphis), November 23, 1948; "D.P.'s Make a Hit in Mississippi," *Courier-Journal* (Louisville), January 17, 1949; "400 More DPs Coming South for New Life," *Tate County Democrat* (Mississippi), April 27, 1949.

7. On the categorization of "displaced persons" and the assumption of responsibility for them by UNRRA, see Chapter 3 of this book. Robert A Divine, *American Immigration Policy, 1924–1952* (New Haven, Conn.: Yale University Press, 1957), 114–28; Gil Loescher and John A. Scanlan, *Calculated Kindness: Refugees and America's Half-Open Door, 1945 to the Present* (New York: Free Press, 1986), 7–8; Malcolm J. Proudfoot, *European Refugees: 1939–1952* (Evanston, Ill.: Northwestern University Press, 1956), 78–93, 189–229, 399–428; Jacques Vernant, *The Refugee in the Post-War World* (New Haven, Conn.: Yale University Press, 1953), 13–23, 54–104; U.S. Senate and House Hearings on the Admission of Displaced Persons, *Congressional Record*, 80th Cong., 2nd Sess., 1948, 6454, 6567, 6893, 7732 (May 26–27, June 2 and 14, 1948). On the international legal status of *non-refoulement* in the early Cold War, see Susan L. Carruthers, "Between Camps: Eastern Bloc 'Escapees' and Cold War Borderlands," *American Quarterly* 57 (2005): 920.

8. Anna D. Jaroszynska-Kirchmann, *The Exile Mission: The Polish Political Diaspora and Polish Americans, 1939–1956* (Athens: Ohio University Press, 2004), 111–12; Loescher and Scanlan, *Calculated Kindness*, 3–7; Proudfoot, *European Refugees*, 214–20.

9. Louise W. Holborn, *The International Refugee Organization: A Specialized Agency of the United Nations, Its History and Work, 1946–1952* (London: Oxford University Press, 1956), 1–53; *U.S. Senate Hearings on H. J. Res. 192, UNRRA Participation*, February 1944 (Washington, D.C.: GPO, 1944), 30.

10. House Hearings on the Admission of Displaced Persons, *Congressional Record*, 80th Cong., 2nd Sess. (June 14, 1948), 7739.

11. American Federation of Labor, "Protection of Migrant and Immigrant Labor"; David Dubinsky (AFL) to Trygve Lie (UN Secretary-General), June 30, 1947, both in Rosenfield Papers, B 1, F UN ECOSOC. Also "Russian Presses Refugee Charges," *New York Times*, November 8, 1947; UN Economic and Social Council, "Report of the Secretary-General on the Allocation of Functions among the Various Organs Concerned in the Field of Migration," May 28, 1948, *Reports of the Economic and Social Council* (Lake Success, N.Y.: UN, 1948).

12. Vernant, *The Refugee in the Post-War World*, 255–734.

13. Carl Bon Tempo, *Americans at the Gate: The United States and Refugees During the Cold War* (Princeton, N.J.: Princeton University Press, 2008), 22–25; Anthony Trawick Bouscaren, *International Migrations since 1945* (New York: Praeger, 1963), 7; Leonard Dinnerstein, *America and the Survivors of the Holocaust* (New York: Columbia University Press, 1982), 137–82, 217–54; DPC, *Memo to America*, 9–41; E. P. Hutchinson, *Legislative History of American Immigration Policy, 1798–1956* (Philadelphia: University of Pennsylvania Press, 1981), 279–82. On a late 1945 executive directive placed by President Harry S. Truman—one that eventually admitted forty thousand European refugees, mostly Jews, into the United States during the two years before the passage of the DP Act—see Dinnerstein, *America and the Survivors of the Holocaust*, 112–13, 118, 140, 163–64, 204–6; Haim Genizi, *America's Fair Share: The Admission and Resettlement of Displaced Persons, 1945–1952* (Detroit: Wayne State University Press, 1993), 61–80.

14. Minutes of the Church World Service Committee on Displaced Persons, December 9, 1948, unprocessed files located at the headquarters of the Church World Service, New York City (hereafter CWS); A. T. Callicott to Ugo Carusi, November 27, 1948; Si Corley to Carusi, November 30, 1948; Carusi to Si Corley, December 10, 1948, all in DPC, B 113, F Mississippi. "DPs in Dixie: Ups—and Downs—Bared," June 30, 1949, *Christian Science Monitor*; "400 More DPs"; "Latvians to Mississippi," November 24, 1948, *Beaumont Texas Journal*; "Bright New World."

15. James C. Cobb, *The Selling of the South: The Southern Crusade for Industrial Development* (Baton Rouge: Louisiana State University Press, 1980); Pete Daniel, *Breaking the Land: The Transformation of Cotton, Tobacco, and Rice Cultures Since 1889* (Urbana: University of Illinois Press, 1985), xiii–xiv, 168–82, 240–49, 262; Bruce J. Schulman, *From Cotton Belt to Sun Belt* (Durham, N.C.: Duke University Press, 1991); Gavin

Wright, *Old South, New South: Revolutions in the Southern Economy since the Civil War* (New York: Basic, 1986).

16. Daniel, *Breaking the Land*, 155–83, 239–52; Robert Korstad and Nelson Lichtenstein, "Opportunities Found and Lost: Labor, Radicals, and the Early Civil Rights Movement," *Journal of American History* 75 (1988): 786–93; H. L. Mitchell, *Mean Things Happening in This Land: The Life and Times of H. L. Mitchell, Co-Founder of the Southern Tenant Farmers Union* (Montclair, N.J.: Allanheld, Osman, 1979), generally, but especially 188–92.

17. "D.P.'s Make a Hit" (quotation). Also A. T. Callicott to Carusi; Carusi to Si Corley; Corley to Carusi, November 30, 1948, all in DPC, B 113, F Mississippi. Also "Bright New World"; "DPs in Dixie"; "400 More DPs"; "Latvians to Mississippi"; minutes of the Church World Service Committee on Displaced Persons, December 9, 1948, CWS. Photographs of Latvian refugees in Nuremberg DP camps show clean-cut and fair (often blond) groups of people, something that may have appealed to Callicott as he considered bringing them to Mississippi communities. See Lutheran World Federation Album, 1947–1949, National Lutheran Council, Records of the Lutheran Resettlement Service, Evangelical Lutheran Church of American Archives (hereafter LRS).

18. Divine, *American Immigration Policy*, 116–17, 126; House and Senate Hearings, *Congressional Record*, 80th Cong., 2nd Sess., 1948, 6585, 8858, 8861–62 (May 27, June 18, 1948). Another two hundred three thousand immigration slots were added to the act when it was amended in 1950. 62 Stat. 1009, 80th Cong., 2nd Sess.; 64 Stat. 219, 81st Cong., 2nd Sess.

19. 62 Stat. 1009, 80th Cong., 2nd. Sess.; 64 Stat. 219, 81st Cong., 2nd Sess.

20. "Senate DP Measure Called Booby Trap and Discriminatory," *Washington Star*, June 7, 1948; House Hearings, 80th Cong., 2nd Sess.; Hearings before the Subcommittee on Amendments to the Displaced Persons Act of the Committee on the Judiciary (Senate), 81st Cong., 1st and 2nd Sess., Congressional Record, March 25, 1949, to March 16, 1950; Genizi, America's Fair Share, 61–111. Dinnerstein, *America and the Survivors of the Holocaust*, 137–82.

21. See, for example, DPC, *Memo to America*, 141–60, 238–41, 267–93; Genizi, *America's Fair Share*, 28–55, 114–201; summary of meeting between Harry N. Rosenfield and American Jewish immigrant aid societies, August 30, 1948, Rosenfield Papers, Chronological File, 1948.

22. DPC, *Memo to America*, 182–210; Milton Friedman, "DP 'Magician,'" August 9, 1951, *Jewish Advocate*.

23. DPC, *Memo to America*, 21–99; O'Connor to Carusi, August 24, 1948, Rosenfield Papers.

24. "Bright New World."

25. The number Callicott was directly involved in recruiting appears to be closer to one thousand, although, as a result of his actions, and the publicity he propagated, over one thousand more DPs were sponsored by Mississippians by autumn 1950. Hopewell

H. Darneille, Jr., "Mississippi State Committee for Resettlement of Displaced Persons," 2–3, DPC, B 113, F Mississippi.

26. "Memorandum of Understanding between the Displaced Persons Commission and the Advisory Committee on Voluntary Foreign Aid of the United States," February 9, 1949, Rosenfield Papers, B 9, F ACVAFS; U.S. DPC Meeting, September 2, 1948, Rosenfield Papers, B 3, F Chronological File, 1948.

27. Callicott to Carusi, November 27, 1948; Carusi to Corley, December 10, 1948; Corley to Carusi, November 30, 1948, all in DPC, B 113, F Mississippi. Also "808 DP's Land at Boston Today," *New York Herald Tribune*, November 19, 1948.

28. "808 D.P.s Land at Boston for New Homes," *New York Herald Tribune*, November 19, 1948; "Rejoicing DPs Welcomed by Boston," *Christian Science Monitor*, November 19, 1948.

29. "Bright New World"; "D.P.'s Make a Hit"; "Latvians to Mississippi," all in Rosenfield Papers, B 28, F January 49. Aroos Benneyan's report on the 'Callicott Resettlement Project in Mississippi, Appendix I, CWS-S-178 to minutes of the Church World Service Committee on Displaced Persons, December 9, 1948, CWS; "Mississippi Town Greets 89 Latvian D.P. Settlers," *New York Herald Tribune*, November 24, 1948.

30. "Latvians to Mississippi" (quotation). Also Aroos Benneyan's report, CWS; "Bright New World"; "D.P.'s Make a Hit in Mississippi"; "Mississippi Town Greets 89."

31. "Latvians to Mississippi" (first quotation); Darneille, Jr., "Mississippi State Committee for Resettlement of Displaced Persons" (second quotation). See also "Bright New World."

32. See, for example, "Excerpts from a Letter from a D.P. in Mississippi," signed "E.C.," undated, but prior to March 6, 1950; Maria Silis to Lauma Kasak, June 17, 1950; Wisconsin DP Committee, B 7, F Lauma Kasak.

33. "D.P.'s Make a Hit."

34. Jason Morgan Ward, "'No Jap Crow': Japanese Americans Encounter the World War II South," *Journal of Southern History* 52 (2007): 75–104.

35. Jeannie M. Whayne, ed., *Shadows over Sunnyside: An Arkansas Plantation in Transition, 1830–1945* (Fayetteville: University of Arkansas Press, 1993).

36. Daniel, *Breaking the Land*, 160.

37. The thirty dollar fee Callicott charged is listed on sharecropping contracts he had the refugees sign at the German port of Bremerhaven, and sometimes even before that at their DP Camp residences. Beyond the other standard items for which the soon-to-be sharecroppers would immediately go into debt—for example, seed, farming equipment, lights, and cows—was an additional fee Callicott charged the refugees for transportation from their port of entry to their new Mississippi homes. See, for example, Edith Terry Bremer (American Federation of International Institutes, in New York City) to Contract between Stanislavs Jermacans and the Delta and Pine Land Co. of Mississippi, February 6, 1950, DPC, B113, F Mississippi; Pauline S. Gardescu (Wisconsin DP Committee), February 28, 1950, Wisconsin DP Committee, B 7, F Lauma Kasak.

38. "D.P.'s Make a Hit"; minutes of the Church World Service Committee on Displaced Persons, December 9, 1948, CWS.

39. "D.P.'s Make a Hit."

40. Mr. Johnston to DP Commission, December 3, 1948; Edward M. O'Connor to Johnston, December 16, 1948; O'Connor to Johnston, January 14, 1949; all in DPC, B 113, F Mississippi. "Memorandum of Understanding between the Displaced Persons Commission and the Advisory Committee on Voluntary Foreign Aid of the United States," February 9, 1949, Rosenfield Papers, B 9, F ACVAFS; minutes of the Church World Service Committee on Displaced Persons, December 9, 1948, CWS; U.S. DPC Meeting, September 2, 1948, Rosenfield Papers, B 3, F Chronological File, 1948.

41. Meeting on Plan for Immigration to the United States, August 9, 1948, Rosenfield Papers, B 9, F ACVAFS; DPC, *Memo to America*, 55-69.

42. On humanitarian norms produced during the era of the First World War, especially through the work of Hoover, see Bruno Cabanes, *The Great War and the Origins of Humanitarianism, 1918-1924* (Cambridge: Cambridge University Press, 2014), 189-247. On the motivations and activities behind the UDHR, see Mary Ann Glendon, *A World Made New: Eleanor Roosevelt and the Universal Declaration of Human Rights* (New York: Random House, 2001); William Korey, *NGOs and the Universal Declaration of Human Rights: "A Curious Grapevine"* (New York: St. Martin's, 1998); Samuel Moyn, *The Last Utopia: Human Rights in History* (Cambridge, Mass.: Belknap Press of Harvard University Press, 2010), 62-71. On the role of human rights in American geopolitical strategies after the war, Elizabeth Borgwardt, *A New Deal for the World: America's Vision for Human Rights* (Cambridge, Mass.: Belknap Press of Harvard University Press, 2005).

43. Cable from Displaced Persons Commission, Frankfurt, to Secretary of State, February 2, 1949; Edward M. O'Connor to Harry Rosenfield and Ugo Carusi, February 3, 1949; Edward M. O'Connor to J. P. Cole, January 26, 1949, all in DPC, B 113, F Mississippi.

44. Dinnerstein, *America and the Survivors of the Holocaust*, 164-65, 244-45; Divine, *American Immigration Policy*, 124, 136, 140.

45. Minutes of DP Commission, February 10, 1949, Rosenfield Papers, B 3, F Chronological File, 1949; Alexander Squadrilli to Ugo Carusi, Harry Rosenfield, and Edward O'Connor, February 3, 1949, DPC, B 113, F Mississippi.

46. "Careful Placing of DP's Is Urged," *New York Times*, October 16, 1948.

47. "Aroos Benneyan's report," CWS.

48. Minutes of a Meeting of the California Displaced Persons Committee, August 31, 1948; Rev. Frederick A. Smith to Harry Rosenfield, December 10, 1948, both in DPC, B 108, California folder.

49. "56 DPs to Settle in Mississippi," *Chicago Defender*, February 19, 1949.

50. See, for example, "Christian Solution," *Phoenix, Arizona Gazette*, July 22, 1949; Rosenfield Papers, B 28, F Newspaper Clippings.

51. "Careful Placing of DP's Is Urged."

52. "Louisiana Story," 5, Rosenfield Papers, B 18, F Louisiana Resettlement Problem; "Low Pay for DP's Laid to U.S. Action," May 4, 1949, *New Orleans Item*; Meeting of the Louisiana State Displaced Persons Commission, December 14, 1949, both in DPC, B

111, Complaint folder; "Report to His Excellency, Most Reverend Joseph P. Rummel, Archbishop of New Orleans Re: Resettlement of Displaced Persons in the New Orleans Area," May 6, 1949. Also "Low Wage Held Sugar Act Fault," May 4, 1949; "No DP Abuse Seen by Msgr. Castel," May 4, 1949; "DPs in the Cane Belt," May 4, 1949, all in *New Orleans Times-Picayune*.

53. Bremer to Gardescu, February 28, 1950; "DPs in Dixie"; "Louisiana Story," 5, Rosenfield Papers; "Priest Finds That DP's Work in 'Semi-Servitude' in South, Their Babies 'Crying for Food, Milk,'" *New York Times*, May 4, 1949; "Report to His Excellency," DPC. .

54. Carusi to Coman, July 1, 1948; Ellis S. Coman to Carusi, June 29, 1948; Minutes of a Meeting of the California Displaced Persons Committee, November 10, 1948; United Press release, July 12, 1948; Edward O'Connor to Harry Rosenfield, November 5, 1948, all in DPC, B 108, California folder; Governor Earl Warren to Ugo Carusi, July 21, 1949.

55. Cindy Cavalita, *Inside the State: The Bracero Program, Illegal Immigrants, and the INS* (New York: Routledge, 1992); Robert S. Robinson, "Taking the Fair Deal to the Fields: Truman's Commission on Migratory Labor, Public Law 78, and the Bracero Program," *Agricultural History* 84 (2010): 382–402.

56. "Canada DP Program Hailed as Success," *Christian Science Monitor*, January 6, 1949; "First of 20 Groups on Way to Quebec from Germany," September 17, 1948, *Reuters News Agency*; Andrew Markus, "Labour and Immigration 1946–49: The Displaced Persons Program," *Labour History* 46 (1984): 73–90; "Russian Presses Refugee Charges," *New York Times*, November 8, 1947; Vernant, *The Refugee in the Post-War World*, 295–314, 340–66, 542–78..

57. DPC, *Memo to America*, v–viii, 1–3, 211–25; Rosenfield, "The DP Program," Rosenfield Papers.

58. "Tea with the Iron Lady," *Baltics Worldwide*, http://www.balticsworldwide.com/vike-freiberga_tea.htm, 2002 (originally published in *Financial Times*), accessed March 19, 2015.

59. Displaced Persons Commission memorandum from Virginia Mosley, March 24, 1949; Displaced Persons Commission telegram to "interested persons," April 21, 1949; Lutheran Resettlement Service, "Progress Report to Lutheran Resettlement Committees," October 17, 1952, LRS, B 1, F Area Committees-General; memorandum from Rosenfield to Edward O'Connor and Ugo Carusi, February 23, 1949; Rosenfield to Ransom Aldrich, April 19, 1949; Rosenfield to Aldrich, April 27, 1949; Harry N. Rosenfield to Charles Gage, February 23, 1949, all in DPC, B 113, F Mississippi.

60. Incoming airgram no. 36–3767 from the Department of State, Division of Communication and Records, Moscow, May 10, 1949, DPC, B 111, Complaint folder; James J. McTigue to Cordelia Cox, May 2, 1949, LRS, B 4, F US Gov. Displaced Persons Commission; Harry N. Rosenfield to Ransom Aldrich, April 25, 1949, DPC, B 111, F Mississippi.

61. Harry N. Rosenfield to Cordelia Cox, April 19, 1949; James J. McTigue to Cordelia Cox, May 2, 1949, both in, LRS, B 4, F US Gov. Displaced Persons Commission. Also

Gregor Sobba, "DPs in Dixie"; "Exploiting DP's Denied," *New York Times*, May 5, 1949; "University of Georgia Displaced Persons Study" précis, September 15, 1952, National Lutheran Conference Records, RG 5/3/2, B 4, F US Gov. Displaced Persons Commission.

62. "DP Sharecroppers Brought to South," *New York Times*, May 14, 1949; Stanislavs Jermacans to Lauma Kasak, January 11, 1950, DPC, F Mississippi.

63. "Report to His Excellency," DPC; Lawrence E. Higgins to Harry N. Rosenfield, May 5, 1949, both in B 111, Complaint folder. Also Guy J. D'Antonio to Harry N. Rosenfield, May 6, 1949; "Louisiana Story," 2, Rosenfield Papers; "'Semi-Servitude' of DPs in South Astounds Priest," AP Press Release, May 3, 1949.

64. Airgram from Moscow, May 10, 1949, DPC, B 111, Complaint folder.

65. Guy J. D'Antonio to Harry N. Rosenfield, May 6, 1949; W. H. Grayson to T. H. Allen (Chief, Wage and Price Division, Sugar Branch, U.S. Department of Agriculture), May 4, 1949, both in DPC , B 111, Complaint folder. Also "DPs in Dixie"; "Low Pay for DP's"; "Low Wage Held Sugar Act Fault"; "No DP Abuse Seen."

66. "Name 3-Man Group to Start Flow of DPs," AP Press Release, August 2, 1948, Rosenfield Papers, B 26, F News Clippings, 1948.

67. "DPs in Dixie"; "Louisiana Plantations Exploiting"; "Louisiana Story," 1, Rosenfield Papers; "Low Pay for DP's"; "Priest Finds"; "Report to His Excellency," DPC.

68. Bremer Gardescu, February 28, 1950; Jermacans and Delta Co. contract; Meeting of the California Displaced Persons Committee, March 10, 1949, DPC.

69. U.S. DPC Meeting, July 12, 1949.

70. Kasak to Shirk, November 13, 1950 (first quotation); "Latvians to Mississippi" (second quotation). Also Kasak to Shirk, November 30, 1950; Bernard J. Maegi, "Dangerous Persons, Delayed Pilgrims: Baltic Displaced Persons and the Making of Cold War America, 1945–1952" (PhD dissertation, University of Minnesota, 2008), 222–23, 230; Shirk to Kasak, January 19, 1951; Andris Stramanis, "Memorial Would Honor Latvians in Mississippi," *Latvians Online*, August 19, 2004, http://latviansonline.com/memorial-would-honor-latvians-in-mississippi/,accessed March 25, 2015.

71. See, for example, Agenda for the Second Session of the Economic and Social Council, April 30, 1946; Department of State memorandum, July 1948; Department of State report, "Background: First Session of the Economic and Social Council"; Paul V. McNutt to Dean Acheson, August 24, 1945; Watson B. Miller (FSA administrator) to Dean Acheson (acting secretary of state), May 21, 1946; Harry N. Rosenfield memorandum, May 14, 1946; Harry N. Rosenfield to McNutt, August 25, 1945; John G. Winant to Watson B. Miller, May 6, 1946, all in Rosenfield Papers, B 2, F UN ECOSOC. On Articles 13 and 25, UNGA, Universal Declaration of Human Rights (1949). On Rosenfield's résumé, "Name 3-Man Group to Start Flow of DPs."

Chapter 5. State of Voluntarism for Hungarians?

1. Elizabeth Clark Reiss, *The American Council of Voluntary Agencies for Foreign Service, ACVAFS: Four Monographs* (New York: The Council, 1985), 20, 54, 68–7; Staff of the Senate Committee on Foreign Relations and the Department of State, *A Decade of*

American Foreign Policy: Basic Documents, 1941–1949 (Washington, D.C.: GPO, 1950), 1268–327; Merle Curti, *American Philanthropy Abroad: A History* (New Brunswick, N.J.: Rutgers University Press, 1963), 487–88; Wallace J. Campbell, *The History of Care: A Personal Account* (New York: Praeger, 1990).

2. Carl Bon Tempo, *Americans at the Gate: The United States and Refugees During the Cold War* (Princeton, N.J.: Princeton University Press, 2008), 34–59; Gil Loescher and John A. Scanlan, *Calculated Kindness: Refugees and America's Half-Open Door, 1945 to the Present* (New York: Free Press, 1986), 45–47.

3. Csaba Békés, "The 1956 Hungarian Revolution and World Politics," *Cold War International History Project* 5 (1996): 5; Charles Gati, *Failed Illusions: Moscow, Washington, Budapest and the 1956 Hungarian Revolt* (Stanford, Calif.: Stanford University Press, 2006), xi–iii, 136, 142; Loescher and Scanlan, *Calculated Kindness*, 53; Janos M. Rainer, "The Hungarian Revolution of 1956: Causes, Aims, and Course of Events," in *The 1956 Hungarian Revolution: Hungarian and Canadian Perspectives*, ed. Christopher Adam et al. (Ottawa: University of Ottawa Press, 2010).

4. Békés, "1956 Hungarian Revolution"; Rainer, "Hungarian Revolution."

5. "Hungary Reds Form New Government"; "New Rebel Gain"; "Women Weep on Last Road into Freedom," *Chicago Daily Tribune*, November 5, 1956. Also Gati, *Failed Illusions*, 2–6, 138–51, 172, 183, 231.

6. Cherne, "They Changed Your Life"; "Hungarian Rebels Still Holding Out; "Women Weep." Also Bon Tempo, "Americans at the Gate," 163–64; "New Rebel Gain."

7. "'Merciless' Steps to Quell Revolt," *New York Times*, November 11, 1956.

8. Gati, *Failed Illusions*, xiv, 71–72, 85, 90–91, 97–99, 141–222; Evan Thomas, "A Singular Opportunity: Gaining Access to CIA's Records," *Studies in Intelligence* 39 (1996): 19–23.

9. "Bring in More Hungarians M'Carthy Asks," *Chicago Daily Tribune*, April 8, 1957.

10. "Budapest Agrees to Take U.S. Aid," *New York Times*, November 18, 1956.

11. American Federation of International Institutes (hereafter AFII), "National Newsletter," April 1957, F 75, Records of the United HIAS Service, RG 245.8, YIVO Archives (hereafter UHS). In the early stages of the conflict especially, many Hungarian border guards turned a blind eye on border crossing, even when their orders directed them otherwise. "Hungary Reds Form New Government"; "New Rebel Gain."

12. Loescher and Scanlan, *Calculated Kindness*, 50–51.

13. James A. Michener, *The Bridge at Andau* (New York: Random House, 1957), 229–30.

14. President's Committee, "Final Report to the President by the President's Committee for Hungarian Refugee Relief," May 14, 1957," B 3, F 27 (hereafter First Aid for Hungary, Final Report); President's Committee, "Outline of the Organization and Work of the President's Committee for Hungarian Refugee Relief in Assisting in Resettlement of Hungarian Refugees," B 3, F 25 (hereafter "Outline of the Organization"), both in Records of First Aid for Hungary, Hoover Institution Archives (hereafter First Aid); Ford Foundation, *Annual Report*, 1957 (New York: Ford Foundation), 41–42; AFII, "National Newsletter," April 1957

and June 1958. See also, for example, "Flood of West's Aid on Way to Hungary," October 29, 1956; "Kadar Seeks to End Strike by Starvation," November 18, 1956; "List Agencies in Hungarian Relief Drive," November 20, 1956; "Nations Rush Medical Help to Hungarians," October 28, 1956; "U.S. Groups Take Aid for Hungary," November 18, 1956, all in *Chicago Daily Tribune*. See also "Hungary Accepts Red Cross Tender of Medical Help," *Washington Post and Times Herald*, October 28, 1956; "Red Cross Drafts Budapest Set-Up," *New York Times*, November 13, 1956; "$20,000,000 U.S. Aid Offered to Hungary," *Los Angeles Times*, November 3, 1956. On the funding of the ICEM, see Michael R. Marrus, *The Unwanted: European Refugees in the Twentieth Century* (New York: Oxford University Press, 1985), 361.

15. "First Aid for Hungary, Final Report"; "List Agencies"; "Outline of the Organization"; "Religious Sponsorship," *Washington Post and Times Herald*, December 26, 1956; "U.S. Groups Take Aid"; Aloysius J. Wycislo, "Escape to America," *Catholic World* 434 (1957): 326–32.

16. "First Aid for Hungary, Final Report."

17. *Hungary's Fight for Freedom: A Special Report in Pictures* (New York: Time, 1956), accessed from B 2, F Publicity Material, Clippings, First Aid; "Ike Opens U.S. to 5,000 Who Fled Hungary," November 9, 1956. Also "American Medical and Food Help Starts," October 29, 1956, "Refugees Fly In," November 25, 1956, both in *New York Times*.

18. Bon Tempo, *Americans at the Gate*, 75–81.

19. The letters were often quite emotional about the plight of the Hungarians, their respective authors addressing Hoover almost as if they knew him personally. The folders cited below also include expressions of gratitude in responses from Hoover. See five files, all labeled "Contribution Files, Lists, General," B 1, First Aid. On Hoover's willingness to serve as a symbol for the cause, see, for example, W. Hallam Tuck to Herbert Hoover, December 3, 1956, B 3, F 26, First Aid. On the gala and Hoover's personal solicitations, see full page advertisement for First Aid for Hungary, Inc. (paid for by Lord and Taylor). The document includes a plea from Herbert Hoover for donations to relieve the Hungarian crisis, calling it "a great challenge and opportunity to all Americans." *New York Herald Tribune*, December 23, 1956; memorandum from Douglas J. Graham to the Board of Directors of First Aid for Hungary, Inc., B 2, F "Galpin, Perrin Correspondence, Herbert Hoover," First Aid; approximately forty letters to Hoover from individuals and companies requesting tickets to the gala found in: B 3, F 19, First Aid.

20. "Fraud Charged in Refugee Aid," *Washington Post and Times Herald*, December 3, 1956 (first quotation); "Donors Are Warned," *New York Times*, December 15, 1956 (second quotation). Also AFII, "National Newsletter," April 1957; "Mayor Calls Red Cross Best Agency for Hungary," *Los Angeles Times*, November 12, 1956.

21. AFII, "National Newsletter," April 1957.

22. U.S. Senate, *Status of the Hungarian Refugee Program*. Also "U.S. Gives Million to U.N. Fund," November 15, 1956; "U.S. Refugee Plan Revised 3d Time," December 6, 1956; both in *New York Times*.

23. "Soviet Denounces Austrian Chiefs," *New York Times*, April 14, 1957

(quotations). "Agreement on Aid to Hungarian Refugees in Austria" (hereafter "Agreement to Aid"), B 2, F "Galpin, Perrin Correspondence, Herbert Hoover," First Aid; "Mayor Calls Red Cross"; "U.S. Refugee Plan Revised."

24. Tracy Voorhees, "Trend of Opinion as to the Inadequacy of Existing Measures for Hungarian Refugees not Coming to the United States," February 22, 1957, B 3, F 25, First Aid.

25. "First Aid for Hungary, Final Report" (first quotation); "Agreement to Aid" (second quotation). Also "Out of Hungary—The Defiant Exiles," *New York Times*, November 25, 1956.

26. Tuck to Galpin, November 19, 1956; Tracy Voorhees to Herbert Hoover, January 13, 1957, both in B 3, F 25, First Aid.

27. The voluntary agencies also aided a much smaller number on non-Europeans during this period, even helping to resettle some Koreans and Chinese in the United States who had been admitted through special procedures. Information Memorandum #84 of the National Council of Churches, March 19, 1954; Bon Tempo, "Americans at the Gate," 94–153; Curti, *American Philanthropy Abroad*, 537–38; CWS; Loescher and Scanlan, *Calculated Kindness*, 44–48.

28. AFII Newsletter, April 1957 and June 1958; "First Aid for Hungary, Final Report"; Tuck to Galpin, November 19, 1956; Arthur A. Markowitz, "Humanitarianism Versus Restrictionism: The United States and the Hungarian Refugees," *International Migration Review* 7, 1 (1973): 58.

29. Herbert Hoover to Herbert Hoover, Jr., November 16, 1956, B 3, F 7, First Aid for Hungary (quotations). Under Secretary of State Hoover, Jr., replaced Secretary of State John Foster Dulles for a month in the late fall of 1956 while the latter recovered from surgery to remove malignant tumors from his intestine. "Dulles Reported in Good Condition after Operation," *Atlanta Daily World*, November 4, 1956; "Hoover Jr. Resigns from State Dept.," *Los Angeles Times*, December 9, 1956; "Reveal Dulles Has Cancer," *Chicago Defender*, November 5, 1956.

30. "Outline of the Organization"; Tuck to Galpin, November 19, 1956 (quotation); Voorhees to Hoover, January 13, 1957. On the role of the voluntary agencies in the admissions process, see Bon Tempo, *Americans at the Gate*, 68–69; "Resettling the Refugees," *Washington Post and Times Herald*, December 24, 1956.

31. "Outline of the Organization"; Tuck to Galpin, November 19, 1956; Voorhees to Hoover, January 13, 1957 (quotation).

32. First Aid for Hungary press release, December 7, 1956, B 2, F Press Releases, First Aid. Also Committee Meeting, Records of Presidential Committees, Commissions, and Boards, Records of the U.S. President's Committee for Hungarian Refugee Relief, Eisenhower Library; President's Committee for Hungarian Refugee Relief; "Refugee Expediter: Tracy Stebbins Voorhees," *New York Times*, November 30, 1956; "Summary of Meeting," December 14, 1956, B 2, F; Tracy Voorhees telegram to Herbert Hoover, November 30, 1956, B 3, F 25, First Aid.

33. "First Aid for Hungary, Final Report"; Voorhees to Hoover, January 13, 1957;

Voorhees telegram to Hoover, November 30, 1956; "Arrivals Mostly Young Men," *New York Times*, December 12, 1956.

34. French to Voorhees, December 1, 1956, B 3, F 27, First Aid (quotations). Also "Report to the President by the President's Committee."

35. Hoover Sr. to Hoover, Jr., November 16, 1956 (first quotation); Tuck to Galpin, November 19, 1956. See also Galpin to Tuck, November 19, 1956 (second quotation), B 3, F 25; Tuck to Hoover, December 3, 1956, B 3, F 26, both in First Aid. For the long working relationships between Galpin, Hoover, and Tuck, see the Biographical Notes in the finding aids for both the Galpin and Tuck Papers at the Hoover Institution Archives.

36. Galpin to Tuck, November 19, 1956.

37. "Resettling the Refugees."

38. Galpin to Tuck, November 19, 1956.

39. Ibid.; Tuck to Galpin, November 19, 1956; Tuck to Hoover, December 3, 1956; Voorhees to Hoover, January 13, 1957; Voorhees telegram to Hoover, November 30, 1956; Voorhees, "Trend of Opinion."

40. On Hoover's World War I experience, see Chapter 1 of this book. On Hoover's humanitarian efforts after World War II, see Timothy Walch, *Uncommon Americans: The Lives and Legacies of Herbert and Lou Henry Hoover* (Westport, Conn.: Praeger, 2003), 76. On Hoover's commissions on the reorganization of federal government, see Joanna Grisinger, *The Unwieldy American State: Administrative Politics since the New Deal* (New York: Cambridge University Press, 2012), 153–94.

41. Hoover Sr. to Hoover Jr., November 16, 1956; Voorhees to Hoover, January 13, 1957; Voorhees telegram to Hoover, November 30, 1956 (quotations), B 3, F 25, First Aid for Hungary.

42. Hoover Sr. to Hoover Jr., November 16, 1956; Voorhees to Hoover, January 13, 1957; Voorhees telegram to Hoover, November 30, 1956 (quotations), B 3, F 25, First Aid for Hungary.

43. Herbert Hoover to Tracy Voorhees, December 4, 1956 (first two quotations), B 3, F 25, First Aid; Hoover Sr. to Hoover, Jr., November 16, 1956 (third quotation); Tuck to Hoover, December 3, 1956. On the multiple relief enterprises that Hoover directed during the World War I period which included the name American Relief Administration, see Chapter One of this book.

44. Hoover to Voorhees, December 4, 1956..

45. Voorhees to Hoover, January 13, 1957 (quotations); Voorhees, "Progress Report on Hungarian Refugees," January 27, 1957, B 3, F 27, First Aid for Hungary. Also "First Aid for Hungary, Final Report"; Herbert Hoover to Mr. President (Dwight Eisenhower), December 27, 1957, B 3, F 6, First Aid for Hungary; "Outline of the Organization and Work of the President's Committee"; Julia Vadala Taft, David S. North, and David A. Ford, *Refugee Resettlement in the U.S.: Time for a New Focus* (Washington, D.C.: New TransCentury Foundation, 1979), 52–53.

46. Hoover to Mr. President (Dwight Eisenhower), December 27, 1956 (quotation).

Also "Outline of Organization"; Voorhees, "Progress Report"; Tracy Voorhees to Mr. President (Dwight Eisenhower), February 27, 1957, B 3, F 25, First Aid.

47. Bon Tempo, *Americans at the Gate*, 66–70.

48. "Refugee Loads Seen on Austria," *Washington Post and Times Herald*, February 21, 1956; Voorhees, "Trend of Opinion."

49. Voorhees, "Trend of Opinion."

50. "Refugee Centers Scored by Priest," *New York Times*, February 20, 1957.

51. "Emergency Refugee Plan for Hungary Is Ending," April 6, 1957; "Refugee Program Slowed, Not Ended, U.S. Officials Say," April 7, 1957, both in *New York Times*. Also "Case Demands Light on Flow of Hungarians," April 7, 1957; "Hungarians Hear U.S. Will Shut its Gate," April 7, 1957, both in *Chicago Daily Tribune*. Also "First Aid for Hungary, Final Report"; "U.S. Betrays Hungarians, Refugees Say," *Washington Post and Times Herald*, April 7, 1957.

52. "Refugee Admission Lag Blamed on Split, Apathy," *Washington Post and Times Herald*, April 7, 1957 (quotation). Also "48 Refugees from Hungary Try Suicide," *Los Angeles Times*, April 7, 1957.

53. AFII Newsletter, April 1957 and June 1958. Also "Pike Cites 'Smear' in Envoy Suicide," *New York Times*, April 8, 1957.

54. "Knowland Urges Cut in Foreign Aid," *New York Times*, April 1, 1957.

55. "United Church Women Put O.K. on Foreign Aid," *Chicago Daily Tribune*, May 1, 1957 (quotations). Also "Laws or Whims," *Washington Post and Times Herald*, April 8, 1957.

56. "Knowland Urges Cut."

57. *Time*, January 7, 1957 and January 6, 1958.

58. James Read (UN Deputy HCR), March 31, 1957; "Refugees Oppose Austria as Home," April 19, 1957, both in *New York Times*. Also "Hungary Held Failing to Lure Refugees Back," *Los Angeles Times*, April 6, 1957.

59. AFII, "National Newsletter," April 1957; "CARE to Withdraw from Part in Aid to Hungarian Refugees," *Chicago Daily Tribune*, May 2, 1957; "First Aid for Hungary, Final Report"; "Final Report to the President by the President's Committee."

60. "Agreement on Aid to Hungarian Refugees in Austria"; John Hutchinson, *Champions of Charity: War and the Rise of the Red Cross* (Boulder, Colo.: Westview, 1997); "Refugee Aid Extended," *New York Times*, April 18, 1957.

61. "Refugees Oppose Austria as Home."

62. "48 Refugees"; "Hungary Held Failing to Lure Refugees Back," *Los Angeles Times*, April 6, 1957; "Refugees Oppose Austria"; "U.S. Betrays Hungarians, Refugees Say," *Washington Post and Times Herald*, April 7, 1957; "Young Refugees Found Disturbed," *New York Times*, June 3, 1957.

63. "48 Refugees."

64. "Refugee Program Slowed, Not Ended, U.S. Officials Say," *New York Times*, April 7, 1957 (quotation). Also "Case Demands Light on Flow of Hungarians," April 7, 1957; "Hungarians Hear U.S. Will Shut Its Gate," April 7, 1957, both in *Chicago Daily Tribune*.

Also "Emergency Refugee Plan for Hungary Is Ending," *New York Times*, April 6, 1957; "U.S. Betrays Hungarians."

65. "48 Refugees."

66. "Refugee Aid Extended"; "Refugees Oppose Austria"; "6,000 Hungarian Refugees Return," *Los Angeles Times*, September 4, 1957; "2,000 Hungarians Quit Refuge in Yugoslavia," *Chicago Daily Tribune*, September 6, 1957. Also "Hungary Refugees Are 90% Resettled," November 3, 1957; "More Exiles for Vienna," May 1, 1957, both in *New York Times*.

67. Knowland Urges Cut"; "Refugee Program Slowed."

68. "Exiles Riot in Austria," *New York Times*, May 8, 1957; "Sentenced Three to Die," *Chicago Daily Tribune*, April 9, 1957.

69. American Council for Nationalities Service, National Newsletter, December 1960, F 77 (UHS).

70. "Budapest Raps U.N. 'Violation,'" *Washington Post and Times Herald*, June 25, 1957 (quotation). Also AFII Newsletter, April 1957 and August 1957; "Up from the Plenum," *Time*, January 6, 1958.

71. On these developments during World War II, see Chapter 3 of this book.

Chapter 6. Freedom Fighters on the American Home Front

1. The film school was the Academy for Theater (or depending on the translation, "Dramatic") and Film Art. "Allen U. Enrolls 5 White Students, Japanese Teacher," *Atlanta Daily World*, September 19, 1957; "Allen U. to Hold Guidance Workshop," *Norfolk Journal and Guide*, September 14, 1957; "Desegregation," *Pittsburgh Courier*, September 14, 1957; "Foreign Students," *Chicago Defender*, September 7, 1957; "Japanese Educator Joins Allen Staff," *Philadelphia Afro-American*, September 14, 1957; "Negro School Asks Why It's Disqualified," *Chicago Daily Tribune*, September 11, 1957; "Probers Quiz Air Consultant," *Washington Post and Times Herald*, September 13, 1957; telephone interviews of Andre Toth by author, May 11 and 15, 2008 (hereafter Toth Interviews). See also "Hungarian Student at Allen University Stirs Race Issue," September 21, 1957; "Hungarian to Study at Allen University," September 7, 1957, both in *Norfolk Journal and Guide*. See also President's Committee, "Final Report to the President by the President's Committee for Hungarian Refugee Relief," May 14, 1957," B 3, F 27 (hereafter "President's Committee, Final Report"); President's Committee, "Outline of the Organization and Work of the President's Committee for Hungarian Refugee Relief in Assisting in Resettlement of Hungarian Refugees," B 3, F 25 (hereafter Outline of the Organization), both in Records of First Aid for Hungary, Hoover Institution Archives (hereafter First Aid).

2. "Hungarian Refugees Blend Easily into U.S. Way of Life," *New York Times*, March 24, 1957.

3. For examples of black civil rights advocates referred to as "freedom fighters," see "Entry of Hungarians Urged," July 13, 1957; "Honored in Rights Issue," May 27, 1957; "Negro Recalls Year in Tennessee School," May 25, 1957, all in *New York Times*.

4. Carl Bon Tempo, *Americans at the Gate: The United States and Refugees During the Cold War* (Princeton, N.J.: Princeton University Press, 2008), 66.

5. Ibid., 65–73, 82–85. Also "First Aid for Hungary, Final Report"; Gil Loescher and John A. Scanlan, *Calculated Kindness: Refugees and America's Half-Open Door, 1945 to the Present* (New York: Free Press, 1986), 49–58; "Outline of the Organization."

6. Bon Tempo, *Americans at the Gate*, 65–73, 82–85; "First Aid for Hungary, Final Report"; Loescher and Scanlan, *Calculated Kindness*, 49–58; "Outline of the Organization."

7. Bon Tempo, *Americans at the Gate*; "First Aid for Hungary, Final Report"; Loescher and Scanlan, *Calculated Kindness*, 49–58; "Outline of the Organization."

8. The Eisenhower administration and other advocates of regularizing the Hungarians' status sparred with opponents in Congress over the issue for many months before the refugees were finally given a pathway to citizenship in summer 1958. Bon Tempo, *Americans at the Gate*, 82–85.

9. "Nixon at Kilmer Greets Refugees," *New York Times*, December 28, 1956; "Outline of the Organization"; Tracy Voorhees, "Progress Report on Hungarian Refugees," January 27, 1957, B 3, F 27, First Aid.

10. Norman L. Zucker, *The Guarded Gate: The Reality of American Refugee Policy* (New York: Harcourt Brace, 1987), 173; Tracy Voorhees to Herbert Hoover, January 13, 1957, B 3, F 25, First Aid.

11. "City Studies Shift in Law to Treat Ailing Refugees," *Washington Post and Times Herald*; "Housing for Refugees," *New York Times*, December 29, 1956; "Public Housing Priority Urged for Refugees," January 5, 1957; "Refugees and Public Housing," January 9, 1957; "Spreading Good Will Around"; "Urges Waiving Relief Rules for Refugees," November 20, 1956, all in *Chicago Daily Tribune*. See also "Seek Priority for Hungarians," *Daily Defender*, January 9, 1957.

12. "City Studies Shift in Law"; "Housing for Refugees"; "Public Housing Priority Urged for Refugees"; "Refugees and Public Housing"; "Spreading Good Will Around"; "Urges Waiving Relief Rules for Refugees"; "Seek Priority for Hungarians."

13. "First Aid for Hungary, Final Report"; "President Greets 7000 Hungarians," *Los Angeles Times*, December 26, 1956.

14. "Little Hungary Refugees Visited by Santa Claus," *Los Angeles Times*, December 7, 1956; "St. Nicholas Visits Refugee Children," *Washington Post and Times Herald*, December 7, 1956.

15. "Text of Nixon's Hungarian Report," *Los Angeles Times*, January 2, 1957 (quotation). Also "Arrivals Mostly Young Men," *Washington Post and Times Herald*, December 12, 1956; Leo Cherne, "They Changed Your Life," *Los Angeles Times*, December 30, 1956; "Hungarian Refugees Blend Easily."

16. "200 in Area Offer Jobs to Hungarians," *Washington Post and Times Herald*, November 27, 1956.

17. "Outline of the Organization and Work of the President's Committee"; "First Aid for Hungary, Final Report"; American Federation of International Institutes, "National Newsletter" (hereafter AFII, "National Newsletter"), April 1957; "IBM Reports," Records of Presidential Committees, Commissions, and Boards; "Statistical Analysis of Refugees Seeking Employment," April 24, 1957, B 18, F.

18. Julia Vadala Taft, David S. North, and David A. Ford, *Refugee Resettlement in the U.S.: Time for a New Focus* (Washington, D.C.: New TransCentury Foundation, 1979), 61.

19. "Disc Jockeys Aid Drive," *New York Times*, December 18, 1956; "From Hungary–New Americans," *Look*, January 22, 1957, 49–55; Paul Comly French to Tracy Voorhees, December 1, 1956, First Aid for Hungary, B 3, F 27; "Hungarians in America: The Fortune of a Family," *Newsweek*, May 20, 1957, 18–43; "Nixon at Kilmer Greets Refugees," *New York Times*, December 28, 1956; "Report to the President by the President's Committee"; "Text of Nixon's Hungarian Report"; *Los Angeles Times*, January 2, 1957; "They Pour in . . . And Family Shows Refugees Can Fit In," *Life*, January 27, 1957, 20–27; "23-Year-Old Heroine Has Become a Model Housewife," *New York Times*, March 24, 1957. For a fascinating examination of the "selling" of the Hungarians to America, Bon Tempo, *Americans at the Gate*, 75–81.

20. Michener, *The Bridge at Andau* (New York: Random House, 1957). On Michener's experiences interviewing the refugees and bringing his accounts to publication see Stephen J. May, *Michener: A Writer's Journey* (Norman: University of Oklahoma Press, 2005), 128–35.

21. "23-Year-Old Heroine."

22. Martin A. Bursten, *Escape from Fear* (Syracuse: Syracuse University Press, 1958), throughout, but especially 193–209.

23. Voorhees, "Progress Report," January 27, 1957.

24. AFII, "National Newsletter[s]," June 1958 (quotation). Also April 1957.

25. "'Hijacker,'" AFII, "National Newsletter," April 1957 (first quotation); Ida Bobula, "Escape to America: The Hungarians One Year Later," *Atlantic Monthly* 201 (January 1958): 62 (second quotation). Also "Hungarian Refugees Blend Easily"; "Outline of the Organization and Work of the President's Committee."

26. "Hungary's Refugees Taking Hold," *Washington Post and Times Herald*, June 1, 1957; Report from International Rescue Committee offices in Washington D.C. to IRC Headquarters (New York), November 1957, Acc. # 82033-73.01, B 2408, F Local Committees, Records of the International Rescue Committee (hereafter "IRC"), Hoover Institution Archives.

27. ACVAFS Report of Fact Finding; AFII, "National Newsletter[s]," April 1957, June 1958, and August 1958.

28. Recession Hurts Hungarian Refugees," *New York Times*, July 14, 1958.

29. "Hungarian Refugees Blend."

30. "Recession Hurts."

31. On the overseas repatriations, see Chapter 5 of this book.

32. "Recession Hurts" (first quotation); AFII, "National Newsletter," June 1958 (second quotation). Also AFII, "National Newsletter[s]," April 1957, June 1958, and August 1958; "40 Hungarians Sent Back for Lie Under Oath," *Chicago Daily Tribune*, May 28, 1957; "Hungarian Refugees Taking Hold"; "101 Refugees Return," *New York Times*, May 25, 1957.

33. "Homesick Refugee Shoots Self," *Washington Post and Times Herald*, July 22, 1957.

34. "3 Hungarians without Jobs Want to Go Home," *Washington Post and Times Herald*, June 12, 1957.

35. "First Aid for Hungary, Final Report."

36. AFII "National Newsletter," June 1958 (quotation). Also AFII "National Newsletter," August 1958; "Hungarian Follow-Up," *Washington Post and Times Herald*, June 14, 1957.

37. U.S. Attorney General William P. Rogers offered the higher number while the United States Committee for Refugees, a private group also closely involved with the matter, indicated the lower figure. Bon Tempo, *Americans at the Gate*, 73–75, 81–85 (Rogers figure); United States Committee for Refugees, "Refugee Admissions to Those of Other Countries," Records of the United HIAS Service, RG 245.8, F 75, YIVO Archives, Center for Jewish History.

38. U.S. Committee for Refugees, "Refugee Admissions to Those of Other Countries."

39. "Hungarian Student"; Louis E. Lomax, "Integration with a Difference," *The Nation* 185 (September 28, 1957); Toth Interview, May 15, 2008. On the political persuasion of many of the Hungarian student protesters see Charles Gati, *Failed Illusions: Moscow, Washington, Budapest, and the 1956 Hungarian Revolt* (Stanford, Calif.: Stanford University Press, 2006), 3–4, 126–35.

40. Toth noted in the cited May 15 interview that the Soviet troops he observed tended to look nervous and unwilling to stray very far from their units, sensing that they were not welcome. Toth Interview, May 15, 2008. Also "Andre Toth Is Unhappy in the Rain," *Philadelphia Afro-American*, September 28, 1957; "Hungarian Student at Allen University Stirs Race Issue," *Norfolk Journal and Guide*, September 21, 1957.

41. "Andre Toth Is Unhappy"; "Hungarian Student"; Toth Interview, May 15, 2008.

42. "Hungarian Student"; Toth Interview, May 15, 2008.

43. Toth Interview, May 15, 2008.

44. The language training sequence Toth was approached about was the second such pilot program for developing language skills. The first had been initiated the month before, in December, at Bard College. "Outline of the Organization"; "Path to U.S. Life Eased for Exiles," both in *New York Times*, January 19, 1956.

45. "Path to U.S. Life"

46. "Hungarians in Vermont," *Washington Post and Times Herald*, April 14, 1957; Toth Interview, May 15, 2008.

47. Lomax, "Integration with a Difference" (quotation). The Department of Health Education and Welfare was also involved in arranging for Toth's scholarship and those for many other refugees. "Allen University," *Chicago Defender*, September 21, 1957; "Hungarian Student"; Lomax, "Integration with a Difference"; IIE website, "History," accessed July 28, 2015, http://www.iie.org/Who-We-Are/History; "Outline of the Organization"; "Probers Quiz"; Toth Interview, May 15, 2008.

48. "AME's Irked," *Philadelphia Afro-American*, September 21, 1957.

49. "Andre Toth Is Unhappy"; "Hungarian Student"; "N.Y.U. to Consider Tuition Aid for Exiled Hungarian Students," *New York Times*, December 2, 1956; "Outline of the Organization"; "Recession Hurts"; "Scholarships: For Hungarians," *Pittsburgh Courier*, December 29, 1956; Toth Interview, May 15, 2008.

50. See, for example, "Allen U. Loses State Rating"; "Andre Toth Is Unhappy"; "Hungarian Student."

51. Jean-Paul Sartre, *La putain respectueuse: Pièce en un acte et deux tableaux* (Paris: Nagel, 1946); Toth Interview, May 15, 2008. Whereas the French word "putain" is more accurately translated as "whore," the common English translation of the play uses "prostitute" in the title.

52. Toth Interview, May 15, 2008.

53. "Allen Prexy Clears 3 of Subversive Charge," *Chicago Defender*, May 3, 1958; Andre Toth Interview, May 11, 2008; "Hungarian Student."

54. "Allen Prexy"; "Allen Students Upset State!" *Pittsburgh Courier*, January 25, 1958; "Hungarian Student"; Toth Interview, May 15, 2008.

55. "Allen U. Enrolls 5"; "Allen U. to Hold"; "Andre Toth Is Unhappy"; "Desegregation," *Pittsburgh Courier*, September 14, 1957; "Hungarian Student"; "Hungarian to Study"; "Japanese Educator."

56. Stephanie Fitzgerald, *The Little Rock Nine: Struggle for Integration* (Minneapolis: White-Thompson, 2006).

57. "Negro School Asks Why It's Disqualified," *Chicago Daily Tribune*, September 11, 1957 (first quotation); "Allen U. Loses State Rating" (second quotation). Also "Allen University"; "Probers Quiz." Callison is quoted slightly differently, though making the same point, in Lomax, "Integration with a Difference," 190.

58. "Dr. Mays," *Pittsburgh Courier*, July 17, 1954; "Integration: A Two Way Street," November 13, 1954; "Seek White Students for Wilberforce U.," January 20, 1945, both in *Chicago Defender*.

59. "Dr. Mayes"; "Integration"; "Philander Smith Graduates First White Student," *Atlanta Daily World*, October 13, 1954.

60. "People Places and Things," *Chicago Defender* June 12, 1954.

61. "Integration."

62. "Andre Toth Is Unhappy" (quotation). Also "Allen U. Enrolls 5"; "Desegregation"; "Hungarian Student"; "Negro School Asks"; "Probers Quiz." Toth explained in two 2008 interviews that the press reports about his time in Hungary and his escape often embellished certain of his experiences, sometimes recording facts incorrectly. He long assumed that certain minor details were in fact mere misunderstandings: a product of his poor English during his first period in the United States when various reporters interviewed him. Other times journalists published specious reports on Toth that could not reasonably have been caused by language barriers but rather a desire to craft a good story that would conform to the political and cultural expectations of a periodical readership in that particular environment. For instance, papers reported that before sailing for the United States Toth made a rendezvous with his French mother in Paris under the Eiffel

Tower. No such thing happened. Toth sailed directly from Bremerhaven to the United States. The Eiffel Tower story likely appealed to the press because it romanticized Toth as a good son with roots in noncommunist Western Europe. In perhaps a more subtle transformation of the facts Toth was often described as an ardent "freedom fighter" and a "bitter foe of communism." While Toth opposed hardline Stalinist communism and the heavy-handed Soviet interventions that historically came with it in postwar Hungary, he also embraced elements of socialism and sympathized with some goals of such reformist Hungarian communists as Imre Nagy. See, for example, "Andre Toth Is Unhappy"; "Hungarian Student"; "Allen U. Loses State Rating." Toth Interviews, May 11 and 15, 2008.

63. "Allen U. Loses State Rating."

64. "Andre Toth Is Unhappy."

65. Toth Interviews, May 11 and 15.

66. Ibid., May 15.

67. AFII, "National Newsletter," June 1958; Bon Tempo, *Americans at the Gate*, 73–75, 82–85; "Fraud Charged in Refugee Aid," *Washington Post and Times Herald*, December 3, 1956; "Spreading Good Will Around," *Chicago Defender*, November 27, 1956.

68. "Andre Toth Is Unhappy"; "Hungarian Student"; "Spotlight on Allen U. President," *Pittsburgh Courier*, January 11, 1958; Toth Interview, May 15, 2008.

69. "Andre Toth Is Unhappy"; "Hungarian to Stay at Negro College," *Washington Post and Times Herald*, September 21, 1957. Toth Interviews, May 11 and 15, 2008. On the intersections of U.S. civil rights and Cold War politics see Carol Elaine Anderson, *Eyes off the Prize: African Americans, the United Nations, and the Struggle for Human Rights, 1944–1952* (New York: Cambridge University Press, 2003); Thomas Borstelmann, *The Cold War and the Color Line: American Race Relations in the Global Arena* (Cambridge, Mass.: Harvard University Press, 2001); Mary Dudziak, *Cold War Civil Rights: Race and the Image of American Democracy* (Princeton, N.J.: Princeton University Press, 2000); Penny M. Von Eschen, *Race against Empire: Black Americans and Anticolonialism, 1937–1957* (Ithaca, N.Y.: Cornell University Press, 1997).

70. "Allen Totals Now over 800 Mark," *Norfolk Journal and Guide*, October 12, 1957.

71. "The Penalizing of Allen University," *Norfolk Journal and Guide*, October 19, 1957.

72. "Says State Asks for Teachers' Ouster," *Chicago Defender*, January 4, 1958. Also "Dr. Veal Defies Governor," January 18, 1958; "Principle or Force?" January 11, 1958, both in *Pittsburgh Courier*. Also Toth Interview, May 15, 2008.

73. Lomax, "Integration with a Difference"; "Hungarian Student."

74. Toth Interviews, May 11 and 15, 2008.

75. Ibid.

Chapter 7. Revolutions in Cuba and Refugee Welfare

1. James Nathan Miller, "Opportunity or Disaster: The Challenge of Cuba's Exiles," *Reader's Digest* (December 1962), 72.

2. American Council for Nationalities Service (hereafter "ACNS"), National

Newsletter, August 1960, F 77, Records of the United HIAS Service, RG 245.8 (hereafter "UHS"), YIVO; "Statement by Rep. Dante B. Fascell," August 21, 1963, IRC, Acc 82033-73.01, B 2406, Records of the International Rescue Committee (hereafter "IRC"), Acc 82033-73.01, B 2407 (hereafter IRC), Hoover Institution Archives; Julia Vadala Taft, David S. North, and David A. Ford, *Refugee Resettlement in the U.S.: Time for a New Focus* (Washington, D.C.: New TransCentury Foundation, 1979), 67; "Address by Abraham Ribicoff," May 15, 1962; U.S. Department of Health, Education, and Welfare Press Release, May 15, 1962, Furman, No. 3-3178, both in Records of the Social Security Administration, Cuban Refugee Program files, Record Group 47.8, B 3, F Resettlement (General), NARA (hereafter SSA).

3. IRC Annual Report, 1962, IRC, B 2407.

4. Miller, "Opportunity or Disaster" (quotation). For another example of High's thinking, a representative of the nongovernmental International Rescue Committee told Congress later that year that the Cuban refugee crisis "could be quickly converted into an opportunity" for the United States to manipulate favorably the political scene not just in Cuba, but throughout "our own hemisphere." "International Rescue Committee Statement Before the Subcommittee on Refugees and Escapees," July 12, 1961, B 2408, IRC.

5. See, for instance, Jens Manuel Krogstad, "After Decades of GOP Support, Cubans Shifting toward the Democratic Party," June 24, 2014, *Fact Tank: News in the Numbers* (Pew Research Center), accessed July 28, 2015; Virginia Yans-McLaurghlin, *Immigration Reconsidered: History, Sociology, and Politics* (New York: Oxford University Press, 1990), 176–77.

6. Federal Bureau of Public Assistance memorandum, "To State Agencies Administering Approved Public Assistance Laws: Cuban Refugee Program," March 17, 1961, unprocessed files located at the headquarters of the Church World Service, New York City (hereafter CWS); Charlotte J. Moore, *Review of U.S. Refugee Resettlement Programs and Policies* (Washington, D.C.: GPO, 1980), 27; "'New Deal' for Cuban Refugees," *Miami Herald*, February 1, 1961.

7. ACNS Newsletter, August 1960; Carl Bon Tempo, *Americans at the Gate: The United States and Refugees During the Cold War* (Princeton, N.J.: Princeton University Press, 2008), 107–10; Gil Loescher and John A. Scanlan, *Calculated Kindness: Refugees and America's Half-Open Door, 1945 to the Present* (New York: Free Press, 1986), 61–62; Felix Masud-Piloto, *Cuban Migration to the U.S., 1959–1995* (Oxford: Rowman and Littlefield, 1996), 32–43; *Review of U.S. Refugee Resettlement Programs*, 27–28; Taft et al., 67.

8. Bon Tempo, *Americans at the Gate*, 107–10, 127–32; Scanlan and Loescher, *Calculated Kindness*, 61; Lars Schoultz, *That Infernal Little Cuban Republic: The United States and the Cuban Revolution*, 82–141.

9. ACNS, National Newsletter, August 1960, R; Bon Tempo, *Americans at the Gate*, 109–10; "Statement by Rep. Dante B. Fascell," August 21, 1963, IRC; Taft, et al., 67; U.S. Department of Health, Education, and Welfare (HEW) Press Releases, September 7, 1961 and May 15, 1962, both in B 3, F Resettlement (General), SSA. A notable exception to

Cubans arriving in the United States without an organized plan for their resettlement was the arrival of over fourteen thousand unaccompanied minors from Cuba, approximately half of whom were taken in by relatives in America with the other half cared for by Catholic charity. Yvonne M. Conde, *Operation Pedro Pan: The Untold Exodus of 14,048 Cuban Children* (New York: Routledge, 1999); Masud-Piloto, *Cuban Migration*, 39–42.

10. Dante B. Fascell, "Resettlement Program for Cuban Refugees," August 10, 1961, *Congressional Record: House* (Washington, D.C.: GPO, 1962), 14238; IRC Annual Report, 1962..

11. ACNS Newsletter, August 1960; Bon Tempo, *Americans at the Gate*, 107–10; Moore, *Review of U.S. Refugee Resettlement Programs*, 27–28; David M. Reimers, *Still the Golden Door: The Third World Comes to America* (New York: Columbia University Press, 1985), 157; Scanlan and Loescher, *Calculated Kindness*, 61–62; Taft, et al., 67.

12. American Immigration and Citizenship Conference (hereafter "AICC"), "Special Information Memorandum to Members," October 28, 1960, F 195, UHS; Bon Tempo, *Americans at the Gate*, 108–10; Scanlan and Loescher, *Calculated Kindness*, 62.

13. "Refugees: A Federal Case," *Miami Herald*, November 17, 1960; Taft et al., 67.

14. See, for example, "Help Us Aid Cubans, Rep. Fascell Asks House," *Miami News*, June 29, 1961; "IRC Statement to Congress," July 12, 1961. Barely over a year later, in October 1961, approximately one quarter of a million Cuban refugees had entered the United States since Castro's assumption of power. Maria Cristina Garcia, *Havana USA: Cuban Exiles and Cuban Americans in South Florida, 1959–1994* (Berkeley: University of California Press, 1996), 13.

15. Taft et al., 68.

16. "Ike's Aide in State on Refugee Problem," *Miami Herald*, November 17, 1960; "IRC Statement to Congress," July 12, 1961; Taft et al., 68.

17. "Keating Scores Kennedy Refusal of Catholic School Aid at Miami," *New York Times*, February 12, 1961.

18. AICC memorandum, October 28, 1960; "Cuban Refugee Aid Groups Go Broke," *Miami Herald*, February 10, 1961; "IRC Statement to Congress," July 12, 1961; "Miami's Refugees Are Going Hungry," *Miami News*, November 11, 1960; Taft et al., 68.

19. AICC memorandum, October 28, 1960; "IRC Statement to Congress," July 12, 1961.

20. "Federal Help Comes on Refugee Problem," *Miami News*, October 31, 1960.

21. AICC letter to members, December 13, 1960; F 70, UHS; William S. Bernard to Members of the Joint AICC-ACVA Committee on DHEW, September 26, 1960, F 70, UHS; "Cuban Refugee Aid Groups Go Broke"; Fascell, "Resettlement Program"; "Recommendations for DHEW Participation in Immigration," April 14, 1959, UHS, F 76.

22. First Aid for Hungary press release, December 7, 1956, B 2, F Press Releases, Records of First Aid for Hungary, Hoover Institution Archives; "How America Responded to Refugee Plight," *Miami Herald*, February 1, 1961; "Refugee Expediter: Tracy Stebbins Voorhees," *New York Times*, November 30, 1956.

23. "How America Responded."

24. Jon L. Regier, "Memorandum on Cubans in Miami, Florida," December 30, 1961, CWS.

25. "Refugees: A Federal Case," *Miami Herald*, November 17, 1960.

26. Taft et al., 70.

27. "How America Responded"; Regier memorandum, December 30, 1961, CWS.

28. "Cuban Needy Given First U.S. Checks," *Miami Herald*, February 27, 1956; "Cuban Refugees Get U.S. Checks," *Miami Herald*, February 25, 1961; "Miami Economy Strained as Cubans Hunt for Jobs," *New York Times*, April 3, 1961.

29. ACNS Newsletter, February 1961, 7; "Eisenhower Asks Cuban Exiles Aid," *New York Times*, November 19, 1961; Fascell, "Resettlement Program."

30. Kennedy to Voorhees, January 28, 1961, UHS, F 196.

31. "Miami Economy."

32. Kennedy to Ribicoff, January 27, 1961, UHS, F 196.

33. "Abraham Ribicoff, 87, Dies," *Washington Post*, February 23, 1998.

34. ACNS Newsletter, February 1961; "Director Chosen for Cuban Relief," *New York Times*, February 2, 1961.

35. Kennedy to Voorhees, January 28, 1961.

36. Fascell, "Resettlement Program"; HEW Press Release, May 15, 1962; Ribicoff Address, May 15, 1962; Taft et al., 70–79.

37. Bon Tempo, *Americans at the Gate*, 121.

38. The burden of proof was on the alien to show that the cause of illness or dependency on public resources did not exist prior to entry. Sections 3, 19, and 221 of the Immigration Act of February 5, 1917; Stephen H. Legomsky, *Immigration and Refugee Law and Policy*, 2nd ed. (Westbury, N.Y.: Foundation Press, 1997), 321–27; U.S. Code Title 8, Section 155 (a) and 136 (i).

39. "'We'll Remember,' Grateful Declare," *Miami Herald*, February 28, 1961.

40. "Cuban Needy"; "Cuban Refugees Get U.S. Checks"; Fascell, "Resettlement Program"; Bonnie G. Steiner to Ann S. Petluck memorandum, February 28, 1961, F 196, UHS.

41. Fascell, "Resettlement Program"; "Refugees Swallow Pride, Line up for Free Food," *Miami News*, April 6, 1961.

42. "Cuban Refugees Being Placed in Federal Jobs to Ease Plight," *New York Times*, March 3, 1961.

43. "'We'll Remember.'"

44. "Ike's Aide in State."

45. Fascell, "Resettlement Program"; "Keating Scores Kennedy."

46. AICC to Members, December 13, 1960; IRC Statements to Congress, July 12, 1961 and December 13, 1961, both in B 2408, IRC; Regier memorandum, December 30, 1961.

47. Steiner to Petluck, February 28, 1961.

48. "Cuban Needy"; "Cuban Refugees Get U.S. Checks"; Fascell, "Resettlement Program"; Steiner to Petluck, February 28, 1961; Taft et al., 72–73.

49. For a sophisticated examination of the adjustment of Cuban refugees' juridical citizenship status, see Bon Tempo, *Americans at the Gate*, 127–32.

50. "Considerations in the Use of Public Assistance for Jewish Aliens Residing in U.S. over Five Years," 1944 (exact date unclear), F 519, Records of the National Refugee Service, RG 248, YIVO.

51. Taft et al., 70–79.

52. "What for Negroes?" *Chicago Defender*, February 21, 1961.

53. "Weighty Questions Pile Up Here as Refugees Flood In," *Miami Herald*, May 23, 1962.

54. "Take a Look at Cuban Relief," *Miami Herald*, October 4, 1961.

55. "U.S. May Deliver Cuba Exiles Here," *New York Times*, December 14, 1961.

56. "Says Cuban Refugees Undermine Negro Workers of Jobs in Florida," December 12, 1961; "3,400 Cuban Refugees Get College Fund Aid from U.S.," October 22, 1961; "Warn Miamians of Cuban Refugees," October 24, 1961, all in *Chicago Defender*. Also Taft, et al., 65–91.

57. "U.S. May Deliver." There was occasional speculation that the Kennedy administration initially resisted that idea of resettlement because it wanted to maintain a large core of Cubans in Miami for the potential help that they might offer in overthrowing Castro, as witnessed the ill-fated Bay of Pigs campaign in April 1961. "Cuban Needy."

58. "Beef-Up of Miami Refugee Aid Pressed," *Miami Herald*, April 12, 1962.

59. "Take a Look."

60. "Address by Abraham Ribicoff," May 15, 1962; DHEW Press Release, May 15, 1962; Marshall Wise to W.L. Mitchell, November 7, 1961, all in SSA, Cuban Refugee Program files, B 3, F Resettlement (General). DHEW Press Release, May 15, 1962. Also "U.S. May Deliver."

61. "U.S. May Deliver"; "Weighty Questions." On dispersal and concerns with "over-population" more generally, see Michael R. Marrus, *The Unwanted: European Refugees in the Twentieth Century* (New York: Oxford University Press, 1985), 114–15.

62. "Beef-Up"; HEW Press Release, May 15, 1962; IRC Annual Report, 1962, B 407, IRC; Ribicoff Address, May 15, 1962; "Statement by Fascell," August 21, 1963; Taft et al., 65–91; "U.S. Steps Up Program to Get Cuban Refugees Settled," *Chicago Defender*, May 16, 1962; Wise to Mitchell, November 7, 1961.

63. "Financial Assistance to Needy Cuban Refugees, Fiscal Years '64 & '65"; Louise J. McDonnell to Regional Representatives, January 21, 1964, both in SSA. Also "Beef-Up"; Cuban Refugee Program files, B 1, F Transitional Allowances and Grants; IRC Annual Report, 1962, B 2407, IRC; "Statement by Fascell," August 21, 1963; Taft et al., 65–91; "U.S. Steps Up."

64. For an interesting discussion of the ways in which the 1966 law afforded Cuban refugees the opportunity to reclaim their Cuban citizenship upon the possible dissolution of the Castro regime, see Bon Tempo, *Americans at the Gate*, 127–32.

65. The best treatment of these issues is Bon Tempo, *Americans at the Gate*, with the following pages dealing specifically with the role played by human rights discourses in

justifying refugee admissions: 133–43, 141–55, 158–62, 174–76. See also Scanlan and Loescher, *Calculated Kindness.*

66. Office of the U.S. Coordinator for Refugee Affairs, "Organizational Location of Refugee Reception and Placement Grants," November 28, 1980, F U.S. Coordinator for Refugees, B 242, IRC. For contracts between the federal government (HEW) and the voluntary agencies into the 1970s, see B 666, IRC. Based on the precedent set with the Cuban Program, the federal government also contracted immediately with American voluntary agencies for the domestic resettlement of Vietnamese, Cambodian, and Laotian refugees after the Vietnam War in 1975. See myriad such contracts in Boxes 664 and 1733, IRC; Contract form between Social Security Administration and voluntary agencies, F Resettlement, B 3, SSA, Cuban Refugee Program files.

67. Deborah Anker and Michael Posner, "The Forty Year Crisis: A Legislative History of the Refugee Act of 1980," *San Diego Law Review* 19 (1981): 43–64; Bon Tempo, *Americans at the Gate*, 173–79, 183–94, 198–205; Arnold H. Leibowitz, "The Refugee Act of 1980: Problems and Congressional Concerns," in *The Global Refugee Problem: U.S. and World Response*, ed. Gil Loescher and John Scanlan (Beverly Hills, Calif.: Sage, 1983); P.L. 96–212, "Refugee Act of 1980," *U.S. Statutes at Large, 1980*, vol. 94, pt. 1 (Washington, D.C.: GPO, 1981); David M. Reimers, *Still the Golden Door*, 189–99; U.S. Department of Health and Human Services, *Refugee Resettlement Program* (Washington, D.C.: GPO, 1985), 1–6.

Epilogue

1. Anastasia Brown and Todd Scribner, "Unfulfilled Promises, Future Possibilities: The Refugee Resettlement System in the United States," *Journal on Migration and Human Security* 2 (2014): 101–20 (quotation 105).

2. Jeremy Hein, *States and International Migrants: The Incorporation of Indochinese Refugees in the United States and France* (Boulder, Colo.: Westview 1993), 59.

3. Carl Bon Tempo, *Americans at the Gate: The United States and Refugees During the Cold War* (Princeton, N.J.: Princeton University Press, 2008), 170.

4. Hein, *States and International Migrants*, 38.

5. Bon Tempo, *Americans at the Gate*, 146, 149–50; John D. Tenhula, "United States Refugee Resettlement Policy as Seen in the Indochinese Refugee Program" (PhD dissertation, Columbia University, 1981), 72, 77–84.

6. A companion bill was passed the same day, which, for purposes of simplicity, may be included in references to the 1975 law. James A. Elgass, "Federal Funding of United States Refugee Resettlement Before and After the Refugee Act of 1980," in *Transnational Legal Problems of Refugees* (New York: Clark Boardman Callaghan, 1982), 182–84. On the exodus and operations of the overseas camps, see Bon Tempo, *Americans at the Gate*, 149, 155–56; Hein *States and International Migrants*, 20–21; Jana K. Lipman, " 'Give Us a Ship': The Vietnamese Repatriate Movement on Guam, 1975," *American Quarterly* 61 (2012): 1–31; Keith St. Cartmail, *Exodus Indochina* (Exeter, N.H.: Heinneman, 1983); Tenhula, "United States Refugee Resettlement Policy," 71–77, 81.

7. As had been the case with Kilmer, a cluster of state and voluntary agencies were responsible for the camps' various operations, including the licensed voluntary agencies and Departments of Defense, Justice, Labor, State, and Health, Education and Welfare. Hein, *States and International Migrants*, 23, 46; Jana K. Lipman, "A Refugee Camp in America: Fort Chaffee and Vietnamese and Cuban Refugees, 1975–1982," *Journal of American Ethnic History* 33, 2 (2014): 57–87; Tenhula, "United States Refugee Resettlement Policy," 77–84.

8. Elgass, "Federal Funding of United States Refugee Resettlement," 182–84; Tab B, "Processing," July 14, 1975, in "Operation New Arrivals—Phase 1," July 1975, F Civil Coordinator's, B 3, Records of the Interagency Task Force for Indochinese Refugees, 1975–'77, RG 220, Entry 38070a, NARA (hereafter, IATF); Tenhula, "United States Refugee Resettlement Policy," 77–94.

9. Tab E, "Breakdowns," July 14, 1975, in "Operation New Arrivals—Phase 1," July 1975; Tab G, "Report from Tram Ngoc Thoi & Do Dinh Duyet," July 6–11, 1975, both in F Civil Coordinator's, B 3, IATF; "131,399 Asian Refugees Now in U.S., Ford Reports," June 23, 1975, and "Ford Calls Progress Good on Resettling Refugees," June 24, 1975, both in *Los Angeles Times*.

10. Bon Tempo, *Americans at the Gate*, 149, 188–89, 198–99; Elgass, "Federal Funding of United States Refugee Resettlement," 183–84; Hein, *States and International Migrants*, 19, 21, 38, 43, 46, 75; Richard J. Irvin and Lois Gambrell, *Refugee Resettlement in the United States* (Huntington, N.Y.: Nova Science, 2013), 9–10. During the six-month gap in federal funding, eleven states composing a significant portion of the Indochinese refugee population (27 percent resided in California alone) refused to continue those government programs aimed at assisting the refugees rather than use their own state funds. Hein, 53.

11. Hein, *States and International Migrants*, 29–30.

12. "McGovern Opposes Airlift," *New York Times*, April 30, 1975 (first quotation); "Refugees and Guilt," *New York Times*, May 11, 1975 (remaining quotations).

13. Tenhula, "United States Refugee Resettlement Policy," 94–98 (second quotation 96); "Refugees and Guilt" (first quotation). See also Bon Tempo, *Americans at the Gate*, 163, 178–79; Hein, *States and International Migrants*, 33–43, 56–61, 67.

14. Tab A, "Closing of Elgin," in July 14, 1975, in "Operation New Arrivals—Phase 1," July 1975, F Civil Coordinator's, B 3, IATF. On the Mariel Boat Lift, see Bon Tempo, *Americans at the Gate*, 179-84.

15. Bon Tempo, *Americans at the Gate*, 146–47, 151, 154–55 (quotation 146). See also Hein, *States and International Migrants*, 23–24, 29–30, 38–43.

16. Bon Tempo, *Americans at the Gate*, 133–43, 147–48, 151–55, 160–62, 165–66; Gil Loescher and John A. Scanlan, *Calculated Kindness: Refugees and America's Half-Open Door, 1945 to the Present* (New York: Free Press, 1986), 95–101. On the rise of human rights politics in 1970s America, among both the grassroots and government officials, see Bon Tempo, "From the Center-Right: Freedom House and Human Rights in the 1970s and 1980s," *The Human Rights Revolution: An International History*, ed.

Petra Goedde and William Hitchcock (New York: Oxford University Press, 2012); Bon Tempo, "Human Rights and the U.S. Republican Party in the Late 1970s," in *The Breakthrough: Human Rights in the 1970s*, ed. Jan Eckel and Samuel Moyn (Philadelphia: University of Pennsylvania Press, 2013); Kenneth Cmiel, "The Emergence of Human Rights Politics in the United States," *Journal of American History* 86 (1999): 1231–50; Bradley R. Simpson, "Denying the 'First Right': The United States, Indonesia, and the Ranking of Human Rights by the Carter Administration, 1976–1980," *International History Review* 31 (2009): 798–826; David F. Schmitz and Vanessa Walker, "Jimmy Carter and the Foreign Policy of Human Rights," *Diplomatic History* 28 (2004): 113–44; Sarah B. Snyder, *Human Rights Activism and the End of the Cold War: A Transnational History of the Helsinki Network* (New York: Cambridge University Press, 2011); Vanessa Walker, "At the End of Influence: Rethinking Human Rights and Intervention in U.S.-Latin American Relations," *Journal of Contemporary History* 46 (2011): 109–35.

17. See also Bon Tempo, *Americans at the Gate*, 150–53, 172; Loescher and Scanlan, *Calculated Kindness*, 133; Tenhula, "United States Refugee Resettlement Policy," 96–97.

18. Charlotte J. Moore, *Review of U.S. Refugee Resettlement Programs and Policies* (Washington, D.C.: GPO, 1980), 35–43, 47–56.

19. Brown and Scribner, "Unfulfilled Promises," 105–6; Elgass, "Federal Funding of United States Refugee Resettlement," 180–83; Hein, *States and International Migrants*, 59. On "$5 to $110," see "Report from Tram Ngoc Thoi & Do Dinh Duyet."

20. Elgass, "Federal Funding of United States Refugee Resettlement," 182–84, 187–88; Hein, *States and International Migrants*, 56, 59–61; Moore, *Review of U.S. Refugee Resettlement*, 43–47, 56–61.

21. Bon Tempo, *Americans at the Gate*, 178–83, 187–91; Elgass, "Federal Funding of United States Refugee Resettlement," 188; David A. Martin, "The Refugee Act of 1980: Its Past and Future," in *Transnational Legal Problems of Refugees*, Michigan Yearbook of International Legal Studies (New York: Clark Boardman Callaghan, 1982), 91–92; Moore, *Review of U.S. Refugee Resettlement*, 60–62..

22. Brown and Scribner, "Unfulfilled Promises," 106–9.

23. Ibid. See also Hein, *States and International Migrants*, 61.

24. Brown and Scribner, "Unfulfilled Promises," 109.

25. The primary welfare programs are Medicaid and Temporary Assistance for Needy Families, which succeeded AFDC in 1997 as a result of the 1996 Welfare Act. Don Barnett, "Refugee Resettlement: A System Badly in Need of Review," Center for Immigration Studies website, May 12, 2011, accessed August 14, 2015; "Refugee Resettlement Program; Requirements for Refugee Cash Assistance; and Refugee Medical Assistance," *Federal Register*, March 22, 2000.

26. Barnett, "Refugee Resettlement"; Brown and Scribner, "Unfulfilled Promises," 111–12; Andorra Bruno, "Refugee Admissions and Resettlement Policy," February 18, 2015, Congressional Research Service report RL31269.

27. Brown and Scribner, "Unfulfilled Promises," 110–11.

28. Barnett, "Refugee Resettlement"; Bon Tempo, *Americans at the Gate*, 203–6;

Brown and Scribner, "Unfulfilled Promises," 102, 107, 116–17; U.S. Department of State, "Refugee Admissions Statistics," August 15, 2015, http://www.state.gov/j/prm/releases/statistics/.

29. Jonah Goldberg, "Putting an End to the 'Refugee Crisis,'" *National Review*, September 11, 2015 (quotation); "EU Ministers Discuss Sharing Refugees Among Nations," September 13, 2015; "Syrian Refugee Crisis a No-Win for Obama," September 13, 2015, both in *Washington Times*; "The Politics of the Syrian Refugee Crisis, explained," *Washington Post*, September 11, 2015; "Syrian Refugee Crisis: Thousands March in Solidarity in London and Across Europe," *International Business Times*, September 12, 2015.

30. Mark Krikorian, "Just Say No to Refugee Resettlement," September 11, 2015; Ian Tuttle, "Before Welcoming Thousands of Syrian Refugees, We Should Consider What Somali Immigrants Have Brought the U.S.," September 11, 2015, both in *National Review*; "Putting an End to the 'Refugee Crisis'"; Syrian Refugee Crisis a No-Win for Obama"; Brian Babin, "Push the Pause Button on Refugee Resettlement," *In the News*, August 14, 2014.

31. "The Ethnicity of San Bernardino Shooters Doesn't Matter," *Newsweek*, December 4, 2015; "San Bernardino Attack Drawn into Republican Calls to Halt Refugee Intake," *The Guardian*, December 7, 2015; "Tashfeen Malik Got Resident Status Via Marriage," *Los Angeles Times*, December 4, 2015.

32. Emma Lazarus, "The New Colossus," in *Emma Lazarus: Selected Poems and Other Writings* (Peterborough, Ont.: Broadview, 2002).

ACKNOWLEDGMENTS

Master violinist and Russian refugee Jascha Heifetz is rumored to have coined the joke about "practice" offering the best route to Carnegie Hall. Considering that Heifetz first headlined the famed Manhattan venue when he was only eighteen years old, one can't escape the humbling conclusion that some people need less practice than others. While lacking the grandeur of performing at Carnegie, writing a book about refugees like Heifetz has certainly required a lot of practice, and with it, abundant help from others.

In part a history of the helpful and harmful consequences of institutional action, this book has thankfully benefited considerably from the support of many institutions. The Institute for Historical Studies at the University of Texas provided me with a critical year to concentrate on the book, along with a marvelously invigorating intellectual environment in which to build its potential. Similar thanks goes to both the UT History Department and the Reinventing Diplomacy symposium at the LBJ School of Public Affairs. I should also recognize two of Austin's other venerable institutions, live music venues and food trucks, both of which helped me recharge after long days of writing. At the University of Cincinnati, I am indebted to support from the Taft Research Center, University Research Council, and especially, the Department of History, whose collegiality and generosity has proven invaluable. Just down the street, the American Jewish Archives has lived up to its reputation as a world class research repository and model of professionalism. Earlier stages of this project were nurtured by support from the University of Chicago, Social Science Research Council, Miller Center of Public Affairs, Harry S. Truman Presidential Library, Hurst Summer Institute in Legal History at the University of Wisconsin, Immigration History Research Center at the University of Minnesota, and Newberry Library.

Though most are not mentioned here, the many archives listed in the book's citations were essential. The same applies to the skilled assistance of the archivists at each, a noble profession if there ever was one. I owe a special thanks to someone who introduced me to a less formal sort of archives, John Backer, who spent six decades helping refugees through his work with the Church World Service at its New York City headquarters. When I began research on the work that served as a foundation for the book, John graciously offered me his extensive knowledge of refugee aid initiatives, the keys to a nearly forgotten closet full of organizational records, and a month's access to a conference room boasting a lovely view of the Hudson River. It proved a comforting way to embark on a study chronicling so much discomfort.

The book has incorporated the guidance of many people: most known to me, some not. Carl Bon Tempo not only wrote a terrific book on United States refugee affairs, which allowed me to engage with his keen insights and chart new territory, but has been an engaging colleague and friend. Many have offered close readings of my work, giving constructive criticism and encouragement at various stages of the project, including Bill Novak, Mae Ngai, Michael Geyer, Jim Sparrow, Jeremi Suri, Elizabeth Borgwardt, Elisabeth Clemens, Akira Iriye, Barbara Welke, Brian Balogh, Chris Capozzola, Kate Weaver, Jason Parker, and Robert Hutchings. Among my colleagues at the University of Cincinnati who have supported this book in various ways, special mention should be made of Willard Sunderland, whose tremendous intellectual vigor matches his generous spirit. Providing important editorial and research assistance were Peter Agree, Alison Anderson, Boyd Holmes, Tracy Kellmer, and Bert Lockwood. Any mistakes are, of course, mine.

Close friends, family, and other loved ones have been especially critical in reminding me not only that academic history can and should speak to a diversity of audiences, but that I could keep my wits about me during the process of producing that history. Special gratitude and much affection goes to Ashley Duncan, Josh Goldberg, Panda Porter, Marion Rife, and Kyle Volk. This book is dedicated to Catherine Porter Small and Greg Porter, two master teachers who taught me the joy of sharing the fascinating and important wonders of all things past and present.